VOICES FOR PEACE

VOICES FOR PEACE
An Anthology

Edited by Anna Kiernan

Scribner

First published in Great Britain by Scribner, 2001
An imprint of Simon & Schuster UK Ltd
A Viacom Company

1 3 5 7 9 10 8 6 4 2

Simon & Schuster UK Ltd
Africa House
64–78 Kingsway
London WC2B 6AH

www.simonsays.co.uk

Simon & Schuster Australia
Sydney

A CIP catalogue record for this book is available from the British Library

ISBN 0-7432-3066-3

Typeset by Palimpsest Book Production Limited,
Polmont, Stirlingshire
Printed and bound in Great Britain by
Omnia Books Limited, Glasgow

CONTENTS

Three

Publisher's Note

The terrorist attacks of September 11 united the world in its condemnation of such breathtaking acts of malice. New Yorkers hugged strangers in the streets and the Big Apple, briefly, became a village. In the numbed aftermath of the bombing, a neighbourly peace emerged. But the rhetoric for war, for a 'crusade' against terrorism, was soon to the fore and the ramparts were drawn up again and the bombs fell.

The issues in this particular war are complex. And a growing number of people want them debated. The contributors to this anthology do not speak as one voice, but they have in common the desire to explore more humane, thoughtful and just ways of reacting to the atrocities of September 11. Some are experts in their fields of interest, such as Islam, international law, the Middle East or military studies, others have a strong connection with human rights organizations and still others represent the arts and humanities – playwrights, poets, actors, songwriters and novelists. Their viewpoints, backgrounds, creeds and beliefs are wonderfully disparate, a hymn to peace in itself, but also universally eloquent and passionate. We thank them so much for taking the time to contribute to

Voices for Peace. Thanks also go to War Child for their positive reception of the project and their helpfulness at every stage.

We hope that this anthology will help to engender the debate that democracy has so far denied us, and that it will lead to a discussion of the wider issues and cultural questions which frame this 'war against terrorism', issues which will not disappear with military victory on either side. All hope that this war will end quickly and with as little human suffering as possible, but should this come to pass, achieving a meaningful, lasting peace will entail a long, hard-fought battle that we can ill-afford to ignore.

Helen Gummer
Non Fiction Publisher
Simon & Schuster UK

If we could love even those who have attacked us, and seek to understand why they have done so, what then would be our response? Yet if we meet negativity with negativity, rage with rage, attack with attack, what then will be the outcome? These are the questions that are placed before the human race today. They are questions that we have failed to answer for thousands of years. Failure to answer them now could eliminate the need to answer them at all.

The Dalai Lama

One

Only thin smoke without flame
From the heaps of couch-grass;
Yet this will go onward the same
Through Dynasties pass.

Yonder a maid and her wight
Come whispering by:
War's annals will cloud into night
Ere their story die.

'In Time of
"The Breaking of Nations"',
Thomas Hardy

Lessons We've Learnt

If someone attacks your country, it's because of your country's good qualities not its bad ones.

When someone may have committed a crime, drop bombs on the country where he lives.

Extradition of a suspect to a third country is not acceptable if the evidence is not very good.

Better get him in your own country where you know he's guilty.

It is better to do something that makes things worse than to do nothing.

In a democracy, the leader decides whether to go to war.

Killing innocent people is an attack on civilization unless your side does it, then it's collateral damage.

The Pentagon and the twin towers were nothing to do with the military or capitalism.

Terrorism is killing by people without planes of their own.

Bombing and causing death by starvation win hearts and minds.

Strawberry jam and face wipes save millions from famine.

Countries that abuse human rights can be attacked if they don't have much support or sell us oil.

If there's a country you've been bombing for ten years, evidence is likely to emerge that it needs attacking some more.

New foreign policy that emerges after terrorism was always in place because terrorism can't achieve anything.

The risk of starvation for millions is less than the risk of hesitation for a leader.

Talking to the enemy is difficult; so is killing them, but it makes better television.

War is different from terrorism because war is bigger.

Caryl Churchill

Address to Media Workers
Against the War (MWAW)

One of the many disadvantages of the present situation is that we have to endure endless television footage of President Bush. Bush has a look on his face that is usually interpreted as a sign of distress at what happened on September 11. It is only after you've seen him again and again that you realize that the look does not represent distress at all. What it represents is panic: panic that he will not be able to summon up a word that even remotely approximates to the message he wishes to convey. So, for instance, in his first appearance after the atrocity in New York, he referred to the 'cowardly acts' of the terrorists. Someone might have taken him on one side and said well, you know, George, the people who hijacked the airliners are all dead by their own hand. You can call them lots of things, but you can't really call them cowards. So 'cowards' came down to 'folks', and then in one desperate moment 'evil doers'. This same uncertainty and vacillation seemed to paralyse the reaction to the bombings in New York so that for a moment it was possible to hope that there might, somewhere in the bowels of the United States government, be some grain of sanity.

All those hopes were a bit sad, really. Having an

imbecile for a president is a little embarrassing for the military-industrial complex that governs the US. So now we are at war, apparently to root out the horror of New York. I would define that horror as reckless bombing without warning which leads to the mass murder of innocent people. As a result, every night on the television there are the familiar pictures of explosions in the night air, superannuated generals discussing tactics, endless talk about precision bombing, targeting terrorists, humanitarian missions, international law. And already we can see what it all means: reckless bombing without warning which leads to the mass murder of innocent people.

There is another feature of war that is also familiar: the awful unanimity of people who call themselves our representatives. On Monday, the day the war broke out in Afghanistan, lots of speeches were made by MPs of all parties. Not a single voice was raised against the waging of war by Britain, the United States and other Western countries against one of the poorest countries on earth. Tony Blair can go on saying, until he strangles in his own rhetoric, that we are not waging war on the Afghan people, but all the brilliant brains among his advisers cannot explain how you drop bombs on Afghan cities without killing Afghan people. He can talk about humanitarian aid, but cannot explain how the dropping of food rations can feed 7 million starving people, many of them rushing desperately away from their homes to avoid the bombs.

Not a single voice was raised in Parliament against the declaration of war. On that unanimous afternoon last Monday, there was only one rude noise. It came from Paul Marsden, the Labour MP for Shrewsbury and Atcham. Mr Marsden, a mild enough man, asked on a point of order if perhaps there might be a vote. 'There is,' he said, 'growing disquiet that for the third time Parliament has been recalled, yet Honourable Members have been denied a vote on this war. Can you confirm to me that there will be no vote?' Here is the reply of Mr Speaker, guardian of the cradle of British democracy: 'It seems that the Honourable Gentleman is getting advice already. Procedural advice is best given privately at the chair. If the Honourable Gentleman wishes to come to the chair I will give him some private advice.' I heard that exchange on the radio; the Speaker's answer was greeted with howls of mirth from the Honourable Members, delighted that such an impertinent suggestion from a little-known backbencher should be so firmly put in its place. The result is that British forces have gone to a war in a far-off country for which there is little justification, and their and our representatives are not even allowed a vote on the matter.

This unanimity does not reflect what is going on in the country at large. The opposition to these attacks goes very deep, far deeper than any of the government ministers imagine. It is only a sign of the deep unease, doubt and, in some cases, fear that nags at the minds of ordinary people as they go to their daily jobs.

Some say: what is the alternative? The New York massacre was a terrible event and we are asked – well, what would you do? Would you appease the terrorists, leave the field open to them? Our reply is no, not at all. We can suggest to Bush, Blair and all the rest of them a whole series of policies that, we guarantee, would do immeasurably more to stop terrorists than bombing the countries in which they live. First, cut off your aid to the state of Israel and its merciless persecution of the Palestinian people. Stop grovelling to the war criminal Sharon. Stop shaking his blood-stained hand. Do all that is in your power to stop Mr Putin and his KGB in Russia from slaughtering and torturing the people of Chechnya. For that matter stop propping up dictatorships in Pakistan, Saudi Arabia and South Asia. Above all, instead of talking yet again about a new world order, set about dismantling economic and social priorities which divide the world, yes even our own world in Britain and in the United States, into classes: grossly rich minorities in power selling each other the weapons of mass destruction so that they can more ruthlessly control and punish the landless unarmed masses of the dispossessed. These are policies that hold out some hope of subverting terrorism. They are the exact opposite of the policies pursued by our governments. There is a most vital and urgent need to turn the hearts and minds of the British people against individual terrorism of the type that bombed New York and state terrorism of the type that is bombing Afghanistan.

Ten years ago, as the bombs started to rain down on Baghdad, John Pilger and I wrote a letter to the *Guardian* asking anyone who worked in the media and who shared our disgust at the war to come and talk to us in the Conway Hall. Five hundred people turned up that night and there and then we formed Media Workers Against the War. Our aims were simple: in general to oppose the war by every means at our disposal and in particular to do so in the media.

The situation today is far more intense than it was ten years ago. People are at once far more anxious and far more angry. Anti-war groups are forming all over the country. Media Workers Against the War will be part of a grand alliance of everyone against this war. It needs to be more effective, more powerful than before. We can and must challenge the government and force them, by the sheer weight of public pressure, to get their bombs and missiles out of Afghanistan and concentrate on economic and social policies that will lead to a world free from capitalist exploitation and free from racism, barbarism and terrorism.

Paul Foot

Redressing the Balance

It was in a slum in the Indian city of Bhopal, among the survivors of history's greatest industrial disaster, that I saw the horrifying images of September 11. I witnessed live coverage of the dreadful terrorist attacks on New York and Washington on television in the company of men and women who had undergone a similar apocalypse eighteen years previously. Their crisis resulted from a gas leak from an American pesticide plant built almost in the heart of their city that killed between 16,000 and 30,000 people.

Of course, the tragedy bore no resemblance to the appalling attack by Osama bin Laden's men. The American engineers who had deactivated all the safety systems of their hi-tech Indian plant in order to cut costs had no intention of killing anyone. Nevertheless their foolish negligence caused five or six times as many deaths as the terrorist attacks in New York and Washington.

But who remembers Bhopal? Who ever led a world-wide crusade to bring those who were responsible for that crime – and it was a crime – before a court, so that their victims might at least know how and why their disaster came about? Warren Anderson, the

President of Union Carbide at the time of the catastrophe, fled from his Florida retreat when Interpol issued a warrant for his arrest. The authorities concerned are not interested in knowing where he is hiding and the Bhopal victims have no hope of ever obtaining his extradition. What is more, no international body is backing their efforts. There is nothing very unusual about that. After all, what is an Indian life worth? The *Wall Street Journal* tried to work it out once: 'Given that an American life is worth approximately 500,000 dollars and that India's GNP is only 1.7% of that of the United States, it may be estimated that an Indian life is only worth 8,000 dollars.'

The Bhopal martyrs never had the opportunity to prick the conscience of the universe. They were the victims of what is coyly referred to as an 'industrial accident', whereas the World Trade Center martyrs are those of a deliberate act of terrorism. Above all, though, the Bhopal martyrs had the misfortune of being predominantly poor. And it is a well-known fact that the voices of the poor do not carry much weight in this world, when a billion men, women and children do not have access to drinking water; a quarter of the inhabitants have less than one dollar a day to survive on and where one child in a rich country consumes as much as fifty times more than a child in the Third World.

It was despicable religious fanaticism that armed the New York and Washington assassins. But from where did these fanatics draw their resolve, if not from the poverty and injustice that afflicts a broad area of our planet? I would not want to be in Calcutta on the day when a figure with the charisma of Gandhi, but the violence of Osama bin Laden, rallies the slum-dweller to revolt. On that day the Park Street shop windows, brimful of luxury goods, and the villas in the smart neighbourhoods will be pillaged and their owners massacred in an explosion of rage, that has been stifled for too long. The revolt of the poor of Calcutta might then spread throughout India and the world, extending everywhere that downtrodden, despised and humiliated people decide that they have had enough of their inhumane living conditions.

To understand the causes of the violence that brings daily bloodshed to the land where prophets and Christ himself preached love and reconciliation we must look to the lives led by Palestinian refugees who are squatting in sordid ghettos. Look to Mother Teresa's soup kitchens in the poorest areas of London, New York, Paris, Rome or Rio de Janeiro to assess the state of extreme despair in which a substantial proportion of humanity finds itself.

In New York's Bronx district, less than an hour's journey from the twin towers, I was shocked to encounter misery, poverty and a wretchedness beyond mere financial deprivation. When people find themselves cut off from all humane reference points, bereft of identity, religion, nationality, family, past and future, they become pariahs. Should we really be surprised when fanatics, under the guise of perverted religious ideals, have no reservations about tying sticks of dynamite to their waists in the middle of innocent crowds or hijacking passenger planes to launch them at targets which represent the values they abhor?

The problems of poverty and injustice in two-thirds of our planet remain unresolved. At the beginning of this millennium, the greatest and primary challenge confronting the West is how to share its abundance with less fortunate countries. Procedures must be established to ensure that the proceeds reach those for whom they are really intended. The question remains: can we act before it is too late? For only when the millions of underprivileged in the world have won their right to dignity and happiness may we glimpse the dawn of true peace between peoples.

Dominique Lapierre

Ledbury Street

I wrote this story for the Artthrob: Defining a Nation tour, but feel that the events it depicts are relevant to the current situation concerning Muslims in this country. Although Britain is very much a multicultural society in terms of diversity, tolerance of varied cultures has never been anywhere near total, even in the most ethnically strong areas. The recent riots in Oldham and the Brixton nail bombing attack are testimony to that fact. My story is an appeal for tolerance from all sides, and a hope that, as individuals, we begin to see all people in the same way instead of making assumptions based on perceived class, creed, racial and sexual generalizations. If we can't get over that most basic and fundamental of human urges – to make someone else the enemy – then maybe we are doomed indeed.

*   *   *

I remember Ledbury Street like every day was yesterday, and the years were simply hours, the decades morning, afternoon, night. I grew from a child to become a teenager and eventually a man on that row of council houses, a suburban road in the midst of urban decay. Ledbury Street was a Garden of Eden, slap-bang in the middle of the sprawling concrete jungle that was London. A quiet cul-de-sac, where us kids were in training for the world that we'd one day inhabit as full-grown adults. The community around us was rich and varied; this, like everything else on my road was broken down and duplicated, so we became miniature doppelgängers of the society surrounding us.

Recently, a local reporter came down and interviewed Ledbury Street's residents. He was writing a piece on the changing face of Britain and felt our street was a microcosm of multicultural society. I had lived there so long I remained loyal to the image we strove to maintain and didn't challenge him on his view. If he really knew what Ledbury Street was like, I'm sure his story would have radically changed, and changed for the worse. I often wondered if he would have reported what he found. For life in Ledbury Street was not as it seemed.

My parents moved on to the street sometime in the early 70s. They had worked for years, buying our house on a modest mortgage. I was three years old at the time. My brothers were six and nine. I never found out if the three-year gaps were fate, or one of mum and dad's elaborate 'plans'. They were teenage sweethearts, whose affection had never waned, and they'd come to England in the 60s full of expectation. Despite the hardships of the ice-cold climate, they found somewhere to live, jobs and friends. My home was a happy one, my upbringing influenced by hard work.

The difference in our ages was sufficient to make my brothers and myself semi-strangers for most of our lives. We had varying tastes in music, clothes and friends. I never felt left out, for I had my own little gang of child-hood buddies, all of us closer than the fingers on one hand. The local council used our road as a testing ground for race relations; I swear there were families from almost every country on earth. It was made up of Irish, Italian, Spanish, Moroccan, English, West Indian, Pakistani, African, Chinese. It's true to say that to us kids, these differences didn't mean a thing, though by the time we were old enough for primary school, we did notice. Over the years, they enhanced our friend-ships. I learnt to say *Bacra di culo* and *Hacclada Nebe* . . . which means kiss my arse in Italian, fuck off in Moroccan. My education was sweeter than nectar, and just as plentiful. I wallowed in a sea of cultures and language.

Of course, out of all those kids, there were a few closer to me than the others. Some of them became friends that I still possess today. Fate had thrown us together, so we discovered life at the same time, but from separate angles that were reinforced by the teach-ings of our families. I'm sure my thirst for travel was preceded by my experiences, whetting my appetite like my first sip of lager, aged nine.

There was Danny Rosenfield, the cockney kid that lived next door, with his twin sister, older brother and taxi-driver dad. His mother was a dinner lady at the local secondary school. Some evenings she'd send Danny's twin, Charlotte, to our house with left-over pudding, which made her a firm favourite with us boys. The Rosenfields were your typical East End characters – loud and chirpy, more like Barbara Windsor than

Dirty Den. Already on Ledbury when we arrived, my parents always reminded me that Danny's family came over on our first day, welcoming us to the street.

There were three Asian families on our road, but only one with a kid my age; Kabil, a crazy, perform-any-dare type of guy, who I loved to bits. He was a natural artist at heart, drawing portraits, caricatures and still-life pictures with a breathtaking talent that astounded everyone who saw them. His family was made up of three older brothers, two younger sisters. His father was a schoolteacher, his mother a house-wife, and they got on with everyone.

These boys were my closest friends. We made sure we went to the same secondary school, though we couldn't quite manage the same classes. I was split from the others and so made friends with a Black kid called Arron who lived on the estate behind Ledbury. Within no time, he was a regular visitor to our road. He made friends with Kabil and Danny and hung out with us as if Ledbury Street was his second home.

I must have been around fourteen that hot summer when everything changed. We were enjoying our six-week school holiday. I'd called for Arron early and we were walking towards Danny's house, talking loud, eager to play football and smoke weed in the nearby park. When we got to his front gate, we saw Danny's twin Charlotte sitting with her friends, a group of Black girls, on a multitude of deck-chairs. They were all dressed in summer clothing, shorts and T-shirts. The girls jumped to attention, but it wasn't for my benefit.

I forgot to tell you about Arron. The girls were mad

for him. He was the colour of manila, with an even white smile, curly black hair and large Bambi-brown eyes. He had long, curling eyelashes that really belonged on a girl. Girls wrote their initials on walls beside his, but Arron wasn't watching any of them. There was only one girl he liked – Charlotte, my best friend's sister.

Like a dark storm cloud brewing in the sky, the results of that day were inevitable. Arron sat beside Charlotte, making her blush, his intention plain. None of the girls was interested in me, so I went inside to talk to my mate. When we came out to the garden, the Black girls were still there, but Charlotte and Arron were gone.

The effects were almost immediate. Danny's reaction was one of deep anger, which I couldn't really work out. I mean, his sister had dated guys before – there were even some who claimed to have slept with her – and Danny had never gone mad, not once. Charlotte was her own person and the 'big brother' act didn't wash with her, especially since she was the eldest by two minutes. Danny insisted we look for the couple; we did, but never found them. Sometime that evening they came back hand-in-hand, treating each other with gentle affection. I found myself noticing the abrupt difference between their entwined brown and white fingers. I saw the anger on Danny's face and suddenly realized why.

The Rosenfields, as one, rallied against the relationship. Arron wasn't allowed in the house. Danny's older brother would bully him at school and on the streets; I caught him at it on many occasions. Of course, this reaction split the street into two very definite camps – those that agreed with the Rosenfields and those who did not. Charlotte and Arron refused to be cowed by this display of open racism and continued to see each other in secret, despite her parents. I grew closer to Charlotte as time went by; she was scared by her family's reaction, especially her father's. She realized they'd always harboured views she'd been unaware of.

This appalled my family. My father changed his tune, swearing that I was to stay away from Danny as long as Arron wasn't good enough for his sister. There became something of a feud, complete with snide glances, veiled threats and even a pushing and shoving match one time. Luckily, violence never erupted, but it was a close thing. Then something worse happened. Charlotte fell pregnant.

There was uproar for three months. Charlotte was ordered to stay in the house, with Arron visiting again and again, to be turned away each time. He'd come by my house and break down in tears in front of my trembling mother, saying he only wanted to do right by his son (he kept insisting the child was a boy). Then one day, Charlotte emerged from the house as if everything was back to normal. The gossip spread at once; she'd had an abortion, a miscarriage, a phantom pregnancy . . . One thing everyone was sure she *didn't* have was a baby. She went back to school in time for her mocks and passed.

This was a major blow to the sensitive racial balance on Ledbury Street. Families withdrew into their own homes; Black and White kids simply refused to mix. Charlotte was ostracized by her Black friends for at least a year, then they forgave her and accepted her as an honorary rudegyal. Charlotte left Ledbury Street not long after her exams. I heard she married an African and emigrated. As for my friendship with Danny and Kabil, it was never the same again. Kabil, in the same class as Danny, had sided with him throughout. This was something that amazed me and I didn't recover. We said hello when we saw each other, but we never hung out. I found a new set of friends through Arron, and they were all Black. Arron sunk into a depression from which I thought he'd never recover; he left school and got into the Nation, but left after six months. Last time I saw him, he was living in Finsbury Park with some Jewish girl. They wanted kids, but said they'd have them when they left the United Kingdom for good.

Courttia Newland

Scribes of the New Racism

September 25, 2001: Seidnaya is a Greek Orthodox convent in Syria, three hours' walk from Damascus. The monastery sits on a great crag of rock overlooking the orchards and olive groves of the Damascene plain, more like a Crusader castle than a place of worship.

According to legend, the monastery was founded in the sixth century after the Byzantine Emperor Justinian chased a stag on to the top of the hill during a hunting expedition. Just as Justinian was about to draw his bow, the stag changed into the Virgin Mary, who commanded him to build a convent on the rock. The abbey quickly become a place of pilgrimage. To this day streams of Christian, Muslim and Druze pilgrims trudge their way to Seidnaya from the mountains of Lebanon and the valleys of the Syrian jebel. A couple of years ago, while on a six-month tramp around the Middle East, I went to spend a night within its walls.

By the time I arrived at the abbey church, it was after eight o'clock on a dark and cold winter night. Two nuns in black veils were chanting from a lectern, while a priest, hidden behind the iconostasis, echoed their chants in a deep, reverberating bass. The only light came from a few flickering lamps suspended on gold chains.

Inside the church I witnessed a small miracle. The congregation in the church consisted not principally of Christians but almost entirely of heavily bearded Muslim men and their shrouded wives. As the priest circled the altar with his thurible, filling the sanctuary with great clouds of incense, the men bobbed up and down on their prayer mats as if in the middle of Friday prayers in a great mosque. Their women mouthed prayers from the shadows. Closely watching the Christian women, a few went up to the icons hanging from the pillars; they kissed them, then lit a candle and placed it in front of the image.

At the end of the service I saw a Muslim couple approach one of the nuns. The woman was veiled; only her nose and mouth were visible through the black wraps. Her husband, a burly man who wore his straggly beard without a moustache, looked remarkably like the wilder sort of Hezbollah commander featured in news bulletins from southern Lebanon. But whatever his politics, he carried in one hand a heavy tin of olive oil and in the other a large plastic basin full of fresh bread loaves, and he gave both to the nun as an offering, bowing his head as shyly as a schoolboy and retreating backwards in blushing embarrassment.

It was an extraordinary sight, yet this was, of course, the old way. The Eastern Christians, the Jews and the Muslims have lived side by side in the Levant for nearly one and a half millennia and have only been able to do so because of a degree of mutual tolerance and shared customs unimaginable in the solidly Christian West. The same broad tolerance that had given homes to the hundreds of thousands of penniless Jews expelled by the bigoted Catholic kings of Spain and Portugal protected the Eastern Christians in their ancient homelands despite the Crusades and the almost continual hostility of the Christian West.

Every schoolchild knows that the closest medieval Europe ever came to a multicultural or multi-religious society was Islamic Spain and Sicily; but it is perhaps less well known that, as late as the eighteenth century, European visitors to the Mogul and Ottoman Empires were astounded by the degree of religious tolerance that they found there. As Monsieur de la Motraye, a Huguenot exile escaping religious persecution in Europe, put it: 'There is no country on earth where the exercise of all religions is more free and less subject to being troubled than in Turkey.' If that coexistence was not always harmonious, it was at least a kind of pluralist equilibrium that simply has no parallel in European history.

I have been thinking of Seidnaya a lot since the atrocity at the World Trade Center. Since then we have seen virulent Islamophobia, as a hundred 'experts' in Islam have popped up to offer their views on a religion few seem ever to have encountered in person. A whole series of leaders and comment pieces have denounced Islam, while always being careful to state that the fundamentalists and terrorists do not, of course, represent the views of 'decent Muslims'.

Prejudices against Muslims and the spread of idiotic

stereotypes of Muslim behaviour and beliefs have been developing at a frightening rate in the last decade, something the horrific assault on the World Trade Center can only exacerbate. Anti-Muslim racism now seems in many ways to be replacing anti-Semitism as the principal Western expression of bigotry against 'the Other'.

The horrific massacre of 8,000 Muslims, some unarmed, at Srebrenica in 1995, never led to a stream of pieces about the violence and repressive tendencies of Christianity. Equally the extraordinary size and diversity of the Islamic world should caution against lazy notions of a united, aggressive Islam acting in concert against 'the Judaeo-Christian West'.

Islam is no more cohesive than Christendom: neither is it a single, rational, antagonistic force. We are different from the Swedes, the Serbs and the fundamentalist evangelicals of the American Midwest; so the Indonesians are totally different from the Mauritanians and the Hezbollah headbangers of Lebanon. There is no such thing as 'the Muslim mind', anti-democratic, terrorist, primeval in its behaviour, or however else it is portrayed, versus a rational, peace-loving 'Christian mind'. The Islamic world, for better or worse, is much like anywhere else in the developing world.

For 1400 years there has been a debate within Islam between liberal and orthodox approaches. What is clear, in recent years, is that insensitive and clumsy Western interference in the Islamic world almost always strengthens the hands of the fundamentalists and the conservatives against those who represent more liberal and enlightened interpretations of Islam.

Already we are seeing Pakistan being pushed to the verge of a fundamentalist Islamic revolution as its military government is bullied into helping the Americans against their Afghan kinsmen. Insensitive rhetoric of the kind we have seen in the press, and the use by President Bush of the word 'crusade', can only strengthen the hands of the fundamentalists, fatally weakening the secular states of the region. Most Muslim states would support a precise surgical assault on Osama bin Laden's al-Qaeda network; they would not put up with a large-scale ground war in Afghanistan or Iraq. We must proceed with the greatest of caution. Such a war is much more likely to destabilize the entire region than to achieve the intended aims.

William Dalrymple

Talking About Emotions

As I write this, Tony Blair's speech to the Welsh Assembly is being broadcast live on radio. Concerned that British support for the US-led air strikes against Afghanistan is waning, the Prime Minister is attempting to stiffen the nation's moral fibre and get people 'to stay the course'. 'It is important,' he is saying, 'that we never forget why we have done this, never forget how we felt as we watched planes fly into the trade towers, never forget those answerphone messages, never forget how we imagined how mothers told their children they were going to die.' The intention is clearly to invite a gut-level response and comes close to encouraging revenge.

At the same time as Blair was putting the finishing touches to his speech, a reporter in Kabul was filing a story on the latest US air strikes. It is worth quoting the piece at length, partly because it plainly contradicts US Defense Secretary Donald Rumsfeld's claim that the Taliban are manipulating journalists by getting women to sit by bomb sites and shed tears of manufactured grief; partly because, unusually in the reporting of the war so far, it acknowledges that 'their' dead had loves and histories, just like 'ours'; but also because it is a perfect illustration that the other side too have emotions.

American air strikes meant to punish the Taliban spilled over today into residential neighbourhoods here, killing thirteen civilians. It was the second time in two days that missiles have hit homes and killed residents . . . Weeping families buried their dead within hours of the morning bombardment . . . 'I have lost all my family,' said a sobbing woman in the Qalaye Khatir neighbourhood on Kabul's northern edge. 'I am finished.' After the morning strikes, a father hugged the dead body of his son, who looked barely two. Women slapped themselves with grief. One 13-year-old boy, Jawad, bandaged and bloody from the strike, asked about his relatives – not knowing he was the only survivor in his nine-member family. Jawad lay semiconscious in his bed in Wazir Akbar Khan hospital in Kabul. A neighbour, Muhammad Razi, explained to a journalist that Jawad was unaware of all that had happened. 'He asked me, "How is my family?"' Mr Razi whispered. 'I said: "They are all OK. You were walking in your sleep, and you fell down the well by your house, and I rescued you."' . . . In Washington, Pentagon spokesmen had no immediate comment on the latest strikes and the civilian casualties involved. The Pentagon has stressed that civilians are never deliberately targeted.

It is possible that Mr Razi will come to the semi-conscious Jawad's hospital bedside to bring him the comforting news that he wasn't deliberately targeted. Who knows, it may even be possible that Mr Razi will tell Jawad of Blair's speech today, from which Jawad will learn that the West is 'morally right' and, if he only makes the effort to understand, he will accept the reasons for the unfortunate obliteration of his family.

It is, however, as we all know, much more likely that Jawad – if his hospital is not bombed and he has the good fortune to survive a conflict we are now being told may last for our lifetimes – will also 'never forget'. He will never forget that he once had a home, that he once had parents and brothers and sisters. And like the father cradling his 2-year-old son, like the 'finished' woman who lost all her family, he will never forget that an American bomb blasted those he loved to bits and a British Prime Minister went on radio to emote about morality and right and justice.

If Jawad rejects the Pentagon's bland avowals and Blair's words as hypocrisy and cant, if he grows up with a visceral hatred of America and Britain and the West, who will blame him? Who in the West would dare say to him, 'I know we killed your family, Jawad, but Britain is your friend. America is your friend'? The dead cannot bear grudges, but those who loved them can, and do. That's what tends to happen when you bomb people.

We are being urged never to forget. Emotions are being deliberately heated. Is this really the way to go? The Irish experience strongly suggests it is not. The high emotions sparked by deaths on 'our' side resulted directly in deaths on 'theirs'. 'We' struck back. 'They' struck back again, only harder this time. Before we knew it we were in what the rest of the world was telling us was a 'self-perpetuating cycle of violence'. British politicians whose emotions were not quite at the same pitch condemned 'tit-for-tat' killings and wondered why the two communities could not forgive, forget and, like decent, civilized people in the rest of the decent, civilized world, move on.

There were many reasons why they could not – injustice and discrimination, being among the most important. But just as important was the emotion which sustained and fuelled the conflict. Emotion, as the Prime Minister's advisers, if they are doing their jobs properly, should very quickly point out to him, works on both sides, 'ours' and 'theirs'. When what we feel becomes what is true and what is true becomes what is right, barbarism and savagery are validated. Emotion blots out understanding, analysis, good sense. It makes a thousand times more difficult the serious business of resolving conflicts and ending enmities and hatreds. Emotional responses cannot be turned on and off when political practicalities and military exigencies demand reversals in policy. We are accustomed to talking about 'taking the heat out of a situation' in order to find political settlements. Emotion does the opposite of this.

Do we never forget the dead? Is it right that the dead must always be remembered? In Ireland, the memory of the executed rebel leaders of the 1916 Rising helped create and sustain the Anglo-Irish war of independence, in which yet more volunteers fell. They in turn were remembered (indeed, very recently ten of the Irish fallen were remembered in a state ceremony, which attracted much hostility from anti-Republican commentators). In the Troubles there are so many to remember. Just look in the In Memoriam columns of the newspapers.

I can remember one of the dead very clearly, though he was no more than an acquaintance. I said good evening to him as I was on my way to the pictures with my girlfriend. This was March 1974. On the bus on the way back, we heard a thunderous blast. I jumped off and ran towards the sound of the explosion. Dazed people, covered in dust, a few crying but most merely numb (the grey men and women making their way north after the attacks on the World Trade Center were eerily familiar to me). A Loyalist gang had rolled a beer keg filled with explosive into Conway's bar on the Shore Road, near where I lived. The dead man had calmly and bravely picked it up and taken it outside. The bomb went off in his arms and he was, literally, blown to pieces. The next morning firemen scraped sticky bits of what looked like burned rubber from the walls of the bar and shops. They scraped and dug this man's blasted, charred flesh in the way you do when you are stripping wallpaper, and with as much ceremony. They had seen it all before. But among those who knew the dead man was there an emotional response? Of course there was. I heard what people were saying. I felt in my own bones horror and anger. I don't know if there was a death on 'their' side directly attributable to this death on 'ours', but at the very least it kept alive the fears and hatreds on which the conflict thrived.

It has taken more than a generation for the emotions provoked by deaths like this to subside to the point where negotiation and the pursuit of peaceful methods has all but replaced retaliation and revenge. The heat is slowly being taken out of the equation. Blair has played his part in this. And the dead? They are not yet forgotten, and perhaps they never will be. But at least their deaths are no longer being used – emotionally, as some would say; cynically as others might – to legitimize the infliction of yet more deaths.

Tony Blair has made high moral purpose and emotion his rhetorical trademark. Until now when it has missed its target – as at the Women's Institute fiasco – the collateral damage has been minimal and the main casualty has been the Prime Minister himself. But this is different. Lives are at stake, 'ours' and 'theirs'.

Ronan Bennett

The Perils of Selective Grief

Dare to suggest that there may just possibly be a slight link between America's past behaviour and the hijackings, and out pour the accusations. Such people are guilty of 'foaming malevolence' according to one paper. Because all decent reporters know the only humanitarian response is to shake your head, mutter a sentence containing the words 'evil' and 'monsters' and demand that someone somewhere gets bombed.

Maybe they argue amongst themselves, these types. Perhaps they approach a fellow columnist and say 'How callous to describe the terrorists as "evil" when they're at least "despicably evil": though I care more than anyone because I wrote "words can't describe this despicable evil". Top that.'

Strangely, many of those who appear the most horrified haven't always been so sensitive about the loss of innocent lives. They managed to watch the Gulf War on telly, for example, and even seemed to enjoy the experience. I wonder whether Iraqi TV showed the New York disaster in the same way we covered the bombing of Baghdad. Maybe a panel of experts sat around a table chatting about the extraordinary accuracy of the pilots, while the presenter said 'And we're being

35

told that so far there's not a single Iraqi casualty, so that really is fantastic news isn't it?'

Some people are almost poetic in their selective grief. On Radio 4 one morning we were treated to an 'adviser' to Vladimir Putin, sombrely running through his evils and despicables, beside himself with bewilderment at how anyone could cause such carnage. Well, if I was his counsellor I might suggest he work through his confusion by asking the bloke he advises, who slaughtered 50,000 civilians in the town of Grozny. Not that I'm calling him a hypocrite as maybe he only advises Putin on traffic-flow issues, but it does make you wonder who's going to pop up next. 'With us in the studio is Harold Shipman, who's issued his own statement condemning the terrorists' "appalling disregard for human life". Harold, thank you for joining us on this awful, awful occasion.'

Some Palestinians were so malicious they danced in the streets, raged the newspaper that screamed 'Gotcha!' following the drowning of 300 conscripted Argentinians. It could be argued that was different, as they weren't civilians. But the 500 women and children blasted by a cruise missile in a Baghdad bomb shelter certainly were. As were countless Nicaraguans, or the million Vietnamese, such as the victims in this account of the My Lai massacre: 'The killings began without warning. Soldiers began shooting women and children who were kneeling, weeping and praying round a temple. Villagers were killed in their homes. Helicopters shot down those who fled. Many of the GIs were laughing, "Hey, I got me another one. Chalk one up for me".

Soldiers took breaks to rest and smoke before resuming the killing.'

Maybe this was a long time ago and therefore irrelevant to today's story, except that when George Bush Sr launched the war against Iraq, he promised this 'won't be like Vietnam, where we were fighting with one hand tied behind our back'. And this has summed up their attitude ever since: 'we lost in Vietnam because we were too bloody liberal'. All that stopping for fags between killings, it's no wonder they lost.

Then there was Chile and Lebanon and so on; thousands of innocent people with innocent families, amongst them firemen and fathers and people with faces who were never displayed on the centre pages of the *Daily Mail*, never to be remembered during minute silences at the start of football matches.

So how can it be explained, this erratic caring of Presidents and advisers and those who are opposed to foaming malevolence? Could it be that their grieving is, perchance, in some way politically motivated? That they weep not for the devastated families, shell-shocked citizens and unimaginable torment of the victims, but in horror and disbelief that this could happen in America?

Now the selective grievers demand retribution, and don't seem too bothered whom it is against. The implication is that anything less than devastation of somewhere or other would be showing a lack of respect for the victims. Like manipulative teenage lovers, they're pleading 'Go on, you'd do it if you *really* cared.'

So, it looks as if Afghanistan will do for a start.

Though I can't see the point in bombing buildings there as the Taliban seem happy to blow them up themselves. After a cruise-missile strike, they'd probably send Bush a note saying 'Cheers George, that saved us doing that infidel street, with its provocative curvy bit.'

So now atrocity is likely to be answered with atrocity, together with all the inevitable webs of lies bound up as part of a package. Already we're told the CIA satellites can 'pinpoint a cigarette'. Really? Yet they haven't the foggiest idea where Osama bin Laden is. I suppose the one thing they didn't reckon on was that he doesn't smoke. If only he stopped for one occasionally between killings they'd have him in a flash.

We can be, and as humans should be, extraordinarily moved by all the victims. But if we're only extraordinarily moved by the victims on one side, we're at least halfway to foaming.

Mark Steel

The Case for Disenthralment

I wish to raise a dissenting if broadly peace-minded voice. Those who destroyed the World Trade Center and killed so many thousands are not, in my view, open to mediation and negotiation. If they find another target of opportunity they will strike at it just as ruthlessly. That target is more likely to be civilian than military. There will be further casualties. Here we are in a new world, a world of asymmetric warfare in which the traditional brokering of ceasefires and compromises simply does not apply. The United Nations has been sidelined, not just by the decision of the principal target and the last remaining superpower, but also by the revolutionary nature of the conflict itself.

The events of September 11 represented the most devastating attack on the continental United States by an outside power since the British burned the White House in 1812. With the exception of the Civil War the Americans have waged their wars abroad, often at sacrificial cost, but the homeland was untouched. It was also scarcely conceivable, because of the dynamics of democracy, that force would not be met with force. President Jimmy Carter was denied a second term because of perceived weakness in dealing with the hostage crisis in Tehran in 1980. This time the bombs were bound to fall, and they did.

I do not doubt that in this case the use of force against force is justified, if only to take the initiative from those who seek to destroy us. The option of inaction is not available. It is a principle of warfare that, if you wait for bad things to happen, bad things will happen. Any government's primary duty is to protect its people, whether from threats new or old. If it fails in that it will fall. Another principle of warfare is that a military operation, if it is to succeed, needs an achievable objective. To take two examples from World War II: the Dieppe raid did not have an achievable objective; the Normandy landings did. The question in this case is: what is the achievable objective of the American bombing campaign, other than to satisfy a need to avenge the deaths of New York's firefighters – and to rally support for the enemy when the bombs go astray? From my personal experience of warfare, I am as unconvinced about the bombing strategy as about the deployment of ground troops, other than small groups of special forces as advisers to anti-Taliban units or on limited and specific missions informed by good intelligence.

I doubt very much whether a ground campaign, fighting from cave to cave, is operationally possible. Military commanders try to avoid street fighting, because of the cost in lives. Cave fighting against the soldiers of the jihad, except on limited operations and with accurate intelligence, seems equally questionable. A further inhibition belongs to the nature of asymmetric warfare.

The two sides are not in fact evenly matched in their military cultures. Casualties matter so much more to one than to the other.

This is not Hollywood. There is no Rambo or Terminator to save the day for the Americans after the last commercial break. This is the real world. And in the real world there is an imbalance of forces, with the firepower favouring one side and the fanaticism another. If we seek to wage a conventional war we may not even win in conventional terms. We should know that and understand it.

It would be wiser, in my view, to think of this thing differently, and to go back for a paradigm to the American Civil War. At the height of that terrible conflict the American president made a speech which Aaron Copland included in the narration for his 'Portrait of Abraham Lincoln', and which speaks to our present predicament as eloquently as anything I have come across. Lincoln said: 'As our case is new, we must think anew and act anew. We must disenthrall ourselves.'

We, too, could use some disenthralment from the view that armed conflict has to end with the victory of one side over another, or with a peace agreement, or with both. This one may not. I expect this campaign, which is as much a clash of ideas as of arms, to endure in one form or another for the rest of my life – and I am not planning to meet my Maker imminently. It will certainly not satisfy the clamour of the media, in an age of rolling news and ratcheting expectations, for quick results and a Kosovo-style conclusion. It may possibly happen that extraordinary luck and intelligence will deliver up Osama bin Laden, dead or alive – but if dead, others will take the martyr's place; if alive, the conflict will continue and no international criminal court yet exists before which he could be brought. (The Americans themselves opposed its establishment.)

We could use some further disenthralment from the idea that technology conquers all, and that wars can be waged without costs and casualties – on our own side, that is. It is worth remembering that the attack on the World Trade Center was not the only case of mass murder in recent years. Rather more people, about 7000, were killed in the Srebrenica massacre of 1995. Yet we responded to one with bombs and missiles, aircraft carriers and commando raids – and to the other with a shrug of the shoulders. We walked away from a UN-declared safe area, in a country that had more than 30,000 UN troops in it. It was as if we were saying, British and French and Dutch lives matter on one scale of values, and Bosnian lives on another. So today, New York is worth going to war for, and if as many innocent lives are lost in Afghanistan that's just collateral damage. We stand for certain values in the Western democracies, or at least we claim to, and if in defending those values we sacrifice them, then we revert to the notorious Vietnam example of saving a village by destroying it. George Orwell is worth rereading in this context. In his marvellous essay on 'Politics and the English Language' the euphemism was 'pacification'. Today it's 'collateral damage'.

In the matter of disenthralment, we should also disenthral ourselves from the notion that we in the Western
democracies enjoy peace and freedom as a God-given
right. Of course we don't. Peace and freedom, as we
understand them, are not a right but a privilege. They
have to be fought for; politically if we can, but militarily if we cannot, and certainly not taken for granted.
If we take them for granted we shall surely lose them.
Perhaps we have just grown soft and complacent. We
have such a stronger sense of our rights than we do of
our obligations. My own view, from where I have been
and what I have seen since the end of the Cold War,
is that the new world order is immeasurably more
dangerous than the old. We have been living in a fool's
paradise or golden age – perhaps the same thing seen
from a different angle. There is not one of us whose
life is not touched and changed by the present emergency. It is a wake-up call to us all. For that reason
alone we have to hope that some good will come of it.

I should make it clear that I am not writing here for
UNICEF, whom I am proud to serve as an occasional
envoy and witness. But six weeks after the disasters in
New York and Washington, it was a journey for
UNICEF that brought home to me the gravity and
novelty of the challenge we face. It is time to throw
the rulebooks away. Neither Clausewitz nor manuals
of peacekeeping have anything to teach us.

The frontier chosen by UNICEF was a place where
it was (and still is) active, together with the British
medical charity MERLIN. It was a flood plain of the
Pyandzh River between Afghanistan and Tadjikistan,

43

where at least 10,000 refugees were seeking shelter, with more arriving daily. It was a no man's land in a double sense. The Afghans had fled from a Taliban-held area, and had nowhere else to go. On a 300 foot escarpment above them the border was sealed not by Tadjik but by Russian troops. In the sense of realpolitik, it was Russia's southern frontier, closed to refugees, closed to Islamic fundamentalists, and to just about everyone except (occasionally) the volunteers from these two charities carrying out a programme of immunization. The flood plain was also a no man's land in that it had previously been thought uninhabitable. Now the Afghans were digging in for the winter, living in holes in the ground covered with river grasses, building mud huts against the winter weather. Water was scarce except from the river itself, under Taliban gunfire. There was little food but bread and oil, and not much of that. The sinister symptoms of scurvy were showing themselves.

I drove back north through part of Tadjikistan that used to be a desert. After two years of drought and the collapse of its Soviet irrigation system, it was returning whence it came, as much of a desert as large parts of Uzbekistan, Pakistan and Afghanistan itself. Misery and warfare march in the same legion. We ignore them at our peril. The time is long past when we could say, 'if we leave the world alone it will leave us alone'. It won't.

And then it occurred to me that in a sense we have been here before. This is the second time in a little over ten years that the British and Americans have gone to

44

war in a desert. The difference is that, unlike the Gulf, this is a desert with millions of people living in it; and among them are the soldiers of the jihad, who will not be minded to throw down their arms in the face of superior firepower.

Time to think anew and act anew – to disenthral ourselves.

Martin Bell

We're All in this Together Now

The terrible events of September 11 fulfilled many predictions about the nature of future conflict. For years, experts had been suggesting that if we were to face some form of attack in future, it would probably not be by other nation states, but by 'non-state actors', flitting like shadows across physical borders or, now, ghostlike through cyberspace. They might be 'super-terrorists' using weapons of mass destruction – nuclear, biological or chemical. Future conflict would no longer be between broadly symmetric armed forces, arrayed across the landscape in similar ways, using broadly similar technology and tactics. Whatever differences there might be between them in numbers and quality, these ponderous military organisms had still been designed, trained and equipped to fight mirror images of themselves. Instead, future conflict would be 'asymmetric', with the protagonists using very different means to achieve very different ends.

In all this, the 'experts' were right. Tragically, their discourses were not precise enough to prevent what they had foretold. The attack on New York City's World Trade Center, in particular, released as much energy as a small nuclear weapon. Not for nothing was the base of the World Trade Center dubbed 'Ground Zero' – a phrase borrowed from the arcane theology of nuclear strategy. All the military power of the United States – its thousands of nuclear warheads, its carrier battle groups, its armed forces prepared to operate on the digital battlefield – was powerless to prevent the crudest of attacks. The West's own technology – airliners, tall buildings – was turned against it by determined men armed only with knives, working, maybe, in loose affiliation with an elusive controller. The attacks were blamed on a 'non-state actor', Osama bin Laden, who does appear to be the culprit. The United States has been unable to find, never mind hit, that non-state actor, it has attacked the benighted country where he is believed to be concealed, like James Elroy Flecker's prophet, 'guarded, in a cave'.

But the response to this tragedy needs to be different and asymmetric as well. There are signs that, so far, it has not been. Initially, the United States was more cautious than some of us feared it might be. There was no initial fusillade of cruise missiles, which would have achieved nothing. American and British politicians and senior military officers stressed that the military action was only a small part of the overall response. Wise counsel seemed to have prevailed. But on October 7 the bombing began. They did it in the same old way. The way they did it in the Gulf. The way they did it in Yugoslavia. First of all, take out the air defences. Then take out the command and control. And then? Take out ghosts? Take out shadows?

The lesson is clear to anyone who wants to see. The

required response to the events of September 11 is not primarily a military one. The right response mirrors something that has been happening in the aftermath of conflict around the world. When armies, navies and air forces work together, we call it 'joint'. When many nations work together, we call it 'combined'. And when many different agencies work together, we call it 'integrated' – multi-agency.

The response to September 11 involved, initially, the fire service and medical agencies. It involved police and criminal investigators, the FBI and other intelligence services, and their work continues. It involves airline security. It involves diplomats. It involves financial institutions, traditionally loath to reveal details of accounts, in tracking down suspected terrorist funds. As fear spread of an armed response against Afghanistan – and none of the perpetrators of the September 11 atrocities, it must be remembered, was Afghan – the refugee crisis in Afghanistan, already dire after twenty years of war and three of famine, became worse. This, in turn, brought in international organizations like the United Nations Commission for Refugees; national donors, like USAID and the United Kingdom's Department for International Development; the non-governmental organizations like the International Red Cross, Oxfam, Médecins Sans Frontières and War Child, to whom the royalties of this book will be donated.

As a gesture, the US Air Force has been dropping aid to some areas of Afghanistan, while bombing others. The Taliban government, it has been reported, has burned some of the aid, while the United States has bombed other aid supplies by mistake. It is not a good start and the former American action violates one key principle in the aid business. If you mix food and firepower, blankets and bombs, baby milk and bullets, you risk compromising the wider aid effort. Aid workers may need to work with the military. But if their work becomes too closely identified with the military, they will lose their impartiality, at least while bombing is still going on. They will become part of the war, and therefore even more vulnerable.

But what of the most important component, the people of Afghanistan itself? The people whom the United States and its allies are trying to persuade to hand over the prime suspect and change their form of government. Will they be persuaded?

We had already begun to learn these lessons in the peace-building operations underway in Africa and south-east Europe. General Sir Mike Jackson, who commanded the force that went into Kosovo in 1999, compared such an integrated, multi-agency force to a rope. The combined strength of the strands exceeded the sum of the strands individually. In post-conflict, peace-building situations, the military forms a strand of this rope, but only one. Once the security framework is established, police are needed more than soldiers. And courts. And an independent judiciary. And prisons. We can begin to draw the rope. A red strand for the soldiers, black for the judges, dark blue for police. The international organizations, perhaps a light blue strand, the colour of the United Nations. The non-governmental organizations silver, for they operate using the money they raise. The national donors gold, for they donate money.

Most important, are the people of the country, the local authorities and the ordinary people. They run down the middle of the rope, and all the other strands touch them.

It is important that no one strand is too thick because that distorts the rope, and makes it burn those who hold it. The military, which has the advantages of a coherent structure and centralized communications, is sometimes impatient and dismissive of the other strands of the rope. They, conversely, are resentful at what may be seen as the military's desire to run everything.

But this tension may be creative. In all the peace-keeping and peace-building operations I have witnessed I have been deeply moved by how soldiers take to humanitarian operations. There is a view in certain quarters that 'peacekeeping is for wimps'. Not true. The 'peacekeeping is for wimps' view has been supported by the performance of some armies which have specialized in peacekeeping and humanitarian operations at the expense of basic military skills. Others – notably the Americans – take a very gung-ho view and, partly out of concern about casualties, and partly for cultural reasons, do not interact with the local community. This causes the rope to fray.

But all the evidence indicates that the most effective peacekeepers are hard, well-trained, disciplined profes-sional soldiers. Nobody with any sense would say that the Royal Marines are 'wimps'. Yet in Kosovo the Marines threw themselves enthusiastically into helping

War Child build children's playgrounds as part of the general drive to establish normality after the conflict there. When older youths started vandalizing the playgrounds, the Marines, with their usual brand of lateral thinking, came up with a 'hotline' so local people could alert them.

Some of those same Royal Marines may be among the specialist Arctic and mountain warfare troops likely to be deployed to Afghanistan this winter. Peacekeeping is not for wimps.

Some people may take issue with my application of the principles of peacekeeping and humanitarian operations to the wide-ranging conflict against the perpetrators of the September 11 atrocities. But I believe many of the principles we have learned about peace-building in various post-conflict operations are applicable to new-style conflict, and vice versa. Certainly, the old principles of war, starting with 'selection and maintenance of the aim', apply well to peace-building and humanitarian operations. Similarly, the integrated approach involving all agencies, which we have learned in peacekeeping and humanitarian work, can be adapted to the integrated struggle against terrorism. The conventional military may have a role, but it may not be that big.

This is where I believe we may be going wrong. The military operation may be occupying too much of our attention and too many resources. The declared aim was, initially, to dismantle the 'integrated air defence network'. The Afghans probably do not have an integrated air defence network and, even if they did, it was not responsible for the September 11 attacks. Of course, the shadowy work of the criminal investigation, the intelligence agencies and the banks is unlikely to be advertised and, even if it were, does not make good television. Planes taking off from aircraft carriers and bombs hitting targets do make good television. It may be that the military campaign is largely for public consumption, and also a deception – a distraction from other operations underway. But unfortunately it is killing innocent people. And, with no discernible success to report from the military component of the integrated operation, the media has focused on the mistakes, thus beginning to imperil the public support on which it depends. There must be another way.

My colleagues and I in the field of Defence and Security Studies are frequently asked to comment on current operations. Sometimes, we are invited to discussion programmes to put forward the case for military action. It is assumed, for understandable reasons, that my colleagues and I will take this point of view. Not always. I am a military analyst and I have seen war. But war is not always the right way to solve the problem – and never the only way. The first principle of war is selection and maintenance of the aim or, as the Americans say, the objective. What is our objective? What is bombing Afghanistan doing to attain it? I hope the governments involved know the answer.

Professional soldiers make the best peacekeepers. They are also the last people to want to go to war – again, for obvious reasons. You might think that Karl von Clausewitz (1780–1831), the pre-eminent Western military thinker and philosopher, would have been an unstinting advocate of military solutions. Not so. 'The main lines of every major strategic plan,' he wrote in a letter of 1827, 'are largely political in nature . . . According to this point of view, there can be no question of a purely military evaluation of a great strategic issue, nor of a purely military scheme to solve it.' Some may have been deluded by eleven years of one-sided military successes into thinking that war is an easy option. Most of our leaders have no experience of it. Clausewitz did, as did the Chinese philosopher-general Sun Tzu. 'Weapons,' he wrote in the fourth century BC, 'are tools of ill omen. War is a grave matter; one is apprehensive lest men embark upon it without due reflection.' And further on, the general has a surprising observation. 'To win one hundred victories in one hundred battles is not the acme of skill. To subdue the enemy without fighting is the acme of skill.' Clausewitz and Sun Tzu would have been very wary of what our leaders are doing, right now. But then, they were soldiers.

Chris Bellamy

Not in My Name

It is naive to suggest that you can fight a conventional war against terrorism. Conventional war is state-sponsored terrorism anyway. Special intelligence should locate Osama bin Laden, and whoever else is responsible for the appalling senseless tragedy of September 11, and bring them to justice, without risking the lives of innocent children through a pointless bombing campaign.

Our military resources should be deployed to escort food and aid convoys to Afghanistan, so that a population half the size of London's doesn't die this winter.

Marches, demonstrations and direct action are a waste of time, not least because the press largely ignores them. In a recent march in London, a reported 20,000 people showed up, taking up around five hours out of each of their days. This is the equivalent of at least three working lifetimes. Instead we need to re-involve ourselves in the democratic process or else risk losing it.

We have already witnessed Tony Blair's decision to support American military action in Afghanistan without a parliamentary vote. Such undemocratic action must be countered through people writing, e-mailing and phoning elected representatives to express doubts and dissent. Pressure groups should demand that the concerns of real people are represented in the senates, congresses and parliaments of the world.

Democracy can be defined as a government by the people for the people that takes into account the views of minorities. Let's stop whinging and get on with demonstrating our democratic rights, otherwise *Voices for Peace*, and other such ventures, will become a travesty of what they purport to be.

The West's handling of the current crisis fails to intelligently address the indisputable importance of human life. Our civilization is on the verge of meltdown as the powers-that-be waste huge amounts of money and resources on war: resources that could have been usefully channelled into feeding the starving and repairing our damaged planet. We are faced with a choice: kowtow to materialism, despotism and nihilism or embrace democracy, activity and solidarity. Which is it to be? It is up to us to decide and make it happen.

Katharine Hamnett

Diaries from the Front Line

Tuesday, September 25, 2001

I visited Peshawar today to recruit some workers and doctors to work in the camps. Although jobs are scarce, I used to get a lot of eager recruits to do the job, but this time people had their concerns and I found them reluctant to go inside the camps. Security was their main concern. But I still found a couple of doctors and others willing to accept the jobs.

Despite all the media hype and threats, I actually saw people of all colours and creeds roaming around in the markets and hotels, most of them journalists. One rather elderly French journalist was all set to go into Afghanistan. I tried to talk him out of it, reminding him of all the possible dangers, but he had been there before and was quite confident about the Taliban's behaviour, if 'approached appropriately'. I could not find out the meaning of appropriate approach in that context.

I met a few officials from UN agencies and refugee administration departments. They are expecting about 1.5 million people to migrate in as soon as the border opens. The figure was 7 million when the Soviets entered Afghanistan in 1979. By and large, people in the city were doing what they would be doing on a normal Tuesday.

*   *   *

Monday, October 8, 2001
Finally it has happened. Last night at around 9 p.m. I heard the news on a special bulletin on TV. Although it was expected, I had been hoping that something good would happen to avoid the whole issue, but it never did. I spent a very uncomfortable night thinking about the worst possibilities. I remembered the war of 1971 with India; I was about eight at that time but the horrors still linger in my memory. The air attacks, the sirens, the bunkers and most of all the anxiety in the family were very vivid. I strongly wished that my children would never have to live with such memories.

This morning everybody was looking up the newspapers and discussing the events. The most asked question was: 'What will happen now?' One of my friends commented that whatever may be the outcome of the war we, the Pakistanis, will be the worst affected. This is even more troubling when we realize that our nation is just an innocent bystander which happens to be in the region of a war.

Sunday, October 14, 2001
It is growing more and more frustrating now. Today is the third time I have had to cancel my visit to the refugee camps to arrange supplies of medicine, etc. This is because of increasing threats of violence in the Northwest Frontier near the Afghan border. My kids have been bombarded with so much war and terrorism talk that they now know about Osama, Bush and various warplanes.

The opinion of people varies from place to place.

Most of my medical colleagues are confused and apprehensive. One of my patients, who had been living in Kabul, has fled the city with her family and is now living here. In her own childlike way, she narrated the first night of attacks on Kabul: 'It was fire all over the skies with a lot of strange noises. I was scared.' I could see the horror in her eyes.

Wednesday, October 17, 2001
Finally today I was able to visit the refugee camp. The delay was quite frustrating because of one or another reason. There were no new faces, probably because of the closure of the border. Not many new people have been able to get into Pakistan. But a lot more are expected any day.

The aid is trickling in but, to my mind, in a very haphazard way. One of my friends, in the health department dealing with aid agencies, was really frustrated. 'How is this going to benefit any Afghanis if we cannot get ourselves out of these bureaucratic channels?' he said, while throwing a bundle of proposals on his desk. In the camp I was rather surprised to note that Afghan refugees were rather wary about the US strikes on the Taliban. I expected them to be strongly supportive of the war, being one of the most affected groups of people, but they were not. An old man remarked, 'I would never let anybody invade my homeland, whosoever it may be.'

Assad Hafeez

Nile Blues

Right there, at my feet, the Nile spreads out in a shimmering, flowing mass. The water reflects the lights of small boats, of floating restaurants, of the bridges flung across the river. From the centre rises Gezira island, on it the lit-up dome of the Opera House and the tall slim lotus of the Cairo Tower. The scene is spectacularly beautiful, and over it all hangs the thick pall Cairenes call 'the Black Cloud'. No one seems certain where it comes from. They say it's the farmers burning husks of rice in Sharqiyya province. They say it's Cairo rubbish burning in several places – two of the fires out of control. They say it's a component in the new unleaded petrol. It hangs over everything but Cairenes live with it, because – so far – they can still breathe.

'I don't know who I feel more alienated from, the Americans or the Taliban,' says Nadra. She hitches her heel to the seat of her chair, hugs her knee to her chest. 'The Americans' language is so sleazily self-laudatory.' Nadra and her American husband are photographers. He has been in San Diego for three months. She was supposed to join him on September 15 and they had planned to come back together in January. But now she can't bring herself to go. 'Do you watch CNN?' she asks. 'Should journalists collude with government? Or do the media have an agenda of their own? They're trying to frighten us all so we each stay in our little hole and don't talk to each other.' She tells me that on September 12 she received international calls from seven agencies, all working for clients in the American media. 'Go out,' they said, 'and photograph the people rejoicing in the streets.' 'But nobody's rejoicing in the streets,' she said. 'In the coffee-shops then. Photograph the people laughing and celebrating in the coffee shops.' 'People are glued to their TVs,' she told them, 'Everybody's in shock.' Still they pressed her. Eventually, she said if they wanted her photographs they could send her to Jenin (on the West Bank) and she'd photograph Israeli tanks entering the city.

That was my first night in Cairo. The city is, as usual, humming with energy. The Cairo film festival awards its special jury prize to the Iranian director Tahmina, who is in trouble in Iran for including a shot of two chador-clad women handing out communist leaflets in her film, *The Hidden Half*. The Hanager theatre workshop is showing an Egyptian *Phaedre*. The feast of the Lady Zeinab, granddaughter of the Prophet and one of the most popular members of his household, is reaching its climax with thousands of people from all over the country converging on al-Sayyida, the district which contains her mosque and bears her name. The walls of downtown Cairo are chaotic with posters for the trade union elections due to take place in a few days. The demonstrations that have so far been contained within the campuses of Cairo's five universities ebb and flow with news of Afghan civilian casualties and new Israeli incursions into Palestinian towns.

Over the next two weeks I sense a mood that is not explosive but tense, expectant. There is also puzzlement, a deep exhaustion and a cold, amused cynicism. Nobody even bothers to discuss the 'clash of civilizations' theory except to marvel that the West wastes any time on it at all. Can't they see, people ask, how much of their culture we've adopted? Practically every major work of Western literature or thought is translated into Arabic. The Cairo Opera House is home to the Cairo Symphony Orchestra and the Egyptian Ballet as well as the Arab Music Ensemble. English is taught in every school and the British Council in Cairo is the largest of their operations worldwide because of its English language courses. Yes, there are aspects of Western society that we don't like, they say, but they are the aspects that the West itself regards as problematic: widespread drug abuse, violent crime, the disintegration of the family, teenage pregnancies, lack of sense of community, rampant consumerism. What's wrong with not wanting those for ourselves?

The 'Islam versus the West' theory is dismissed by both Muslim and Christian clerics. In an interview with al-Jazeera, Sheikh Qaradawi echoes what Nadra has been saying: 'It is unfair to lump people together in one basket,' he says. 'The American people are the prisoners of their media. They're ordinary people, concerned with their daily lives, with earning a living. We must try to reach them through debate, not through hostility.' Sayed Hasan Nasrallah, secretary-general of Hizbollah warns: 'We should not deal with this war [in Afghanistan] as if it is a Christian war against Islam.'

A columnist in *al-Ahram*, the major national newspaper of Egypt, reminds readers that in 1977, when Anwar Sadat made his peace visit to Israel, the Coptic Pope, Shenuda III, insisted that no Arab Christian would visit Jerusalem until they could visit alongside the Muslims.

We are fourteen people sitting down to dinner at the Arabesque: Egyptians, Palestinian, American and Iraqi. On the table is a choice of wine, water and guava juice:

'It's sheer ignorance this equation of the East with Islam.'

'Where did Christianity come from in the first place?'

'Bethlehem, Beit Sahour, Beit Jala, all essentially Christian Palestinian towns, bombarded by the Israelis every day.'

'And where do they think we are, the twelve million Egyptian Christians, in all this?'

'And the Jews would have still been here if it hadn't been for the creation of Israel.'

One of the gravest fears in Egypt is of the threat Islamic extremism poses to the fourteen centuries of national unity between Egyptian Copts and Egyptian Muslims. The 'clash of civilizations' rhetoric coming out of the West, the transformation of Osama bin Laden from a fringe figure into a hero, the shoehorning of what people see as a political and economic conflict into a religious mould, are all appallingly dangerous for the very fabric of Egyptian society, where the two communities are so intertwined that they share all the rituals of both joy and sorrow; where Christian women visit the mosque of Sayyida Zainab to ask for needed help and Muslims visit the Church of Santa Teresa, the Rose of Lisieux, to plead for her aid.

Bush and Blair's repeated affirmations of the essential goodness of Islam are seen as so much hot air designed to appease the uneducated masses who, naturally, will never believe them. People smile as they remind you of the German propaganda asserting that 'Hajji Muhammad Hitler' was a true friend of Islam, or the rumour put about by the French 150 years earlier that Bonaparte had converted to the 'true faith'. Religion, people believe, is being used both as a smoke-screen and a mobilization device. When, people ask, has Osama bin Laden ever spoken of Iraq or Palestine? Only after the bombings started. His mission, essentially, was to get the Americans out of Saudi Arabia; now he is playing the West at its own game, and the millions of aggrieved, desperate young Muslims across the world are likely to believe him.

'And what does your chap think he's up to? What's his name?' I'm asked.

'Blair?' I venture.

'Yes. Is he outbidding the Americans? He comes over here with a list of names he wants handed over and six of them are in the Sudanese cabinet.'

There is general incredulity at Tony Blair's gung-ho stance and Britain's seeming eagerness to be part of the conflict. Someone asks me what public opinion in the United Kingdom is really like. We talk about the anti-war demonstrations, reminiscent of the Suez crisis.

Returning from the Middle East after his first whirl-wind visit last month, the Prime Minister seemed to think that his problem was one of communication. He has suggested that Britain needs to do more PR in the Arab world. Well, his personal efforts have been a resounding failure. Why is he rushing around with such zeal? Why does he look so pleased with himself? A cartoon in a newspaper has a flunky saying to a government minister: 'But of course there's nothing wrong with your excellency taking a second job to augment your income. Look at the British Prime Minister – he's got an extra job as PR manager for America's campaign in Afghanistan.' Blair might save the Downing Street spin doctors' efforts for internal affairs. Spin will get nowhere with people who have for a long time not trusted their governments – far less the governments of the West.

Nobody condones what is happening in Afghanistan. Anger is given more edge, yes, by the fact that it is a Muslim country, but more by the perception that the Afghan people have been used and abused for more than twenty years. Everyone is aware of the responsibility of the United States in creating the circumstances for the appearance of the Taliban, who are then pointed at as proof of the backwardness of Islam in general.

Yet Afghanistan, before the Russian invasion, was finding its own way towards modernity; otherwise, how come there are so many Afghan women professionals in the opposition camped up north?

An article in the Egyptian press maps the relationship between oil, arms and key members of the American administration. Not a conspiracy theory, rather a practical acknowledgement that 'oil, defence and politics . . . are not mutually exclusive interests'.

Nobody is surprised by this. After all, a democracy where you need millions of dollars to get into the White House is hardly likely to be free of corporate influence. But a journalist asks why America needs a pretext at all. Why paint itself into a corner with all the 'bin Laden dead or alive' rhetoric? Maybe we understand why it needs Russia and Europe on board but why the pressure on the Arab countries? Is it necessary? Several letters in *al-Ahram Weekly* suggest that not everyone thinks so. In the past five weeks the paper has received hundreds of hostile letters from Westerners – many of them taking that classical orientalist image of a penetrative relationship between West and East to contemporary levels of openess and violence.

Why does America assume conflict and confrontation with the Arab world? My aunt reminds me of the crowds that welcomed Richard Nixon, then the US president, to Egypt in 1974: 'Remember all the talk of USAID and the democratizing process and how the coops were full of American chickens? America was synonymous then with plenty, with progress and liberalization. But none of it came through.' My aunt is a doctor but right now she's lying in bed with a drip attached to her arm. Her left hand is swollen with a bad infection and a powerful antibiotic is blasting its way through her veins. Her son has had to scour Cairo and pay over the odds because the public-sector lab that produces the drug has just burned down. Next the lab will be sold at a rock-bottom price to a well-connected private investor, many of its workforce will be laid off and the medicine, when production is resumed, will be more expensive than before. This is part of the privatization process, the economic 'reforms' the country is being pushed into. 'None of it came through.' In fact, I remember wondering, when I first came in touch with USAID in 1980, why – if it was such a benevolent operation – did its officials seem so jittery? Why did they drive around in black-windowed limos? And why had their embassy been turned into a marine-guarded fortress?

Over Turkish coffee in the Café Riche, Ahmad Hamad, who works for Legal Aid (a non-government organization funded by a sister NGO in Holland) reminds me of the US-encouraged domestic policies of President Anwar Sadat. People were ready to give them a try. America was democratic and free and more fun than the dour, totalitarian Russians. But what 'democratization' amounted to was a clampdown on all left-wing, Nasserist and pan-Arab views and organizations, and eventually on all oposition. 'They nurtured the Islamists as a way of hitting the left. They created and funded Islamist organizations. They manipulated elections so that Islamists took control of the student unions and the professional syndicates. What they didn't understand was that Islamists took themselves seriously and eventually, of course, they assassinated Sadat himself.' It is the same game that the United States played in Afghanistan: to fund and aid an 'Islamist' opposition to the Russians and fail to recognize the consequences.

Since the three attacks by armed Islamist extremists on tourists in Egypt in the mid-90s, the tourist industry has become extremely sensitive. Last week some 50 per cent of its employed workers were forced to take indefinite unpaid leave. For the self-employed there is hardly any work. Entire resorts in Sinai are closed down. Around 2 million Egyptians rely directly on tourism for their livelihoods, and the worry in the country is palpable.

Practically every American, or American-influenced intervention in Egypt has been bad for every one of the 65 million Egyptians – except the few thousand who have become fabulously wealthy in the new economy. Debt-ridden farmers, disenfranchised workers, the decimated middle class, the silenced intellectuals and students – all of them will tell you they have America's influence to thank for their problems. Yes, Egyptians have internal problems with their government and inter-Arab problems with their neighbours, but these problems are made ever more intractable by American intervention. And then there's the question of Palestine.

Egyptian official media, on the whole, play down what is happening in the Palestinian territories. Egyptian television, for example, does not show the images of brutality, destruction and grief coming out of the West Bank and Gaza. Yet half of Cairo is tuned in to the al-Jazeera satellite channel. On top of every building you can see the dishes facing up towards ArabSat. And every taxi driver you talk to says: 'Isn't that terrorism what they're doing to the Palestinians?'

The Egyptian Committee for Solidarity with the Palestinian Intifada (ECSPI) formed itself in October 2000 to provide humanitarian aid to the people of the West Bank and Gaza. It now has volunteers in every city across Egypt. When I meet four of its members in a coffee shop they are shadowed by a chap from the State Security Service, who sits down at the next table. Their phones are bugged and their every move is monitored. The people I meet are two men and two women. One of the women, May, is Christian, the other, Nadia, is a Muslim in a complete veil. She tells me she used to be my student, and it turns into a joke since there's no way I can recognize her. The ECSPI volunteers go into the towns and villages to collect donations for the Palestinians. 'There isn't a house that doesn't give us something,' May tells me, 'and people have so little. We collected three tonnes of sugar half-kilo by half-kilo.'

On September 10 a long-planned petition on behalf of the Palestinian people was due to be handed in to the American Embassy in Cairo. As the delegation met in Tahrir Square it grew to some 300 people. The police surrounded it and refused to let it proceed. A group of ten was chosen and headed for the embassy, where the ambassador refused to meet them and the embassy refused to take delivery of the petition.

America's support for Israel is a dominant issue in Egyptian–American relations. I have not had a conversation in Cairo where it has not come up. When American officials talk about the lives lost in New York and Washington, about New Yorkers' inalienable right to freedom of movement, about US citizens' right to safety, a voice inside the head of every Arab will echo: 'True. And what about the Palestinians?' President Bush has spoken for the first time about a 'Palestinian state', but he has not used the word 'viable'. People remember that when the West was drumming up the coalition against Iraq it made noises about Palestine and set up the Madrid conference, resulting in the Oslo agreements, which have been disastrous for peace. They suspect a similar agenda now. Yet the hope is that if one good thing can come out of the current horrors it would be that America recognizes that a truly workable formula for a reasonably just peace has to be imposed on the Israeli–Palestinian conflict.

A few days after the failed attempt to deliver the petition, Farid Zahran, vice-chair of the organization, was abducted by State Security and vanished for three weeks. He was released only after 250 members of ECSPI and Legal Aid insisted on turning themselves in to the public attorney, signing an affidavit against themselves that they were complicit with Zahran in whatever he was accused of. 'It was a warning,' Nadra says. 'We'll let you carry on collecting medicines and stuff, but any attempt to mobilize the street and we'll come down on you hard.' This is made possible by the emergency laws operating since the assassination of Sadat in 1981 and further strengthened by anti-terrorism laws formulated in the mid-90s – essentially the same type of laws that are under discussion now both in the United States and here in the United Kingdom.

People I speak to are alarmed at the prospect of Americans giving up their civil liberties. 'It's one of the organizing principles of their society,' someone says. 'How will their society hold without it?'

An article in the Egyptian press publishes a report that Americans, apparently, are 'cocooning'. They're staying at home, hiring videos, talking to each other, visiting family and friends nearby and buying only what they need. It seems, to the Egyptian reader, like a good way to live. But the report is alarmed; two-thirds of the American economy is consumer spending, if people don't get out there to the malls the economy will collapse. People feel sorry for them. The poor Americans, they say, they're whipped out to work more and earn more, then they're whipped out to spend it; is that the freedom they're so proud of?

I walk down Sheikh Rihan with a young American graduate student who tells me that he had been approached to be interviewed on NBC. They called him for a pre-interview, he says. He kept his answers neutral, but truthful. In the end they said they'd call him back – they never did.

There is general agreement among people who have access to Western media that Americans are being kept ignorant. 'They're under media siege,' was how one journalist put it.

'Our only hope,' Nadra says, 'is to talk to them.

Sensible people everywhere should make themselves heard so that we don't personally witness the end of the world.'

A young, slim, professional woman in casual trousers and a loose shirt, the canvas bag slung over her shoulder bulging with lenses, tapes, papers and somewhere, I suppose, a comb and some lip salve. I watch her walk away from me down the avenue of flame-trees. Is the road tightening round her? Narrowing down? Or is it just my perspective?

Ahdaf Soueif

Two

And blood in torrents pour
In vain – always in vain,
For war breeds war again.

'War Song', John Davidson

The Bigger They Come,
The Harder They Fall

Still the enemy, says *The Times*. As if you can. 'The foes of democracy must face a united assault,' the paper adds, as though anyone has the least idea who makes up this prowling host or where its encampment is to be found.

'Unsheathe the terrible swift sword,' cries the *Daily Telegraph*, omitting to offer further news of the miracle weapon. 'A broad coalition of all peace-loving states must be built to defeat this enemy,' writes Ehud Barak in *The Times*, apparently unaware some of them would object to the inclusion of his own country in that list.

Spare us this nonsense.

'What happened on September 11, 2001,' even Hugo Young writes in the *Guardian*, 'changed the course of human history' and 'punctured the dream' of American isolation: 'Disengagement is not an option.' In the same paper James Rubin, former spokesman for President Clinton, declares that ground troops could be used: 'It's not retribution, it's pre-emption.'

Crush terrorism? Purge fundamentalists? Impose Pax Atlantica on a continent peppered by bandit states and religious maniacs? Spread Christian–liberal order across a savage world by force of arms? Kipling, thou should'st be living at this hour.

This is babble, dangerous babble. This is bawling nonsense. What gets into the collective head of the political class and its commentariat, shooting off their mouths at times like these? Do they think a terrorist is like a pin in a tenpin bowling alley: one down, nine to go? Do they want to give Osama bin Laden his own Bloody Sunday? Do they not know that when you kill one Osama bin Laden you sow twenty more? Playing the world's policeman is not the answer to that catastrophe in New York. Playing the world's policeman is what led to it.

September 11 is a consequence of trying to impose world order, not a wake-up call to redouble the attempt. September 11 is a demonstration of what you can never achieve with armies, spies, coalitions, conferences and international muscle, not an argument for buying more.

September 11 reminds us of another giant in history, a tower of a man brought down by a well-aimed airborne projectile from the sling of a slim young zealot. But in that case we are on the side of the zealot; in this our condolences are for the giant. Both stories would teach that the bigger they come the harder they fall. But did we not know that already? September 11 teaches us nothing we did not already know.

We know – do we not? – that the infrastructure of a modern capitalist state is essentially unguarded, and unguardable. We cannot be body-searching each other all day; we could not bar from employment any jobseeker who was Muslim because he might already be, or later become, a secret fundamentalist.

We know – do we not? – that borders cannot be sealed. Is the whole forty-year experience of Berlin insufficient to teach us that even a ruthlessly authoritarian power struggles to make an impregnable wall across one city?

From another mental compartment, curiously sealed from the echo of calls to halt the free movement of terrorists, comes a recollection that the British and French governments appear unable to seal the mouth of one tunnel just beyond our shores. What hope the land borders of Central Asia? We know – do we not? – that 40,000 NATO troops in tiny Kosovo are unable to stop KLA Albanian terrorist weapons crossing freely into Macedonia. We know – do we not? – that an imperial Britain was unable to contain so much as one terrorist uprising in little Cyprus; that we barely beat the Boers in South Africa and never beat the Mau Mau in Kenya, Jewish terrorists in Palestine or the bombers in Aden; and that Algerian terrorism wrecked much of the last century for France.

In every case the terrorists' pursuer governed the place. And we are going to have them 'stamped out' in Iraq and Afghanistan, where we do not? Dream on, Tony.

We know – do we not? – that even the watchful state can seldom find those who are determined to work unseen. In Britain we cannot so much as keep tabs on a few wretched asylum-seekers who slip away into the crowd when their applications are refused. Nor need a potential terrorist be an illegal immigrant: he may have entered lawfully, or have citizenship. We know – do we not? – we cannot keep them out and we know we cannot find them when they are in.

We know – do we not? – that with every year that passes, every thousandth link-up to the Internet, every millionth new mobile phone, it becomes less necessary for conspirators to meet physically in one place in order to conspire. The day is coming, perhaps has already come, when terrorists will not need to gather in camps. There will be no HQs to bomb, no cells to track down, no tents to ransack. The concept of 'host' country as geographical location for a terrorist group may already be too weak to bear weight, certainly too weak to justify revenge-bombing of the uninvolved. All we will be able to allege will be the 'hospitality' or 'ambiguity' shown by some governments to shadowy figures who flit in and out of their territories. The IRA, for instance, flitting in and out of America and raising funds. Shall we bomb Washington? Should we bomb Dublin? Should white supremacist South Africa have bombed London when black freedom fighters with bases here killed innocent people there? We have got a cheek – have we not? – to declare that the Americans should 'make no distinction between the perpetrators of a terrorist atrocity and the government which gives it shelter'. London and the capitals of Europe offer some of the world's best havens for terrorists and freedom fighters seeking neutral countries from which to hatch their campaigns.

For we know – do we not? – that no ghost of an international consensus will ever be reached about who are the goodies and who are the baddies in the world of violent protest. One man's terrorist is another man's freedom fighter.

Making these distinctions the grounds for invasion will sow the most monstrous sense of injustice among nations who think differently.

Of course, we must catch and disable terrorists where we can. Of course, there is a moral case for trying to snuff out those who threaten our world. There was a moral case for American policy in Vietnam. But if America failed to remove the Vietcong from South-East Asia, and if Russia cannot even remove terrorists from Chechnya and all but foundered in the attempt to subdue Afghanistan, why and how do a series of explosions in America suddenly make possible a new Pax Atlantica imposed worldwide by an American-led group of nations of which Britain now yaps to be a leading member?

It is not the case that terrorism can never be stamped out by sheer force; rather it is the case that without locating, surrounding, isolating and ruthlessly exterminating the whole group, the attempt – particularly if made by a foreign power – is likely to fail; and in failing, to energize and remotivate the cause, spreading its appeal and acting as a recruiting sergeant for its leaders. The West is in no position to trample across the East with the necessary vast manpower, firepower and local intelligence. All we would do is infuriate the Muslim world and drive moderates into the arms of extremists. That is Osama bin Laden's hope.

Instead we should ask what makes a Muslim terrorist. It is rage. Can we understand the rage? Surely we can.

Many in the Middle East, including many who are not extremists, resent American involvement there, propping up favoured states and undermining others. Few Muslims – even among those America supports – can be comfortable with this; many are angered, and a hard core are enraged.

A drawing-in of horns by the West would take the heat from this anger. After America's immediate lashing-out (and perhaps after securing the extradition of Osama bin Laden himself), I believe such a partial retrenchment may take place. And after September 11, and the horrible, horrible deaths of thousands of innocent people, one thing will be certain: the world will be the same again after all.

Matthew Parris

'William Blake Says: Every Thing that Lives is Holy'

Long live the Child
Long live the Mother and Father
Long live the People

Long live this wounded Planet
Long live the good milk of the Air
Long live the spawning Rivers and the
mothering Oceans
Long live the juice of the Grass
and all the determined greenery of the Globe

Long live the Elephants and the Sea Horses,
the Humming-Birds and the Gorillas,
the Dogs and Cats and Field-Mice –
all the surviving animals
our innocent Sisters and Brothers

Long live the Earth, deeper than all our thinking

we have done enough killing

Long live the Man
Long live the Woman
Who use both courage and compassion
Long live their Children

'To Whom It May Concern'

It is not and never has been a poem about the Vietnam War. I've never been to Vietnam. It is a poem about sitting comfortably in a safe country and sometimes wishing that the news of the murderous world would stop. It is a poem about the times when we wish to be cut off from the truth. It is a poem about the necessity for the truth.

I was run over by the truth one day.
Ever since the accident I've walked this way
    So stick my legs in plaster
    Tell me lies about Vietnam.

Heard the alarm clock screaming with pain,
Couldn't find myself so I went back to
    sleep again
    So fill my ears with silver
    Stick my legs in plaster
    Tell me lies about Vietnam.

Every time I shut my eyes all I see is flames.
Made a marble phone book and I carved
    all the names
    So coat my eyes with butter
    Fill my ears with silver
    Stick my legs in plaster
    Tell me lies about Vietnam.

I smell something burning, hope it's just
    my brains.

They're only dropping peppermints and
  daisy-chains
    So stuff my nose with garlic
    Coat my eyes with butter
    Fill my ears with silver
    Stick my legs in plaster
    Tell me lies about Vietnam.

Where were you at the time of the crime?
Down by the Cenotaph drinking slime
    So chain my tongue with whisky
    Stuff my nose with garlic
    Coat my eyes with butter
    Fill my ears with silver
    Stick my legs in plaster
    Tell me lies about Vietnam.

You put your bombers in, you put your
  conscience out,
You take the human being and you twist
  it all about
    So scrub my skin with women
    Chain my tongue with whisky
    Stuff my nose with garlic
    Coat my eyes with butter
    Fill my ears with silver
    Stick my legs in plaster
    Tell me lies about Vietnam.

Adrian Mitchell

An Eye for an Eye

The events of September 11 were truly horrific and the resultant international outrage is understandable, especially in America. But we should fully understand why Osama bin Laden took such dramatic terrorist action against America and the Western world. We in Britain have had terrorist activities on our doorstep for more than thirty years and have not yet totally eradicated terrorism from Northern Ireland. Why, then, should we believe that we can do so in Afghanistan, a place so culturally, politically and geographically removed from our island nation?

Religious and nationalistic prejudices seem to be the root cause of most terrorist activities. Britain's ongoing diplomatic negotiations between Protestants and Catholics has helped mollify the situation in Ireland, and has significantly contributed to the decommissioning of weapons. Such negotiations and the developments they boast must be observed in our present conflict with international terrorism. America has funded and supported Israel (and also the IRA) and this has disgusted the Muslim world. There are many other aspects of the US foreign policy that, understandably, it rejects.

However, I don't believe any country can conduct a

'war' against terrorism. The 'eye for an eye' argument cannot be successful in a modern world. Such archaic views will only stimulate further racial and religious tensions. You cannot conduct a 'war' against people's deeply held beliefs. War only convinces them that their belief is correct and results in such views being even more deeply felt.

Whilst I understand that the people responsible for masterminding the events of September 11 are murderers and need to be brought to justice, I also believe that declaring war on a whole country and killing the innocents of that county can only escalate terrorism and international aggression.

The only solution is for the Christian and Jewish worlds to begin to understand the Muslim world and vice versa. They can then consider making the necessary compromises to allow them to live in peace with respect for each other's beliefs. A lot of talking must be done to achieve this.

In New York recently I saw a piece of graffiti which said, 'An eye for an eye can make everybody blind'. War is certainly not a solution where diplomacy and negotiation are options.

Terence Conran

Peace. What is that?

Peace. What is that?

Something I have taken so much for granted in all my forty-six years on our planet. I have never had to endure the suffering experienced by millions and it intrigues me how I could have managed to avoid the implications of warfare so easily.

The possibility of a completely different reality began to dawn on me one Sunday afternoon a few weeks ago in the supermarket. While trailing through the corridors of tins and packaging, I wondered what would happen if the whole system suddenly stopped? Could I take the children and flee to another country where no bombs would fall and where no deadly chemicals could reach us?

And then what?

How would we live?

What about money? With the world economy crashed, there would be no handy cashpoint in the high street. The high street might no longer exist. I wondered if perhaps I ought to withdraw some cash now and stash it safely somewhere.

Where though? Under the mattress? Far too risky. I remembered that's what people did in World War II. Yes, in easily secreted pockets. Then I realized I was being too ludicrous, too paranoid. How ridiculous. The image of a wheelbarrow piled with roubles for the price of a loaf of bread and scores of downtrodden people queuing for endless hours at the rumour of potatoes raced through my mind.

What else? What else?

No electricity; no heating; no light. Remember to stock up on candles and matches. Bad water – probably contaminated.

Food. Should we start planting now? I've never grown a thing in my life. Plants wilt when they hear me coming.

School. Well, it would probably be shut down. Wouldn't it?

Transport. Would there be any petrol?

I'm making a record but there'd be no music industry. Will anyone survive to hear this small masterpiece anyway?

And what would happen if you got ill? A toothache or sudden appendicitis? How would you get any medicine with the chemist closed and no supplies available?

A plethora of potentially irresolvable dilemmas invaded my brain.

And, of course, I haven't even mentioned the big issue.

Mainly the d-word. That terrible something that happens to us all. Don't know where, don't know when. Only, surely, not everybody all at once. Visions of Armageddon.

*   *   *

A few months ago I had an incredibly vivid and disturbing dream. I seemed to be standing outside on a bright sunny day somewhere in the City of London. Through the buildings, in the distance, I suddenly realized that a massive fireball was heading rapidly in my direction. I spun round and saw lots of people running out of the tube station in panic.

'What's happening?' I called out to the man nearest me.

'That's it! It's all over!' he said.

And I woke up instantly with my heart pounding, having just witnessed the end of the world.

How do you stop terrorism? Go to war with it?

'Come out, come out wherever you are . . . We're gonna get you!'

I'm sorry, but I just don't get it.

Annie Lennox

The Case for Collateral Repairs

Nothing symbolizes the futility of this war like the yellow ration packs drifting from American planes on to the minefields of Afghanistan. Their purpose, the US government told us, is to show that the allied forces are not attacking the Afghan people; that the war is being waged for their good as well as ours; that the United States' concern to overthrow the Taliban is matched by its concern to rescue the people from their misery. If this is so, the yellow bags could scarcely be more suggestive of political failure.

The United Nations estimates that there are 7.5 million hungry people in Afghanistan. One person requires 18 kg of food per month to survive. If the United Nations' projections are correct, and some 1.5 million people manage to leave the country, around 6 million starving people will be left behind. Afghanistan requires 580,000 tonnes of food to see its people through the winter, as well as tarpaulins, warm clothes, medicines and water supply and sanitation equipment. In the middle of winter in the Hindu Kush there is snow up to your neck. Many of these supplies, in other words, could have been delivered to the vulnerable people only if they had been brought into Afghanistan before the middle of November. Even without a war, an operation of this size would have pressed at the margins of possibility. But military action has prevented all but a fraction of the necessary supplies from entering in time.

Instead, the people of Afghanistan have been bombed with peanut butter and paper napkins, in the packs fluttering out of the sky. The US Department of Defense has announced that it possesses a total of 2 million of these bags, which it might be prepared to drop. If so, and if, miraculously, all of them reach those who need them most, they could feed 27 per cent of the starving for one day.

But some of these rations will, of course, be lost. Many, perhaps most, will be eaten by people who are not in immediate danger of starvation, as they are more mobile than the seriously hungry and better able to reach the packs. Some will remain untouched. One of the warring factions may discover that an effective means of eliminating its enemies is to remove the contents of these packs and replace them with explosives. This is just one of the problems associated with dispensing kindness at 20,000 feet: no one can be completely sure whose generosity they are about to enjoy.

The usefulness of any feeding programme, moreover, is greatly diminished if it is not carefully targeted. People in different stages of starvation require different preparations. Children, especially infants, are more vulnerable than any others. Yet all the packs being dropped on Afghanistan are identical, and all are equipped only to feed adults. The packs contain medicine as well as food, but unlike aid workers on the ground, the pilots delivering them can offer no diagnosis. This blanket prescription is likely to be either useless or dangerous.

So Western governments have terminated what may have been an effective humanitarian programme and replaced it with a futile gesture. The bombing raids, moreover, have persuaded tens of thousands to flee from their homes. Yet Afghanistan's borders with the Central Asian Republics and Pakistan were closed by order of the United States: the refugees have nowhere to go. The military strikes, the US Defense Secretary Donald Rumsfeld announced, would 'create conditions for sustained . . . humanitarian relief operations in Afghanistan'. They have, so far, done precisely the opposite.

But the real purpose of the food drops is not to feed the starving, but to *tell* them they are being fed. President Bush explained one Sunday that by means of these packages, 'the oppressed people of Afghanistan will know the generosity of America and our allies'. In fact, what they know is that gestures will not feed them because hunger brooks no tokenism.

Since the attacks on New York, many of us have argued that the only effective means of dealing with the Taliban, Osama bin Laden and al-Qaeda is through humanitarian, rather than military intervention. A vast delivery of aid, dragging the population back from the brink of famine, would show the people that, unlike the Taliban, the West is on their side. The Taliban thrive on the fear of outsiders, which, as far as Afghans are concerned, has so far been amply justified. A massive aid programme, coupled with some astute diplomatic work, would provide us the best chance of overthrowing the Taliban and capturing the suspects.

Thanks to the linkage established by both Bush and Blair between aid and ordnance (i.e. dropping both bombs and ration packets), which sounds so bold and compassionate at home, this option is now less workable than it was before the bombing began. Moreover, time is running out rapidly for the Afghan people and the chances of getting food to all who need it are diminishing by the day. Even so, it remains the only humane and intelligent approach for dealing with both the country's crisis and the West's need to free itself from terrorism.

Predictably, most mainstream commentators have written off these views as hopelessly naive and idealistic. And it's true that the success of this approach is far from assured. But there is surely no notion as naive as that which supposes that you can destroy a tactic (such as terrorism) or an idea (such as fundamentalism) by means of bombs or missile strikes or special forces. Indeed, even the Pentagon now lists its military choices under the heading AOS: All Options Stink. If military intervention succeeded in delivering up Osama bin Laden and destroying the Taliban, it's hard to see how this could fail to encourage retaliatory strikes all over the world.

Nor is it entirely clear that the attacks on Afghanistan will bring down the maniacs who govern it. Britain and the United States have been bombing Iraq for the past ten years, only to strengthen Saddam's grip. There are many in Washington who privately acknowledge that Castro's tenure has been sustained by US hostilities and embargoes. Had the United States withdrawn its forces from Guantanamo Bay, opened its markets and invested in Cuba, it would have achieved with generosity what it has never achieved with antagonism. There is plenty of evidence to suggest that, as a result of the attacks on Afghanistan, the Afghans are siding with the lesser Satan at home against the Great Satan overseas.

Conversely, Britain's Conservative government responded to the riots of the 1980s by regenerating the mauled estates until other cities complained that the only way to gain funding was to run amok. But the government had understood that while rioters may be encouraged by the residents of depressed and decaying estates, they are fiercely resisted by people whose prospects are brightening.

Some might argue that showering Afghanistan with food rather than bombs would create an incentive for further acts of terror. But Osama bin Laden has no interest in the welfare of the Afghan people. Like the Taliban, the social weapons he deploys are misery and insecurity. He seeks not peace, but war. While Western aggression has been driving Afghans into the arms of the Taliban and their guests, a coherent programme of Western aid would divide the Afghan people from the Taliban predators.

Such an aid programme would, of course, take time and it's not hard to see why the American people want instant results. But justice requires patience, and infinite justice requires infinite patience. The great advantage of this strategy is that it's safe. Far from spawning future conflicts, it is likely to defuse them. Far from immersing a new generation in hatred of the West, it's likely to inculcate a hatred of those who would deprive them of friendly contact with outsiders. Far from triggering fundamentalist uprisings all over the Muslim world, it could lead to a new understanding between cultures, even a sense of common purpose. The likes of Osama bin Laden would then have nowhere to hide. And there's an accidental by-product,which has nothing to do with the West's strategic objectives. Rather than killing thousands more civilians, we could save the lives of millions. Let's make this the era of collateral repair.

George Monbiot

The Grammar of the War on Terrorism

What really alarms me about President Bush's 'War on Terrorism' is the grammar. How do you wage war on an abstract noun? It's rather like bombing Murder.

'We're going to bomb Murder wherever it lurks,' announced President Bush. 'We are going to seek out the Murderers and the would-be Murderers wherever they are hiding and we are going to bring them to justice. We are also going to bomb any government that harbours Murderers and Murderers-to-be.'

The other thing that worries me about Bush and Blair's 'War on Terrorism' is: how will they know when they've won it?

With most wars you can say you've won when the other side is either all dead or surrenders. But how is 'Terrorism' going to surrender? It's well known, in philological circles, that it's very hard for abstract nouns to surrender. In fact it's very hard for abstract nouns to do anything at all of their own volition, and hard for even trained philologists to negotiate with them. It's difficult to find their hide-outs, useless to try and cut off their supplies or intercept their paths of communication, and it's downright impossible to try and make them give in. Abstract nouns simply aren't like that.

I'm afraid the bitter semantic truth is, you can't win against these sort of words – unless, I suppose, you get them thrown out of the Oxford English Dictionary. That would show 'em.

A nearby Professor of Ontological Semiotics (currently working on finding out what his title means) informs me that World War II was fought against an abstract noun: 'Fascism' – remember? But I point out to him that that particular abstract noun was cunningly hiding behind the very real persona of Nazi Germany. In 1945 we simply had to defeat Nazi Germany to win. In President Bush's 'War on Terrorism' there is no such solution in sight. He can say: 'We will destroy Terrorism. And make no mistake we shall win!' until the chickens come home to roost, but the statement is about as meaningful as saying: 'We shall annihilate Mockery' or 'We shall deride Persiflage'.

Actually, the very word 'Terrorism' seems to have changed its meaning over recent years. Throughout history, Terrorism has been a favourite tool of governments – one thinks, for example, of Edward III's *chevauchée* across Normandy in 1359 (or possibly one doesn't). But in its current usage, 'Terrorism' cannot be committed by a country. When the United States bombed the pharmaceutical factory in the Sudan on the mistaken advice from the CIA that it was a chemical weapons factory, *that* was not an act of Terrorism. It was pretty stupid. It probably killed thousands of sick people, by destroying their medical supplies, but it was not an 'Act of Terrorism' within the current meaning of the word, because the US government did it officially. *And* they apologized for it. That's very important. No self-respecting Terrorist ever apologizes. It's one of the few things that distinguishes legitimate governments from Terrorists.

So it was really difficult for President Bush to know whom to bomb after the World Trade Center outrage. If a country like Bermuda or New Zealand had done it then it would have been simple – he could have bombed the Bahamas and Australia. It must have been really irritating that the people who perpetrated such a horrendous catastrophe were not a nation. What's more Terrorists – unlike a country – won't keep still in one place so you can bomb them. Terrorists have this annoying habit of moving around and sometimes of even leaving the country. It's all very un-American (apart from the training, that is).

On top of all this, you really have no idea who the Terrorists are. At least I assume the CIA and the FBI had no idea who the World Trade Center Terrorists were – otherwise they'd have stopped them getting on the planes in the first place. It's in the very nature of Terrorists not to be known until they've committed their particular Act of Terrorism. Otherwise they're just plain old Tim McVeigh who lives next door, or that nice Mr Atta who's taking flying lessons.

Well, you may say, there's that not-so-nice (although rather good at propaganda) Osama bin Laden – we know he's committed Acts of Terrorism and intends to do so again. Fine. At least we know one Terrorist. But kill him and you still haven't killed Terrorism. In fact you haven't even begun to kill Terrorism. That's the trouble with declaring war on Terrorism. Being an abstract noun it cannot be defined by individuals or organizations.

Mr Bush and Mr Blair must be the first heads of state to lead their countries into a war in which they don't know who the enemy is.

So let's forget the abstract noun. Let's rename President Bush's war for him, let's call it the 'War on Terrorists' – that sounds a bit more concrete. But actually the semantics get even more obscure. What exactly does President Bush mean by 'Terrorists'? He hasn't actually defined the term for us, so we'll have to try and work out what he means from his actions.

Judging from President Bush's actions, the Terrorists who instigated the attack on the World Trade Center all live together in camps in Afghanistan. There, apparently, they've all stuck together, after their successful mission, hanging around in these 'camps' so that we can go and bomb the hell out of them. Presumably they spend the evenings playing the guitar and eating their chow around the campfire. In these 'camps', the Terrorists also engage in 'training' and stockpiling weapons, which we can obliterate with our cluster-bombs and uranium-tipped missiles. Nobody seems to have told the President that the horrors of September were perpetrated with little more than a couple of dozen knives. I suppose the United States could bomb all the stock-piles of knives in the world, but I have a sneaking feeling it's still not going to eradicate any Terrorists.

Besides, I thought the Terrorists who crashed those

planes into the World Trade Center were living in
Florida and New Jersey. I thought the al-Qaeda
network was operating in sixty-four countries includ-
ing the United States and many European countries,
which even President Bush might prefer not to bomb.
But no, President Bush, the US Congress, Prime
Minister Blair and pretty much the entire House of
Commons are convinced that Terrorists live in
Afghanistan and can be bombed from a safe distance.
What we are witnessing is clearly yet another exam-
ple of a word changing its meaning.

It's often said that 'in War the first casualty is
Grammar'. President Bush's 'War on Terrorism' is no
exception. Statements no longer mean what they used
to mean. For example, people keep saying to me: 'We've
got to carry on as normal.' What are they talking about?
The World Trade Center has been destroyed with the
loss of thousands of lives and the United States and the
United Kingdom are currently bombing Afghanistan.
That doesn't sound like a definition of 'normal' to me.
Why should we pretend that it is?

And what is meant by: 'We mustn't give in to the
Terrorists'? We gave in to the Terrorists the moment
the first bombs fell on Afghanistan, and the instiga-
tors of September 11 must have been popping the
corks on their non-alcoholic champagne (I speak
metaphorically of course). They have successfully
provoked the United States into attacking yet another
poor country it didn't previously know much about,
thereby creating genuine revulsion throughout the
Arab world, ensuring that Islam is destabilized and

that support swings in favour of the Islamic fundamentalists. Words have become devalued, some have
changed their meaning and the philologists can only
shake their heads and wonder whether it isn't all just
a huge grammatical mess.

Terry Jones

First Writing Since

1.

there have been no words
i have not written one word.
no poetry in the ashes south of canal street.
no prose in the refrigerated trucks driving debris
    and dna.
not one word.
today is a week, and seven is of heavens, gods,
    science.
evident out my kitchen window is an abstract
    reality.
sky where once was steel.
smoke where once was flesh.
fire in the city air and i feared for my sister's life in
    a way never before.
and then, and now, i fear for the rest of us.
first, please god, let it be a mistake, the pilot's heart
    failed, the plane's engine died.
then, please god, let it be a nightmare, wake me
    now.
please god, after the second plane, please, don't let
    it be anyone who looks like my brothers.

i do not know how bad a life has to break in order
    to kill.
i have never been so hungry that i willed hunger.
i have never been so angry as to want to control
    a gun over a pen.
not really.
even as a woman, as a palestinian, as a broken
    human being.
never this broken.
more than ever, i believe there is no difference.
the most privileged nation, most americans do not
    know the difference between indians, afghanis,
    syrians, muslims, sikhs, hindus.
more than ever, there is no difference.

2.

thank you korea for kimchi and bibim bob, and
    corn tea and the genteel smiles of the wait staff
    at wonjo.
smiles never revealing the heat of the food or how
    tired they must be working long midtown shifts.

thank you korea, for the belly craving that brought
    me into the city late the night before and
    diverted my daily train ride into the world trade
    center.
there are plenty of thank-yous in ny right now.
thank you for my lazy procrastinating late arse.
thank you to the germs that had me call in sick.

thank you, my attitude, you had me fired the week
    before.
thank you for the train that never came, the rude
    nyer who stole my cab going downtown.
thank you for the sense my mama gave me to run.
thank you for my legs, my eyes, my life.

3.
the dead are called lost and their families hold up
    shaky printouts in front of us through screens
    smoked up.
we are looking for iris, mother of three.
please call with any information.
we are searching for priti, last seen on the 103rd
    floor.
she was talking to her husband on the phone and
    the line went.
please help us find george, also known as adel.
his family is waiting for him with his favourite
    meal.
i am looking for my son, who was delivering coffee.
i am looking for my sister girl, she started her job
    on monday.
i am looking for peace.
i am looking for mercy.
i am looking for evidence of compassion.
any evidence of life.
i am looking for life.

4.

ricardo on the radio said in his accent thick as
yucca, 'i will feel so much better when the first
bombs drop over there. and my friends feel the
same way.'

on my block, a woman was crying in a car parked
and stranded in hurt.

i offered comfort, extended a hand she did not see
before she said, 'we're gonna burn them so bad, i
swear, so bad.'

my hand went to my head and my head went to
the numbers within it of the dead iraqi children,
the dead in nicaragua.

the dead in rwanda who had to vie with fake sport
wrestling for america's attention.

yet when people sent e-mails saying, this was bound
to happen, let's not forget u.s. transgressions, for
half a second i felt resentful.

hold up with that, cause i live here, these are my
friends and fam, and it could have been me in
those buildings, and we're not bad people, do not
support america's bullying.

can i just have a half second to feel bad?

if i can find through this exhaust people who were
left behind to mourn and to resist mass murder, i
might be all right.

thank you to the woman who saw me brinking my
cool and blinking back tears.

she opened her arms before she asked 'do you want
a hug?'

a big white woman, and her embrace was the

kind only people with the warmth of flesh
can offer.
i wasn't about to say no to any comfort.
'my brother's in the navy,' i said. 'and we're arabs.'
'wow, you got double trouble.'
word.

5.
one more person ask me if i knew the hijackers.
one more motherfucker ask me what navy my
brother is in.
one more person assume no arabs or muslims were
killed.
one more person assume they know me, or that i
represent a people.
or that a people represent an evil.
or that evil is as simple as a flag and words on a
page.
we did not vilify all white men when mcveigh
bombed oklahoma.
america did not give out his family's addresses or
where he went to church.
or blame the bible or pat robertson.
and when the networks air footage of palestinians
dancing in the street, there is no apology that
these images are over a decade old.
that hungry children are bribed with sweets that turn
their teeth brown.
that correspondents edit images.

that archives are there to facilitate lazy and
    inaccurate journalism.
and when we talk about holy books and hooded
    men and death, why do we never mention the
    kkk?
if there are any people on earth who understand how
    new york is feeling right now, they are in the west
    bank and the gaza strip.

6.
today it is ten days.
last night bush waged war on a man once openly
    funded by the cia.
i do not know who is responsible.
read too many books, know too many people to
    believe what i am told.
i don't give a fuck about bin laden.
his vision of the world does not include me or those
    i love.
and petitions have been going around for years
    trying to get the u.s. sponsored taliban out of
    power.
shit is complicated, and i don't know what to think.
but i know for sure who will pay.
in the world, it will be women, mostly coloured and
    poor.
women will have to bury children, and support
    themselves through grief.
'either you are with us, or with the terrorists' –

meaning keep your people under control and your
   resistance censored.
meaning we got the loot and the nukes.
in america, it will be those amongst us who refuse
   blanket attacks on the shivering.
those of us who work towards social justice, in
   support of civil liberties, in opposition to hateful
   foreign policies.
i have never felt less american and more new yorker,
   particularly brooklyn, than these past days.
the stars and stripes on all these cars and apartment
   windows represent the dead as citizens first, not
   family members, not lovers.
i feel like my skin is real thin and that my eyes are
   only going to get darker.
the future holds little light.

my baby brother is a man now, and on alert, and
   praying five times a day that the orders he will
   take in a few days' time are righteous and will not
   weigh his soul down from the afterlife he deserves.
both my brothers – my heart stops when i try to
   pray – not a beat to disturb my fear.
one a rock god, the other a sergeant, and both
   palestinian, practising muslims, gentle men. both
   born in brooklyn and their faces are of the
   archetypal arab man, all eyelashes and nose and
   beautiful colour and stubborn hair.
what will their lives be like now?
over there is over here.

7.

all day, across the river, the smell of burning rubber
and limbs floats through.
the sirens have stopped now.
the advertisers are back on the air.
the rescue workers are traumatized.
the skyline is brought back to human size.
no longer taunting the gods with its height.
i have not cried at all while writing this.
i cried when i saw those buildings collapse on
themselves like a broken heart.
i have never owned pain that needs to spread
like that.
and i cry daily that my brothers return to our
mother safe and whole.
there is no poetry in this.
there are causes and effects.
there are symbols and ideologies.
mad conspiracy here, and information we will
never know.
there is death here, and there are promises of more.
there is life here.
anyone reading this is breathing, maybe hurting, but
breathing for sure.
and if there is any light to come, it will shine from
the eyes of those who look for peace and justice
after the rubble and rhetoric are cleared and the
phoenix has risen.
affirm life.
affirm life.

we got to carry each other now.
you are either with life, or against it.
affirm life.

Suheir Hammad

Where does the Bombing Stop?

New York is very important to me. It was where, in the 60s, I did my growing up and where I met my husband. Our courtship took place up the highest buildings we could find. Of course the World Trade Center wasn't opened until 1973 so that had to wait till we had a child or two who whooped their way to the top. Manhattan wound its way into my heart as an old friend or close relation and, although I return much less often now, it's the only other city, apart from London, where I could imagine myself living. My first novel was set there. My newest novel tells the story of three women: one of them is Chicago born who becomes a doctor in New York.

Like so many people linked by television around the world, I watched the second airplane crash into the World Trade Center and then stared with mesmerized horror as the tragedy unfolded. I spent that terrible afternoon with a friend who feared for the safety of her son in Washington. I will never forget the images that were projected into our safe little Notting Hill Gate flat. No reminder will ever be needed, however much time passes.

As soon as I could take in the disaster which had

not, in any obvious sense, affected me personally, I realized I must touch base in New York, pay a bit of homage in its time of trouble for what it has given me. So my ticket is booked and I'll spend that wonderful celebration of Thanksgiving with close friends in Manhattan.

I write the above at some length to explain that my attitude to what has followed September 11 does not show a lack of feeling for what America has suffered. Nevertheless, almost immediately, I felt a dreadful anxiety that the US response would not mitigate the tragedy but increase it. The use of the word 'war' by President Bush and others seemed unreal and therefore dangerous. War against whom? Many others, I know, shared the same fear that the US response would be a wild bellow of rage, expressed by immediate and thoughtless action. This anxiety was made worse by our Prime Minister (for whom I voted) declaring total support for whatever Bush and his administration planned.

It seemed tasteless and unsympathetic to contradict Tony Blair's statement that the whole free world had been attacked. The obvious truth, that America, in particular, had been attacked for her role in various Arab countries, including, of course their support of Israel, and, more generally, for her perceived veneration of the great god Capitalism, could not be stated without feeling traitorous to our stricken friends across the Atlantic.

Also, one could hardly avoid a feeling that common justice, if one could leave out emotions, demanded that something should be done in retaliation for so many deaths. In this situation, it was a relief when no instantaneous military action took place. It was a further relief when 'the war' became 'the war against terrorism'. War was being used in a much wider sense than usual, as one might speak about 'war against drugs'. Using that sense, it seemed that our political leaders, with Blair at the helm of those European countries canvassed for support, were taking a properly moral and sensibly statesmanlike line. As support was requested in countries, such as Syria and the all-important Pakistan, it seemed that the all-powerful United States had entered a new era in which they recognized the importance of co-operation with other countries.

When the bombing started, this changed. At first, the arguments in its favour seemed fairly clear. The American people simply would not stand for a government that, in their eyes, did nothing after such a horrific violation of their lives. Anti-terrorist activity had to be seen to be believed. Many people, when I expressed opposition to the bombing, asked me 'Well, what would you do then?' This has never seemed sound reasoning. You don't spend weeks bombing a poor and suffering country because you can't think what else to do. There is no justification for a war founded on such thinking – if, as we are told, we are now at war.

Tony Blair often uses the Kosovo analogy to point out that doubters then would have halted the bombing which led to the overthrow of the Milosevic regime. I do not accept this argument, as it happens, but I note that, during those bombing raids, the word 'war' was never used. So why are we at war now? It seems to be an effort to encourage the British public into believing that we are under threat in order to stimulate greater support for the bombing.

If so, this behaviour is very odd from a government whose duty, one would have thought, was to keep their countrymen confident, if vigilant. During the worst of the IRA bombing campaigns in London, every effort was made to downplay their effect. As I remember very well, there would on occasion be an explosion which hardly made the news. Fear was not considered a proper tool in the running of a country.

I was born during World War II and, as a baby in Oxford, can remember almost nothing about it. But, growing up in London where bomb craters lingered on for years, and entertained by a decade of war films, I was perhaps inoculated from the kind of panic to which some people now seem rather proud of confessing. Of course, if we are at war, then fear is a proper reaction. But a mother fleeing from American bombs in Afghanistan might find it rather hard to understand.

The real problem, I believe, is that we are not clear about the objectives of the military action. I have always understood that a just war needs, as one of its principles, a reasonable chance of success. But the first stated aim of the action was to catch Osama bin Laden which, perfectly clearly, had less than a reasonable chance. The second aim, to bring down the Taliban, possibly has more chance, although there is no particular sign of it as I write today. If a war is not just, it is not war, it is something else – maybe revenge.

We cannot really know what is happening in

Afghanistan. Perhaps by the time this is published, the Taliban will have fallen and a respectable government will be found to rule in their place. Perhaps our extraordinarily brave soldiers will capture Osama bin Laden. Capture or kill. But that's another argument. If that happens, like Kosovo, military force will have been deemed a success.

So where does it stop? It is estimated that six thousand innocents died in New York and Washington. How many more must die to pay for their loss? Should we be bombing with our hearts or our heads?

Is bombing the Taliban and the downtrodden citizens the way to defeat terrorism? Judging by the reaction from various interested parties round the world, it seems hardly likely. On the contrary, it may be just the way to encourage further outrages as terrible as the World Trade Center attacks. So where does the bombing stop?

As my 95-year-old mother, acclaimed biographer of that great general, the Duke of Wellington, put it to me: 'When human beings try to effect just retribution, it almost always picks up injustice along the way. I'm very keen on the idea of justice but I think in the present situation military action is far more likely to prolong violence rather than produce peace. So I would advocate some just, non-violent retribution.'

These are clearly not fighting words, although my mother is no pacifist. Yet it is interesting that just a few days ago, our former Chief of the Defence Staff, General, the Lord Guthrie, writing about Wellington, in his estimation the greatest British soldier, noted that one of his strengths was in knowing when *not* to fight a battle, however tempting. It seems this is a lesson not learnt by our present leadership.

A final image that gives me hope is of Westminster Cathedral's Choir School flying back to London from a tour of America on the eve of All Saints Day (Hallowe'en). The choir is composed of boys aged between eight and twelve whose parents had resisted panicking and sent them across the Atlantic. The pilot realized they would pass over the graveyard of the World Trade Center, so asked them a favour. The plane flew over that place of misery with young voices singing *Our Father*.

Rachel Billington

First Betrayal

I've lived my whole life in New York, and this in and of itself makes it a rarity that I visited the observation deck, a major tourist attraction of the World Trade Center, in August, just a month before the towers were destroyed. I'd taken two Italian tourists there at approximately 9.00 in the morning. The weather that day was as glorious as it would be on September 11, as it has remained since for the most part throughout the autumn, a meteorological mockery of the terrible events forthcoming: the escalation of war and our continued bereavement over the more than several thousand dead. But on what would be my last visit to that renowned vantage point, I contemplated the grandeur of the skyline to the north, and then the adjacent glass and metal twin of the tower on which I stood, able to marvel at the extraordinary feat of design and architecture that raised them so high. At the very back of my mind was the sense that some people in the world saw these twins as Babel towers.

After all, the first bombing of the World Trade Center on a frigid snowy February morning in 1993 actually occurred while I was riding the subway en route to one of the twin buildings. Shortly after the explosion, and even before the rescue units mobilized, I surfaced into

121

the concourse of shops, which have now been crushed under tons of rubble. These thoroughfares, normally glutted with people, were a deserted, smoke-filled netherworld. Sensing that something potentially catastrophic had happened, but maintaining the dead calm that many of the recent survivors have described, I broke into a trot and jogged towards the nearest exit, where an entering phalanx of firefighters yelled at me to leave the building.

My two Italian friends had never been up in a skyscraper before, much less one of the tallest in the world. Exuberant as small children, they handed me their camera and, making burlesque gleeful faces, balanced on one foot as though they were falling off the observation deck while I took pictures of them against the crystalline skyline. Then we went down to the plaza where they sprawled on the benches in the sun and I clicked away more photos. It was their first visit to America.

'You Americans, you have such big hearts,' these friends remarked to me later that day. With any sophisticated European invariably comes their world-weary view of our culture. 'You do care about your fellow man, you have more charities than any other country, you donate all sorts of aid to the rest of the suffering world. But then you are so obsessed with youth and beauty, you are so competitive. You want not just to be rich or famous, but the richest, the most famous. And being the world's cultural leader you set the stage for the rest of us. Why do you Americans go through life at such a fast pace?' one of my Italian friends asked shyly and then turned philosophical. 'Perhaps it's because in modern times you've never been occupied by a foreign power, never feared annihilation the way we did during World War II, never had your cities attacked and bombed, your citizens killed in the streets. These are humbling things. They make you want to stop, take stock of life, to take the time for a three-hour lunch.' And then she laughed.

A few days before the attack on the World Trade Center I was sitting in a church just outside of Boston watching a friend of mine, a 34-year-old bride, walking down the aisle. People had travelled from all over the world to her wedding, including a handful of friends from California. Three days later some of these wedding guests, confirmed on one of the California-bound flights that crashed into the World Trade Center, decided at the last minute to go home a day early. In the midst of the wedding procession, I found myself scrolling back six weeks earlier in the summer when I was witnessing a starkly different scenario. I was watching a woman I loved, as emotionally close to me as my own sister, a woman the same age as this bride, and who was an acquaintance of hers, dying in a hospital after years of suffering one cancer-related illness after another. These are the bookends of the summer, I naively told myself at that September 8 wedding: one month, a woman swathed in hospital white and tethered to oxygen hoses is fighting to breathe; the next month, a woman wearing a white dress is getting married. When I saw the bride's mother smiling, I recalled my friend's mother, the night her daughter died, keening over her lifeless body. She wept with an agonized note of grief that pierced me through and reverberates now as I think of the thousands of mothers throughout the world mourning over their missing and murdered children who lie buried in rubble at the fallen towers.

Now when I look towards what used to be the World Trade Center, the memory continuing to haunt the sky like phantom limbs, my first thought is a selfish one: no longer will I be able to site them when I go for a run through Little Italy and Chinatown, to gaze up at these particularly American monuments with the heady sense that is so much a part of the nature of New York City, a place where one can transit numerous world cultures in just a few blocks. But then I remember the admonishing words of my Italian friends, 'these are humbling things', a viewpoint emanating from a country that only sixty years ago was ruled by a fascist regime while being bombed by the Allies. Up until recently, it was far too easy for us Americans to delude ourselves into thinking that we were immune to the sorts of political troubles that brewed civil unrest and war in the rest of the world. We are caught now in this moment of anguished realization, like a young lover broken hearted by our first betrayal. While we are hardening ourselves to what may come next, even bearing wounds that will likely test our limits, so many things – our cultural supremacy, the lives of the rich and famous, our dream of the perfect life – already seem to matter less. Perhaps we've begun to understand that we live in the world rather than in America.

Joseph Olshan

11 September 2001: Firebirth

This is the moment when
The 21st century was born
When the mood of the world
Was altered and torn.
Often we wonder when time's
Change finds its visible form
When what will be the future
Horror or grace reveals its norm.
A rage beyond dreams, a rage
That has hopelessness as its cage
Where pain that makes men
Think living worse than death
Humiliation worse than hope
Despair without end
Dialogue banned by the power
Of deafness, a greater anger
Than the world has dreamed
Has impacted on the glass towers
Of the world's concentrated powers.

New fire-time was born from
The collision of unimaginable grace
And impossible fear; there ought

To be a limit to the ghosts
That we no longer hear;
Four planes create the grim
Shadow of the apocalypse here
With the dead whose death
Encompasses the globe in sorrow;
But sorrow deeper than hope
Has given birth to a war
Beyond the known scope
Of the known wars that feed
On the corpses that await
In our dreams and our eyes.
Let's prepare graves in the skies.
An eye for an eye has mad
Mathematics now; injustice
Has changed the world's liberty
Has brought from the nightmare
Of terrorism, an unsuspected tyranny.

Not listening has made our world
Encircled with fires from on high;
Below we shrink into shadows.
Below the refugees gather and die.
We have lost control of our freedoms
Surrendered our future to inflated
Vengeance in the kingdoms.
Beware the base of great sorrow.
We are losing our tomorrow.
The millennium today was born.
The dream of heights is shorn.
Towers of peace are invisible in space.

Hear the weeping of the race
Where power crushes seeds with tanks.
The dead burn silence in the banks.
Shadows and dying birds;
Flowers and murdered herds.
Here new time has begun.
Here is the firebirth of a new sun.
Strike a resonant gong.
Utopia will not burn a song.

Ben Okri

The Invisible Women

In one ward lay a woman named Dery Gul, about thirty years old, with her 10-year-old daughter, Najimu, and a baby named Hameed Ullah. The little girls have bruised and cut faces. But to understand how lucky they were you only have to look at their mother. Her face is half-covered with bandages, her arm wrapped in plaster. 'The bomb burned her eyes,' says the doctor, 'The whole right side of her body is burned.' The reason Ms Gul is so battered and her daughters so lightly injured is because she cradled them.

Richard Lloyd Parry, *Independent*,
on the victims of American bombing raids,
October 25, 2001

Even before September 11, the situation of women in Afghanistan was, not to put too fine a point on it, diabolical. They were the invisible, inaudible women. They were seen briefly in documentaries flitting through rubble-strewn cities, shrouded in grey, watching the world as through a prison grille, unable to work, unable to be educated, unable to move around without a male relation, liable to savage beatings if they showed their fingers or feet or the shape of their bodies as they walked.

As our politicians would like to forget, the power of the mujaheddin was bolstered by the West during the war with the Soviet Union. Our leaders could only support those men who joined the armed struggle by entirely ignoring their treatment of women. If the women are ignored now, the world will be adding evil to evil. For years, millions of women in Afghanistan have had little, had to look forward to in their lives but fear – and now the West is adding the threat of bombing raids.

I believe that the invisible, unheard deaths of women and children in Afghanistan will lie like a stain on the conscience of the world, and on the consciences of us lucky women in the West. We are visible, we are audible. So perhaps we have a moral duty to speak up for those invisible, inaudible women.

Already it is clear that fewer women than men in the West support the killing of innocent people. A survey of public attitudes in Britain at the end of October showed that only 19 per cent of women wanted the bombing to continue without a pause, as compared to 40 per cent of men (*Guardian*, October 30, 2001). At the very least, women who do not support this war should now find the courage to stand up and say, as Professor Robin Therkauf, who was widowed in the World Trade Center disaster, said, 'The last thing I want is for more widows and fatherless children to be created in my name.'

All wars kill people. But certain actions, certain situations, make the deaths of women and children more likely. Bombing raids on towns are always going to cause civilian deaths – any other expectation is simply ludicrous. The United States is even using indiscriminate missiles, the notorious cluster bombs, that that can kill and maim people up to 100 metres from the point of detonation. What's more, unexploded bomblets from cluster bombs sit beaneath the soil, like landmines, for years. At the end of October the United Nations Office of the Co-ordination of Humanitarian Affairs reported that cluster bombs were dropped over Herat, in western Afghanistan, and a village was littered with unexploded bomblets. These weapons are still killing one civilian a week in Kosovo (*The Times*, October 25, 2001). Human rights organizations throughout the world have called for a ban on their use. And yet they have now been used in Afghanistan, the most heavily mined country in the entire world.

But the most numerous victims of our actions will probably not be the people caught by stray or dud bombs. They will be, rather, the people caught by hunger and cold. Even before the bombing campaign began, the United Nations believed that there were 7.5 million hungry people in Afghanistan. You've probably read that figure before. But it's impossible really to imagine 7.5 million hungry people; from the viewpoint of our comfortable lives it is almost impossible to imagine even one truly hungry person.

Many of them are women and children; widows whose lives have already been broken by the evil of the Taliban and rival factions, living in desperate camps or ruined villages, seeing their last hope of survival dwindle as the expensive bombs flash in the sky. As I write, aid into Afghanistan has already been reduced to a trickle – not just because the lorries can't get across the border, but also because the food can't be delivered where it is needed or is being looted by soldiers. Already deaths from starvation are being reported by aid agencies, but of course most people who starve to death in Afghanistan will never be reported. They will die unseen, unheard in the frozen mountains.

She was a widow with five mouths to feed, her man killed by the Taliban. One of her children, a boy, had no toes. The Taliban had burnt down the house and he had been asleep inside a cot, her neighbours said. The woman did not speak for herself, only gathered her shawl around her face, and continued her lullaby. None of her children had shoes or cold weather clothes. Last winter, in this one camp, 12 miles south of the River Derya – known to the ancients as the Oxus – forty children and twenty mothers with newborn babies died. Their graves are earth mounds, a few marked by flags, on the slopes of the dust-blown hill.
John Sweeney, *Observer*, October 21, 2001

Yet we in the West are being asked to accept with an easy conscience the sufferings of millions of civilians, the majority of them women and children and old people. At the outset of almost every war in modern history, people are told that this war must be fought in order to defend the peace. This suffering is necessary, because it will lead to an end to suffering. This danger is unavoidable, in the pursuit of a safer world.

Indeed, the moral fervour of our leaders now must be more or less unmatched in recent times. And they are, at the moment, carrying the majority of their people with them. They have convinced us that after the deaths of thousands of civilians in America, it is a moral imperative that more civilians should die. They have made us believe that these deaths are just a necessary stage in the campaign against terror, after which will come peace and security for the West – not to mention the rebuilding of the Afghan state.

If we were sure that violence was the only means to such an end, I guess we would all be able to steel ourselves against the suffering of the innocent women of Afghanistan. Yes, if we were so sure, then we would look into the eyes of the children in the refugee camps, peering from our television screens, and say that their deaths were worthwhile because of the generations yet unborn who will live safer lives because of the American bombs. Then we would all read the tale of the mother burnt almost to death while cradling her children as the missiles blazed, saying to ourselves that her suffering, though regrettable, was necessary. But we should only so harden our hearts if we are certain that sending cluster bombs rocketing into villages is definitely more effective than diplomacy, sanctions, intelligence, aid, education, negotiation, bargaining, bribery and any other non-violent methods of dealing with the situation.

My husband, Tom Theurkauf, lost his life in the World Trade Center disaster. If we succumb to the understandable impulse to injure as we have been injured and in the process create even more widows and fatherless children, perhaps we will deserve what we get.

      Robin Theurkauf, widow and mother of three children, and Professor of international law

But if there is any possibility that other methods might have worked as effectively, then these deaths are as unnecessary as the deaths of the civilians in America. And then this horror should cry out to us with the same force of evil as that horror. And we should be as shocked, as grieving for those innocent people as we were for those who died the day the towers went up in smoke. We should speak in tones as outraged about their broken lives, their sobbing children, their bereaved parents. We should find our dreams as interrupted, and our waking hours as haunted, as all our nights and days were then.

There have, as always, been alternatives to war at every stage. But negotiation and diplomacy were pushed off the agenda before they could possibly have had a chance to work. When, on October 14, the Taliban's deputy prime minister proposed discussing the possibility of delivering Osama bin Laden to a neutral county, George W. Bush said, 'When I said no negotiations I meant no negotiations'. We have to ask why using any means other than violence was so quickly dismissed by our leaders.

If we are serious about destroying this terrorist group, we should have pursued every possible diplomatic path to that end before blundering into war. Certain aspects of the terrorists' support have not yet been openly discussed by American or British politicians. Consider the fact that more than half of the nineteen men who took part in the attacks on September 11 are believed to be from Saudi Arabia. But although the Saudi royal family has, over the years, channelled millions of dollars into fundamentalist groups including al-Qaeda, the American and British governments continue to support the Saudi leadership. We are ignoring the protection that al-Qaeda has received from sources far richer and more powerful than the Taliban, in order to pretend that there is no alternative to war with a poor and desperate country.

Not only do we have to wonder whether there were alternatives to war, we also have to ask if this bombing may end up being positively counter-productive. By turning Afghanistan into a graveyard we are choosing to consolidate support for extreme anti-American groups in many parts of the world. In Pakistan, the mood among many people is hardening against the West, as is shown by attacks on churches and thousands of young men flocking to the borders to fight with the Taliban. We must wonder why we are choosing action that will naturally have the paradoxical effect of strengthening an enemy that only needs a few cells of like-minded people to continue its murderous enterprise. We must ask why we have chosen to fight a sentiment – dislike of America – with the very action that will increase rather than decrease that sentiment.

> The mother of the seven dead children stood watching as the bodies of the youngsters were pulled from a smouldering building and wrapped in shrouds. 'What shall I do now? Look at their savagery,' she said. 'They killed all of my children and my husband. The whole world is responsible for this tragedy. Why are they not taking any decision to stop this?'
>
> Andrew Buncombe, *Independent*,
> on a scene described by witnesses in Kabul,
> October 29, 2001,

Giving diplomacy another chance might not have worked immediately, but bombing does not work immediately. Our leaders are asking us to prepare for a war that may be weeks, months, years long, to have courage, and to be patient. But the root of the word patient is *patior*, I suffer. Very few of us are now being asked to suffer. Rather, we are asking others, millions of others, to suffer for us.

When we heard the voices of Afghan women, we have heard voices of reason and hope. The Revolutionary Association of the Women of Afghanistan, an organization founded in 1977 to fight for women's rights, still works towards equality for women. They oppose the Taliban, and many have lost their lives in that opposition as they secretly educate women and children in defiance of the Taliban and expose the crimes of their rulers. One spokeswoman for the organization, Fatima, said in an interview, 'We are so sorry for the victims of this terrorist attack. We can understand their sorrow because we also suffered this terrorism for more than twenty-three years.' But they also oppose the American attacks on Afghanistan. 'Our people have to burn in the flame of war,' said Fatima. 'And all the doors are closed.'

Interestingly, both George Bush and Osama bin Laden have used similar language to insist that we must all now take sides. 'In this conflict, there is no neutral ground,' said Bush. 'The world is divided into two camps, the camp of the faithful, and the camp of the infidel,' said Osama bin Laden. But many women and children in Afghanistan are now caught between the two camps, and many will die there without ever being seen, or being heard.

> We are condemming an attack of the US on Afghanistan, because it won't be the Taliban but our people who will be the victims.
> Fatima, spokeswoman for the
> Revolutionary Association of
> The Women of Afghanistan,
> in an interview on *salon.com*

Natasha Walter

A Time of Gifts

The patterns of human history mix decency and depravity in equal measure. We often assume, therefore, that such a fine balance of results must emerge from societies made of decent and depraved people in equal numbers. But we need to expose and celebrate the fallacy of this conclusion so that, in this moment of crisis, we may reaffirm an essential truth too easily forgotten, and regain some crucial comfort too readily forgone. Good and kind people outnumber all others by thousands to one. The tragedy of human history lies in the enormous potential for destruction in rare acts of evil, not in the high frequency of evil people. Complex systems can only be built step by step, whereas destruction requires but an instant. Thus, in what I like to call the Great Asymmetry, every spectacular incident of evil will be balanced by 10,000 acts of kindness, too often unnoted and invisible as the 'ordinary' efforts of a vast majority.

We have a duty, almost a holy responsibility, to record and honour the victorious weight of these innumerable little kindnesses, when an unprecedented act of evil so threatens to distort our perception of ordinary human behaviour. I have stood at Ground Zero, stunned by the twisted ruins of the largest human structure ever destroyed in a catastrophic moment. (I will discount the claims of a few biblical literalists for the Tower of Babel.) And I have contemplated a single day of carnage that America has not suffered since battles that still evoke passions and tears nearly 150 years later: Antietam, Gettysburg, Cold Harbor. The scene is insufferably sad, but not at all depressing. Rather, Ground Zero can only be described, in the lost meaning of a grand old word, as 'sublime', in the sense of awe inspired by solemnity.

In human terms, Ground Zero is the focal point for a vast web of bustling goodness, channelling uncountable deeds of kindness from an entire planet – the acts that must be recorded to reaffirm the overwhelming weight of human decency. The rubble of Ground Zero stands mute, while a beehive of human activity churns within, and radiates outward, as everyone makes a selfless contribution, big or tiny according to means and skills, but each of equal worth. My wife and stepdaughter established a depot on Spring Street to collect and ferry needed items in short supply, including face masks and shoe pads, to the workers at Ground Zero. Word spreads like a fire of goodness and people stream in, bringing gifts from a pocketful of batteries to a $10,000 purchase of hard hats made on the spot at a local supply house and delivered right to us.

I will cite but one tiny story, among so many, to add to the count that will overwhelm the power of any terrorist's act. And by such tales, multiplied many millionfold, let those few depraved people finally understand why

140

their vision of inspired fear cannot prevail over ordinary decency. As we left a local restaurant to make a delivery to Ground Zero late one evening, the cook gave us a shopping bag and said: 'Here's a dozen apple brown betties, our best dessert, still warm. Please give them out to the rescue workers.' How lovely, I thought, but how meaningless, except as an act of solidarity, connecting the cook to the clean-up. Still, we promised that we would make the distribution, and we put the bag of twelve apple brown betties atop several thousand face masks and shoe pads. Twelve apple brown betties into the breach. Twelve apple brown betties for thousands of workers. And then I learned something important that I should never have forgotten – and the joke turned on me. Those twelve apple brown betties went like literal hot cakes. These trivial symbols in my initial judgement turned into little drops of gold with a rainstorm of similar offerings for the stomach and soul, from children's postcards to cheers by the roadside. We gave the last one to a firefighter, an older man in a young crowd, sitting alone in utter exhaustion as he inserted one of our shoe pads. And he said, with a twinkle and a smile restored to his face: 'Thank you. This is the most lovely thing I've seen in four days – and still warm!'

Stephen Jay Gould

Three

Though leaves are many, the root is one;
Through all the lying days of my youth
I swayed my leaves and flowers in the sun;
Now I may wither into the truth.

'The Coming of Wisdom with Time',
W. B. Yeats

Collective Passion

Spectacular horror of the sort that struck New York (and to a lesser degree Washington) has ushered in a new world of unseen, unknown assailants, terror missions without political message, senseless destruction. For the residents of this wounded city, the consternation, fear and sustained sense of outrage and shock will certainly continue for a long time, as will the genuine sorrow and affliction that such carnage has cruelly imposed on so many.

The national television reporting has, of course, brought the horror of those dreadful winged juggernauts into every household, unremittingly, insistently, not always edifyingly. Most commentary has stressed, indeed magnified, the expected and the predictable in what most Americans feel: terrible loss, anger, outrage, a sense of violated vulnerability and a desire for vengeance and unrestrained retribution. There has been nothing to speak of on all the major television channels but repeated reminders of what happened, of who the terrorists were (as yet nothing proven, which hasn't prevented the accusations being reiterated hour after hour), of how America has been attacked, and so on. Beyond formulaic expressions of grief and patriotism,

145

every politician and accredited pundit or expert has dutifully repeated how we shall not be defeated, not be deterred, not stop until terrorism is exterminated. This is a war against terrorism, everyone says, but where, on what fronts, for what concrete ends? No answers are provided, except the vague suggestion that the Middle East and Islam are what 'we' are up against, and that terrorism must be destroyed.

What is most depressing, however, is how little time is spent trying to understand America's role in the world and its direct involvement in the complex reality beyond the two coasts that have for so long kept the rest of the world extremely distant and virtually out of the average American's mind. You'd think that 'America' was a sleeping giant rather than a superpower almost constantly at war, or in some sort of conflict, all over the Islamic domains. Osama bin Laden's name and face have become so numbingly familiar to Americans as in effect to obliterate any history he and his shadowy followers might have had (for example, as useful conscripts in the jihad raised twenty years ago by the United States against the Soviet Union in Afghanistan) before they became stock symbols of everything loathsome and hateful to the collective imagination. Inevitably then, collective passions are being funnelled into a drive for war that uncannily resembles Captain Ahab in pursuit of Moby Dick, rather than what is in fact going on, an imperial power injured at home for the first time, pursuing its interests systematically in what has become a suddenly reconfigured geography of conflict, without clear borders, or visible actors.

Manichaean symbols and apocalyptic scenarios are bandied about with future consequences and rhetorical restraint thrown to the winds.

Rational understanding of the situation is what is needed now, not more drum-beating. George Bush and his team clearly want the latter, not the former. Yet to most people in the Islamic and Arab worlds, the official United States is synonymous with arrogant power, known mainly for its sanctimoniously munificent support not only of Israel but of numerous repressive Arab regimes, and its inattentiveness even to the possibility of dialogue with secular movements and people who have real grievances. Anti-Americanism in this context is not based on a hatred of modernity or technology-envy as accredited pundits like Thomas Friedman keep repeating; it is based on a narrative of concrete interventions, specific depredations and, in the cases of the Iraqi people's suffering under US-imposed sanctions and US support for the 34-year-old Israeli occupation of Palestinian territories, cruel and inhumane policies administered with a stony coldness.

Israel is now cynically exploiting the American catastrophe by intensifying its military occupation and oppression of the Palestinians. Since September 11, Israeli military forces have invaded Jenin and Jericho and have repeatedly bombed Gaza, Ramallah, Beit Sahour and Beit Jala, exacting great civilian casualties and enormous material damage. All of this, of course, is done brazenly with US weaponry and the usual lying cant about fighting terrorism. Israel's supporters in the United States have resorted to hysterical cries like 'we are all Israelis now', making the connection between the World Trade Center and Pentagon bombings and Palestinian attacks on Israel an absolute conjunction of 'world terrorism', in which Osama bin Laden and Arafat are interchangeable entities. What might have been a moment for Americans to reflect on the probable causes of what took place, which many Palestinians, Muslims and Arabs have condemned, has been turned into a huge propaganda triumph for Sharon; Palestinians are simply not equipped both to defend themselves against Israeli occupation in its ugliest and most violent forms *and* the vicious defamation of their national struggle for liberation.

Political rhetoric in the United States has overridden these things by flinging about words like 'terrorism' and 'freedom', whereas, of course, such large abstractions have mostly hidden sordid material interests, the efficacy of the oil, defence and Zionist lobbies now consolidating their hold on the entire Middle East and an age-old religious hostility to (and ignorance of) 'Islam' that takes new forms every day. The commonest thing is to get TV commentary from, run stories, hold forums, or announce studies on Islam and violence or on Arab terrorism, or any such thing, using the predictable experts (the likes of Judith Miller, Fouad Ajami and Steven Emerson) to pontificate and throw around generalities without context or real history. Why no one thinks of holding seminars on Christianity (or Judaism for that matter) and violence is probably too obvious to ask.

It is important to remember (although this is not at

all mentioned) that China will soon catch up with the United States in oil consumption, and it has become even more urgent for the United States to control both Persian Gulf and Caspian Sea oil supplies more tightly: an attack on Afghanistan, including the use of former Soviet Central Asian republics as staging grounds, therefore, consolidates a strategic arc for the United States from the Gulf to the northern oil fields that will be very difficult for anyone in the future to pry loose. As pressure on Pakistan mounts daily, we can be certain that a great deal of local instability and unrest will follow in the wake of the events of September 11.

Intellectual responsibility, however, requires a still more critical sense of the actuality. There *has* been terror, of course, and nearly every struggling modern movement at some stage has relied on terror. This was as true of Mandela's ANC as it was of all the others, Zionism included. And yet, bombing defenceless civilians with F-16s and helicopter gunships has the same structure and effect as more conventional nationalist terror. What is especially bad about all terror is when it is attached to religious and political abstractions and reductive myths that keep veering away from history and sense. This is where the secular consciousness has to step forward and try to make itself felt, whether in the United States or in the Middle East. No cause, no God, no abstract idea can justify the mass slaughter of innocents, most particularly when only a small group of people are in charge of such actions and feel themselves to represent the cause without having been elected or having a real mandate to do so.

Besides, much as it has been quarrelled over by Muslims, there isn't a single Islam: there are *Islams,* just as there are Americas. This diversity is true of all traditions, religions or nations, even though some of their adherents have futilely tried to draw boundaries around themselves and pin their creeds down neatly. Yet history is far more complex and contradictory than to be represented by demagogues who are much less representative than either their followers or opponents claim. The trouble with religious or moral fundamentalists is that, today, their primitive ideas of revolution and resistance, including a willingness to kill and be killed, seem all too easily attached to technological sophistication and what appear to be gratifying acts of horrifying symbolic savagery. (With astonishing prescience in 1907, Joseph Conrad drew the portrait of the archetypal terrorist, whom he calls laconically 'the Professor', in his novel *The Secret Agent*; this is a man whose sole concern is to perfect a detonator that will work under any circumstances and whose handiwork results in a bomb exploded by a poor boy sent, unknowingly, to destroy the Greenwich Observatory as a strike against 'pure science'.) The New York and Washington suicide bombers seem to have been middle-class, educated men, not poor refugees. Instead of getting a wise leadership that stresses education, mass mobilization and patient organization in the service of a cause, the poor and the desperate are often conned into the magical thinking and quick bloody solutions that such appalling models provide, wrapped in lying religious claptrap. This remains true in the Middle East generally, Palestine in particular, but also in the United States, surely the most religious of all countries. It is also a major failure of the class of secular intellectuals not to have redoubled their efforts to provide analysis and models to offset the undoubted sufferings of the large mass of their people, immiserated and impoverished by globalism and an unyielding militarism with scarcely anything to turn to except blind violence and vague promises of future salvation.

On the other hand, immense military and economic power such as the United States possesses is no guarantee of wisdom or moral vision, particularly when obduracy is thought of as a virtue and exceptionalism believed to be the national destiny. Sceptical and humane voices have been largely unheard in the present crisis, as 'America' girds itself for a long war to be fought somewhere out there, along with allies who have been pressed into service on very uncertain grounds and for imprecise ends. We need to step back from the imaginary thresholds that supposedly separate people from each other into supposedly clashing civilizations and re-examine the labels, reconsider the limited resources available, decide somehow to share our fates with each other as in fact cultures mostly have done, despite the bellicose cries and creeds.

'Islam' and 'the West' are simply inadequate as banners to follow blindly. Some will run behind them, of course, but for future generations to condemn themselves to prolonged war and suffering without so much as a critical pause, without looking at interdependent histories of injustice and oppression, without trying for common emancipation and mutual enlightenment seems far more wilful than necessary. Demonization of the Other is not a sufficient basis for any kind of decent politics, certainly not now when the roots of terror in injustice and misery can be addressed and the terrorists themselves easily isolated, deterred or otherwise put out of business. It takes patience and education, but is more worth the investment than still greater levels of large-scale violence and suffering. The immediate prospects are for destruction and suffering on a very large scale, with US policy-makers milking the apprehensions and anxieties of their constituencies with cynical assurance that few will attempt a counter-campaign against the inflamed patriotism and belligerent war-mongering that has for a time postponed reflection, understanding, even common sense. Nevertheless, those of us with a possibility for reaching people who are willing to listen – and there are many such people, in the United States, Europe and the Middle East, at least – must try to do so as rationally and as patiently as possible.

Edward W. Said

War is Easy

On the morning of September 11 I travelled from our home in Suffolk and drove into the heart of the Lincolnshire countryside. It was a gentle autumn day and I enjoyed being alone for a while listening to music on my car radio.

The conference I was about to address was already in session when I arrived. A lecture was being given on the chilling subject of Biological and Chemical Terrorism. After lunch I was due to speak on International Terrorism. The participants were drawn from different parts of the country and had responsibility for disaster planning in their respective counties. Just as I was about to get to my feet someone came into the room and calmly announced that a plane had crashed into the World Trade Center and there was a major disaster in New York. At first I wondered if some sort of exercise was being given to the group. If so it seemed remote and somewhat far-fetched. We trooped out of the room and made our way to the gym where there were plenty of large-screen TV sets. It took but a second to realize that this was no exercise. As we were watching, one of the gym members wandered in and sat on the rowing machine. 'Do you mind turning the sound down,' he said, 'I'd like to get on with my exercise.'

We stared at him in amazement and then realized that perhaps he thought we were absorbed in watching a fictional movie. We returned to the conference room and rarely have I given a lecture that had such immediate relevance.

Travelling home I dispensed with the music and listened to the news as the full horror of the event unfolded. Back in Suffolk there was an e-mail from a friend in America. 'I think I've lost forty of my colleagues,' he wrote, 'probably more.'

There can be few people who were not surprised by the sheer scale of the attack and only the most callous could feel no sympathy for the innocent individuals caught in an event that will scar many for life. It took a day or so for the full horror of the incident to sink in. Gradually the United States homed in on a prime suspect and Osama bin Laden was identified as public enemy number one. President Bush, either in anger, ignorance or more likely a mixture of both, came out with injudicious language and spoke of a 'crusade' against terrorism. Eventually his scriptwriters got to him and his utterances improved somewhat. As Osama bin Laden, the Taliban and Afghanistan loomed into focus one hoped against hope that America would keep calm and not retaliate. Then the bombs began to drop and we were at 'war', albeit a war that hardly fitted any previous definitions given to armed conflict.

The first and most obvious question to ask is whether or not bombing Afghanistan is the best way to prevent terrorism. I would suggest it is not. In fact I would go further and say that there is a very real possibility that it will lead to further terrorist acts.

It is difficult for the average American to understand the depth of feeling there is across the developing world against the United States. Understandably, rich and powerful nations are bound to attract some degree of envy, but the feelings of many run deeper than that. Acts of terrorism are symptomatic of a far graver problem. In part it lies with the perceptions of many. Take Pakistan. There, many of the population feel used by America. They say that they were used when it suited the Americans and when they were no longer useful they were dropped. They remind us that when the battle against communism was being fought on Afghan soil the United States armed and supported the Taliban and hailed Osama bin Laden as a freedom fighter.

In the Arab world, despite the complexity of the Middle Eastern conflict, the perception of millions is that America has not been an honest broker and has been partial to Israel partly because of the Jewish vote in the United States. This may or may not be accurate but it is the perception of many and thus needs to be taken seriously.

The poor of this world lack military and economic power. Islam brings many of them together and enables them to have a feeling of belonging to a global community of faith. It is hardly surprising that in such a situation violent opportunists seek theological justification for their actions, build on the frustrations of the poor and succeed in demonstrating that the most powerful nation on earth is in fact totally vulnerable. While most Muslims will certainly deeply deplore the loss of innocent lives in New York, nevertheless there will be an underlying sympathy with the terrorists simply because they have been able to demonstrate that the poor are not completely without power. It is highly likely that every time an innocent person dies in Afghanistan as a result of Western military action, more young people will be recruited into the ranks of terrorism. The approach of the West towards Osama bin Laden has succeeded in mythologizing him to an absurd degree. He may be rich and clever but we can be sure that he is not the only rich, clever individual determined to teach the West a lesson. Whether by design or not, the West has been drawn into the inter-tribal conflict that constitutes Afghanistan. The ability of the Northern Alliance to govern more effectively than the Taliban is questionable and, should the Taliban be decimated, as seems likely at the time of writing the roots of the problem will persist.

There is no easy and simple answer to the problem of terrorism but there are ways we can begin to deal with the root of the problem. First, the root issues of poverty and injustice have to be addressed. America must enter into responsible dialogue with the Arab League, Islamic nations and the developing world in general. They must be assisted in partnership to deal with some of the problems that cripple their development. Global companies, rightly or wrongly, are seen as ruthless exploiters of the poor and vulnerable. They are also seen as contributing, by fair means or foul, to the massive wealth of the West. At the recent summit meetings on global trade the media gave much attention to the violence perpetrated by the demonstrators. True, the behaviour of a minority was appalling and dominated the headlines. Perhaps equal attention ought to have been given to the reasons for the protests. Injustice and the economic might of the international corporations that seem to swamp local aspiration are points that spring to mind. It is only by removing the justification for terrorist acts that terrorism can eventually be reduced.

President Bush has already indicated in a telephone conversation with the King of Morocco that the United States might well reconsider its attitude to the UN resolutions referring to Israel and Palestine. The complexity of that situation is formidable and it is by constantly using justice as a baseline that progress can be made. If it is true that the CIA have now been given a 'licence to kill' in respect of Osama bin Laden then the consequences of this action are terrifying. What right will the United States have to speak out against any other nation that adopts a similar action in respect of individuals they regard as terrorists? Without a doubt America has to review its whole attitude to the United Nations and to international law. America must be clear in its commitment to the United Nations. Certainly reform is needed in that body but effective reform can only come about when member states understand the absolute necessity for such an organization in today's world and are determined to play their full part along with their dues.

September 11 has demonstrated that clearly we need a new global order. The moral mess that passes for international affairs must be cleaned up and this will be a long, painful and difficult task. I am not without hope. The incident in New York was a tragedy and I weep for the victims. I also weep for the innocent man, woman or child in Afghanistan who will die as a result of a Western bomb paid for in part by my taxed income. However, it is possible for new hope to emerge from the ashes of despair. September 11 was indeed a wake-up call. To make war is easy. To make peace is much more difficult. Let us pray for statesmen of sufficient wisdom and stature to help us move forward into a world of justice and, hopefully, greater peace.

Terry Waite

The True, Peaceful Face of Islam

There are 1.2 billion Muslims in the world, and Islam is the world's fastest-growing religion. If the evil carnage we witnessed on September 11 was typical of the faith, and Islam truly inspired and justified such violence, its growth and the increasing presence of Muslims in both Europe and the United States would be a terrifying prospect. Fortunately, this is not the case.

The very word Islam, which means 'surrender', is related to the Arabic *salam*, or peace. When the Prophet Muhammad brought the inspired scripture known as the Koran to the Arabs in the early seventh century AD, a major part of his mission was devoted precisely to bringing an end to the kind of mass slaughter we witnessed in New York City and Washington. Pre-Islamic Arabia was caught up in a vicious cycle of warfare, in which tribe fought tribe in a pattern of vendetta and counter vendetta. Muhammad himself survived several assassination attempts, and the early Muslim community narrowly escaped extermination by the powerful city of Mecca. The Prophet had to fight a deadly war in order to survive, but as soon as he felt his people were probably safe, he devoted his attention to building up a peaceful coalition of tribes and achieved victory by an ingenious and inspiring campaign of non-violence. When he died in 632, he had almost single-handedly brought peace to war-torn Arabia.

Because the Koran was revealed in the context of an all-out war, several passages deal with the conduct of armed struggle. Warfare was a desperate business on the Arabian Peninsula. A chieftain was not expected to spare survivors after a battle, and some of the Koranic injunctions seem to share this spirit. Muslims are ordered by God to 'slay [enemies] wherever you find them' (4:89). Extremists such as Osama bin Laden like to quote such verses but do so selectively. They do not include the exhortations to peace, which in almost every case follow these more ferocious passages: 'Thus, if they let you be, and do not make war on you, and offer you peace, God does not allow you to harm them' (4:90).

In the Koran, therefore, the only permissible war is one of self-defence. Muslims may not begin hostilities (2:190). Warfare is always evil, but sometimes you have to fight in order to avoid the kind of persecution that Mecca inflicted on the Muslims (2:191; 2:217) or to preserve decent values (4:75; 22:40). The Koran quotes the Torah, the Jewish scriptures, which permits people to retaliate eye for eye, tooth for tooth, but like the Gospels, the Koran suggests that it is meritorious to forgo revenge in a spirit of charity (5:45). Hostilities must be brought to an end as quickly as possible and must cease the minute the enemy sues for peace.

Islam is not addicted to war, and jihad is not one of

its 'pillars', or essential practices. The primary meaning of the word jihad is not 'holy war' but 'struggle'.
It refers to the difficult effort that is needed to put
God's will into practice at every level – personal and
social as well as political. A very important and much
quoted tradition has Muhammad telling his companions as they go home after a battle: 'We are returning
from the lesser jihad [the battle] to the greater jihad',
the far more urgent and momentous task of extirpat-
ing wrongdoing from one's own society and one's own
heart.

Islam did not impose itself by the sword. In a statement in which the Arabic is extremely emphatic, the
Koran insists: 'There must be no coercion in matters
of faith!' (2:256). Constantly Muslims are enjoined to
respect Jews and Christians, the 'People of the Book',
who worshipped the same God (29:46). In words
quoted by Muhammad in one of his last public sermons,
God tells all human beings: 'O people! We have formed
you into nations and tribes so that you may know one
another' (49:13) – not to conquer, convert, subjugate,
revile or slaughter but to reach out towards others with
intelligence and understanding.

So why the suicide bombing, the hijacking and the
massacre of innocent civilians? Far from being endorsed
by the Koran, this killing violates some of its most
sacred precepts. But during the twentieth century the
militant form of piety often known as fundamentalism
erupted in every major religion as a rebellion against
modernity. Every fundamentalist movement I have studied in Judaism, Christianity and Islam is convinced that

161

liberal, secular society is determined to wipe out religion. Fighting, as they imagine, a battle for survival, fundamentalists often feel justified in ignoring the more compassionate principles of their faith. But in amplifying the more aggressive passages that exist in all our scriptures, they distort the tradition.

It would be as grave a mistake to see Osama bin Laden as an authentic representative of Islam as to consider James Kopp, the alleged killer of an abortion provider in Buffalo, NY, a typical Christian, or Barauch Goldstein, who shot twenty-nine worshippers in the Hebron mosque in 1994 and died in the attack, a true martyr of Israel. The vast majority of Muslims, who are horrified by the atrocity of September 11, must reclaim their faith from those who have so violently hijacked it.

Karen Armstrong

The Right to Judge?

Therefore you have no excuse, O man, whoever you are, when you judge another; for in passing judgement upon him you condemn yourself, because you, the judge, are doing the very same things. – Romans 2:1

There are things we can all do to prevent repeats of the evil felt on September 11. Through increased personal responsibility we can reduce the likelihood of future attacks and so reduce the amount of destruction and pain that they cause. We might prevent them happening altogether. Our effectiveness in this will depend in part upon our understanding of the place of war and the place of blame.

We live in an imperfect world. The imperfection is not the presence of armies but the need for armies. It would be better if the Taliban would engage fully in diplomacy, if al-Qaeda would be willing to negotiate. But you cannot negotiate with 'Death to America'. And in a better world the Taliban would never have been able to take power in Afghanistan. If we were all more concerned about our neighbours' welfare then we would not have tolerated the entrenchment of this unspeakably cruel regime in the first place. But we missed that. So now we must deal with the present reality.

It will help us for the future, though, if we remember that the whole world is becoming increasingly interdependent. The political climate of *every* country affects all other countries. Who, in August 2001, would have suggested that global security could hang on the political openness of Tadjikistan and Uzbekistan? How many people recognized then that the structures of power in Pakistan are of vital interest to the entire world?

So let us be reminded that injustice anywhere is a threat to justice everywhere. If we avoid this truth then conflict becomes inevitable.

There is a wishful and dangerous fallacy about the accomplishment of peace. Very simply, we know that in Utopia there would be no war and therefore no need for soldiers or guns. And so some conclude that if we rid ourselves of soldiers and guns then that is a step in the right direction, that our world will more closely resemble Utopia. This is wrong. It is like saying that in the perfect world there would be no sickness and therefore no need for doctors and medicine. Would we make our world better then by getting rid of doctors and medicine? No. We are not in the perfect world. It is because of past wrongs, because of the faults of all of us, that we find ourselves in situations where our options are ones that will cause pain and injustice. Here we must seek the lesser of evils.

A second obstacle to us finding a solution is if we

misunderstand the place of blame, either by exonerating those who support terrorists or by heaping all the blame on America. These two mistakes are usually connected.

Although everyone I have spoken to condemns the attacks on September 11 as inexcusable, there are too many who then immediately try to excuse them, claiming that those who support terrorists have 'legitimate grievances', that they are sorely oppressed.

But what should we think of elderly men, of community leaders, who go berserk in the street, burning flags and effigies of human beings and chanting 'Death to America'? These grown men behave like this in front of children. Such acts are breathtakingly irresponsible. Is it all right to fill children with hatred because one feels a legitimate grievance?

If we think the behaviour of the fanatics is understandable then we deny their very humanity. To absolve these men, to take them out of the moral loop, to set them aside from blame, is to make them alien. They have freewill. They make choices. This is precisely what makes them human. If in some patronizing folly we wish to absolve them, we end up absolving them not of guilt but of their humanity. I think people who do this don't quite realize what a threat we are under.

If people refuse to acknowledge the terrorists' culpability this means heaping all the blame on the United States.

I think this comes partly from the commendable trait of siding with the underdog against the powerful. But virtue is not inherent in challenging the powerful. We are called to align ourselves to truth and justice, and when the cause of the powerful is good, then we should support it.

Of course, America is not perfect. Of course, America's foreign policy has caused damage. But does this alone account for the great hatred and prejudice against America? More likely it is jealousy and something even worse. As long as Europeans can blame America for the world's problems then we don't have to face our own culpability. This I think is the greatest stumbling block to informed debate on the whole subject. Intelligent and educated people across the world seem to need an excuse to avoid the truth of their own responsibility. This is moral cowardice. And the fashionable technique today for those who want to avoid responsibility is an unending tirade against the United States (a tirade which obscures their valid points).

For balance, allow the Islamic fundamentalists to be human – allow them some blame. Allow Americans to be human – give them some credit. We all saw on September 11 what America is really made of. We saw the truest nature of the American people. It is those fire and police officers who disregarded their own lives in their rush to save the lives of others. It is those men and women on the aeroplanes who did not resort in their final minutes to panic and screaming. Instead they telephoned their families to speak of their love. It is the outstanding heroism of men like Todd Beamer who overcame the hijackers on the plane brought down in Pennsylvania. It is the awesome dignity and restraint of an administration that has withstood such cruelty and hatred without lowering itself to the same. That is America. That is mankind.

So if we are not confused by the question of war, and if misplaced blame does not distract us, then we can more effectively address the solution.

We are all responsible for the state of the world.

The fact that there exists such injustice in the world, that there is such unfathomable suffering, is a consequence of the fact that every single one of us is flawed. We all do wrong, we all contribute to the world's problems. It is no excuse if we think our own wrongdoing is minor in comparison with another's.

There are terrible problems in the world: devastating occurrences of injustice, exploitation, terrorist attacks. All result from widespread instances and huge, long-term accumulations of greed, intolerance and hatred, to which we all contribute. They are not the results of isolated acts by individuals utterly steeped in these vices. Nobody is that powerful.

The problem is vice. The solution is virtue. The problem is deceit, pride, anger, greed. The solution is honesty, humility, compassion, courage.

Government has a role to play in tackling our problems. But it is a limited role. The more important part, the very thing that human beings need more than anything else in the world, is something which government cannot give. It is love.

And love is not merely a spiritual abstract; it has the most pragmatic and concrete of consequences. What does it mean to love one's neighbour? What does it mean, for example, to love a child in Afghanistan? Well, the answer is not so difficult. It means the same thing as loving our own children. Do we love our children? Well, we make sure that they do not go hungry. We tend them when they are sick. We strive to keep them safe from attack, from exploitation. And if our children are safe and well and fed, then the next thing which parents all round the world want for their children is education. Education is a powerful defence against tyranny.

It is not impossible to achieve these things but international organizations and state institutions alone cannot do it. The task is too vast. It needs to be driven by love, by individuals. It will happen when millions, billions of people put their minds and energy and resources in to making it happen. What do we have to do in life that is more important than supporting our brothers' welfare?

Our everyday actions shape the world we live in. Every person who has travelled abroad or met foreigners in the United Kingdom has affected international relations. When we travel abroad do we treat local people with respect, with kindness, with interest? A thousand tourists who do this will have a bigger impact on building up goodwill than all the diplomatic efforts of an ambassador. The Foreign Office will do everything they can to keep a strong relationship between Pakistan and the United Kingdom. But this task would be infinitely easier if every Brit who had travelled through Pakistan had treated all the locals they met with great respect and with kindness. For then it would be far more difficult for fanatics to dance in the street drawing crowds calling for death to the West. This is important. If those crowds were ever to grow unmanageable, then it is conceivable that Osama bin Laden's supporters would get their hands on nuclear bombs. Could that possibly happen because we waltz arrogantly through other people's countries utterly indifferent to their terrible poverty, wishing only to indulge our cameras, stomachs and throats without a care for local life? That is not loving our neighbour, and it breeds a deadly resentment.

Or what about at home? What if we were all more welcoming to immigrants here? What if we made more effort in helping them to integrate? Then would it not be more difficult for terrorist groups to find alienated and disaffected young men who they could brainwash with their blasphemous corruption of Islam? Maybe we cannot stop every last person from being recruited, but we can do much to reduce the support for organizations bent on terror and disorder. The stronger and deeper our relations are with the Muslim world then the more difficult it will be for terrorists to find environments of support and complicity for them to move in.

And as for war, it matters how every one of our soldiers chooses to fight. We need a military that can discriminate between Taliban soldiers and Afghan civilians. Otherwise the war is pointless and impossible. To achieve this takes incredible intelligence work, incredible science in developing sufficiently accurate ordnance and incredible dedication from pilots and crews upon whose every effort the final result depends.

Each of us, however far removed, has an effect. Our efforts can only ever be drops in the ocean, but when millions of people are willing to make that effort, then the ocean is mighty indeed.

If we want to fight against wickedness in the world, if we want to reduce the amount of evil, then there is only one place where we are guaranteed success. That is in the fight against the wickedness in our own hearts. Each of us has greed, and pride, and anger, and hatred. We can all strive to overcome these faults and there is no one in the world but ourselves who can stop us from succeeding.

To change the world, change oneself. Learn to love.

James Mawdsley

Hearts and Minds:
Avoiding a New Cold War

This is a different kind of war. That much of what we are being told, at least, is true. And because of that, a different kind of analysis is required.

The single most common question anti-war activists are confronted with is, 'What's your solution?' Although many elements of a sensible solution have been offered, the anti-war movement has reached no general consensus on the fundamentals.

In the past, activists who critiqued and/or resisted unjust US foreign policy and militarism faced three main scenarios in which US actions were blatantly unjust and the raw exercise of US power was obviously wrong:

1. US attempts to overthrow democratically elected governments, such as Iran in 1953, Guatemala in 1954, and Chile in 1973.

2. US wars against national liberation movements, such as Vietnam in the 1960s, or against attempts to consolidate national liberation, such as Nicaragua throughout the 1980s.

3. US wars in response to clearly illegal acts, but where the US short-circuited negotiations and used indiscriminate, gratuitous violence that killed huge numbers of civilians (directly and indirectly), such as in the Gulf War in 1991.

In all those cases, there was no threat to the people of the United States, even though many of the interventions were carried out in the context of the Cold War project of making people afraid of threats-that-might-come. The solutions were simple – in the first two cases, no intervention by the United States and in the third, diplomacy and negotiations within the framework of international law while keeping the United States from unilateral military action.

But this war was sparked by attacks on US soil, and people feel threatened and afraid, for understandable reasons.

In a climate of fear, it doesn't matter to many that the military strategy being pursued by the United States is immoral (the civilian death-toll from bombing and starvation resulting from the attack will no doubt reach into the tens, possibly hundreds of thousands without immediate action) and ineffective (it will most likely breed more terrorism, not end it). Americans are confronted with a genuine threat and want to feel safe again.

As a result, proposals offered by some in the anti-war movement have been difficult for the public to take seriously. It is clear that pacifism is only of interest to the few in the United States. That is not said out of disrespect for principled pacifists who consistently reject violence, but simply to point out that any political argument that sounds like 'turn the other cheek' will be ignored. It is also hard to imagine how it would have an impact on the kind of people who committed the crime against humanity on September 11.

The only public display of pacifism that would be meaningful now would be for pacifists to put their bodies on the line, to put themselves somewhere between the weapons of their government and the innocent victims in Afghanistan. Short of that, statements evoking pacifism will be worse than ineffective; they will paint all the anti-war movement as out of touch with reality.

Also inadequate are calls for terrorism to be treated solely as a police matter in which law enforcement agencies pursue the perpetrators and bring them to justice through courts, domestic or international. That is clearly central to the task but is insufficient and unrealistic; the problem of terrorist networks is a combined political and criminal matter and requires a combined solution.

So, what should those who see the futility of the current military strategy be calling for?

First, we must support the call made by UN-affiliated and private aid agencies for an immediate bombing halt to allow a resumption of the serious food distribution efforts needed to avoid a catastrophe.

There will need to be a transitional government, which should be – as has been suggested for the past decade – ethnically broad-based with a commitment to allowing international aid and basic human rights. It must, however, be under UN auspices, with the United States playing a minimal role because of its history of 'covert' action in the region. It should also be one that does not sell off Afghanistan's natural resources and desirable location for pipelines on the cheap to multi-national corporations.

While all that goes forward, the United States should do what is most obviously within its power to do, to lower the risk of further terrorist attacks: begin to change US foreign policy in a way that could win over the people of the Islamic world by acknowledging that many of their grievances – such as the sanctions on Iraq, the presence of US troops in Saudi Arabia, Israel's occupation of and aggression against Palestine – are legitimate and must be addressed.

This shouldn't be confused with 'giving in to the terrorists' or 'negotiating with Osama bin Laden'. It is neither. It is a practical strategy that demonstrates that a powerful nation can choose to correct policies that were rooted in a desire to extend its dominance over a region and its resources and are now not only unjust but untenable. It is a sign of strength, and it is the right thing to do.

Some have argued against any change in US foreign policy in the near term. International law expert Richard Falk wrote in *The Nation*, 'Whatever the global role of the United States – and it is certainly responsible for much global suffering and injustice, giving rise to widespread resentment that at its inner core fuels the terrorist impulse – it cannot be addressed so long as this movement of global terrorism is at large and prepared to carry on with its demonic work.'

In fact, the opposite is true: now is precisely the time to address these long-term issues.

Here we can actually take a page from 'liberal' counter-insurgency experts who saw that the best way to defeat movements of national liberation was to win the hearts and minds of people rather than try to defeat them militarily. In those situations, as in this one, military force simply drives more people into resistance. Measures designed to ease the pressure toward insurgency, such as land reform then and changing US Middle East policy now, are far more likely to be effective. The alternative in Vietnam was a wholesale attempt to destroy civilian society – 'draining the swamp' in Donald Rumsfeld's phrase. The alternative now would be unending global war.

In the past, such strategies were part of a foreign policy 'debate' in which the end goal of US economic domination of Third World countries was shared by all parties, and so they were entirely illegitimate. Now, it is different – these terrorists are not the voice of the dispossessed and they are not a national liberation movement. Their vision for their own societies is grotesque.

But they do share something with the wider populace of their countries.

There is tremendous justified anger in the Islamic world at US foreign policy. For the vast majority of the populace, it has not translated to anger at the United States as a nation or at Americans as a people. For groups like al-Qaeda, it has. Their aims and methods are rejected by that majority, but the shared anger at US domination provides these terror networks their only cover. A strategy to successfully 'root out' those networks must isolate them from the populace by eliminating what they hold in common. It is necessary to get the co-operation not just of governments of Islamic nations but of their people as well. The only way is to remove their sources of grievance.

These changes in policy must be preliminary to a larger change. The United States must drop its posture of the unilateralist, interventionist superpower. In lieu of its current policy of invoking the rule of law and the international community when convenient and ignoring them when it wishes, it must demonstrate a genuine commitment to being bound by that law and the will of the international community in matters of war and peace.

Many have said of the Afghans, and perhaps by extension of many other deprived peoples, 'Feed them and you'll win them over'. This attitude dehumanizes those people. Nobody will accept bombs with one hand and food with the other. Nor will anyone feel gratitude over food doled out by an arrogant superpower that insists on a constant double standard in international relations and makes peremptory demands of other nations on a regular basis. To win the support of Afghans and others for the long term, which will be necessary to substantially reduce the danger of terrorism, the United States must treat other peoples with dignity and respect. We must recognize we are simply one nation among many.

This strategy will not win over Osama bin Laden or other committed terrorists to our side; that's not the objective. Instead, we have to win over the people.

The choice we face as a nation is similar to that faced at the end of World War II. The capitalist West, the Communist world, and many of the colonies had united to defeat fascism. That could have been the basis of building an equitable world order, with the United States helping to equalize levels of wealth and consumption around the world. Had that path been taken, the world would be a far safer place today, for Americans and others.

Instead, US leaders chose the path of the Cold War, which was not so much an attempt to contain Soviet-style communism as it was to destroy any example of independent development in the Third World, to extend and entrench our economic superiority. That effort harmed democracy in our country and in others, killed millions, and has led in the end to the creation of new and terrifying threats to all our safety.

Government officials are already speaking as if we are fighting a new Cold War, with President Bush calling the war on Afghanistan 'the first battle of the war of the twenty-first century'.

We cannot let history repeat itself.

Rahul Mahajan and Robert Jensen

Real Aid, Fair Trade and the Green Renaissance

Whether science and society like it or not the results of the human genome project proved the dream of genetic determinism to be dead. All people are members of a single species sharing 30,000 genes that code some 300,000 proteins, the stuff of life. From the moment of their inception these proteins are subject to moulding by the environment within the cell, which is itself at the mercy of the wider environment in which the person lives. The truly staggering diversity of people thus came about as the descendants of Eve began to meet the challenge of the different environments they encountered in their race across the world.

This world is now falling apart environmentally, socially and ethically. Stock exchanges, insurance companies, businesses and people, both rich and poor, are now having to grapple with the problems caused by gross disruption of climate and weather and by over-grazing, over-fishing, soil erosion, eutrophication, pollution, Aids and terror. Even the richest economies are running out of water and more and more of their farmers can no longer make a viable living. Rural communities are in disarray, while graffiti and negative equity stain suburbia as inner cities fall into decay.

There are already solutions to all environmental problems in the pipelines of research and development. Wave power, which could produce the base load of electricity needed to service a modern world of 10 billion people, would be a prime source, with solar power, offshore wind and co-generation from waste, topping up local supplies. Fuel cells could replace the pollution problems of internal combustion with pure water vapour, integrated crop management and hi-tech hydroponics to close the water and the pollution cycles. As these new technologies become integrated into the market place, millions of jobs will be created.

Across the world tens of thousands of partnerships of people and businesses, both great and small, and governance at all levels, are beginning to think globally and act locally. I like to call this mass movement of people the Green Renaissance.

The quick profiteers and green doomsayers, who resort to scaremongering, often on issues of marginal concern, either ignore the fact that an environmental awakening is forthcoming or intone that 'it is too little too late'. I agree that it is not yet happening fast enough, either for the right reasons or on a grand enough scale, but at least these grass roots stirrings are now in the public domain. It is my firm belief that when people are fired not by the divisive spirit of revolution but the spiritual reunion of a renaissance, much can be achieved. Peace must happen now because the longer we wait the more difficult it will be.

The bombing in Afghanistan must stop and the supplies of relief and aid be significantly increased. This war is one more symptom of the disparity between the haves and have nots of the world, in which at least 16,000 children die every day for want of basic health care and food and 600 die every hour for want of potable water.

To address this crisis, all the world's wilderness areas that are still in a viable state must be saved. Such areas include estuaries, sea grass beds and reefs and the fisheries that depend on them. For they are the world bank of genetic information, the only viable investment we have which will allow rehabilitation of the vast areas of the world that are in need of stabilization. The costs of buying up the logging rights on all old growth forests now under threat are miniscule compared to the downstream effects of their continued destruction.

The same common sense economics suggest that if the recommendations of the Kyoto protocol were implemented, conservation and the necessary rehabilitation of the environment could be funded through the much discussed carbon sequestration tax. This tax would create millions of jobs in the rural areas of desperately poor countries through planting and managing forests. Reforestation would stabilize soils and whole watersheds, improving local climates and downstream water supplies and fisheries, while giving the wealthy world the time to invest in alternative sources of energy as quickly as possible.

Those nations rich in fossil fuels have nothing to fear for most are also rich in alternatives. Once they stop wasting these precious resources on the production of energy then their true value as feedstock for the plasto-chemical lifestyles of the twenty-first century can be realized. The thriving recycling plastic industry may result in fossil fuel being reclassified as a 'quasi-renewable resource'.

With modern methods of satellite surveillance, all this could be monitored in the detail it deserves, as could overfishing. The immense subsidies, which are driving this industry to the wall of extinction, could then be spent putting all fish and shellfish farms on closed circuit, 'flowgro' systems thus avoiding pollution of our rivers and inshore waters. The crop could be fed on earthworms and rotifers, themselves fed on cardboard, treated grey water and other organic waste. Not on capelin and sandeel, small fishes that are crucial steps in the marine food-chain which feeds the larger fish of commerce.

Another source of funding could come from the oil companies themselves, many of which are already starting to broaden their portfolios into alternatives. At the moment pure dogma is forcing them to waste energy and landfill space through recycling redundant oil rigs at immense cost, (an estimated £22 billion for the North Sea fields alone), with no researched, let alone proven benefit to the marine environment. Surely it makes more economic sense to clean them up and make them safe? Then, artificial reefs to enhance marine life and fisheries and test rigs for wave power and hydrogen production could be developed, as is now being done in the United States. Part of the money so saved could be used to more rapidly broaden the investment base of these industries and fund other aspects of real marine conservation, which must include giving local fisheries back to local communities.

As tourism was the world's biggest industry before the events of September 11 and as it is an industry that in part depends on a rich and thriving heritage of culture, custom, cuisine, landscape, and biodiversity, it must be reconfigured as soon as possible. Nature can be seen as a great healer, teaching people to love and respect each other's ways of life amongst rich and poor alike. The increasing expenditure on gardens and gardening and the increasing popularity of botanic gardens and nature-based theme parks in the West shows that the desire to till the soil and recreate Eden here on earth is still a natural impulse.

The growing world demand for organic food, traditional medicine and fair trade artifacts are beginning to put into question the destruction of age-old crafts, customs and practices. Fair trade is already revitalizing thousands of village communities across the globe. Real aid, which recognizes and rewards intellectual property, could speed up these processes, giving the developing world the breathing space it needs to decide its own future courses of action. The dropping of food supplies in Afghanistan is good news indeed but real aid, putting village communities back into self-sufficient working order, must figure in the order of the way ahead.

It is my hope that the present crisis will catalyse a new deal for all creeds and kinds. A centre of Real Aid and Fair Trade, not rotten to the core with profit for profit's sake but a flagship of sustainable redevelopment, where local people and local environments will always call the shots, could mean that all the sorrow felt has not be in vain.

David Bellamy

The Jihad for Peace

The word Islam has the dual meaning of 'peace' and 'submission'. Islam seeks peace not just for its own sake; it is an essential precondition for and consequence of submission to the 'will of God', the creation of the circumstances in which the life of faith can be implemented in all aspects of human existence. So, why does Islam today appear to be synonymous with violence? And why are those who claim to be following the 'will of God' so bent on the path of war?

As Anwar Ibrahim, the former Deputy Prime Minister of Malaysia, asked in an article written from prison, how 'in the twenty-first century, the Muslim world could have produced a bin Laden'; or, as many supporters of Anwar, whose only crime is standing up against the corruption and despotism of Mahathir Muhammad, Malaysia's incumbent Prime Minister for the last two decades, are asking: why is the Muslim world so crammed with despots, theocrats, autocrats and dictators? Or, to put it another way: why have Muslim societies failed so spectacularly to come to terms with modernity?

These are not new questions. But after September 11, they have acquired a new poignancy and a much

185

broader currency. However, such debate and earnest discourse has some notable features. For the most part, Muslim intellectuals and writers living and working in the West conduct the debate, though they enjoy a readership and close links within the Muslim world. The reason is not hard to find. Living in the West requires a direct response to the circumstances and human dilemmas of modernity; it allows more ready access to sources of Muslim scholarship than in most Muslim countries; within the Muslim world dissent, wide-ranging intellectual inquiry and argument has little if any public scope. So the central debate on the contemporary meaning of Islam is, in its most challenging form, doubly marginal. It occurs outside Muslim nations, where any attempt to apply its ideas is blocked by existing power structures and entrenched vested interests. In the West, as it is the concern of a minority, it is almost inaudible and invisible. Furthermore from a Western perspective it is not consistent with popular perceptions of Islam or the realpolitik of relations with the Muslim world.

Defining the predicament of modern Muslim nations and Islam in the modern world is not difficult. Ascribing reasons is an equally effortless procedure. We have tended to look to outsiders for answers to these questions. It is apparent, despite all the posturing of governments, that the fate of the Muslim world is affected and determined by decisions taken elsewhere, creating a widespread sense of dispossession and powerlessness.

Therefore, much energy goes into critique of the actions and consequences of the centres of power, the nexus of Western government, economy, industry and popular culture where modernity is manufactured and exported to its recipients in the Muslim world. For example, Muslims are quick to point out the double standards of America, both in its domestic rhetoric and foreign policy. The American support for despotic regimes, its partiality towards the Israelis and a long series of covert operations have undermined democratic movements in the Muslim world. There is truth in these assertions. But such truths cannot explain or provide all the answers. Indeed, the most significant answers lie deep within the history, social practice and intellectual and political inertia of Muslims themselves. Holding a mirror to our faults is something we Muslims are just too reluctant to do. But unless we re-examine our own assumptions, our own perceptions of what it means to be a Muslim in the twenty-first century, peace – in any meaningful sense – will continue to elude us.

The question of peace, then, is tied up with a re-examination of the meaning and nature of Islam in contemporary times. The Muslim world has no doubt that its identity is shaped by the best religion with the finest arrangements and precepts for all aspects of human existence and the most glorious of all human histories. Muslim rhetoric is shaped by the ideals of Islam where all is sacred, nothing secular and justice the paramount duty. The problem, as all concerned acknowledge, is that Muslims, as individuals and nations, are neither expressly Islamic nor all that just. The problem of flawed humanity is answered, in the deepest core of Muslim being, by the unquestionable need to be more Islamic. So, we are constantly retreating to a more and more romanticized notion of 'Islam'. Time after time, we have watched as the definition of what is 'Islamic' in contemporary times and circumstances is shrunk and reduced to pathological levels. Our most sacred concepts have been monopolized and hijacked by undereducated 'clerics', by obscurantist 'sheikhs' and 'ulama' (scholars), fanatics and madmen.

This process of reduction itself is also not new. But now it has reached such an absurd state that the very ideas that are supposed to take Muslims towards peace and prosperity are now guaranteed to take them in the opposite direction. From the subtle beauty of a perennial challenge to construct justice through mercy and compassion, we get mechanistic formulae fixated. The extremes are repeated by people convinced they have no duty to think for themselves because all questions have been answered for them by the classical ulamas, far better men long dead. And because everything carries the brand name of Islam, to question it or argue against it is tantamount to voting for sin.

Peace will elude the Muslim world as long as Muslims continue to perform violence on our own ideas and concepts. Let me illustrate the nature of this violence by looking at two very common Muslim concepts: the notions of jihad (struggle) and ijma (consensus) that shape much of Muslim identity and outlook. Jihad has now been reduced to the single meaning of 'Holy War'. This translation is perverse not only because the concept's spiritual, intellectual and social components have been stripped away, but also it has been reduced to war by any means, including terrorism. So anyone can now declare jihad on anyone, without ethical or moral rhyme or reason. Nothing could be more perverted or pathologically more distant from the initial meaning of jihad. The primary meaning of jihad is peace, not war. Peace and justice are the core values of the message of Islam. Thus war cannot, nor has it ever been, an instrument of Islam. Muslim polities have been no strangers to war, like any other societies, but conversion to Islam is unequivocally declared by the Koran and understood by the community to be a matter of private, personal conscience between each individual and God. The entire history of human experience testifies that war instigates, perpetuates and compounds all the conditions that negate justice and are not peace. War demeans the dignity of the human person, which Islam explicitly seeks to nurture and promote. Even if jihad is reduced to the sole meaning of war, it cannot be war by any or all means. The rules of engagement established by Prophet Muhammad are well known to all Muslims and the basis on which even the Taliban's clerics had to condemn the terrorist attacks in America and declare them unethical. The most central notion of Islam is tawheed, usually translated as unity of God. But this unity extends to, indeed demands, moral and ethical unity: Islam insists that there cannot be a distinction between ends and means, and that just causes must be pursued by just means.

Given the violence done to the notion of jihad, it is hardly surprising that in modern times no call for jihad has translated into securing justice for anyone, least of all those on whose behalf and in whose interests it has been proclaimed. A central principle of our faith has become an instrument of militant expediency and morally bankrupt. Those who call Muslims to jihad are dead to compassion and mercy, the most essential values by which justice and peace must and should be sought.

Similarly, the idea of ijma, the central notion of communal life in Islam, has been reduced to the consensus of a select few. Ijma literally means consensus of the people. The concept dates back to the practice of Prophet Muhammad himself as leader of the original polity of Muslims. When the Prophet Muhammad wanted to reach a decision, he would call the whole Muslim community – then, admittedly not very large – to the mosque. A discussion would ensue; arguments for and against would be presented. Finally, the entire gathering would reach a consensus. Thus, a democratic spirit was central to communal and political life in early Islam. But over time the clerics and religious scholars have removed the people from the equation – and reduced ijma to 'the consensus of the religious scholars'. Not surprisingly, authoritarianism, theocracy and despotism reign supreme in the Muslim world. The political domain finds its model in what has become the accepted practice and metier of the authoritatively 'religious' adepts, those who claim the monopoly of exposition of Islam. Obscurantist mullahs dominate Muslim societies and circumscribe them with fanaticism and absurdly reductive logic.

The way to peace requires Muslims to move in the

opposite direction: from reduction to synthesis. Ordinary Muslims around the world who have concerns, questions and considerable moral dilemmas about this current state of affairs must reclaim the basic concepts of Islam and reframe them in a broader context. Ijma must mean participatory consensus leading to participatory and accountable governance. Jihad must be understood in its complete spiritual meaning as the struggle for peace and justice as a lived reality for all people everywhere.

More specifically, we need to declare jihad for peace. In its original multidimensional meaning, jihad must involve Muslims in concerted, co-operative endeavour to combat poverty, disease, the indignity of unemployment, the lack of educational opportunity and provision, the underachievement of economic institutions, all aspects of corruption, denials of basic rights to freedom and the oppression of women – all those things that afflict Muslim societies everywhere. And this jihad has to be conducted by intellectual and moral means. When the deformed political institutions of our nations impede the process of peace and justice, we have a duty to peacefully work together to bring meaningful change based on programmes of remedial action. Jihad for peace also involves intellectual efforts for peace, including the construction of a discourse for peace. When the inequities of the global system impede our efforts to bring improvement to the needy, it becomes a matter of jihad for every Muslim to engage in dialogue and not be satisfied with self-righteous denunciation. In such a jihad, it becomes a supreme duty of the ummah, the international Muslim community, to be part of the world community of faiths, nations and peoples. The essence of the Koranic vision is the duty of believers to take the lead in forming new coalitions across all dividing lines to promote what is right, and prevent what is wrong.

Muslims have no monopoly on right, on what is good, on justice, or the intellectual and moral reflexes that promote these necessities. The Koran calls on Muslims to set aside all sectarianism and work with people of good conscience whoever they may be, wherever they are, to serve the needs of the neediest. This, for me, is the true jihad, the jihad that is crying out for the attention of Muslims everywhere.

Movement towards synthesis requires the interplay of another central Islamic concept, namely: ijtihad. Ijtihad means 'reasoned struggle for understanding', struggle to comprehend the contemporary meaning of Islamic precepts and principles. It is a cognate of jihad, one that expands the meaning of the term. Interpretation of the meaning of Islam is an act of culpable negligence by educated Muslims the world over. We have left the exposition of our faith in the hands of undereducated elites, religious scholars whose lack of comprehension of the contemporary world is usually matched only by their disdain and contempt for all its ideas and cultural products. Islam has been permitted to languish as the professional domain of people more familiar with the world of the eleventh century than the twenty-first century we now inhabit. And this class has buried ijtihad – a conventional source of Islamic law and wisdom as well as the basic conceptual instrument for adjusting to change – into frozen and distant history.

The betrayal of ijtihad has enabled obscurantism to dominate the life of Muslim communities. It has lead to the pernicious irreligion of the Taliban who deny women the right to education and work in direct violation of the responsibilities laid upon women by the Koran. They are akin to all those religious adepts who complain that democracy and human rights are 'infidel inventions' because their terminology and institutional form are not shaped in the conceptual framework of Islam. This is the unreason that has become the prime obstacle to the reasoned struggle of one fifth of humanity to live in dignity, freedom, justice and peace.

The events of September 11 make it clear that ordinary Muslims cannot be complacent about the interpretations of their faith. We have to find a way to unleash the best intentions, the essential values of Islam, from the rhetoric of war, hatred and insularity that is as much the stock in trade of mullahs as it is of unenlightened policy advisers in the United States. That means all educated and concerned Muslims must take responsibility for authoring twenty-first-century interpretations of the basic concepts of Islam. From the ubiquitous and reductive idea of jihad as Holy War we must move to a more holistic notion of jihad for peace. From a reductive interpretation that limits ijma to an authoritarian elite, we must develop contemporary, effective and operable models for democratic and participatory notions of consensus. Finally, we must revive ijtihad as the dynamic principle for seeking a more humane understanding of our faith. In short, we have to go forward to the intrinsic meaning of Islam: peace.

Ziauddin Sardar

Society is Only as Strong as
its Weakest Link

The events of the morning of September 11 stand out with a surreal, terrifying clarity. All too predictably real and human, however, has been the confused course of subsequent events. Despite assurances that the US military wasn't about to fire a $20 million rocket at a $10 tent, that is exactly what is happening. One early casualty of the terrorist attacks was supposed to be irony. But irony is thriving, when brutalized Afghan people, who have been denied adequate access to education or the media, find themselves suffering again for an unclear war aim. In that, they share something with the thousands of innocent Americans who died on September 11.

The mass suffering of innocents has always been part of what's often referred to as war's 'collateral damage'. Correct me if I'm wrong, but it seems that only during the last century have civilian populations become particular targets in times of conflict. In the new century even more so, and the military mentality that plans for a war between opposing armies, suitably equipped and defined, is irrelevant. Nothing made this more obvious than the American administration's obsession with a multi-billion dollar missile defence shield at the same time as a handful of knife-wielding fanatics were planning to bring the country to a standstill with not much more than $100,000 and a plan that was inconceivably audacious in its simplicity.

So the answers to the terrifying questions posed by September 11 clearly involve alternatives to the attitudes that prevailed prior to the attacks. I feel everyone is lost. An eye for an eye inevitably leads to blindness, but I know that as much as I deplore the military response we have seen to date, the apocalyptic nihilism we're confronted by isn't about to be placated by traditional diplomacy. Along with many people who normally share my anti-war sentiments, I accept that some kind of punitive action is necessary, but it can't be based on the 'give 'em hell Harry' approach that favours missiles over on-the-ground human intelligence.

It is also quite clear that the conflict between the Israelis and Palestinians must finally be settled: a challenge almost as enormous as the consequences if it is not resolved. After years of being content to play the easily distracted policeman of the world, America has woken up to the fact that it is also a citizen of that world. There are no longer conflicts that can be dismissed as local. In this respect, interconnectedness is potentially as much a weakness as a strength in the modern world.

But I prefer to focus on the area where I feel reassured that I can make a contribution. I am a born trader. Trade is one of the oldest and most honourable human endeavours. The ethical business movement seeks to preserve it as such, as something that protects and promotes human rights, justice and widening economic opportunity. September 11 and subsequent events have presented a challenge to our values. The values of freedom and fairness, not the prime motivators greed and exploitation, must become the transparent motivation for globalizing the world.

Prevalent global business practices have exacerbated crime, poverty, disease and social disparity. Such businesses are characterized by forced labour, sweatshops, child labour, the poisoning of air, water and land, the dislocation of entire communities, brutal dictatorships and gross inequalities of wealth. We like to think multinationals operate within the law. But what are their values? Do they include human rights and democracy? How do their global policies affect the rights of indigenous people and rural farmers? The perfect paradigm is the role of the oil multinationals, particularly in Burma, Nigeria and the Middle Eastern countries, places where the United States and the United Kingdom are now desperately trying to claim allies. Just look at how our representatives remain silent about human rights abuses in Saudi Arabia. At the very least, the silence makes the West morally inconsistent. The roots of hatred for Western policies are quite comprehensible when one experiences at grass-roots level the negative impact of globalization's stock in trade.

Organized crime, the drug trade, the black market in weapons, toxic waste and ozone depleting chemicals, the sex industries in Eastern Europe and the Orient, and sweatshop economies everywhere, are mobilizing worker armies of poorly monitored and dangerously

neglected urban squatters, refugees and economic immigrants on behalf of the global shadow economy. Five or
so years ago, Manuel Castells, a sociology professor at
Berkeley, made some profound observations about the
twentieth century being shaped by 'the excluded excluding the excluders', with non-partisan terrorism as their
most likely weapon. The roots of future conflict are to
be found not among these dispossessed and poor but
within the current global policies that create them and
will eventually provoke them into retaliation.

A society is only as strong as its weakest link.
September 11 proved that even the Western world's
strongholds become vulnerable when the weakest links
in the world are ignored. I can't help but feel that there
would be much less support for terrorists if their powerful targets were helping weak nations deal with debt,
famine, Aids, the drug trade and all the detritus that the
West has heaped on them over the decades. As one highly
decorated retired general, who is opposed to the bombing, recently told the *Guardian*: 'Those who have food,
security and prospects will not want to kill or be killed.'

So, how will this ideal situation be brought about?
I believe it is crucial to keep rural life vital and
therefore abate the surge of millions into the squalor
of overpopulated cities. Political stability and sustainable democracy can be helped by preventing conflict
created by prevailing business practices. Every bit of
pressure helps: campaigning for an end to arms; refus-
ing to trade with despots and human rights abusers;
finding an alternative to the major economic planning
models; setting up small-scale, fair-trade initiatives or

networking and sharing best practices with socially responsible businesses.

We need to recognize the rights and contributions of indigenous peoples who bring life-affirming leadership to the task of conserving the earth and its creatures. We need to understand that indigenous wisdom constitutes one of human society's most important and irreplaceable resources. We also need to embrace the fact that gender balance is essential to sustainable development: women's roles, needs, values and wisdom are especially central to decision-making for a new global reality. Women should be involved on an equal basis with men at all levels of policy-making, planning and implementation.

The global economic impact of women can be felt in the small-scale, grass-roots initiatives that women have been so instrumental in establishing in the majority of the world. Initiatives such as The Body Shop's Community Trade programme deal directly with economically marginalized communities and co-operatives around the globe. It is clear that economic opportunity means much more to women than money. It is empowering because it fosters the fundamentals of self-esteem: education, health care, cultural community and the chance to protect the past while shaping the future.

A sense of community is one of the so-called feminine values that ethical business thinkers actively promote. Such values reflect intimate personal and cultural attributes, which are in many ways the reverse of the global market syndrome, in its distance, impersonality and feckless capitalism. I have no doubt that feminized economic activity and economic relations are a desirable and workable way forward and that female financial pioneers will fundamentally change global economics.

We must shift from a private greed to a public good, for the sake of millions of lives. Issues such as the redistribution of wealth and economic globalization have moved up the political agenda, because a global community which doesn't address them is a dangerous place. However small-scale, initiatives which hold out the chance for economic independence can provide communities with the ability to guarantee their environment and their cultural identity – and, therefore, their future.

Ultimately, there is no other way to restore the sense of security and stability that the Western world lost in September 2001.

Anita Roddick

Pandora's Box

War on Terrorism

Since the atrocities on September 11 in America, more innocent people continue to die each day. Victims are being buried in New York, Washington and Pennsylvania and also in Tel Aviv, Kabul and Jalalabad. Pandora's Box has been opened and the violence is escalating unabated. The question is how can the lid be closed? Violence breeds violence and for all the grand rhetoric of Prime Minister Tony Blair a new world order is not waiting around the corner.

West versus East

The political leadership in Britain fails to truly understand the Muslim world, while President Bush struggles to find Islamic states on a world map. It is an indictment of the current and past foreign policies of Western countries that humanitarian gestures to developing nations in no way deliver global justice or eliminate poverty, disease and oppression.

The causes of terrorism are broad and deep. There is no excuse for killing, injuring or threatening individuals, but it is futile for a war to be declared on terrorism when you cannot fight and destroy the use of violent tactics designed to fulfil political ends.

It is first necessary to isolate the individuals by tackling the root causes. There will always be terrorists but they will not always enjoy popular support. Terrorists prey on oppressed people from whom they take succour. Remove the oppression through peaceful means and a key pillar of terrorism falls away. The answer to the brutal conflict in and around Israel is to create a new State of Palestine next to the State of Israel, sharing Jerusalem. Peace will only be achieved when the poison of tit-for-tat killing is ended and for that to happen the Israeli government has to recognize the Palestinian right to self-determination.

In the West most people, including government politicians and their advisers, fail to comprehend the Muslim world and faith. According to Gai Eaton, in *Islam and the Destiny of Man*, Muslims identify someone in terms of the religion into which they are born rather than in terms of their nationality. Even atheists and agnostics are still regarded as belonging in the Christian world.[1]

That is why support will grow when Muslims are being killed in Afghanistan and elsewhere while the sympathy for the United States may be waning. You cannot wipe out 1400 years of religious and political history and 100 years of US foreign policy with a few soundbites in the twenty-first century.

Economic Globalization

While Western children walk around in £100 trainers produced for a wage pittance by workers in poor countries, 30,000 children in developing nations die every day from preventable diseases.[2]

Although the British government has helped lead the campaign to reduce Third World debt, there is a long way to go to end the cycle of unsustainable repayments. Each day developing nations repay £40 million to the wealthy West; money that they simply cannot afford and which fails to dent the mountain of money they owe.[3]

With a higher incidence of natural disasters such as earthquakes, droughts, floods and cyclones, developing nations endlessly struggle to provide schools, hospitals, basic sanitation and clean water supplies.

The United States refusal to back the Kyoto Protocol, which in itself still does not adequately address the generally agreed increases in climate change, is symptomatic of their isolationist policies pre-September 11. This approach is underpinned by the hypocrisy of such battles as that at the World Trade Organization, where Bush's administration tried to stop Brazil and South Africa from trying to bypass pharmaceutical company patents to allow HIV/Aids drugs to be produced cheaply, to allow the treatment of the millions of infected victims in their continents. Yet now the United States blithely talks of ignoring the Cipro, anti-anthrax pill patent to allow mass production to counter the terrorist threat to their citizens.

A handful of rich countries come close to fulfilling their obligations to the United Nations by paying 0.7 per cent of their Gross Domestic Product to poor countries. After seven years of a Labour government barely half that target will be paid each year by Britain.

Dominant international institutions such as the World Trade Organization, International Monetary Fund and World Bank require radical reform to allow poor countries a fair opportunity to access much needed funds without the onerous and despised ties to the Structural Adjustment Programmes.

The Limitations of British Parliamentary Democracy

So how do we demonstrate that the secular and democratic world poses a challenge to the Islamic world? By arresting hundreds of Muslims and detaining them for questioning in dawn raids across Britain in the aftermath of the terrorist attacks? Through the Home Secretary launching a new 'anti-democracy' bill in Parliament? By deporting asylum seekers without appeal, while police powers to trawl through retained computer data on British citizens are explicitly promised and compulsory identification cards are discussed? Such measures will erode freedoms and increase powers to control the British people.

But at least the mother of all parliaments has voted for this war in Afghanistan? At least the elected representatives of the people have had their say and debated a motion setting out support for the government's actions? In fact, the House of Commons has had three emergency recalls and is still subjected each week to grand statements on international developments by the Prime Minister and his ministers. But, as Members of Parliament, we have been refused the right to vote on whether or not we want this war.

Is there a precedent for voting in Parliament for a war? Ironically the then Conservative administration allowed a vote on the Gulf War to endorse UN Security Resolution 678 and accepted a humanitarian amendment by the then Labour opposition.[4]

The Royal Prerogative dates back to 1688 and the Glorious Revolution. Then, the dictatorial powers of the monarch were given to the Prime Minister of the day. In its day it was radical stuff and 100 years later inspired an American constitution that enshrined inalienable rights to its new frontier citizens (excluding native Americans).

Now, over three centuries later, Britain staggers on with the same ailing and failing democracy. Parliament is a lame duck institution with no written constitution and the Royal Prerogative extends so widely that its parameters are unknown.[5]

In the first emergency debate following the recall of Parliament back from its ridiculously long summer recess on September 14, I urged caution on the Prime Minister. By the third recall I demanded Parliament be given the right to vote on the war. The suggestion was brushed aside and on a point of order I later again asked the Speaker for a vote. I was ruled out of order and the House of Commons' Honourable Members jeered and laughed at the temerity of the demand.[6]

The world teeters on the brink of a terrible war between West and East, the American president declares a 'crusade', hundreds die in bombing raids and 2.5 million Afghans are threatened with starvation this winter, while American and British serviceman risk their lives. And British MPs think this is funny.

A New British Written Constitution

It is time for a Constitutional Commission (note: not a Royal Commission) to draw up proposals for a written constitution. Parliamentary renewal should include fixed term parliaments and prime ministers, rights of Parliament to recall itself, to authorize a declaration of war or military action, to veto prime ministerial appointments, to strengthen the Select Committee system and to reform the 'whipping' system so that backbenchers are given genuine rights to speak and vote freely.

The partial reform of the House of Lords is welcomed but it needs to be replaced with the introduction of a democratically elected Senate. The detested dictatorial powers of the Royal Prerogative should be consigned to history and a new Bill of Rights and improved freedom of information would give new enforceable rights to British citizens.[7]

A written constitution would provide the structural framework in Parliament for reinvigorating our democracy. But by itself it will not persuade people that they should take an active part in politics. In the 2001 general election barely half the voters in Britain bothered to vote for their next government. Two-thirds do not vote in local elections and over three-quarters did not see the point of voting in the 1999 European elections. It is clear the present democratic systems have failed.

Politics and politicians need to become relevant to local people in British communities. Only then will the nation truly feel empowered to make changes in conjunction with its government. That it takes less time to set up an e-mail account than for MPs to queue through the lobbies, casting a single vote in an archaic voting method, suggests that we must implement radical changes to procedural protocol in the Commons.

Referendums on key issues and public petitioning that forces parliamentary debates would help to deliver a modern democracy for the twenty-first century. But MPs should also be more accountable to their constituents, with minimum standards laid down for their performance. Annual reports on MPs' work should be published so that by demonstrating their accountability, MPs might begin to reconnect with disaffected citizens.

A Strong, Ethical United Nations

The implications of renewing Britain's democracy (and other democracies faced with similar disillusioned voters) must be extended to the international community. There has to be a reaffirmation of commitment to the one organization responsible for international peace and security. The United Nations was born in 1942. Three years later at the San Francisco conference it adopted its Charter. Apart from several amendments this has remained the bedrock of hope for a peaceful world.[8]

While nation states pay lip-service to the United Nations, rich nations ride roughshod over the spirit and text of the Charter. Henry Kissinger has said that realpolitik must be given a clear priority over the idealism of striving to conquer global evils.[9]

There is a glimmer of hope that with reform and the advent of a global economy and increasing trade, the West will see the need to reaffirm the importance of the United Nations, not least in order to protect and enhance its economies. But so far the war in Afghanistan shows that old habits die hard. UN Security Council Resolutions passed in the weeks after the terrorist attacks expressed sympathy for the US victims, confirmed the right to self-defence and declared that all necessary steps should be taken to counter the terrorism. At no point do those texts make mention of authorizing military action in Afghanistan or anywhere else.[10]

There is no UN mandate for the bombing or landing of troops inside the desperate country where one in four, including 300,000 children, starve each year. This winter an additional 100,000 children could die because the bombing is preventing food from getting through to them. An Oxfam worker has said 'We all know we don't have enough food for the winter [in Afghanistan]. Some people know that if this situation continues they will not survive.'[11]

The vague words and bullying of other states have

given carte blanche to the West (i.e. the United States and Great Britain) to do as they see fit. Although Australia, Belgium and France promise military support there is no promise of any Islamic states forming a military coalition.

Is there an alternative to the present action? I think so. There needs to be an emergency meeting of the UN General Assembly to agree the principle of military action to bring the culprits for the terror attacks on the United States to justice and to authorize the creation of an international criminal tribunal to give legal basis to this action.

International Criminal Tribunal

The British Foreign Secretary in the House of Commons on October 8 poured scorn on the idea of an international court to hear the evidence and indict those responsible for the American atrocities. He cited the example of the Lockerbie aeroplane bombing under the jurisdiction of a Scottish court (albeit held in The Netherlands) as the excuse not to invoke an international court. He explained that such a court could be set up after military action. However, earlier that day the Prime Minister had said that it was 'not a very serious consideration' to have to worry about indicting those alleged to be responsible.[12]

It is clear that the prime suspect will be executed through military action and a 'fair' trial is not an option. But even if it was, the suggestion that a US court should try those responsible shows the naive thinking in the

West. With a highly charged situation, how would Muslims react to an American judge and jury sitting and passing judgement? An international criminal tribunal in the absence of a permanent court (which the United States continues to block) is the credible way forward.[13] Such tribunals based upon UN Security Council Resolutions are successfully working to prosecute the criminals in the former Yugoslavia and Rwanda. One thousand two hundred staff work systematically and fairly to indict those responsible for their murderous deeds and bring them to justice.[14]

A proper mandate set out in arrest warrants would allow the international community to see the transparency and strictly judicial basis to the subsequent action. The US and British governments have refused to allow an international criminal tribunal to be set up and the only 'evidence' they produced was a document with some partial facts. That evidence was prefixed with: 'This document does not purport to provide a prosecutable case against Osama bin Laden in a court of law.'

Is it not a terrifying day for democracy when politicians arbitrarily decide someone's guilt and issue an execution order?

United Nations Security Council

As the international criminal tribunal meets, the UN Security Council should agree a new resolution to authorize specific military action under Article 43 of the UN Charter. This does not authorize unilateral or even multilateral action but lays down in precise terms how the Security Council can take control of any agreed military actions. With the assistance of a Military Staff Committee (Articles 46–8), consisting of chief staffs of the Permanent Members of the Security Council, the United Nations on behalf of the international community would decide the nature and limit of actions to be taken.

Special forces may have to be used to enforce the UN arrest warrants, but they would have an international legality and it is likely that bombing would be declared illegal.

Conclusion

East and West, peoples of all ethnicities, faiths, cultures and beliefs should aspire to a state of mutual respect and understanding. For this to occur, international law must be upheld and enforced through the United Nations.

Radical reform is long overdue to redistribute the wealth of the rich and invest in saving lives and building the infrastructure for the future. A new commitment by the West to the United Nations is needed to turn fine words into courageous actions in order to help developing nations eliminate hunger, disease and deprivation. Only then can terrorism be prevented and international peace achieved.

Paul Marsden
Member of Parliament for
Shrewsbury & Atcham

SOURCES

1 *Islam and the Destiny of Man*, by Gai Eaton
2 UNICEF report, 1998
3 'HIPC – flogging a dead process', report by Jubilee Plus, 2001
4 Hansard, debate, 21 January 1991, Column 113
5 Hansard, Prime Minister written reply, 16 October 2001
6 Hansard, debate, 8 October 2001, Column 829
7 *A Written Constitution for the United Kingdom*, by IPPR, 1993
8 United Nations Charter, 1945 (amended 1965, 1968)
9 *Diplomacy*, by Henry Kissinger, 1994
10 UN Security Resolutions 1363 and 1373
11 'The humanitarian situation in Afghanistan and on its borders', by Oxfam International
12 Hansard, debate, 8 October 2001, Column 820
13 *Adapting the UN to a Postmodern Era*, ed. W. Andy Knight, 2001, p. 99
14 The International Criminal Court Bill, House of Commons Library paper 01/39, 2001

Make Law, Not War

On an international level, making law is much harder than making war. The immediate and rightful response to the atrocity of September 11 was to demand 'justice', but that word sounded, in some powerful mouths, like the cry of the lynch mob for summary execution, assassination squads and the prime suspect's head on a plate. If any silver lining is ever to be found in those grotesque pictures of the black cloud over New York City, it can only come from a commitment to a system of global justice which alone offers a principled method of punishing what truly amounts to a crime against humanity.

The confusion over what 'justice' requires became acute when America chose 'Operation Infinite Justice' as its first brand name for the bombing of Afghanistan. It made no philosophical sense, because human justice is both finite and fallible. More importantly, it begged the question – which Western leaders have so notably failed to address – of exactly what procedure they proposed to adopt to persuade the rest of the world that their cause is right. NATO's attack on Serbia was justified in order to stop ethnic cleansing in Kosovo: Milosevic on trial was an early war aim that has now come to pass. The economic war on Libya found its objective, and its resolution, in the Lockerbie Tribunal. This war on terrorism can only be 'won' by putting in place an effective – and, necessarily, a fair – system for punishing the authors of atrocities and hence deterring those minded to perpetrate them in the future.

International Law, it must at once be acknowledged, justifies breaching 'state sovereignty' – the refuge of scoundrels like Pinochet and Milosevic – when force is necessary in self-defence or to punish a crime against humanity. The International Court of Justice declared in 1949, in a ruling sought by Britain when its ships in the Corfu Channel were attacked from Albania, that every state has a duty to prevent its territory being used for unlawful attacks on other states. In 1980, after the hostage taking at the US Embassy, the same court ruled that Iran was responsible for a failure in 'vigilance' and a toleration of terrorism. It follows that the right of self-defence (preserved in Article 51 of the UN Charter) permits the United States to resort to force for the limited purpose of doing Afghanistan's duty, after that state refused to extradite Osama bin Laden and to close down his camps.

But America's legal right of self-defence does not stretch to overthrowing a government or embarking on an indefinite bombing campaign. The precedent which places the severest legal limit on the US attack was established by its own protest against Britain's sinking in 1837 of a US steamboat (the *Caroline*) which was aiding rebels in Canada: both governments agreed that self-defence must be based on a necessity which is 'instant, overwhelming, leaving no choice of means, and no moment for deliberation'. Self-defence is a blunt and somewhat primitive doctrine, which leaves too much scope to the subjective assessment of a self-defender bent on revenge.

A more modern, and more sophisticated, legal justification for an armed response is provided by the emerging human rights rule that requires international action to prevent and to punish 'crimes against humanity'. The September 11 atrocities, like the bombings of the US embassies in Kenya and Tanzania in 1998, precisely fit the definition, which covers not only genocide and torture but 'multiple acts of murder committed as part of a systematic attack against a civilian population'. It was to punish such crimes in Kosovo that NATO breached Serbian sovereignty, and the same principles should apply (and this time, there is Security Council backing) to the attack in Afghanistan.

But this means, importantly for the present conflict, that the attack on Afghanistan must have a legitimate objective, defined in terms of the justification for the incursion. If, as President Bush insists, that objective is justice, there must be produced not only presumptive evidence of guilt but also a fair procedure for bringing the suspects to trial.

I have anxiously considered the case against Osama bin Laden and the Taliban leadership tabled in the UK Parliament in October 2001. It is not 'evidence' so much as argument based on similar facts, matters of record, and intelligence analysis: even so, it shows in blood-curdling detail that Osama bin Laden has consistently incited the murder of Americans and has confessed to involvement in the 1998 US embassy bombings in East Africa. To dismiss the case against his organization for responsibility over September 11 as 'circumstantial' is to miss the point: in proving conspiracy, as every criminal lawyer knows, circumstantial evidence is often more credible than fallible human testimony. It amounts at the very least to a *prima facie* case of mass murder for racist motives, and it has become more compelling since. Osama bin Laden stands accused not merely as a peripatetic gang leader, but as a state actor: a crucial ally and agent of the Government of Afghanistan. The Taliban leadership stands similarly accused, of aiding and abetting his preparations for a genocidal jihad against Americans (and anyone else who happens to get in the way).

These charges are as grave, and as well-substantiated, as those against Karadic and Mladic over Srebrenica (where seven thousand Muslim men and boys were exterminated), and against Milosevic and his political and military leadership for the ethnic cleansing of Muslims in Kosovo. What is common to all these crimes is that they are 'against humanity' precisely because the fact that fellow humans can conceive and commit these diminishes us all. As defined by the 1998 Rome Treaty for an international criminal court, a 'crime against humanity' includes a systematic attack deliberately directed against a civilian population involving acts of multiple murder. The evidence against Osama bin Laden and the Taliban leadership for involvement in such a crime committed on September 11 demands to be answered at a trial. Whether, when it is fleshed out and forensically tested, it would create a certainty of guilt must be a matter for a court. But which court? Milosevic is on trial in The Hague, and Karadic and Mladic (NATO willing) cannot be far behind. But what court awaits the Taliban and Osama bin Laden?

It is at this point that an embarrassed silence descends on the war leadership. For all the talk of 'justice', the preferred option appears to be a cold-blooded killing of Osama bin Laden and a mere removal of the Taliban leadership, supplanted either by a US-imposed puppet government or (more likely) a UN protectorate. The only 'trial' conceivably on offer is before a jury empanelled in New York. The plain fact is that a jury trial in New York, with a death sentence upon conviction, will not provide a forum where justice can be seen to be done.

A New York jury will be too emotionally involved in the events to consider the evidence dispassionately. (For this reason, those accused of IRA crimes in Britain were never tried in the cities they were alleged to have bombed.) It may be doubted whether any American jury could put aside the prejudice against the 'prime suspect' created by their media and by their leader's demands for his 'head on a plate'. The spectacle which would follow – a death sentence by lethal injection – is too grotesque to contemplate. The only 'guilty' verdict which can persuade the world of Osama bin Laden's guilt will not be delivered in one word from 'twelve angry men', but will be closely and carefully reasoned, delivered by distinguished jurists, some from

Muslim countries, at an international criminal court.

There is just such a court in the planning stages, building upon the precedents set by The Hague tribunal in its 'ad hoc' jurisdiction over state actors accused of crimes against humanity in ex-Yugoslavia and Rwanda. Its statute, approved by 120 nations in Rome in 1998, affords all basic rights to defendants, in trials before three international judges and appeals to a further five. It has protocols for evaluating the kind of hearsay evidence which may be necessary to prove terrorist conspiracies, and which protect the recording of electronic intercepts and other fruits of secret intelligence gathering. It was, in fact, first suggested (by Mikhail Gorbachev) as a means of punishing international terrorists. Its statute has so far been ratified by forty-two nations (including Britain, France and Russia). It will come into existence when sixty nations ratify – on present indications, by the end of 2002.

The obvious opportunity created by the coalition against terrorism forged after September 11, supported by all permanent members of the Security Council, was to bring the International Criminal Court (ICC) into being immediately, with a retrospective mandate to investigate, try and punish the perpetrators and abettors of terrorist actions against the US. The problem, ironically, is that the most formidable opponent of the ICC has been the Pentagon, allied with the Jesse Helms faction of the Republican party, obsessed with the notion that US sovereignty would be degraded if an American were ever indicted as a war criminal. Their latest wheeze has been to promote in Congress the misnamed 'American Servicemembers Protection Act', designed to sabotage the court by withdrawing US co-operation and even permitting the President to use force to free any American ever 'captured' by The Hague Tribunal. One would have hoped that the message of September 11 – that we need much more, not less, inter-national co-operation to ensure that perpetrators have no place to hide – would have led to the abandonment of the irresponsible initiative. Yet only a fortnight later – on 25 September 2001 – George W. Bush gave this 'bomb The Hague' bill his support.

This self-indulgent isolationism demonstrates how remote the Bush administration still is from giving any real support to international criminal justice. We owe that very idea to President Truman, who insisted on the Nuremberg trials against the opposition of Churchill (who wanted the Nazi leaders shot on sight). He did so because 'undiscriminating executions or punishments without definite findings of guilt, fairly arrived at, would not sit easily on the American conscience or be remembered by our children with pride'.

Perhaps it needs Mr Blair to remind the President of how 'the American conscience' once cooled the British desire for revenge and created a court at Nuremberg whose judgement stands as a landmark in civilization's fight against racially-motivated terror. Its legacy requires the arrest of Osama bin Laden for the crimes of 1998 as much as 2001 – and of his aiders and abettors, the Taliban mullahs who so misused the state power they arrogated to themselves. But the force that is designed to achieve it, through the bombing of Afghanistan and the collateral killing and maiming of innocent civilians, can only be justified if the overall objective is to put on a fair trial the men accused of crimes against humanity. Unless and until this becomes a war aim, stated and stuck to irrespective of any opportunity for summary execution, the war will have as much to do with 'justice' as the Red Queen's cry in *Alice's Adventures in Wonderland*: 'Sentence first – trial later.'

Geoffrey Robertson

The Presence of Justice

We all long for peace. But peace can be a deceptive and dangerous word. When Hitler invaded Czechoslovakia all he asked was to be left in peace. When terrorists hide away, again, all they ask is to be left in peace. When Martin Luther King was in prison because of his work for civil rights, a group of white pastors wrote to tell him to stop disturbing the peace. He wrote back to say: 'Peace is not the absence of tension but the presence of justice.' Certainly, in the Bible, peace is always inseparable from justice. The great Hebrew word shalom means a just and ordered peace in which every human being is able to flourish.

On this earth, peace and justice will often be in tension. In order to establish a true peace, based on justice, it will sometimes be necessary to disturb the apparent, false peace. But when justice is being sought by the use of arms, as it is at the present moment, two attitudes in particular need to be avoided. First, the idea that right is all on one side. This can lead to a crusade mentality with the idea, in religious terms, that it is a fight on God's side against God's enemies. There is an inevitable ambiguity about all human decision-making that precludes any self-righteousness.

The second approach to be avoided at a time like

this is a refusal to contemplate the difficult, dangerous decisions that have to be made whether we like it or not. All sides to the conflict are flawed, for we live in a fallen world. But there is no moral equivalent between that fragile human achievement which we know as civilization and the terrorism that seeks to destroy it. Our choices have to be made with all the consequences of them realistically considered. As the great theologian and political thinker Reinhold Niebuhr wrote in 1940:

> There is nothing in our Christian faith which allows us to escape the monumental decisions and destinies of history. We must contend against evil, even though we know that we are ourselves involved in the evil against which we contend. We must seek to do the will of God and yet not forget that in his sight no man (not one) living is justified. We must work for the greatest possible justice in human society and yet know that sinful self-interest will corrupt every scheme of justice that we elaborate.

In the world as we have it, it is not possible to contain terrorism without the use of armed force: nevertheless force is only part of the equation. Studies of guerrilla movements and terrorist groups since World War II have shown that their primary objective has always been a political one. They have never been able to win great military victories. Their strategy has been to create enough disturbance and stay in existence long enough until their constituency is widened and their political goal achieved. If this is the nature of terrorism, then counter-terrorist measures need to have the same perspective. In short, the crucial factor is the constituency to which the terrorists are trying to appeal. Whether or not they succeed will depend upon the degree of alienation of that constituency and the extent to which they are able to motivate and mobilize it in their support. Our political leaders well understand this, of course, which is why the United States, together with the crucial support of the United Kingdom, went to so much trouble to build up an alliance and why they will continue to see holding the alliance together as a continuing priority. Governments in many Islamic countries are precarious. It has been said to me by a leading Muslim historian that not a single Islamic government has the support of its people in the current struggle against the al-Qaeda network. Whether or not this is true those governments are certainly caught between appeals from the West and many members of their own population who are strongly anti-American.

If the issue in the world today is primarily political and only secondarily military, then it is the relationship between the Islamic world and the West that really matters. Here, I believe, the Christian churches have a crucial role to play, and in many places they are playing it. In many towns in the United Kingdom, for example, Christian and Muslim communities have been building good relationships.

In 1938, when the Munich Agreement was signed, T. S. Eliot wrote that he experienced a sense of moral shock. It seemed that those opposed to Nazism had nothing better to defend than a cluster of banks and insurance companies and believed in nothing more substantial than a good rate of interest on dividends. The Muslim world also has such criticisms of the West. Leaving aside objections to American foreign policy, which are, of course, very serious and fundamental, there is a widespread sense of distaste at the West's vulgar consumerism. In response to Munich, T. S. Eliot wrote his famous essay on the idea of a Christian society. But what he put forward there could in fact well describe a civilized society. He defined it as one 'in which the natural end of man – virtue and wellbeing in community – is acknowledged for all, and the supernatural end – beatitude – for those who have the eyes to see it'. Over the centuries Islam has also been associated with great civilizations; based at Damascus, Baghdad, Cairo and Constantinople: civilizations from which the West has learnt a lot. It is not necessary to believe with Samuel Huntington that there is an inevitable 'clash of civilizations'. For Christians, Muslims and, indeed, secularists I think can unite around T. S. Eliot's definition. Terrorism seeks to destroy civilization whether it is Christian, Muslim or secular. Christians, Muslims and secularists need to unite in defending civilization against all that threatens it. Alas, we still have a very long way to go before any agreement can be reached about how, now, we can best protect and build up such a civilization. But there could, I believe, be substantial agreement about the nature of civilization and the values which are necessary to sustain it.

The Rt Revd Richard Harries
Bishop of Oxford

The Devil's Complaint

There is an eastern tale about a man who goes to complain to the Devil. Deeply troubled by the suffering he observes in the world, he asks the Devil how it is that he is able to cause so much evil, so much pain, so much chaos.

'I am innocent,' protests the Devil, 'of all these accusations. I am blamed for everything, but I hardly do anything.'

'Explain,' says the man.

'I'll show you,' says the Devil.

Nearby, the Devil finds a large ram, tethered to a stake in the ground. 'Now watch carefully,' says the Devil. 'All I am going to do is loosen the stake slightly – that's all.'

And the Devil loosens the stake.

The ram tosses its head and pulls the stake free. Seeing the open door of its master's house, it wanders inside. By the entrance is a large mirror, and taking the reflection for another ram, the ram charges into it, shattering the mirror into fragments. The owner's wife, running downstairs and seeing her precious family heirloom destroyed, cries to her servants: 'Kill that ram!'

Now the ram had been a special pet of the husband, who returns home and finds his beloved pet has been killed on his wife's order. He is enraged, but his wife shows no remorse.

'I divorce you,' he tells his wife.

The wife moves in with her relatives, who feel she has been unfairly treated, and a delegation is sent to the husband to complain. The husband dismisses them, and protects his home with armed guards. In turn, the opposing relatives arm themselves, and the conflict escalates. Rival houses are burned down, a local man is killed, and a feud ensues, spreading to neighbouring villages. Soon the entire area has divided into warring camps as the casualties mount. The conflict spreads . . .

The Devil turns to the man and says: 'See? How can you blame me for all these terrible things? All I did was loosen a stake!'

The stake has been loosened. War has been declared. Our species has proved itself once again incapable of circumventing the deliberate destruction of human life, and its righteous, sometimes passionate pursuit.

At the same time, people all over the planet – perhaps more people than ever – are asking questions about war: its origins, its results and its possible remedies. Nothing is new in these questions, nor in their likely answers. Just as war has been waged in almost every era, so too have questions regarding validity and alternative strategies for resolving conflict.

I think it is timely to remind ourselves of what is

already known. We know that, under ordinary conditions, war is universally repugnant. We know, generally, that wars cause more problems than they solve. We know of the brutality and injustices that occur during war, of the social and economic disruption which it causes, and of the wholly tragic suffering of the innocent whose lives are shattered by war.

We know, in times when our blood is cooler, about the contagious reductionism by which the 'enemy' becomes a faceless 'evildoer' for whom no punishment is too harsh; about the mass susceptibility of nations to the rhetoric that surrounds war; about the awesome process by which communities, nations and entire continents are swept up in the contagion of conflict.

We know too, as we are made increasingly aware of how small our planet really is, that the fundamental wishes and goals of human beings are not so terribly different in lands and cultures other than our own; to live, in short, and live meaningfully.

And we know even that many people enjoy war – this, perhaps more than any other, is an aspect of human behaviour we are keenest to forget.

How is it that, periodically and in virtually every generation, we remain susceptible to the persuasion that the destruction of human life, together with all of its consequences, is not only desirable but wholly justifiable? And stranger yet, perhaps, that we look back on the more brutal chapters of history with both regret and incredulity, asking ourselves how such things could have happened.

It is the hardest thing to face this question honestly,

and to study it without shrinking from the results. It would be presumptuous to posit an answer; but I believe that, more than ever, it has become our individual responsibility to address this question; no institution can do the job for us. War is a human affliction; it concerns all of humanity. History teaches us that all peoples in every era are susceptible to the pathology of war, and no group or creed should put itself above the need to ask the question. But to be satisfied with an answer in terms of economics, nationality or ideology is insufficient; the problem lies further back, somewhere deeper in human nature.

I believe that an understanding of war – and correspondingly, of peace – must be searched for, observed and pondered in our own individual experience. To do so requires the willingness to examine our own private attitudes and secret prejudices, our convictions and beliefs, our grievances, our susceptibility to powerful emotions (which we may find are not, in the end, our own) – all these and a thousand other very human habits that in ordinary life go largely unquestioned. For the most sincere, to do so will mean meeting face to face not only with human primitivism but, more frighteningly, that prodigious human skill in rationalizing its own most monstrous attributes.

No surprise, perhaps, that humanity has proved a reluctant candidate for the challenge.

But only by meeting it can knowledge – which we do not lack – become understanding, of which we are in dire need – and from which meaningful change in the world itself can spring.

*   *   *

Dare I suggest that some good may be hidden in the present dangers? I do not think it is too much to suggest that we are at some kind of threshold in our potential evolution or at least an opportunity of enormous significance. Suddenly an unprecedented dialogue is taking place around the globe; people are exchanging ideas and concerns across continents.

This is because war has been brought, as it were, to our doorsteps; no longer can countries that formerly felt themselves invulnerable remain so; no longer can they wage war against a distant enemy and remain utterly untouched by the consequences. At no time has the connectedness of the world been felt more keenly. This is good, because we are faced with the necessary challenge of thinking in new ways closer to us all. How are we to protect our livelihoods, if we cannot fence out – or defeat outright – our enemies? Who, indeed – and what – are our true enemies?

And in seeking more creative ways to deliver ourselves from danger, we may discover what those who advocate war are likely to dread: that warfare is an outdated means by which to ensure our common human interests. We may also be led to the conviction that nothing less than a complete overhaul of humanity's ideas about itself is required, and that there is no better time to undertake the task than now.

I believe that an increasing portion of humanity is willing to rise to this challenge. I am personally heartened by the number of people who are shocked at the futility of the present violence; who have no confidence in a military solution, who are convinced of the necessity of re-evaluating our traditionally accepted ideas about solving conflict through conflict, and who are not distracted by issues of politics, doctrine or creed.

Peace is not a utopian dream. It is a universal exigency. But so long as this remains only a concept, rather than a practice, it is wishful thinking.

If we accept the axiom that war is infinitely less desirable than peace – I mean really accept it, and not be derailed by the usual rationalizations for destroying life – we will understand that peace is not only more urgent than ever, but also that its realization can only begin in the individual: the conflicts in human affairs are the mirror of the conflicts in the individual. But so too are their resolutions. Why should peace, instead of war, not be our legacy to our descendants? What holds us back? If societies are prepared to accept the necessity of a long military campaign – why not a long peaceful campaign?

Peace – personal peace, national peace, global peace – is, I believe, largely realizable: it begins here and now, with a choice. For if war is a uniquely human trait, so too is the ability to make choices. At the opposite end of the scale from human barbarity lies human wisdom, which arises from a choice: the choice to observe itself as a species, to step back coolly from itself, to separate, as it were, from itself – and from this wisdom, to learn and grow. Difficult as it is I believe this choice is open to all.

Jason Elliot

A River Runs Through It

In the Jordan Valley, not far from Jericho, on the Israeli-occupied West Bank, a river runs down from the hills.

It's called the Ein Al-Auja – Auja's stream: it shares its name with the village whose fields it watered for generations.

When I (Martin) went there, many years ago, Auja's citrus trees were being abandoned, and many villagers were leaving, too. The stream that had fed their fields had run dry. The reason lay a few miles west, at the end of an uphill track, at the source where the water tumbled out from the hills. The stream head was walled round and guarded by a couple of soldiers. From the nearby slopes, you could see how its flow had been diverted away from its namesake Arab village, and into what were now the lush fields of a new Israeli settlement. A little blue pearl of a swimming pool sparkled among the new buildings.

Some weeks later, I saw a photo of this settlement, or one very much like it, its bright green patchwork an apparent miracle in a dry land. It featured in a tourist leaflet celebrating how Israeli ingenuity had 'made the desert bloom'.

231

I remember wondering whether they'd rename the stream . . . And thinking how bitterly ironic it is, that it's not the supposedly irreconcilable differences between people which pitch them into war, but the things we most have in common – our need for sweet water, good land, and a home . . .

It is of course a mug's game, even at the best of times, to mix realpolitik and the moral high ground. And these are certainly not the best of times. But it's simply impossible *not* to make the connection between our vision of a more compassionate, more equitable, sustainable world – and the events of September 11, and their Afghan aftermath.

At the most basic level, we don't have to look much beyond the Middle East to see how a failure to turn that vision into anything approaching reality can breed conflict. You don't need a degree in environmental management to spot that the refugee camps of the Gaza Strip, for example, are an object lesson in unsustainability – and as such, a perfect seedbed for fanaticism.

This is not for one moment to cast the group of callous murderers who killed thousands in Manhattan as some rather overenthusiastic form of eco-warrior. But the support which men such as Osama bin Laden attract among the poor and the dispossessed is undoubtedly fed by that combination of social injustice and environmental degradation which is the very definition of unsustainable development. In Maoist terms, it's those people who provide the sea of sympathy in which the fish of al-Qaeda swim. And you can't drain that sea by force of arms. Military might can kill individual terrorists (a word strangely reserved almost exclusively for those who attack Westerners): it rarely saps their support. For proof, look at Palestine, where decades of Israeli *force majeure* have only fed successive *intifadas*.

Draining that sea of sympathy must surely include addressing the root causes of injustice and degradation with a resolve which we've sadly lacked to date. At ground level, action programmes on sustainable development can be a crucial part of breaking the vicious circle of poverty, alienation and despair which feeds fanaticism.

We should not, of course, be lured into making too many glib connections here: sympathy for the terrorists' agenda may be strongest in some of the world's poorest countries, but there is no simple link between poverty and terrorism – or indeed, between globalization and poverty. Though this is fiercely contested terrain, most development economists see a positive relationship between international trade and economic growth, reducing rather than increasing absolute poverty. Some have even argued that the reason Afghanistan is so poor is not globalization, but the lack of it.

That said, we in the West haven't properly internalized what it means to live in a global economy. Though its fruits may not be equitably distributed, the hype about its supposed benefits surely is. Once Afghanistan is 'liberated' from the isolationist zealotry of the Taliban, even its remotest villages will over time be exposed to a media onslaught extolling the glories of Western consumerism. For the vast majority, though, the gulf between daily reality and the riches displayed in that onslaught is unimaginably huge. They can all too easily seem no more than a distant dream jealously guarded by the military and financial muscle of America and its allies. So should we really be surprised if the world's 2 billion people surviving on less than $2 a day end up responding with a mix of anger, envy, and intense bitterness? Or that some adopt ideologies that wholly reject Western values, and, *in extremis*, end up as conscripts in the extremists' jihad.

So where does this leave the 'war on terror'?

Well for starters, the much-vaunted talk of a war to safeguard 'democratic values' will mean diddly squat to those who presently have no vote or voice in the new world order, no security of food nor work, no hope of the kind of prosperity which we all but claim as a right, and who rarely register on the G8's radar unless they're dying – or killing – on a CNN scale . . .

Nor are they likely to be impressed by an assertion that we're waging war to protect 'our economy and way of life' – which can all too easily sound as though we're fighting for the freedom to go shopping: for every one of us to own a 4x4 without fear of assault. And which has, it must be said, to be set against the inescapable fact that the apogee of the American way of life á la Bush is deeply unsustainable: the reckless consumption of a hefty chunk of the world's common resources by a relatively small proportion of its people is most emphatically not a cause worth killing for. If this is a battle for 'business as usual', then it can only be a bitterly pyrrhic victory.

What's urgently needed now is for America, and Britain, to articulate a post-war vision which will speak to those far beyond their borders. To their credit, both President Bush and, in particular, Tony Blair in his speech to the Labour conference, have hinted at such a vision – but they could do so much more. They could uncover, and demonstrate, a mixture of compassion and humility which has hardly been the West's forte, but which is a damn fine starting place for any sustained effort to make the world a more sustainable, and hence secure, home. It means a less frenzied promotion of interconnectedness, and a more conciliatory acknowledgement of *interdependence*. One which must, incidentally, be buttressed through strengthened global institutions and agreements. Bush's first few months of US-first unilateralism (during which he abrogated no less than six international treaties) sent out a disastrous message that the rest of the world counted for nothing to the most powerful nation on earth.

We isolate our thinking at our peril, because, as September 11 so viciously demonstrated, we cannot isolate ourselves. No missile defence shield could have halted the terrorists, nor saved the United States from biological attack. And for all we know, the next generation are not being trained in remote camps in Afghanistan, but in the computer departments of American universities. E-terrorism looms large as the next frontier – a frontier quite literally beyond all borders.

So aren't Bush and Blair right to assert that 'terrorism

now poses the greatest single threat to global security'? No: that simply reveals profound ignorance as to what is really undermining it.

This was borne in upon me (Jonathon), very uncomfortably, just a day after the New York and Washington attacks, when a close friend asked why I was more wound up about the 5000 who lost their lives than I was about the 40,000 or so who will have died somewhere in the world on September 11 as a result of preventable or easily treatable diseases. And, according to UNICEF, 50 per cent of those would have been children under the age of five.

The fact that we've all learned to live so easily with such a devastating, daily death-toll speaks volumes. It's morally impossible to argue that the value of one life in Bangladesh or Bolivia is worth less than one in New York or Washington.

This is not for a second to suggest that any course of action that doesn't include bringing justice to those responsible for the murders of September 11 is remotely appropriate. But unless it's pursued in a way which transparently addresses the basic injustices which feed fanaticism – and there is, to be frank, precious little sign of that as we write – then it's only pouring more fertilizer onto those seedbeds of violence. And condemning a lot more people to the repetitive brutalities endured by those who fail to learn from history. It's the strongest case, yet, perhaps, for being tough on crime, tough on its causes.

In this light, reducing our ecological footprint is not some feel-good gesture; it's one of the most persuasive tools of international diplomacy. Applying basic standards of social justice to decisions over international business is not a fad for fans of fair trade: it's our best insurance policy against fanaticism.

Almost without exception, technologies which are environmentally more sustainable are less prone to being hijacked, in any sense of the word, by those intent on harm. No terrorist is going to make governments tremble by threatening to bomb a wind turbine, or release clouds of compost over our cities. Compare that to the destructive potential of nuclear power and toxic chemicals. A more sustainable world is indeed a safer one.

More specifically, this is certain to focus American attention on the vulnerabilities of its addiction to oil. Despite enthusiastic development of its own reserves in Alaska and elsewhere, the United States can never hope to replace its desperate dependence on oil from the Middle East – not while it is so wedded to a carbon economy. That dependence, of course, is the prime reason for the presence of US troops in Saudi Arabia – a presence which, ironically, is one of the chief complaints of Osama bin Laden.

America would love to be self-sufficient in energy; it's just possible that, post-September, it will wake up to the realization that this means a decisive shift away from fossil fuels, towards the combination of renewables and efficiency gains to which it is surprisingly well suited. Against such a backdrop, its reservations about Kyoto would soon, of course, evaporate. And a move in this direction from the world's most powerful economy would surely drive a revolutionary pace of change elsewhere.

There must be a slim hope that the fear of terrorism will, paradoxically, focus attention on the absolute imperative that people with wildly divergent views learn how to talk to each other. One of the surprising triumphs of the sustainable development community is its remarkable progress in developing understanding between people of implacably opposed opinions. There was a time when it would have been inconceivable for industry to sit down with activists: to all intents and purposes, they came from different planets. Yet recent years have seen quite dramatic – and often wholly unsung – breakthroughs in this area, not only between business and campaigners, but within and among communities, too. There's even a village in Israel where Jews and Palestinians have succeeded in living alongside each other precisely as a result of such dialogue.

The trick, it seems, is to start with what we have in common, rather than with the opinions – even the religions – which divide us. And what we have in common are, quite simply, the resources on which all human life depends. We have to find a way to share those equitably, or we will surely go to war over them.

We've said before that it's easy to regard the pursuit of sustainability as a luxury of the good times – something appropriately eclipsed by the hard stuff of human conflict. But surely, now more than ever, the truth is that it's a fundamental prerequisite for that most desperately elusive of shared human desires – peace.

These days we seem to hear a lot about stark choices: about being either 'with us, or against us'. So here's another one, courtesy of Martin Luther King, which might just be a little more poignant for the years ahead: *'We learn to live together as brothers – or we die together as fools.'*

Martin Wright and Jonathon Porritt

Contributor's Notes

KAREN ARMSTRONG

Writer and broadcaster Karen Armstrong is the winner of the Calmus Foundation Annual Award and the Muslim Public Affairs Council Media Award. Her television credits include *The First Christian*, *Tongues of Fire* and she is the author of several books including *Through the Narrow Gate*, *The Gospel According to Woman*, *Muhammad – A Western Attempt to Understand Islam*, *Christianity and Islam* and *Islam: A Short History*.

RONAN BENNETT

Ronan Bennett, whose works include three novels, several screenplays for film and television and a memoir, spent two years of his young adult life in prison as a result of the Troubles in Ireland. Exonerated, he went on to earn a PhD in history at London University. His most recent novel, *The Catastrophist*, was short-listed for the Whitbread novel award. He is a regular contributor to the *Observer*, the *Guardian*, *The London Review of Books* and other publications.

MARTIN BELL

Martin Bell was born in Suffolk in 1938 and served in its Regiment. He worked as a reporter for BBC News from 1962 to 1997 and was assigned to eighty countries and eleven wars, beginning in Vietnam and ending in Bosnia, where he was wounded. In 1997 he left the BBC to stand as an Independent candidate in the Tatton constituency in the General Election; he won by more than 11,000 votes, and so became the only Independent MP in the House of Commons. Bell served on the Standards and Privileges Committee, and was active in a number of causes, including the campaign to win compensation for the former prisoners of war of the Japanese. In 2001, Bell was appointed by UNICEF UK as Special Representative for Humanitarian Intervention. In that capacity, in October 2001, he visited UNICEF projects and Afghan refugees on the border between Afghanistan and Tadjikistan.

CHRIS BELLAMY, PhD

Chris Bellamy is Professor of Military Science at Cranfield University and heads its MSc program in Global Security. Bellamy began his career as a professional soldier, but had to leave the Army on medical grounds. He then pursued a career as an academic and journalist, during which time he found himself in real conflicts. From 1990 to 1997 he was Defence Correspondent for the *Independent* and reported from the Gulf War in 1990–91, from Bosnia from 1992–96, and from Chechnya in 1995.

DAVID BELLAMY, OBE, BSc, PhD, HON FLS

David Bellamy is a lecturer in Botany at the University of Durham, a special professor of Botany at the University of Nottingham and a visiting professor at Massey University. Bellamy is also the director of Botanical Enterprises Ltd, the founder of the National Heritage Conservatory Foundation and the Conservation Foundation. Also a member of various professional committees, Bellamy is the winner of the UNEP Global 500. His television credits include *Life in Our Sea*, *Bellamy on Botany*, *A Welsh Herbal*, and *Paradise Ploughed*. Bellamy is the author of several books including *The World of Plants*, *Il Libro Verde*, *The Queen's Hidden Garden* and *Tomorrow's Earth*.

RACHEL BILLINGTON

Rachel Billington is the author of fifteen novels, two works of non-fiction and eight childrens' books. She is Vice-President of English PEN and co-editor of the national newspaper for prisoners, *InsideTime*. Her new novel, *A Woman's Life*, will be published in February 2002.

CARYL CHURCHILL

Since the mid-70s, Caryl Churchill has ranked among the best-known political playwrights in England. Her work deals with a variety of issues, yet she reaches audiences from across the political spectrum. Her plays include *Owners*, *Traps*, *Shining in Buckinghamshire*,

Vinegar Tom, *Cloud Nine*, *Top Girls*, *Serious Money*, *Mad Forest*, *The Skriker*, *Blue Heart* and *Far Away*.

SIR TERENCE CONRAN

Terence Conran is one of the world's best-known designers, restaurateurs and retailers. He founded the Habitat chain of stores that brought good, modern design within reach of the general population and established the retail group Storehouse, which includes Heal's among others. In the 90s, Conran built another impressive group of companies, Conran Holdings, involved in design, retailing and restaurants. He owns Conran shops and restaurants around the world and his design projects have included Ocean Terminal in Edinburgh, Rex Bar in Iceland, and the Great Eastern Hotel in London. Terence Conran's books include *The Essential House Book*, *Terence Conran on Design*, *The Essential Garden Book*, *Q&A: A Sort of Autobiography* and *Alcazar to Zinc: the story of Conran Restaurants*.

WILLIAM DALRYMPLE

William Dalrymple was born in Scotland and brought up on the shores of the Firth of Forth. He has written a number of highly acclaimed, award-winning books on travel, including *In Xanadu*, *City of Djinns*, *From the Holy Mountain* and *The Age of Kali: Indian Travels & Encounters*. Dalrymple's writing has appeared in national magazines and newspapers such as the *New Statesman* and the *Independent* and he was recently elected the youngest Fellow of the Royal Society of Literature and the Royal Asiatic Society.

JASON ELLIOT

Jason Elliot is the author of the award-winning book on Afghanistan, *An Unexpected Light,* and is currently working on his next book about Iran. Elliot has travelled extensively in countries of the Islamic world over the past fifteen years.

PAUL FOOT

Author, journalist and reporter Paul Foot writes a column for the *Daily Mirror* and *Private Eye.* Foot is the recipient of numerous awards, including Journalist of the Year, the Orwell Prize for Journalism, and Campaigning Journalist of the Decade. He has written many books, including, *Immigration and Race in British Politics, Red Shelley, The Helen Smith Story, Murder at the Farm: Who Killed Carl Bridgewater?* and *Articles of Resistance.*

STEPHEN JAY GOULD, PhD

Stephen Jay Gould is Professor of Geology at Harvard University and is also curator for Invertebrate Paleontology at Harvard's Museum of Comparative Zoology. The author of 300 consecutive essays for his monthly column 'This View of Life' in *Natural History* magazine, Gould has also penned over 20 bestselling books, and has written nearly a thousand scientific papers. In addition, he has received numerous awards, including the MacArthur Foundation Prize Fellowship, the prestigious Medal of Edinburgh, and the Silver National Medal of the Zoology Society of London.

ASSAD HAFEEZ, MD

Dr Assad Hafeez is a paediatrician living in Islamabad. He works with the charity Child Advocacy International providing medical aid to women and children in the Afghan refugee camps on the border between Afghanistan and Pakistan. He contributes regular diary entries to the online publication *Out There News*.

SUHEIR HAMMAD

Suheir Hammad, Palestinian–American poet and political activist, has published a book of poems, *Born Palestinian, Born Black*, a memoir, *Drops of this Story* and is prominently featured in *Listen Up! An Anthology of Spoken Word Poetry*. Hammad is the recipient of the Audre Lourde Writing Award, the Morris Center for Healing Poetry Award and a New York Mills Artist Residency in Minnesota, US. Hammad has read her work on BBC radio, and on stage at the Globe.

KATHARINE HAMNETT

Katharine Hamnett studied fashion at art school in London, then worked as a freelance designer, setting up her own business, Katharine Hamnett Designs, in 1979. She draws inspiration for designs from work-wear and also from social movements, such as the peace movement, which she actively supports. Hamnett's inspiration is evident through her creation of 'logo' T-shirts that advertise social and political messages. Her tops have sported messages including, 'Save the Rainforest', 'Cancel the Third World Debt', 'Life is Sacred', 'Global Aid to Afghanistan Now', and 'Save Democracy'. Hamnett is the winner of the Fashion Designer of the Year award (1984) and the British Clothing and Knitting Council Expert Award. She is currently a professor of Fashion and Textiles at the London Institute.

THE RIGHT REVEREND RICHARD HARRIES, BISHOP OF OXFORD

Before becoming the Bishop of Oxford in 1987, The Right Reverend Richard Harries was the Dean of King's College, a parish priest and lecturer in Christian Doctrine and Ethics. He is a fellow of King's College and an Honorary Doctor of Divinity at the University of London. Harries has written 18 books including *Art and the Beauty of God*, in addition to his numerous contributions to several national newspapers and journals. He is the chairman of the Church of England Board for Social Responsibility, The House of Bishop's Working Party on Issues in Human Sexuality and the Council of Christians and Jews. Harries is also a board member of Christian Aid, the International Interfaith Foundation and a founding member of the Abrahamic Group.

ROBERT JENSEN, PhD

Robert Jensen is an associate professor in the School of Journalism at the University of Texas. He is author of *Writing Dissent: Taking Radical Ideas from the Margins to the Mainstream* and co-author with Gail Dines and Ann Russo of *Pornography: The Production and Consumption of Inequality*. He is a member of the Nowar Collective, and is a regular contributor to newspapers in the United States on foreign policy, politics and race.

TERRY JONES

Writer, film director and performer Terry Jones is best known for his television and film work with *Monty Python*. He directed *Monty Python and the Holy Grail*, *Life of Brian*, *Meaning of Life*, *Personal Services*, *Erik the Viking* and *The Wind in the Willows*. Television credits include *Crusades*, *Ancient Inventions* and *Hidden Histories*. Jones is the author of *Chaucer's Knight*, *Fairy Tales*, *Fantastic Stories*, *Nicobobinus*, *The Curse of the Vampire's Socks*, *The Knight and the Squire*, *The Lady and the Squire*, *Attacks of Opinion*, and *Who Murdered Chaucer?*

DOMINIQUE LAPIERRE

Dominique Lapierre is a former *Paris-Match* correspondent and the author of numerous international bestselling books including *Is Paris Burning?*, *City of Joy*, *Freedom at Midnight*, *O, Jerusalem*, *Beyond Love* and *Five Past Midnight in Bhopal*, several of which have been made into films. A humanitarian and philanthropist, Lapierre donates half his royalties to support humanitarian causes in India.

ANNIE LENNOX

Born and raised in Scotland, Annie Lennox briefly attended London's Royal Academy of Music before joining the band The Tourists in the late 1970s. Best known for her band the Eurythmics, formed with Dave Stewart in 1980, Annie Lennox helped create one of the most popular sounds of the 80s. In 1990, Lennox released her first solo album *Diva*, which sold over two million copies in the United States alone, and was nominated for three Grammy awards. Annie Lennox has also been actively involved in several charity and volunteer organizations, including Greenpeace and Amnesty International.

RAHUL MAHAJAN

Rahul Mahajan is a doctoral candidate in physics at the University of Texas at Austin and serves on the National Board of Peace Action, the largest grass-roots peace organization in the United States and is a member of the Nowar Collective. Mahajan has written for *Newsday*, *Houston Chronicle*, *The Hindu* in India, *Middle East Times* in Egypt, and others. He is the author of the soon to be published *The New Crusade: America's War on Terrorism*.

PAUL MARSDEN, MP

Before his career as a Labour MP for Shrewsbury and Atcham, Paul Marsden worked as a Quality Assurance Manager at Taylor Woodrow Construction, was employed at NatWest Bank, and Mitel Telecoms. As an MP, Marsden has presented bills on Cancer Care, Health Care Standards for the Elderly and Recycling. In 2000, Marsden spoke out on BBC *Panorama* against the government over the fuel crisis and has publicly opposed GM crops and tuition fees. Paul is Vice-Chair of Labour Against the War.

JAMES MAWDSLEY

James Mawdsley was brought up in Lancashire. He went to Bristol University to study physics and philosophy, leaving early to live in Australia. From there he became increasingly involved in the Burmese democracy movement and was subsequently imprisoned by the Burmese government. He is author of *The Heart Must Break*, an account of what he has seen in Burma's border areas and prisons.

ADRIAN MITCHELL, FRSL

Poet and playwright Adrian Mitchell served in the Royal Air Force before becoming a reporter for the *Oxford Mail* and the *Evening Standard*. Mitchell received the Granada fellowship in the Arts at University of Lancaster and a fellowship at the Center for the Humanities at Wesleyan University, USA, and has been awarded an Honorary Doctorate at North London University. Mitchell has been the resident writer at Sherman Theatre and Unicorn Theatre. His plays include *Tyger*, *Man Friday*, *Mind Your Head*, *The White Deer* and *Anna on Anna*. Mitchell has also written for opera and film and is the author of several novels, books of poetry and children's books.

GEORGE MONBIOT, CBE

George Monbiot is an environmental and human rights campaigner and writer. After working on land tenure issues in Asia, Africa and Latin America, he founded a land rights movement in Britain called *The Land is Ours*. Monbiot makes regular radio and TV appearances and writes for the *Guardian* newspaper and is the author of *Captive State*.

COURTTIA NEWLAND

Courttia Newland is the author of titles including *The Scholar* and *Society Within Afrobeat*. Selected by the British Council to represent the new wave of British writing, Newland toured in the Czech Republic with Hanif Kureishi in 1999. He is the co-editor of *IC3: The Penguin Book of New Black Writing in Britain*. Newland has recently cut his teeth in the world of theatre with his company, The Post Office Theatre, Co. His latest novel, *Snakeskin*, is published in Spring 2002.

BEN OKRI, FRSL

Author and poet Ben Okri pursued a career as a presenter and broadcaster at the BBC before becoming a full-time writer. A member of the Society of Authors, PEN International and the recipient of an Honorary Doctorate of literature at the University of Westminster, Okri is the winner of many prizes including the Commonwealth Prize for Africa, the Paris Review Prize for Fiction, the Booker Prize, Premio Grinane Cavour and Premio Palmi. Okri has written several books, including *Flowers and Shadows*, *Incidents at the Shrine*, *An African Elegy*, *Astonishing the Gods*, *Dangerous Love*, *Infinite Riches*, *The Famished Road* and *Mental Fight*.

JOSEPH OLSHAN

Joseph Olshan is the award-winning author of seven novels, including *Clara's Heart*, *Nightswimmer*, and most recently, *In Clara's Hands*. Olshan has also written non-fiction articles and essays for many publications, including the *New York Times Magazine* and the *Washington Post*. Additionally, Olshan is the editorial director of Delphinium Books and lives in New York City.

MATTHEW PARRIS

Matthew Parris is a freelance broadcaster and columnist for *The Times*. Parris is also the recipient of several awards and is the author of books on politics, humour and travel, including *The Great Unfrocked*, *Read My Lips*, *Off Message* and *The Outsider*.

JONATHON PORRITT

Jonathon Porritt is Co-founder and Programme Director of Forum for the Future. He is a leading writer, broadcaster and commentator on sustainable development, and his most recent book is *Playing Safe: Science and the Environment*. In October 2000 he was appointed by the Prime Minister as Chairman of the new UK Sustainable Development Commission. He is also a member of the Board of the South West Regional Development Agency, and is Co-Director of The Prince of Wales's Business and Environment Programme.

GEOFFREY ROBERTSON QC

Geoffrey Robertson is the author of *Crimes Against Humanity: The Struggle for Global Justice*. He is Head of Doughty Street Chambers, a Recorder and Visiting Professor in Human Rights law at Birkbeck College. He has argued many landmark human rights cases in the courts of England and the Commonwealth and in the European Court of Human Rights, and has led missions for Amnesty and Human Rights Watch. He is the author of several legal textbooks, including *Freedom, the Individual and the Law* and *Media Law*, and of a memoir, *The Justice Game*.

ANITA RODDICK, OBE

Anita Roddick opened a small shop in a back street of Brighton selling beauty products made from natural products, not tested on animals, and supplied in refillable containers in 1976. In the Body Shop she created a company with attitude that is known around the world for both its products and its principles. Her dedication to ecology and the Third World has resulted in her book *Take It Personally*, which explores the myths of globalization.

EDWARD W. SAID, PhD

Edward W. Said is a Professor of English and Comparative Literature at Columbia University and has lectured at more than 150 colleges and universities worldwide. He is a regular contributor to the *Guardian*, *Le Monde Diplomatique* and the Arab-language daily *al-Hayat*, printed in every Arab capital in the world. His writing, translated into 14 languages, includes 10 books, among them, *Orientalism*, *The World, the Text and the Critic*, *Blaming the Victims*, *Culture and Imperialism* and *Peace and Its Discontents: Essays on Palestine in the Middle East Peace Process*.

ZIAUDDIN SARDAR, PhD

Ziauddin Sardar is a writer and cultural critic. He has published over 35 books on various aspects of Islam, the Middle East, science policy, culture studies and related subjects including *Postmodernism and the Other*, *Orientalism*, *The Consumption of Kuala Lumpur*, *Introducing Islam*, *The Future of Muslim Civilisation* and *Islamic Futures: The Shape of Ideas to Come*. Sardar is a regular contributor to the *New Statesman* and the *Observer*, and is a Visiting Professor of Postcolonial Studies at City University.

AHDAF SOUEIF

Ahdaf Soueif was born in Cairo and spent part of her childhood in London. She is the author of *Aisha*, *Sandpiper*, *The Map of Love* and *In the Eye of the Sun*, among others.

MARK STEEL

Mark Steel has performed as a stand-up comedian since 1983. He co-wrote and performed four series of *The Mark Steel Solution* and has written and performed three series of *The Mark Steel Lecture* for Radio 4. He has hosted the Radio 5 sports program *Extra Time* and written two books *It's Not a Runner Bean* and *Reasons to Be Cheerful*. Mark Steel writes for the *Guardian*, the *Independent* and the *New Statesman*.

TERRY WAITE, CBE

Terry Waite, envoy of the Archbishop of Canterbury, international humanitarian, and former Beirut hostage is committed to responsible leadership for social justice. As the Archbishop's special envoy, he was particularly involved in negotiations to secure the release of hostages held in the Middle East; between 1982 and the end of 1986, fourteen hostages, for whom he was interceding, were released. Terry Waite was kidnapped in Beirut in January 1987 while involved in secret negotiations to win the release of hostages held in Lebanon. He was not released until November 1991. He is the author of two volumes of memoirs, *Taken on Trust* and *Travels with a Primate*.

NATASHA WALTER

Natasha Walter is the author of *The New Feminism* and editor of *On the Move: Feminism for a New Generation*. She writes a column for the *Independent*.

MARTIN WRIGHT

Martin Wright is Editor of *Green Futures*. Martin has written and broadcast widely on environmental issues in the UK and overseas, has contributed articles and photos to a range of publications, including the *Observer*, *The Times*, the *Guardian*, the *Independant On Sunday*, *Newsweek* and *New Scientist* and won the Environment Council's Science and Environment Journalist of the Year Award. He has written and produced documentaries on these issues for UK independent television, and broadcast on BBC and independent radio, and on the BBC world service.

Editor's Biography

Anna Kiernan is a freelance writer and editor and has reviewed for *The Times Literary Supplement*, *The Big Issue* and *Stealth*, amongst others. She is also a part-time lecturer in Media and Culture at Essex University. Her MA thesis was entitled, 'What does multiculturalism mean for the white literary imagination?'. She is currently working on her first novel.

The appalling events in America were a terrible reminder, if any were needed, of the unstable and violent world we live in. War Child condemns those atrocities, as we do all acts of violence against innocent people the world over.

Conflict is born out of the hatred of adults, but it is invariably children who suffer most. Be it those killed, maimed or orphaned in America, or the millions who continue to suffer in Afghanistan and throughout the world, if we adults do not take an active responsibility for children's well being, the future will offer no more hope than the present.

This should be a time for reflection, not only on our own vulnerability, but also on the precarious existence of the millions of our fellow human beings whose suffering shows no sign of abating.

War Child will continue to work towards a more peaceful world. We will intervene in emergency situations wherever appropriate and effective. In the longer term we continue to focus on education and communications, in the firm belief that ignorance is the life blood of conflict.

War Child is currently working in Central Asia to provide emergency assistance to the people of Afghanistan, and continues to provide long term aid to children and their families in Africa and the Balkans.

War Child
PO Box 20231
London NW5 3WP
Tel. 020 7916 9276
Fax. 020 7916 9280
info@warchild.globalnet.co.uk
www.warchild.org.uk

William Shakespeare's
Macbeth

Tak
offers:

- ext
  ma
- ann
  and
- cross
  sugge
- sugges

Part of the
for all those
the play, bu
surrounds Sh

Alexander Le
Toronto.

Routledge Guides to Literature*

Editorial Advisory Board: Richard Bradford (University of Ulster at Coleraine),
Jan Jedrzejewski (University of Ulster at Coleraine), Duncan Wu (St Catherine's
College, University of Oxford)

Routledge Guides to Literature offer clear introductions to the most widely
studied authors and literary texts.

Each book engages with texts, contexts and criticism, highlighting the range of
critical views and contextual factors that need to be taken into consideration in
advanced studies of literary works. The series encourages informed but independent readings of texts by raagorks. The series encourages informed but independ-
critical issues relevant to the works exam... well as those of critical consensus. Alongside general guides ...
the series includes 'sourcebooks', which allow access to reprinted contextu...
critical materials as well as annotated extracts of primary text.

Available in this series

Geoffrey Chaucer by Gillian Rudd
Ben Jonson by James Loxley
William Shakespeare's The Merchant of Venice: A Sourcebook edited by
  S. P. Cerasano
William Shakespeare's King Lear: A Sourcebook edited by Grace Ioppolo
William Shakespeare's Othello: A Sourcebook edited by Andrew Hadfield
John Milton by Richard Bradford
John Milton's Paradise Lost: A Sourcebook edited by Margaret Kean
Alexander Pope by Paul Baines
Mary Wollstonecraft's A Vindication of the Rights of Woman: A Sourcebook
  edited by Adriana Craciun
Jane Austen by Robert P. Irvine
Jane Austen's Emma: A Sourcebook edited by Paula Byrne
Jane Austen's Pride and Prejudice: A Sourcebook edited by Robert Morrison
Mary Shelley's Frankenstein: A Sourcebook edited by Timothy Morton
The Poems of John Keats: A Sourcebook edited by John Strachan
Charles Dickens's David Copperfield: A Sourcebook edited by Richard J. Dunn
Charles Dickens's Bleak House: A Sourcebook edited by Janice M. Allan
Charles Dickens's Oliver Twist: A Sourcebook edited by Juliet John
Herman Melville's Moby-Dick: A Sourcebook edited by Michael J. Davey
Harriet Beecher Stowe's Uncle Tom's Cabin: A Sourcebook edited by Debra J.
  Rosenthal
Walt Whitman's Song of Myself: A Sourcebook and Critical Edition edited by
  Ezra Greenspan
Robert Browning by Stefan Hawlin

* Some books in this series were originally published in the Routledge Literary Sourcebooks
series, edited by Duncan Wu, or the Complete Critical Guide to English Literature series,
edited by Richard Bradford and Jan Jedrzejewski.

William Shakespeare's
Macbeth
A Sourcebook

Edited by Alexander Leggatt

Routledge
Taylor & Francis Group
LONDON AND NEW YORK

First published 2006
by Routledge
2 Park Square, Milton Park, Abingdon, Oxon OX14 4RN

Simultaneously published in the USA and Canada
by Routledge
270 Madison Ave, New York, NY 10016

Routledge is an imprint of the Taylor & Francis Group

Selection and editorial matter © 2006 Alexander Leggatt

Typeset in Sabon and Gill Sans by RefineCatch Limited, Bungay, Suffolk
Printed and bound in Great Britain by TJ International Ltd, Padstow

British Library Cataloguing in Publication Data
A catalogue record for this book is available from the British Library.

Library of Congress Cataloging in Publication Data
William Shakespeare's Macbeth : a sourcebook / [edited by] Alexander Leggatt.
     p. cm. – (Routledge guides to literature)
   Includes bibliographical references.
1. Shakespeare, William, 1564–1616. Macbeth.   2. Macbeth, King of Scotland,
11th cent. – In literature.   3. Scotland – In literature.   4. Regicides in literature.
I. Leggatt, Alexander.   II. Series.
PR2823.W477 2006
822.3'3–dc22

2005019928

ISBN10: 0–415–23824–2   ISBN13: 9–78–0–415–23824–3 (hbk)
ISBN10: 0–415–23825–0   ISBN13: 9–78–0–415–23825–0 (pbk)

Contents

Modern Criticism   58

The Work in Performance   89

3: Key Passages

4: Further Reading

Illustrations

Editor's Note

Throughout this book including the Key Passages, act, scene and line numbers for *Macbeth* refer to the Arden edition, ed. Kenneth Muir (London: Methuen, 1951, frequently reprinted). In the extracts from criticism and performance reviews, references to this edition have been added to quotations from the play, substituting for the act, scene and line references in the original where these differ. References to Shakespeare plays other than *Macbeth* are to *The Riverside Shakespeare*, ed. G. Blakemore Evans and J. J. M. Tobin (second edition: Boston and New York: Houghton Mifflin, 1997). Unless otherwise specified, footnotes are by the editor of this volume.

Acknowledgements

I am grateful to Duncan Wu and Talia Rodgers for getting me started on this project, and to Duncan Wu, Liz O'Donnell and Routledge's anonymous readers for their very helpful comments on the penultimate version. The errors that remain are my own. The members of the editorial team at Routledge have been patient and supportive, particularly when the curse of the Scottish Play produced an unexpected delay. In particular I wish to thank Fiona Cairns for her help during the middle stages of the project and Liz Thompson for her advice and support throughout. I am also grateful to my wife Anna Leggatt for technical support when the curse struck my own technology.

Excerpts from *Narrative and Dramatic Sources of Shakespeare: Volume VII Major Tragedies: Hamlet, Othello, King Lear, Macbeth*, edited by Geoffrey Bullough. Copyright © 1973 Geoffrey Bullough, reprinted with permission of Columbia University Press and Routledge.

Excerpts from pp. 259–61 of *The Arden Shakespeare: King Henry VI, Part I*, edited by Edward Burns, 2000, Thomson Learning, reproduced with permission of the publisher.

Excerpts from *King James VI and I: Political Writings*, by Johann P. Sommerville, 1994. Copyright © Cambridge University Press, reproduced with permission of the editor and publisher.

'How Many Children Had Lady Macbeth?' from *Explorations: Essays in Criticism Mainly on the Literature of the Seventeenth Century*, by L. C. Knights. Copyright © 1946 L. C. Knights, reproduced with kind permission of C. B. Knights.

Excerpts from 'The Naked Babe and the Cloak of Manliness' THE WELL WROUGHT URN. Copyright 1947 and renewed 1975 by Cleanth Brooks, reprinted by permission of Harcourt, Inc.

From 'Lady Macbeth: "Infirm of Purpose" ' by Joan Larsen Klein in *The Woman's Part: Feminist Criticism of Shakespeare* ed. Lenz, Greene and Neely. Copyright 1980 by Board of Trustees of the University of Illinois. Used with permission of the University of Illinois Press and Joan Larsen Klein.

La Belle, Jenijoy. ' "A Strange Infirmity": Lady Macbeth's Amenorrhea'. *Shakespeare Quarterly* 31:3 (1980), 381–383, 385. © Folger Shakespeare Library. Reprinted with permission of The Johns Hopkins University Press.

Excerpts from Stephen Booth, *King Lear, Macbeth, Indefinition, and Tragedy*, 1983, reproduced with kind permission of the author.

Excerpts from Harriett Hawkins, *Classics and Trash: Traditions and Taboos in High Literature and Popular Modern Genres.* © 1990 Harriett Hawkins, University of Toronto Press, reproduced with permission of the publisher.

Stephen Greenblatt. 'Shakespeare bewitched', from *Shakespeare and Cultural Traditions: The Selected Proceedings of the International Shakespeare Association World Congress, Tokyo, 1991*, ed. Kishi, Pringle and Wells. Copyright © 1994 by Associated University Presses, Inc., reproduced with permission of the publisher.

Excerpts from *Shakespeare's Theatre* by Peter Thomson, 1983, Routledge & Kegan Paul. Copyright © Peter Thomson 1983, reproduced with permission of the publisher.

Excerpts from *Curtains* by Kenneth Tynan. Copyright © 1961 by Kenneth Tynan, reproduced with kind permission of the Estate of K. Tynan.

Goodwin, James. *Akira Kurosawa and the Intertextual Cinema* pp. 178–9, 182–3. © 1993 The Johns Hopkins University Press reprinted with permission of The Johns Hopkins University Press.

Kenneth Rothwell, *A History of Shakespeare on Screen: A Century of Film and Television*, 2nd edition, 2004. © Kenneth S. Rothwell, 1999, 2004, published by Cambridge University Press, reproduced with permission of the author and publisher.

'Double, Double: Trevor Nunn's *Macbeth* for Television' by Marion D. Perret, in *Shakespeare Bulletin* Summer 1992, reproduced by kind permission of *Shakespeare Bulletin*.

Copyright © 1992 from *Suffocating Mothers: Fantasies of Maternal Origin in Shakespeare's Plays, Hamlet to The Tempest* by Janet Adelman. Reproduced by permission of Routledge/Taylor & Francis Group, LLC.

Excerpts from Barbara Everett, *Young Hamlet: Essays on Shakespeare's Tragedies*, 1989, by permission of Oxford University Press.

Excerpts from Julia Lacey Brooke (ed.), *The Tragedy of Macbeth*, 1990, by permission of Oxford University Press.

Excerpts from Derek Jacobi, 'Macbeth' from Robert Smallwood, *Players of Shakespeare 4-Further Essays in Shakespearean Performance by Players with the Royal Shakespeare Company*, 1998, published by Cambridge University Press, reproduced with permission of the author and publisher.

Copyright © 1999 from Shakespeare after theory by David Scott Kastan. Reproduced by permission of Routledge/Taylor & Francis Group, LLC.

Excerpt from A. C. Bradley, *Shakespearean Tragedy: Lectures on Hamlet, Othello, King Lear, Macbeth*, pp. 352–6, © Royal Holloway, University of London. Reproduced by permission of Royal Holloway and Macmillam Publishers Ltd.

Every effort has been made to contact the publishers or copyright holders of reprinted material. The publisher would be pleased to hear from any further copyright holders and to rectify omissions in future reprints.

Illustrations:

Fig 1. From Holinshed's *History of Scotland* (1577). By permission of the British Library (C598. h. 3–4, p. 243)
Fig 2. Photographer Angus McBean. Copyright Royal Shakespeare Company
Fig 3. Joe Cocks Studio Collection. Copyright Shakespeare Birthplace Trust
Fig 4. Photographer Donald Cooper. Reprinted by kind permission of Photostage Ltd.

Introduction

There is a theatrical anecdote, one of many, that sums up the curious power of Shakespeare's *Macbeth*. It concerns a production at the Prince's Theatre in London in 1926, in which Sybil Thorndike played Lady Macbeth and her husband Lewis Casson played Banquo. The production had been accident-prone:

> such terrible things kept on happening that one night Lewis came into her dressing room and said, 'Sybil, the Devil does work in this play – there is horror behind it – we must do something positive against it'. And together they read aloud the 91st Psalm, which calmed and strengthened them.[1]

The psalm in question is a statement of confidence in God's protection. Verses 5 and 11 are characteristic: 'Thou shalt not be afraid for any terror by night: nor for the arrow that flieth by day'; 'For he shall give his angels charge over thee: to keep thee in all thy ways'.

In the theatre *Macbeth* is regarded as a haunted, unlucky play. Stories of accident, illness, even death abound. I recall a production at my own university in which, during rehearsals, the lighting designer broke his ankle and the costume designer suffered a heart attack. Actors consider it bad luck to speak the play's name: it is usually called 'the Scottish play'. It is certainly bad luck to quote it in the dressing room, though there are traditional ways of counteracting the curse. These include quoting an equivalent number of lines from *A Midsummer Night's Dream* or, more elaborately, leaving the dressing room, turning around three times, spitting, swearing and knocking to be readmitted.

Though there are unsupported legends of the curse at work even in the play's first production, including a story that at the first performance the boy actor playing Lady Macbeth fell ill and Shakespeare himself took over,[2] the verifiable stories of misfortune, and the superstition itself, cannot confidently be traced

---

1 Elizabeth Sprigge, *Sybil Thorndike Casson* (London: Victor Gollancz, 1971), p. 111.
2 Richard Huggett, *Supernatural on Stage: Ghosts and Superstitions of the Theatre* (New York: Taplinger Publishing Company, 1975), p. 164. Huggett presents the story as a matter of fact, but there is no evidence for it.

before the 1920s.[3] The sense that evil forces are at work in *Macbeth* may be a product of the aftermath of the First World War, whose horrific death toll produced a new interest in the spirit world, as those who had lost loved ones tried to contact them through ouija boards and table-rapping. Those beliefs have faded (though not vanished); the belief in the *Macbeth* curse remains. So far as we can tell earlier actors – David Garrick, W. C. Macready, Henry Irving – produced the play with no sense that they were courting any special danger. And yet the superstition about *Macbeth*, even if it is more recent than legend would have it, embodies a truth about the play. There is no work of Shakespeare's, and arguably no work of Western art, that evokes such a powerful sense of evil. The dialogue is full of invocations of the powers of darkness (see Key Passages, **p. 142**) and one can sympathize with the belief current among actors that those invocations are genuine, and actually work.

Macbeth was written, probably in 1606, when Shakespeare was at the height of his powers as a writer of tragedy. He had just written *Othello* and *King Lear*; *Antony and Cleopatra* and *Coriolanus* lay ahead. He may also have drawn on *Hamlet*: in its close examination of the mind of a murderer, the play elaborates on the figure of Claudius in the earlier tragedy. However, there is nothing standardized about Shakespeare's tragedies: each is a fresh experiment, with its own distinct methods and atmosphere. *Macbeth* stands out in a number of ways. Not even *Hamlet*, with its striking Ghost, makes such pervasive use of the supernatural. The evil of Iago in *Othello* is a function of his own nature; the evil that grips Macbeth seems to be a force at work in the spiritual world. (Does Macbeth use that force or is it using him? Can we tell?) In its treatment of the supernatural, the play makes fuller use of music and spectacle than the other tragedies do; in this it looks forward to Shakespeare's final romances, especially *Pericles* and *The Tempest*, where music and spectacle present supernatural powers that are more (though not completely) benign.

The play is also unusual in its close concentration on two central figures, Macbeth and Lady Macbeth. *Romeo and Juliet* and *Hamlet* are full of lively, vividly realized secondary characters: the Nurse, Mercutio, Ophelia, Polonius, the Gravediggers. The secondary characters of *King Lear* (Gloucester, Edmund, Edgar, Lear's daughters, the Fool) are so fully developed that the play seems more an ensemble piece than a vehicle for a star actor. In *Julius Caesar* and *Coriolanus* even the nameless citizens have distinctive voices and ideas of their own. It is not that the supporting roles in *Macbeth* are uninteresting or unrewarding. But the focus is so strongly on the two leading characters that the lives of the others seem stunted by comparison. One reason is that the evil which grips Scotland with Macbeth's murder of Duncan is so overwhelming that in the later scenes in particular other characters are swept along with the tide, with little to do but react to what Macbeth has done. Another is that in Macbeth and Lady Macbeth Shakespeare has created, even by his standards, an unusually searching portrait of two people going through a crisis together. We see, with alarming intimacy, what it is like to think of a murder, to do it, and to suffer the consequences. This intimacy includes Shakespeare's most searching depiction of a marriage, and in the

---

3   I owe this observation to Russell Jackson.

pressure Lady Macbeth puts on her husband, and herself, one of his most radical examinations of the whole question of gender, of what it means to be a woman or a man.

In its own time *Macbeth* may have had topical impact. England had a new king, James VI of Scotland, who in 1603 had succeeded Queen Elizabeth as James I of England. The two kingdoms, England and Scotland, were now under a single monarch. A northern country that for the English had been strange and little known, in popular culture the setting of ballads and in history a troublesome enemy, was now politically linked with England, and many Scots had come south with the new King, in search of pickings in a richer land. They were not always welcome: three of Shakespeare's fellow playwrights, George Chapman, Ben Jonson and John Marston, had landed in trouble with the authorities for some anti-Scottish jokes in their 1605 comedy *Eastward Ho*. Chapman and Jonson were imprisoned; Marston fled. Shakespeare was characteristically ambiguous. In the only play he ever set in Scotland, he presents it as a troubled, violent land where evil powers, both human and supernatural, are abroad. But in the survival of the line of Banquo, to which King James belonged, he paid a kind of tribute to the new King; and he played on two of the King's known interests, kingship and witchcraft. James had written treatises on both.[4] Whether the play was written specifically for James, and in any case what James might have thought of it – these remain open questions. But it would have certainly piqued the curiosity of its original audience in its depiction of the history of the country to which, like it or not, they were now joined.

Even if it is a topical work, *Macbeth* is the sort of topical work that can live outside its original context. The near-universality of Shakespeare's appeal is unquestioned, though its causes can be debated. And *Macbeth* is popular, even by his standards. Though it is notoriously difficult for actors and directors, it is one of Shakespeare's most frequently produced plays. In schools, it is one of his most frequently studied. Shakespeare specialists debate whether *Hamlet* or *King Lear* is his greatest achievement; but non-specialists who encounter Shakespeare at school or in the theatre often name *Macbeth* as their favourite Shakespeare play. There is, to begin with, the endless and disturbing fascination of murder itself. We see this fascination at work at every level of culture from Sophocles' *Oedipus Rex* and Dostoevsky's *The Brothers Karamazov* to mass-market paperback whodunits.[5] What does it take for one human being to kill another? What does it mean, and what are the consequences? The story of Macbeth has been re-told in many different cultures. Akira Kurosawa turned it into a film set in mediaeval Japan, in the world of the samurai (see The Work in Performance, **pp. 109–11**). For the stage, Welcome Msomi created a Zulu version, *uMabatha*.[6] Two gangster movies, *Joe Macbeth* (dir. Ken Hughes, 1955) and *Men of Respect* (dir. William

4   He wrote on witchcraft in *Demonology* (1597) and on kingship in *The Trew Law of Free Monarch-ies* (1598) and *Basilicon Doron* (1599). On the latter, see Contemporary Documents, **pp. 30–2**.
5   There is a link between *Macbeth* and detective fiction in James Thurber's short story 'The *Macbeth* Murder Mystery', whose central character, a reader of whodunits, decides that for Macbeth to be Duncan's murderer violates the conventions of the genre (too obvious) and comes up with a different, quite unexpected solution, which I will not reveal.
6   Pretoria: Via Afrika/Skotaville Publishers, 1996. The work was originally created in the 1970s.

Reilly, 1991), use *Macbeth* as a source. A more recent film, *Scotland, Pa.* (dir. Billy Morrissette, 2001), makes a quirkier transfer to small-town Pennsylvania, and to strife in the fast-food business (playing of course on the names Macbeth and McDonald's). Each version, while drawing on its own culture, pays implicit tribute to the basic story of the original play, with its depiction of the human desire for power and the violent consequences of that desire.

In fact the play we think of as Shakespeare's original is also an adaptation. It was published in the Folio of 1623, a posthumous collection of Shakespeare's work put together by two of his fellow actors. The Folio *Macbeth* is the only text we have. In other cases, notably *Hamlet* and *King Lear*, we have Quarto texts as well, and we can see that the Folio text has been cut, possibly by Shakespeare himself. If we had a Quarto text of *Macbeth* would we find that it too was cut in the Folio version? Were there some passages that have now been lost, presumably for ever? Certainly there are additions. There is an unusually strong consensus among scholars that the scenes involving Hecate, with their songs and dances, are not by Shakespeare; they are sometimes attributed to his younger contemporary Thomas Middleton (see The Work in Performance, **pp. 89–90**). At this early date, Shakespeare's interest in music and spectacle was elaborated in his own company's production. After the reopening of the theatres at the Restoration of Charles II in 1660, it was further elaborated by William Davenant's spectacular new version (see The Work in Performance, **pp. 100–6**), which the 'original' Shakespeare was slow to replace. That *Macbeth* creates an urge not just to perform it but to adapt it is a quality it shares with *King Lear* and *The Tempest*. These three works, to an unusual degree, have inspired rewriting, as though later artists, recognizing the power of the original material, want to seize on it and make it their own.

It is the business of this Sourcebook to help readers of our time, especially readers beginning their study of Shakespeare, seize on the play and make it their own. Part 1 puts the play in its original context, with extracts from Shakespeare's primary source, Holinshed's *Chronicles*, and from contemporary documents, theatrical and non-theatrical, that show how Shakespeare's contemporaries thought about some of the play's issues. There is a special emphasis here on witchcraft, as a key to the play's depiction of the power of evil. This is followed by extracts from criticism, from the beginnings of the play's critical reception down to our own time; and in turn by material relating to its performance history. Part 3 presents key passages from the play itself, with commentary designed not just to explain some unfamiliar language but to alert the reader to points of interpretation, and to suggest by example strategies for a fuller reading of the play as a whole.

Through all this material we will see how the play grew out of its world, how its life has continued in the work of readers and performers since then, and how it continues now in our own acts of reading. The issues raised briefly in this intro- duction will recur: the power of evil, the impact of the central characters, the role of gender, the importance of adaptation and interpretation in a play's reception. We shall see how the play has affected other minds, in worlds remote from both Shakespeare's and our own; and the hope is that this will help free the reader's own interpretation of the play, serving as an introduction to an experience that is both disturbing and inexhaustible, the experience of encountering *Macbeth*.

1

Contexts

Contextual Overview

The chief historical event that lies behind the creation of *Macbeth* was the accession in 1603 of James VI of Scotland to the English throne. He took the title James I of England, but he remained King of Scotland, and he brought with him a retinue of Scots, triggering in the English a new, sometimes anxious consciousness of the land to the north to which they were now joined by a shared monarchy. The English had regarded the Scots as a barbarous nation, and they were a traditional enemy. There was a long history of conflict along the border, from cattle raids to outright war. James's mother, Mary Queen of Scots, was a political prisoner in England for eighteen years, and in 1587 Queen Elizabeth finally had her executed. In Shakespeare's *Henry V* the King is warned that before he attacks France he should secure his northern border, for when the English eagle is at prey abroad 'the weasel Scot' (1.2.170) is liable to raid the nest. Yet in the same play a Scot, Captain Jamy, appears as one of King Henry's loyal soldiers. While many of his countrymen were suspicious of their northern neighbours, Shakespeare preserves a characteristic ambiguity about whether the Scots are enemies or friends.

Throughout the 1590s Shakespeare had written a series of English history plays, taking Holinshed's *Chronicle* as his principal source. When in *Macbeth* he turned to Scotland – and this is his only play set in that country – he turned again to Holinshed. The history of Scotland was of course much less well known to his audiences than was the history of England, and as the extracts given here will show, he took even greater liberties than he did in the English history plays, combining characters and events from different reigns into a single story, and suppressing the fact that the historical Macbeth was for much of his reign a wise and just ruler.

The history of Scotland up to Shakespeare's time makes the history of England seem peaceful by comparison. To be king of Scotland was to be a poor insurance risk; in 1607 Sir Christopher Piggott, during a debate on the union of the two kingdoms, told the House of Commons that the Scots 'have not suffered above two kings to die in their beds, these 200 years'. Piggott was rewarded for this historical insight by a stay in the Tower of London,[1] but his sense that Scottish

---

1 A. R. Braunmuller, introduction to the New Cambridge Shakespeare edition of *Macbeth* (Cambridge: Cambridge University Press, 1997), p. 13.

history was a tale of concentrated violence was not far off the truth. The play bears out this impression. It begins in war, with rebellion and invasion. No sooner is peace restored than Macbeth murders Duncan, and while this makes him king it is only the beginning of a line of killings, ending with an invasion by Scottish exiles and English troops in which Macbeth himself is killed. If there is a prospect of a more peaceable Scotland at the end of the play, it lies in the way the new King Malcolm introduces English terminology, turning thanes into earls. England in the play has been a peaceable kingdom under a good king (see Key Passages, pp. 175–7), and Malcolm seems to want to import some of its values. Is there a hint here of James's desire to unite his two kingdoms in one?

At the time of the play's writing, however, England, far from being a peaceable kingdom, had just been through a trauma of its own. In our time we are haunted by 11 September 2001. The equivalent date for the Jacobean English – a date still commemorated in England – was 5 November 1605. A group of Catholic extremists had planned to blow up the King and Parliament with barrels of gunpowder stored in an adjacent building. The plot was foiled at the last minute, and was followed by a series of arrests, interrogations and executions. How much *Macbeth* owes to the Gunpowder Plot is debatable. In 2.3 a drunken porter imagines himself as the porter of hell-gate, admitting damned souls to the everlasting bonfire. One of these is 'an equivocator, that could swear in both the scales against either scale; who committed treason enough for God's sake, yet could not equivocate to heaven' (2.3.9–12). This is frequently taken as a reference to the Jesuit superior Henry Garnet, executed for his role in the Gunpowder Plot. Garnet had written a treatise on equivocation, arguing that a person could tell less than the truth without being guilty of lying, so long as he held the full truth in his heart – an idea that applied particularly to a person under interrogation. Arguably, the witches' prophecies, especially the second set, deal with Macbeth in just this equivocal way (see Key Passages, pp. 167–9). But this sort of riddling goes back at least to classical Greece, with its tales of the oracle at Delphi and the ambiguous pronouncements it made to those who sought its advice. It may be that the chief contribution the Gunpowder Plot made to *Macbeth*, if indeed it made any contribution at all, was a generalized sense of menace and anxiety, the feeling of a kingdom living on its nerves. The shock the discovery of the Gunpowder Plot produced may have an onstage equivalent in the shock produced by Duncan's murder. The fear of living under a tyranny that haunts the second half of the play may link with the fear of what might have followed the Gunpowder Plot. The political atmosphere of the time was not unlike that of the Cold War in the middle of the twentieth century, and part of the atmosphere of terror the play generates is political terror.

In any case the play is not overtly about the Gunpowder Plot. The connection, if any, operates at a general, even subliminal level. In fact acting companies had to beware of being too topical. Less than two years after James came to the throne Shakespeare's own company had produced *The Tragedy of Gowrie*, evidently based on a plot (not long previously, in 1600) to assassinate King James. The play was suppressed. Since the text is lost, we can only guess at the cause of the offence; but we have evidence from other cases of censorship that the authorities did not like the representation of living persons on the stage, and to deal too directly with contemporary events was to court trouble. The paradox is that

James had on his accession taken the acting companies under royal patronage; and Shakespeare's company, who performed *The Tragedy of Gowrie*, was the King's Men. They may have intended to compliment their new patron by showing the defeat of a conspiracy against him. But even a compliment could cause trouble if it involved dramatizing events that were too close to home. The events of *Macbeth* are well in the past.

Some scholars have speculated that *Macbeth* was written as a compliment to King James, and designed to appeal to his interests.[2] Probably the strongest argument for this view is the survival of the line of Banquo, which became the House of Stuart to which King James belonged. Banquo's line is dramatized in the cauldron scene, in the vision of eight kings, the last holding a magic glass that shows an even longer procession, stretching 'to the crack of doom', some with 'two-fold balls and treble sceptres' that figure not only the union of England and Scotland under James but the spread of empire (4.1.117–21). This is certainly a tribute to the royal house to which the King belonged; and Banquo's fertility may also acknowledge the fact that James, unlike the three childless Tudors who preceded him, had two sons.

James's interest in the nature of kingship is another possible link with the play. He had years of experience as King of Scotland before he came to England, and regarded himself as an expert on the art of monarchy, on which he was inclined to lecture. He believed kings were divinely appointed, and answerable not to any human authority, but to God alone. While still in Scotland, he wrote treatises on kingship, *The Trew Law of Free Monarchies* (1598) and *Basilicon Doron* (1599); and once he came to England he lectured Parliament on the subject.[3] The mystique that surrounds Duncan – his murder is a violation of 'The Lord's anointed Temple' (2.3.69) – may feed into James's view of the divine right of kings. However, no such divine right protects Macbeth when his subjects, joined with the English, rise against his tyranny. Even without James's theory of kingship the official doctrine proclaimed in the churches of England by the 'Homily against Disobedience and Wilful Rebellion' (1570) was that the people had no right to rebel even against a wicked king. God had appointed him, and God would deal with him. Malcolm and Macduff do not wait for God. *Macbeth* lines up most directly not with the divine right theory of *The Trew Law of Free Monarchies* but with the more pragmatic *Basilicon Doron*, James's advice to his son Prince Henry on the art of government. The extract given here (see Contemporary Documents, **pp. 30–2**), with its contrast of good and evil rulers, serves as a gloss on the contrast between Macbeth on the one side and, aligned against him, Duncan, the English King Edward and the hope that rests on Malcolm. In any case Shakespeare did not have to wait for the accession of King James to start thinking about kingship: he had already written nine English history plays. *Richard II* presents his most searching examination of the institution, with a tense

2 For a long time the most influential study in this vein was Henry N. Paul, *The Royal Play of Macbeth* (New York: Macmillan, 1950). Paul's argument – which includes imagining that King James himself commissioned the play – now seems exaggerated.
3 James's views are conveniently collected in King James VI and I, *Political Writings*, ed. Johann P. Sommerville (Cambridge: Cambridge University Press, 1994).

opposition of the claims of divine appointment and political ability that goes far beyond anything in *Macbeth*.[4]

Another of James's interests was witchcraft, and in this case the play draws closer to him. The persecution of witches was widespread in England, and while in theory it was possible for a man or a woman to be a witch, in practice the accused were mostly women. The crimes they were accused of were at the local, domestic level: ruining crops, killing cattle, causing impotence. Witch trials seem to have been the product of hostility between neighbours in local communities. We glimpse this level of witchcraft in 1.3 of the play (see Key Passages, **pp. 132–4**), and in the extract given here from a later play, *The Witch of Edmonton* (see Contemporary Documents, **pp. 32–6**). In both cases the witches' powers are real; but we can also see a shadow of what may have been the actual situation: an unpopular old woman, at odds with her neighbours, becomes their scapegoat when crops fail or cattle die. Reginald Scot, in *The Discovery of Witchcraft* (1584), warned his countrymen against believing in the power of witches. King James, on the other hand, was a believer, and in his *Demonology* (1597) he argued against Scot, claiming that witches had real power, which came from the Devil. At first glance, *Macbeth* appears to side with James: the witches' prophecies do come true. But in the action itself the witches do no direct harm; it is Macbeth who does the killing. In 1.3 they make threats about what they are going to do to the sailor's wife; but we never see them do it. In one of the critical extracts later in this volume, Stephen Greenblatt argues that the play is in fact quite tentative about the belief in witchcraft (see Modern Criticism, **pp. 83–6**). On the issue of witchcraft as on the issue of kingship, *Macbeth* in the last analysis is not King James's play but Shakespeare's, with all the ambiguity, the refusal of commitment, we expect from him.

That having been said, the witches are still a powerful, haunting presence; their role in the action is arguably even more disturbing because we cannot quite pin it down. And they bring into focus other anxieties: a fear of the supernatural; a fear of female power, exercised from the margins in a male-dominated world; and more fundamentally the fear of whatever is other, strange, unnameable. Lady Macbeth has no direct dealings with the witches, but throughout the history of the play's reception, as we shall see, she has aroused profound disturbance by her refusal to play the silent, submissive, nurturing role assigned to women by generations of conventional thinking. In that way she links with the witches, who are women but do not look like women, who have a profound and destructive effect on the war hero Macbeth, and who live a strange, half-glimpsed life of their own on the margins of the world, disappearing from sight but never from thought. When they vanish, we do not know where they go; and when Lady Macbeth dies, we do not know how. This anxiety about the other ran deep in Shakespeare's culture, and he himself had already tapped into it: in the extract from *Henry VI Part One* given here (see Contemporary Documents, **pp. 28–30**), and in the story reported early in *Henry IV Part One* of dead English soldiers castrated by Welsh

---

4   For David Scott Kastan's view of the problematic relationship between *Macbeth* and James's view of kingship, see Modern Criticism, **pp. 86–8**.

women (1.1.43–6). On this issue, as on kingship, Shakespeare did not have to wait for the accession of James.

The extracts from contemporary documents given here concentrate on the issue of witchcraft, since this is where the play responds most vividly to its surrounding culture. *Newes from Scotland* (see Contemporary Documents, **pp. 25–8**) is particularly important. It shows the anxiety produced by witchcraft, and the anxieties about sex and gender that cluster around it. It shows witches operating not just at the domestic level, as in most English witch trials, but at the level of royalty, as in *Macbeth*. It depicts King James's interest in the subject, and his credulity. Finally, it gives a glimpse, before James's accession, of that strange kingdom to the north. The accession of James in 1603 may indeed have encouraged a new focus on kingship and witchcraft, two of his pet subjects; it certainly triggered a new interest in Scotland. But if *Macbeth* is a compliment to the new King, the patron of Shakespeare's company, it is (appropriately) a somewhat equivocal one; and it draws on anxieties that already ran deep in its own culture.

Chronology

Bullet points are used to indicate events in Shakespeare's life, asterisks to denote historical and literary events.

1558
* Accession of Queen Elizabeth

1564
• William Shakespeare born on or near 23 April, in Stratford-upon-Avon

1568
• William Shakespeare's father John becomes Bailiff of Stratford

1577
• John Shakespeare falls on hard times, increasingly troubled by debt
* First publication of Holinshed's *Chronicles*

1582
• William Shakespeare marries Anne Hathaway

1583
• Birth of Shakespeare's daughter Susannah, six months after the marriage

1584
* Publication of Reginald Scot's *Discovery of Witchcraft*, urging a sceptical view of witchcraft

1585
• Birth of the twins Hamnet and Judith; after this the Shakespeares have no more children

1586
• Around this time Shakespeare leaves Stratford; nothing is known of his whereabouts for the next six years

1587

*   Queen Elizabeth orders the death of Mary Queen of Scots, mother of King James VI of Scotland

*   Second edition of Holinshed's *Chronicles*; this edition is the principal source for *Macbeth*

1588

*   Defeat of the Spanish Armada

1591

*   First publication of *Newes from Scotland*, an account of Scottish witchcraft

1592

•   Shakespeare attacked by a jealous older playwright, Robert Greene; we know from this that he is now active as a playwright in London, and beginning to make his name

1593

*   Death of Christopher Marlowe, Shakespeare's leading predecessor

1594

•   Formation of the Chamberlain's Company; Shakespeare is a 'sharer' (shareholder)

1596

•   John Shakespeare granted a coat of arms and the right to style himself Gentleman, an important step up the social ladder for him and his son William

•   Death of Shakespeare's son Hamnet

1597

*   King James publishes *Demonology*, urging a serious view of witchcraft

1598

•   Frances Meres, in *Pallas Tamia*, praises Shakespeare as 'among the English ... the most excellent' author of comedy and tragedy, ranking him with the great classical authors

1599

•   Opening of the Globe Playhouse, which was to be the principal venue for Shakespeare's work

*   Publication of James VI, *Basilicon Doron*

1600

*   The Gowrie conspiracy, an unsuccessful attempt to assassinate King James

1601

•   Death of John Shakespeare

1603
* Death of Queen Elizabeth; James VI of Scotland becomes James I of England
• Shakespeare's company taken under royal patronage, becoming the King's Men

1605
* Discovery of the Gunpowder Plot, an attempt by Catholic conspirators to blow up the King and Parliament

1606
• Shakespeare writes *Macbeth*

1608
• Birth of Shakespeare's granddaughter Elizabeth Hall (with her death in 1670, Shakespeare's line will die out); death of Shakespeare's mother Mary

1610
• Around this time Shakespeare may have returned to Stratford to live, though he maintains interests in London

1611
• Simon Forman records seeing a performance of *Macbeth* at the Globe
* Publication of the King James Bible

1616
• Death of William Shakespeare on 23 April at Stratford-upon-Avon

1623
• Posthumous publication of Shakespeare's collected works, the Folio, in which *Macbeth* is published for the first time

Source

From **Raphael Holinshed [and others],** *The Chronicles of England, Scotlande, and Ireland* (1587 edn), Vol. II. Reprinted in Geoffrey Bullough, ed., *Narrative and Dramatic Sources of Shakespeare,* Vol. VII (London: Routledge and Kegan Paul, 1973), pp. 480–99

Holinshed's *Chronicle* was Shakespeare's principal source for his English history plays, and for *Macbeth*. It had several authors, but Holinshed's role as compiler makes it convenient to use his name for the whole collection. Shakespeare drew principally on two sections of the history of Scotland, the story of the murder of King Duff, and the story of Macbeth himself. Just before the extract given below, Holinshed recounts that King Duff became afflicted with a strange illness, which his people blamed on a group of witches living in the town of Forres. Donwald, the captain of the castle of Forres, who was loyal to the King, learned of the witches' plot against the King's life through a soldier who was having an affair with one of the witches' daughters. At Donwald's instigation a party of soldiers broke into the witches' house and found them casting spells against the King. They were burning a wax image of him, and as it burned the King's fever worsened. The image was broken, the witches were executed, and the King was cured. The extract takes up the story at the point where King Duff, his energy restored, puts down a rebellion and the previously loyal Donwald turns against him.

But howsoever it came to passe, truth it is, that when he was restored to his perfect health, he gathered a power of men, & with the same went into Murrey land against the rebels there, and chasing them from thence, he pursued them into Rosse, and from Rosse into Cathnesse, where apprehending them, he brought them backe unto Fores, and there caused them to be hanged up, on gallows and gibets.

Amongst them there were also certeine yoong gentlemen, right beautifull and goodlie personages, being neere of kin unto Donwald capteine of the castell, and had beene persuaded to be partakers with the other rebels, more through the fraudulent counsell of diverse wicked persons, than of their owne accord: whereupon the foresaid Donwald lamenting their case, made earnest labor and

sute to the king to have begged their pardon; but having a plaine deniall, he
conceived such an inward malice towards the king, (though he shewed it not
outwardlie at the first) that the same continued still boiling in his stomach, and
ceased not, till through setting on of his wife, and in revenge of such unthankeful-
nesse, hee found meanes to murther the king within the foresaid castell of Fores
where he used to sojourne. For the king being in that countrie, was accustomed to
lie most commonlie within the same castell, having a speciall trust in Donwald, as
a man whom he never suspected.

But Donwald, not forgetting the reproch which his linage had susteined by the
execution of those his kinsmen, whome the king for a spectacle to the people had
caused to be hanged, could not but shew manifest tokens of great griefe at home
amongst his familie: which his wife perceiving, ceassed not to travell with him,[1]
till she understood what the cause was of his displeasure. Which at length when
she had learned by his owne relation, she as one that bare no lesse malice in hir
heart towards the king, for the like cause on hir behalfe, than hir husband did for
his friends, counselled him (sith the king oftentimes used to lodge in his house
without anie gard about him, other than the garrison of the castell, which was
wholie at his commandement) to make him awaie, and shewed him the meanes
wherby he might soonest accomplish it.

Donwald thus being the more kindled in wrath by the words of his wife, determined to follow hir advise in the execution of so heinous an act. Wherupon
devising with himselfe for a while, which way hee might best accomplish his
cursed intent, at length he gat opportunitie and sped his purpose as followeth. It
chanced that the king upon the daie before he purposed to depart foorth of the
castell, was long in his oratorie at his praiers, and there continued till it was late in
the night. At the last, comming foorth, he called such afore him as had faithfullie
served him in pursute and apprehension of the rebels, and giving them heartie
thanks, he bestowed sundrie honorable gifts amongst them, of the which number
Donwald was one, as he that had beene ever accounted a most faithfull servant to
the king.

At length, having talked with them a long time, he got him into his privie
chamber, onelie with two of his chamberlains,[2] who having brought him to bed,
came foorth againe, and then fell to banketting with Donwald and his wife, who
had prepared diverse delicate dishes, and sundrie sorts of drinks for their reare
supper or collation,[3] wherat they sate up so long, till they had charged their
stomachs with such full gorges, that their heads were no sooner got to the pillow,
but asleepe they were so fast, that a man might have remooved the chamber over
them, sooner than to have awaked them out of their droonken sleepe.

Then Donwald, though he abhorred the act greatlie in his heart, yet through
instigation of his wife, hee called foure of his servants unto him (whome he had
made privie to his wicked intent before, and framed to his purpose with large
gifts) and now declaring unto them, after what sort they should worke the feat,
they gladlie obeied the instructions, & speedilie going about the murther, they
enter the chamber (in which the king laie) a little before cocks crow, where they

---

1   Work on him.
2   Attendants in his bedchamber.
3   A light meal eaten late in the evening.

secretlie cut his throte as he lay sleeping, without anie buskling[4] at all: and immediatlie by a posterne gate they caried foorth the dead bodie into the fields, and throwing it upon an horsse there provided readie for that purpose, they convey it unto a place, about two miles distant from the castell, where they staied, and gat certeine labourers to helpe them to turne the course of a little river running through the fields there, and digging a deepe hole in the chanell, they burie the bodie in the same, ramming it up with stones and gravell so closelie, that setting the water in the right course againe, no man could perceive that anie thing had beene newlie digged there. This they did by order appointed them by Donwald as is reported, for that the bodie should not be found, & by bleeding (when Donwald should be present) declare him to be guiltie of the murther. For such an opinion men have, that the dead corps of anie man being slaine, will bleed abundantlie[5] if the murtherer be present. But for what consideration soever they buried him there, they had no sooner finished the worke, but that they slue them whose helpe they used herein, and streightwaies thereupon fled into Orknie.

Donwald, about the time that the murther was in dooing, got him amongst them that kept the watch, and so continued in companie with them all the residue of the night. But in the morning when the noise was raised in the kings chamber how the king was slaine, his bodie conveied awaie, and the bed all beraied[6] with bloud; he with the watch ran thither, as though he had knowne nothing of the matter, and breaking into the chamber, and finding cakes of bloud in the bed, and on the floore about the sides of it, he foorthwith slue the chamberleins, as guiltie of that heinous murther, and then like a mad man running to and fro, he ransacked everie corner within the castell, as though it had beene to have seene if he might have found either the bodie, or anie of the murtherers hid in anie privie place: but at length comming to the posterne gate, and finding it open, he burdened the chamberleins, whome he had slaine, with all the fault, they having the keies of the gates committed to their keeping all the night, and therefore it could not be otherwise (said he) but that they were of counsell in the committing of that most detestable murther.

Finallie, such was his over earnest diligence in the severe inquisition and triall of the offendors heerein, that some of the lords began to mislike the matter, and to smell foorth shrewd tokens, that he should not be altogither cleare himselfe. But for so much as they were in that countrie, where hee had the whole rule, what by reason of his friends and authoritie togither, they doubted to utter what they thought, till time and place should better serve thereunto, and heereupon got them awaie everie man to his home. For the space of six moneths togither, after this heinous murther thus committed, there appeered no sunne by day, nor moone by night in anie part of the realme, but still was the skie covered with continuall clouds, and sometimes suche outragious windes arose, with lightenings and tempests, that the people were in great feare of present destruction.

Monstrous sights also that were seene within the Scotish kingdome that yeere were these, horsses in Louthian, being of singular beautie and swiftnesse, did eate

4   Commotion (the deed is done swiftly and silently).
5   In the sleepwalking scene (see Key Passages, **pp. 177–80**), Lady Macbeth is astonished by the amount of blood that has issued from Duncan's body (5.1.38–9). Shakespeare uses the belief that a corpse will bleed in the presence of its murderer in 1.2 of *Richard III*.
6   Stained, fouled.

their owne flesh, and would in no wise taste anie other meate. In Angus there was
a gentlewoman brought foorth a child without eies, nose, hand or foot. There was
a sparhawke[7] also strangled by an owle. [. . .]

Culen, King Duff's successor, was advised by his bishops that the omens would
not cease until Duff's murderers were found and punished. Donwald fled. His
wife was captured and confessed under torture. Donwald was shipwrecked and
captured, and he and his wife, together with the servants who carried out the
murder, were executed. Their entrails were thrown into the fire, and sections of
their bodies were displayed throughout the kingdom as a warning against regicide. King Duff's body was recovered from the riverbed and properly buried, at
which point the sky cleared and the omens ceased.

Much of Shakespeare's dramatization of Duncan's murder is drawn from this
account. (Holinshed's account of Duncan's murder is quite brief by comparison.)
Shakespeare's debts include the role of Lady Macbeth, the murder of the grooms
of Duncan's chamber, and the omens that follow the murder (see Key Passages,
pp. 150–4). Holinshed's brief statement that Donwald 'abhorred the act
greatly in his heart' is expanded into Macbeth's prolonged struggle with his
conscience. But Shakespeare removes the servants who do the killing, making
Macbeth himself responsible for the murder, and Duncan's body is not removed
or concealed: it stays in the bedchamber, a source of immediate horror.

Shakespeare also took some details from the story of Culen's successor King
Kenneth, who had his nephew Malcolm, Prince of Cumberland, poisoned in
order to ensure the succession of his own son. Kenneth's conscience troubled
him and one night, unable to sleep, he heard a voice threatening God's vengeance. Macbeth too hears voices, and suffers from insomnia. Kenneth
confessed to a bishop and did penance; but he was murdered in revenge by
Malcolm's mother.

When Holinshed turns to the story of Duncan and Macbeth, it begins as a
contrast between the characters of the two men, the gentleness of Duncan and
the cruelty of Macbeth. Broadly speaking, the play develops this view; but Lady
Macbeth's complaint that her husband is too full of the milk of human kindness
(1.5.17) suggests that he has picked up some of the quality of Duncan in the
chronicle, making him a more mixed character and the contrast with Duncan
less formulaic.

After Malcolme[8] succeeded his nephue Duncane, the sonne of his daughter
Beatrice: for Malcolme had two daughters, the one which was this Beatrice, being
given in mariage unto one Abbanath Crinen, a man of great nobilitie, and thane
of the Isles and west parts of Scotland, bare of that mariage the foresaid Duncane;
The other called Doada, was maried unto Sinell the thane of Glammis, by whom
she had issue one Makbeth a valiant gentleman, and one that if he had not
beene somewhat cruell of nature, might have beene thought most woorthie the

7   Sparrowhawk.
8   Malcolm II, who reigned from 1005 to 1034; not to be confused with the play's Malcolm.

government of a realme. On the other part, Duncane was so soft and gentle of nature, that the people wished the inclinations and maners of these two cousins to have beene so tempered and enterchangeablie bestowed betwixt them, that where the one had too much of clemencie, and the other of crueltie, the meane vertue betwixt these two extremities might have reigned by indifferent partition in them both, so should Duncane have proved a woorthie king, and Makbeth an excellent capteine.[9] The beginning of Duncans reigne was verie quiet and peaceable, without anie notable trouble; but after it was perceived how negligent he was in punishing offendors, manie misruled persons tooke occasion thereof to trouble the peace and quiet state of the common-wealth, by seditious commotions which first had their beginnings in this wise.

Banquho the thane of Lochquhaber, of whom the house of the Stewards is descended,[10] the which by order of linage hath now for a long time injoied the crowne of Scotland, even till these our daies, as he gathered the finances due to the king, and further punished somewhat sharpelie such as were notorious offendors, being assailed by a number of rebels inhabiting in that countrie, and spoiled of the monie and all other things, had much a doo to get awaie with life, after he had received sundrie grievous wounds amongst them. Yet escaping their hands, after hee was somewhat recovered of his hurts and was able to ride, he repaired to the court, where making his complaint to the king in most earnest wise, he purchased at length that the offendors were sent for by a sergeant at armes, to appeare to make answer unto such matters as should be laid to their charge: but they augmenting their mischiefous act with a more wicked deed, after they had misused the messenger with sundrie kinds of reproches, they finallie slue him also.

Then doubting not but for such contemptuous demeanor against the kings regall authoritie, they should be invaded with all the power the king could make, Makdowald one of great estimation among them, making first a confederacie with his neerest friends and kinsmen, tooke upon him to be chiefe capteine of all such rebels, as would stand against the king, in maintenance of their grievous offenses latelie committed against him. Manie slanderous words also, and railing tants this Makdowald uttered against his prince, calling him a faint-hearted milkesop, more meet to governe a sort of idle moonks in some cloister, than to have the rule of such valiant and hardie men of warre as the Scots were. He used also such subtill persuasions and forged allurements, that in a small time he had gotten togither a mightie power of men: for out of the westerne Isles there came unto him a great multitude of people, offering themselves to assist him in that rebellious quarell, and out of Ireland in hope of the spoile came no small number of Kernes and Galloglasses,[11] offering gladlie to serve under him, whither it should please him to lead them.

Makdowald thus having a mightie puissance about him, incountered with such of the kings people as were sent against him into Lochquhaber, and discomfiting them, by mere force tooke their capteine Malcolme, and after the end of the battell smote off his head. This overthrow being notified to the king, did put him

9 This is the situation at the beginning of the play, each man in his proper role.
10 The House of Stuart, to which King James belonged. The vision of a line of kings in 4.1 makes the link between Banquo and the reigning monarch (see Key Passages, p. 169).
11 Foot soldiers and horsemen.

in woonderfull feare, by reason of his small skill in warlike affaires. Calling therefore his nobles to a councell, he asked of them their best advise for the subduing of Makdowald & other the rebels. Here, in sundrie heads (as ever it happeneth) were sundrie opinions, which they uttered according to everie man his skill. At length Makbeth speaking much against the kings softnes, and overmuch slacknesse in punishing offendors, whereby they had such time to assemble togither, he promised notwithstanding, if the charge were committed unto him and unto Banquho, so to order the matter, that the rebels should be shortly vanquished & quite put downe, and that not so much as one of them should be found to make resistance within the countrie.

And even so it came to passe: for being sent foorth with a new power, at his entring into Lochquhaber, the fame of his comming put the enimies in such feare, that a great number of them stale secretlie awaie from their capteine Makdowald, who neverthelesse inforced thereto, gave battell unto Makbeth, with the residue which remained with him: but being overcome, and fleeing for refuge into a castell (within the which his wife & children were inclosed) at length when he saw how he could neither defend the hold anie longer against his enimies, nor yet upon surrender be suffered to depart with life saved, hee first slue his wife and children, and lastlie himselfe, least if he had yeelded simplie, he should have beene executed in most cruell wise for an example to other. Makbeth entring into the castell by the gates, as then set open, found the carcasse of Makdowald lieng dead there amongst the residue of the slaine bodies, which when he beheld, remitting no peece of his cruell nature with that pitifull sight, he caused the head to be cut off, and set upon a poles end, and so sent it as a present to the king who as then laie at Bertha. The headlesse trunke he commanded to bee hoong up upon an high paire of gallowes. [. . .]

After the suppression of Makdowald's rebellion, the next challenge was an invasion by Sueno, King of Norway. At the cost of some narrative confusion, Shakespeare has the rebellion and the invasion taking place simultaneously, increasing the pressure on Scotland and heightening the sense of Macbeth's achievement as a warrior (see Key Passages, **pp. 128–32**). Holinshed notes that even the usually passive Duncan was galvanized into action by the threat from Norway. He led one-third of the Scottish power himself, entrusting the other two-thirds to Macbeth and Banquo. Defeated by Sueno, Duncan retreated to the castle of Bertha (the modern Perth) where Sueno besieged him. Duncan defeated Sueno by trickery, pretending to negotiate terms of surrender with him, and sending him ale and bread for his army. The ale and bread were drugged; as soon as the drug took effect Duncan sent for Macbeth, who finished off the invaders. Sueno and ten others, the only survivors, escaped. (The only hint of this in Shakespeare is Lady Macbeth's drugging the grooms, who in the story of King Duff are simply made drunk.) The Scottish victory was followed by a Danish invasion, instigated by King Canute of England to avenge his brother Sueno. Macbeth and Banquo defeated this invasion, and the result was a peace treaty in which the Danes vowed never to invade Scotland again. These foreign dangers disposed of, the next threat to Scotland was internal. (See Key Passages, **pp. 132–9**.)

Figure 1 **Macbeth and Banquo encounter the witches (Holinshed's**
History of Scotland, 1577).

Shortlie after happened a strange and uncouth woonder, which afterward was the
cause of much trouble in the realme of Scotland, as ye shall after heare. It fortuned
as Makbeth and Banquho journied towards Fores, where the king then laie, they
went sporting by the waie togither without other companie, save onelie themselves, passing thorough the woods and fields, when suddenlie in the middest of a
laund, there met them three women in strange and wild apparell, resembling
creatures of elder world, whome when they attentivelie beheld, woondering much
at the sight, the first of them spake and said; All haile Makbeth, thane of Glammis
(for he had latelie entered into that dignitie and office by the death of his father
Sinell.) The second of them said; Haile Makbeth thane of Cawder. But the third
said; All haile Makbeth that heereafter shalt be king of Scotland.

Then Banquho; What manner of women (saith he) are you, that seeme so little
favourable unto me, whereas to my fellow heere, besides high offices, ye assigne
also the kingdome, appointing foorth nothing for me at all? Yes (saith the first of
them) we promise greater benefits unto thee, than unto him, for he shall reigne in
deed, but with an unluckie end: neither shall he leave anie issue behind him to
succeed in his place, where contrarilie thou in deed shalt not reigne at all, but of
thee those shall be borne which shall govern the Scottish kingdome by long order
of continuall descent. Herewith the foresaid women vanished immediatlie out of
their sight. This was reputed at the first but some vaine fantasticall illusion by
Mackbeth and Banquho, insomuch that Banquho would call Mackbeth in jest,
king of Scotland; and Mackbeth againe would call him in sport likewise, the
father of manie kings. But afterwards the common opinion was, that these women
were either the weird sisters, that is (as ye would say) the goddesses of destinie, or
else some nymphs or feiries, indued with knowledge of prophesie by their necro-
manticall science, bicause everie thing came to passe as they had spoken. For
shortlie after, the thane of Cawder being condemned at Fores of treason against

the king committed; his lands, livings, and offices were given of the kings liberalitie to Mackbeth.

The same night after, at supper, Banquho jested with him and said; Now Mackbeth thou hast obteined those things which the two former sisters prophesied, there remaineth onelie for thee to purchase that which the third said should come to passe. Whereupon Mackbeth revolving the thing in his mind, began even then to devise how he might atteine to the kingdome: but yet he thought with himselfe that he must tarie[12] a time, which should advance him thereto (by the divine providence) as it had come to passe in his former preferment. But shortlie after it chanced that king Duncane, having two sonnes by his wife which was the daughter of Siward earle of Northumberland,[13] he made the elder of them called Malcolme prince of Cumberland, as it were thereby to appoint him his successor in the kingdome, immediatlie after his deceasse. Mackbeth sore troubled herewith, for that he saw by this means his hope sore hindered (where, by the old lawes of the realme, the ordinance was, that if he that should succeed were not of able age to take the charge upon himselfe, he that was next of bloud unto him should be admitted) he began to take counsell how he might usurpe the kingdome by force, having a just quarell so to doo (as he tooke the matter) for that Duncane did what in him lay to defraud him of all maner of title and claime, which he might in time to come, pretend unto the crowne.

The woords of the three weird sisters also (of whom before ye have heard) greatlie incouraged him hereunto, but speciallie his wife lay sore upon him to attempt the thing, as she that was verie ambitious, burning in unquenchable desire to beare the name of a queene.[14] At length therefore, communicating his purposed intent with his trustie friends, amongst whome Banquho was the chiefest, upon confidence of their promised aid, he slue the king at Enverns, or (as some say) at Botgosuane, in the sixt yeare of his reigne. Then having a companie about him of such as he had made privie to his enterprise, he caused himselfe to be proclaimed king, and foorthwith went unto Scone, where (by common consent) he received the investure of the kingdome according to the accustomed maner. The bodie of Duncane was first conveied unto Elgine, & there buried in kinglie wise; but afterwards it was removed and conveied unto Colmekill, and there laid in a sepulture amongst his predecessors, in the yeare after the birth of our Saviour, 1046.

Malcolme Cammore and Donald Bane the sons of king Duncane, for feare of their lives (which they might well know that Mackbeth would seeke to bring to end for his more sure confirmation in the estate) fled into Cumberland, where Malcolme remained, till time that saint Edward the sonne of Etheldred recovered

---

12 Wait.
13 This makes Malcolm half-English, and the Siwards who accompany his invasion of Scotland are his relatives. Shakespeare does not stress Malcolm's English connection as such, but his decision at the end to introduce the English title of earl into Scotland (5.9.28–30; this detail is also in Holinshed) suggests an Anglicizing of his new kingdom.
14 Shakespeare's Lady Macbeth never declares such an ambition for herself; her focus is entirely on Macbeth's becoming king (see Key Passages, pp. 139–43). Holinshed has at this point a marginal note, 'Women desirous of high estate', making Lady Macbeth's ambition for herself the occasion for a conventional generalization. Shakespeare's character is in this sense less conventional.

the dominion of England from the Danish power, the which Edward received Malcolme by way of most friendlie enterteinment: but Donald passed over into Ireland, where he was tenderlie cherished by the king of that land. Mackbeth, after the departure thus of Duncanes sonnes, used great liberalitie towards the nobles of the realme, thereby to win their favour, and when he saw that no man went about to trouble him, he set his whole intention to mainteine justice, and to punish all enormities and abuses, which had chanced through the feeble and slouthfull administration of Duncane. [. . .]

Macbeth was initially a strong and just king, bringing peace and order to Scotland. He made many laws for the common good, strengthening both the crown and the church, and increasing the rights of women to inherit property. Holinshed, however, treats this part of his reign sceptically, and Shakespeare suppresses it altogether.

These and the like commendable lawes Makbeth caused to be put as then in use, governing the realme for the space of ten yeares in equall justice. But this was but a counterfet zeale of equitie shewed by him, partlie against his naturall inclination to purchase thereby the favour of the people. Shortlie after, he began to shew what he was, in stead of equitie practising crueltie. For the pricke of conscience (as it chanceth ever in tyrants, and such as atteine to anie estate by unrighteous means) caused him ever to feare, least he should be served of the same cup as he had ministred to his predecessor.[15] The woords also of the three weird sisters, would not out of his mind, which as they promised him the kingdome, so likewise did they promise it at the same time unto the posteritie of Banquho. He willed therefore the same Banquho with his sonne named Fleance, to come to a supper that he had prepared for them, which was in deed, as he had devised, present death at the hands of certeine murderers, whom he hired to execute that deed, appointing them to meete with the same Banquho and his sonne without the palace, as they returned to their lodgings, and there to slea them, so that he would not have his house slandered, but that in time to come he might cleare himselfe, if anie thing were laid to his charge upon anie suspicion that might arise.

It chanced yet by the benefit of the darke night, that though the father were slaine, the sonne yet by the helpe of almightie God reserving him to better fortune, escaped that danger: and afterwards having some inkeling (by the admonition of some friends which he had in the court) how his life was sought no lesse than his fathers, who was slaine not by chancemedlie[16] (as by the handling of the matter Makbeth woould have had it to appeare) but even upon a prepensed[17] devise: whereupon to avoid further perill he fled into Wales.

---

15 Shakespeare's Macbeth expresses a similarly worded fear of being made to drink from the poisoned chalice he himself has prepared (1.7.10–12).
16 i.e., partly (but not entirely) by accident.
17 Premeditated.

Macbeth began a reign of terror, taking pleasure in killing his nobles and enriching himself with the estates of his victims. To reinforce his tyranny he built a strong castle on the hill of Dunsinane, demanding that his thanes contribute to its construction. Macduff refused to take part. (In the play, this becomes Macduff's refusal to attend the banquet on the night of Banquo's murder.) This refusal, coupled with the prophecy of certain wizards that Macduff would kill him, made Macbeth suspicious of Macduff to the point where he could not bear to look at him. He would have killed him except for a witch's prophecies that Macbeth could never be slain by one born of woman, and would never be vanquished until the wood of Bernane came to the castle of Dunsinane. In Holinshed the prophecies do not come, as they do in Shakespeare, from the three weird women who make the first predictions; but his memory that those predictions came true has given Macbeth a general trust in wizards and witches.

Emboldened by these prophecies, Macbeth increased his tyranny. Macduff fled to England, to join Malcolm; in response, Macbeth slaughtered Macduff's family (see Key Passages, **pp. 170–5**). At this point Shakespeare, who normally handles Holinshed with a certain amount of freedom, begins to follow him closely. In 4.3, the scene in England, Malcolm tests Macduff by pretending to be the epitome of evil, unfit to govern. Only when Macduff finally cracks and agrees that Malcolm should never be king does Malcolm admit that it was a ruse, a test of Macduff's nature, made necessary by the number of times he has been tempted by spies from Macbeth. The unusual length and slowness of Shakespeare's 4.3 may be in part because of the closeness with which he follows Holinshed's dialogue. Holinshed's account continues as the play does, with Malcolm's successful invasion, the failure of the prophecies on which Macbeth has depended, and his death at Macduff's hands.

Contemporary Documents

From **Newes from Scotland, Declaring the Damnable life and death of Doctor Fian, a notable Sorcerer, who was burned at Edenborough in January last. 1591. Which Doctor was regester to the Divell that sundry times preached at North Barrick Kirke, to a number of notorious Witches. With the true examinations of the saide Doctor and Witches, as they uttered them in the presence of the Scottish King** . . . (1591). Reprinted in Barbara Rosen, ed., *Witchcraft* (The Stratford-upon-Avon Library, 6: London: Edward Arnold, 1969), pp. 194–7

This account of the examination of a group of witches bears on *Macbeth* in a number of ways. The obscene sexuality of the witches' dealings with the devil is characteristic of popular belief. Shakespeare transforms it into the less graphic but more profoundly disturbing sexuality of Lady Macbeth's invocation of the spirits to transform her body (1.5.40–50; see Key Passages, **p. 142**). This in turn lends an undercurrent of sexuality to Duncan's murder. Agnes Tompson's confession of a design to kill the King links witchery and regicide, a link that operates more indirectly in the play: the witches' first set of prophecies provokes Macbeth to kill Duncan; their second set of prophecies foretells his own death. The King in question is James VI of Scotland; we see in this account his fascination with witchcraft. There are more detailed links: the witches' claim to be able to sail in sieves and to control the winds is picked up by Shakespeare's witches (1.3.8–17; see Key Passages, **pp. 133–4**). These witches use toad venom; Shakespeare's witches use a toad steeped in its own venom as the first ingredient of their brew (4.1.6–9; see Key Passages, **p. 165**). More generally, the pamphlet shows the mingled fascination and anxiety witchcraft produced in the minds of Shakespeare's contemporaries. We may also note the distance between its tabloid sensationalism and the more profound horror of the play.

This aforesaid Agnes Sampson, which was the elder witch, was taken and brought to Holyrood House[1] before the King's Majesty and sundry other of the

---

1   The royal palace in Edinburgh.

nobility of Scotland, where she was straitly examined; but all the persuasions which the King's Majesty used to her with the rest of his Council might not provoke or induce her to confess anything, but stood stiffly in the denial of all that was laid to her charge. Whereupon they caused her to be conveyed away to prison, there to receive such torture as hath been lately provided for witches in that country.

And forasmuch as by due examination of witchcraft and witches in Scotland it hath lately been found that the Devil doth generally mark them with a privy mark, by reason the witches have confessed themselves that the Devil doth lick them with his tongue in some privy part of their body before he doth receive them to be his servants; which mark commonly is given them under the hair in some part of their body whereby it may not easily be found out or seen, though they be searched; and generally so long as the mark is not seen to those which search them, so long the parties that hath the mark will never confess anything—therefore by special commandment this Agnes Sampson had all her hair shaven off in each part of her body, and her head thrawen[2] with a rope according to the custom of that country, being a pain most grievous which she continued almost an hour, during which time she would not confess anything until the Devil's mark was found upon her privities; then she immediately confessed whatsoever was demanded of her, and justifying those persons aforesaid to be notorious witches.

Item, the said Agnes Tompson was after brought again before the King's Majesty and his Council, and being examined of the meetings and detestable dealings of those witches, she confessed that upon the night of All Hallow's Even last, she was accompanied as well with the persons aforesaid as also with a great many other witches to the number of two hundred; and that all they together went by sea, each one in a riddle or sieve, and went in the same very substantially with flagons of wine, making merry and drinking by the way in the same riddles or sieves, to the kirk[3] of North Berwick in Lothian; and that after they had landed, took hands on the land and danced this reel or short dance, singing all with one voice:—

Commer[4] go ye before, commer go ye;
If ye will not go before, commer let me.

At which time she confessed that this Gillis Duncan did go before them playing this reel or dance upon a small trump,[5] called a Jew's trump, until they entered into the kirk of North Berwick.

These confessions made the king in a wonderful admiration, and sent for the said Gillis Duncan, who upon the like trump did play the said dance before the King's Majesty, who, in respect of the strangeness of these matters took great delight to be present at their examinations.

Item, the said Agnes Tompson confessed that the Devil being then at North Berwick kirk attending their coming in the habit or likeness of a man, and seeing

2   Twisted.
3   Church.
4   Whoever comes.
5   Trumpet.

that they tarried over long, he at their coming enjoined them all to a penance, which was that they should kiss his buttocks in sign of duty to him; which being put over the pulpit bar, everyone did as he had enjoined them. And having made his ungodly exhortations, wherein he did greatly inveigh against the King of Scotland, he received their oaths for their good and true service towards him, and departed; which done, they returned to sea, and so home again.

(At which time the witches demanded of the Devil why he did bear such hatred to the King, who answered 'by reason the King is the greatest enemy he hath in the world'; all which their [c]onfessions and depositions are still extant upon record.)

Item, the said Agnes Sampson confessed before the King's Majesty sundry things which were so miraculous and strange as that his Majesty said they were all extreme liars; whereat she answered 'she would not wish his Majesty to suppose her words to be false, but rather to believe them, in that she would discover such matter unto him as his Majesty should not any way doubt of.'

And thereupon taking his Majesty a little aside, she declared unto him the very words which passed between the King's Majesty and his Queen at Oslo in Norway the first night of their marriage, with their answer each to other; whereat the King's Majesty wondered greatly, and swore by the living God that he believed that all the devils in hell could not have discovered the same, acknowledging her words to be most true; and therefore gave the more credit to the rest which is before declared.[6]

Touching this Agnes Tompson, she is the only woman who by the Devil's persuasion should have intended and put in execution the King's Majesty's death, in this manner:

She confessed that she took a black toad and did hang the same up by the heels three days, and collected and gathered the venom as it dropped and fell from it in an oyster shell, and kept the same venom close covered until she should obtain any part or piece of foul linen cloth that had appertained to the King's Majesty, as shirt, handkercher, napkin, or any other thing; which she practised to obtain by means of one John Kerrs, who being attendant in his Majesty's chamber, [she] desired him for old acquaintance between them to help her to one, or a piece of, such a cloth as is aforesaid, which thing the said John Kerrs denied to help her to, saying he could not help her to it.

And the said Agnes Tompson by her depositions since her apprehension saith, that if she had obtained any one piece of linen cloth which the King had worn and fouled, she had bewitched him to death, and put him to such extraordinary pains as if he had been lying upon sharp thorns and ends of needles.

Moreover, she confessed that at the time when His Majesty was in Denmark she, being accompanied with the parties before specially named, took a cat and christened it, and afterward bound to each part of that cat the chiefest parts of a dead man, and several joints of his body; and that in the night following, the said cat was conveyed into the midst of the sea by all these witches sailing in their

6   [Rosen's note.] In her very next statement Agnes admits to 'old acquaintance' with an attendant in the King's chamber, who may well have accompanied the king on his journey to Oslo. Since privacy in a mediaeval castle was only a relative term and depended mainly on the curtains of a four-poster bed, James's surprise is a trifle naive.

riddles or sieves as is aforesaid, and so left the said cat right before the town of Leith in Scotland.

This done, there did arise such a tempest in the sea as a greater hath not been seen; which tempest was the cause of the perishing of a boat or vessel coming over from the town of Burnt Island to the town of Leith, wherein was sundry jewels and rich gifts which should have been presented to the now Queen of Scotland, at Her Majesty's coming to Leith.

Again it is confessed, that the said christened cat was the cause that the King's Majesty's ship, at his coming forth of Denmark, had a contrary wind to the rest of his ships then being in his company, which thing was most strange and true, as the King's Majesty acknowledgeth; for when the rest of the ships had a fair and good wind, then was the wind contrary, and altogether against his Majesty. And further, the said witch declared, that his Majesty had never come safely from the sea, if his faith had not prevailed above their intentions.

Moreover, the said witches being demanded how the Devil would use them when he was in their company, they confessed that, when the Devil did receive them for his servants, and that they had vowed themselves unto him, then he would carnally use them, albeit to their little pleasure, in respect of his cold nature; and would do the like at sundry other times.

From **William Shakespeare, *King Henry VI Part One*** (c.1590), ed. Edward Burns (London: Thomson Learning, 2000), pp. 259–61 (5.2.22–50)

This early history play of Shakespeare (though whether he was the sole author is frequently disputed) concerns the Hundred Years War, in which England struggled to hold on to its possessions in France. One of the play's most striking characters is the woman known to history as Joan of Arc, a country girl who claimed she had a mission, given her by the saints who appeared to her, to drive the English out of France. Though she was eventually defeated, imprisoned and executed, she began with some remarkable military victories. In 1920 she was canonized. In the play she is Joan La Pucelle (the virgin; 'Puzel' in this edition). Far from being the saint of tradition she gets her power from evil spirits; the play is just patriotic enough to suggest that if the English are defeated it must be by diabolical intervention. Far from being a virgin, she is sexually promiscuous. The connection of black magic and sex returns in *Macbeth*.

In the extract given here, Joan, defeated in battle, calls the devils to her aid. To that extent she anticipates Lady Macbeth's invocation of the spirits in 1.5 (see Key Passages, **p. 142**). Like Lady Macbeth she commits her body to the powers of evil. But while Lady Macbeth's spirits remain unseen, Joan's spirits appear on stage; and while the inhuman energy Lady Macbeth shows after her invocation suggests that in some way it has worked, Joan's spirits proclaim by silence their refusal or inability to help. Like Macbeth, but more simply and directly, Joan is betrayed by the evil powers she trusted. All this makes this scene a forerunner of some key ideas in *Macbeth*; it can be taken as an example of Shakespearean recycling, in which motifs from early work reappear transformed. In particular, the externalization of evil in the appearance of stage devils is replaced by an evil that is more alarming because it is internalized and unseen. As in *Newes from Scotland*, the character of Joan also plays on the audience's anxieties about women, sex and witchcraft, particularly when they appear in combination.

Alarum. Excursions. Enter JOAN Puzel.

JOAN

The regent[1] conquers and the Frenchmen fly.
Now help, ye charming spells and periapts,[2]
And ye, choice spirits that admonish me   24
And give me signs of future accidents.[3]   *Thunder.*
You speedy helpers, that are substitutes
Under the lordly monarch of the north,[4]
Appear, and aid me in this enterprise.

Enter Fiends.

This speedy and quick appearance argues proof
Of your accustomed diligence to me.   30
Now, ye familiar spirits, that are culled
Out of the powerful regions under earth,
Help me this once, that France may get the field.

They walk, and speak not.

O hold me not with silence over-long:
Where I was wont to feed you with my blood,   35
I'll lop a member off and give it you
In earnest[5] of a further benefit
So you do condescend to help me now.

They hang their heads.

No hope to have redress? My body shall
Pay recompense if you will grant my suit.   40

They shake their heads.

---

1 The Duke of York, leader of the English power.
2 [From Burns's note.] Written charms, inscribed on a bandage and wrapped around a part of the body which they were deemed to protect.
3 Events.
4 The traditional location of evil. In *Paradise Lost* Satan assembles his rebellious forces in the north of Heaven. It is probably no coincidence that *Macbeth*, the Shakespeare play with the strongest sense of evil, is set in Scotland.
5 Promise.

Cannot my body nor blood sacrifice
Entreat you to your wonted furtherance?[6]
Then take my soul – my body, soul, and all –
Before that England give the French the foil.[7]   *They depart.*
See, they forsake me. Now the time is come   45
That France must vail[8] her lofty-plumed crest,
And let her head fall into England's lap.
My ancient incantations are too weak,
And hell too strong for me to buckle[9] with.   49
Now, France, thy glory droopeth to the dust.   *Exit.*

From **King James VI and I, *Basilicon Doron*** (1599). Reprinted in Johann P. Sommerville, ed., King James VI and I, *Political Writings* (Cambridge: Cambridge University Press, 1994), pp. 20–1, 51

King James, who was not yet King of England but had many years' experience as King of Scotland, wrote *Basilicon Doron* as advice to his son Prince Henry on the art of monarchy. (Henry, who died in 1610, never became king.) The extract given here bears on *Macbeth* in its contrast of a good king with a usurping tyrant. It is the contrast between Macbeth on the one hand and Duncan, Edward the Confessor and (his subjects hope) Malcolm on the other (see Key Passages, **pp. 175–7**). The thinking is formulaic and conventional, and includes a cautionary note, characteristic of James and of the more conservative political thought of his time: no matter how wicked a tyrant is, it is unlawful for his subjects to rise against him. No such scruples restrain Macbeth's enemies in the play (and even James admits that to kill a tyrant wins general approval in the world). Good kings, James asserts, live happily and die peacefully; in the exceptional cases in which they die by treason, the traitor is punished with infamy – as Macbeth is after killing Duncan. James's contrast of virtuous and vicious rulers puts the moral underpinnings of the play in their starkest form, and his account of the way good kings gain their subjects' love anticipates Macbeth's lament that he lacks 'honour, love, obedience, troops of friends' (5.3.25). The play is perhaps closest to this passage in the scene in England, where Malcolm accuses himself of all the vices of a tyrant (4.3.57–100).

For the part of making, and executing of Lawes, consider first the trew difference betwixt a lawfull good King, and an vsurping Tyran, and yee shall the more easily vnderstand your duetie herein: for *contraria iuxta se posita magis elucescunt*.[1] The one acknowledgeth himselfe ordained for his people, hauing receiued from

---

6   Customary help.
7   Defeat.
8   Lower.
9   Struggle

---

1   [Sommerville's translation.] Opposites placed next to each other become more apparent.

God a burthen of gouernment, whereof he must be countable: the other thinketh his people ordeined for him, a prey to his passions and inordinate appetites, as the fruites of his magnanimitie:[2] And therefore, as their ends are directly contrarie, so are their whole actions, as meanes, whereby they preasse to attaine to their endes. A good King, thinking his highest honour to consist in the due discharge of his calling, emploieth all his studie and paines, to procure and maintaine, by the making and execution of good Lawes, the well-fare and peace of his people; and as their naturall father and kindly Master,[3] thinketh his greatest contentment standeth in their prosperitie, and his greatest suretie in hauing their hearts, subiecting his owne priuate affections and appetites to the weale and standing of his Subiects, euer thinking the common interesse his chiefest particular: where by the contratie, an vsurping Tyran, thinking his greatest honour and felicitie to consist in attaining *per fas, vel nefas*[4] to his ambitious pretences, thinketh neuer himselfe sure, but by the dissention and factions among his people, and counter-faiting the Saint while he once creepe in credite, will then (by inuerting all good Lawes to serue onely for his vnrulie priuate affections) frame the common-weale euer to aduance his particular: building his suretie vpon his peoples miserie: and in the end (as a step-father and an vncouth hireling) make vp his owne hand vpon the ruines of the Republicke.[5] And according to their actions, so receiue they their reward: For a good King (after a happie and famous reigne) dieth in peace, lamented by his subiects, and admired by his neighbours; and leauing a reuerent renowne behinde him in earth, obtaineth the Crowne of eternall felicitie in heauen. And although some of them (which falleth out very rarelie) may be cut off by the treason of some vnnaturall subiects, yet liueth their fame after them, and some notable plague faileth neuer to ouertake the committers in this life, besides their infamie to all posterities hereafter: Where by the contrarie, a Tyrannes miserable and infamous life, armeth in end his owne Subiects to become his burreaux:[6] and although that rebellion be euer vnlawfull on their part, yet is the world so wearied of him, that his fall is little meaned[7] by the rest of his Subiects, and but smiled at by his neighbours. And besides the infamous memorie he leaueth behind him here, and the endlesse paine hee sustaineth hereafter, it oft falleth out, that the committers not onely escape vnpunished, but farther, the fact will remaine as allowed by the Law in diuers aages thereafter. It is easie then for you (my Sonne) to make a choise of one of these two sorts of rulers, by following the way of vertue to establish your standing; yea, incase ye fell in the high way, yet should it be with the honourable report, and iust regrate of all honest men. [. . .]

In a later passage, James gives his son pious advice that has a particular application to Macbeth. Arguably, the witches' prophecies precipitate Macbeth's killing

2 Affected greatness (normally the word means princely virtue; it is ironic here).
3 Lady Macbeth cannot kill Duncan because he reminds her of her father (2.2.12–13; see Key Passages, **p. 152**).
4 [Sommerville's translation.] By lawful or unlawful means.
5 State.
6 Hangmen.
7 Complained of.

of Duncan; while we learn that he has entertained such thoughts before, in theatrical terms his encounter with the witches is the starting point. Of the prophecies in the cauldron scene, the first ('Beware Macduff') triggers the most vicious act of Macbeth's tyranny, the murder of Macduff's family; and he repeats the second and third, with their false promises of safety, with an obsessiveness that makes him look mad.

Take no heede to any of your dreames, for all prophecies, visions, and prophet-icke dreames are accomplished and ceased in Christ: And therefore take no heede to freets[8] either in dreames, or any other things; for that errour proceedeth of ignorance, and is vnworthy of a Christian, who should be assured, *Omnia esse pura puris,*[9] as *Paul* sayth; all dayes and meates being alike to Christians.

From **Thomas Dekker, John Ford and William Rowley, *The Witch of Edmonton*** (1621), ed. Simon Trussler and Jacqui Russell (London: Methuen Student Editions, 1983), pp. 20–6 (2.1.1–36, 100–79)

Shakespeare's witches appear fully formed in the opening scene of *Macbeth*. They have no past, no history; there is no explanation of how they became witches, and even their identities are somewhat mysterious. The word 'witch' is used only once in the play's dialogue (1.3.6); elsewhere they are called, with variations, the weird sisters. They have no proper names, only numbers. *The Witch of Edmonton*, a collaborative play written almost a generation after *Macbeth*, presents a revealing contrast. In the extract given here we see, in effect, the making of a witch. An unpopular old woman, thinking herself (with cause) wronged by her neighbours, curses them; and so her reputation as a witch is established. In reality, events like these were probably re-enacted in village after village. Elizabeth Sawyer has a name, and a clear social reality. There is no question of her vanishing mysteriously as Shakespeare's witches do, and we cannot imagine her sailing in a sieve.

Yet her curses call up a real devil, in the form of a black dog. In the first scene of *Macbeth*, Shakespeare's witches hear the calls of their attendant spirits, called familiars, Paddock the toad and Graymalkin the cat. But the audience never sees them, and may not hear them (see Key Passages, **p. 128**). We see and hear the dog, and it has a distinctive voice of its own: curt, cold and ironic. In the speech that leads to the dog's entrance, Mother Sawyer declares that if she is going to be called a witch she might as well be one. Reputation becomes reality. She has heard stories of witches' familiars. The stories become reality. Lady Macbeth's invocation of the spirits is focused on her own body and what she wants as a high matter of state, nothing less than the murder of a king. Mother Sawyer is a creature of her society, and so in a sense is the evil she conjures up,

---

8   Anything supernatural.
9   To the pure all things are pure.

created from the resentments of village life and stories told around the fire. Supernatural evil has here a down-to-earth quality it lacks in *Macbeth*, though in Shakespeare's 1.3 we get a glimpse of something like Sawyer's story in the encounter between the witch and the sailor's wife (see Key Passages, **pp. 132–4**). At the same time *The Witch of Edmonton*'s analysis of the making of a witch has a sophistication that makes it very different from the sensationalism of *Newes from Scotland*. In the end, Elizabeth Sawyer suffers a fate equivalent to those of Joan la Pucelle (see Contemporary Documents, **pp. 28–30**) and Macbeth; the devil turns against her, and she is tried and executed as a witch.

Enter Elizabeth Sawyer, gathering sticks

MOTHER [SAWYER].
    And why on me? Why should the envious world
    Throw all their scandalous malice upon me?
    'Cause I am poor, deform'd and ignorant,
    And like a bow buckl'd and bent together
    By some more strong in mischiefs than myself?
    Must I for that be made a common sink
    For all the filth and rubbish of men's tongues
    To fall and run into? Some call me witch,
    And being ignorant of myself, they go
    About to teach me how to be one; urging
    That my bad tongue, by their bad usage made so,
    Forespeaks[1] their cattle, doth bewitch their corn,
    Themselves, their servants, and their babes at nurse.
    This they enforce upon me, and in part
    Make me to credit it.

Enter Old Banks.

                 And here comes one
    Of my chief adversaries.

BANKS.   Out, out upon thee, witch!
MOTHER.   Dost call me witch?
BANKS.   I do, witch, I do, and worse I would, knew I a name more hateful. What makest thou upon my ground?
MOTHER.   Gather a few rotten sticks to warm me.
BANKS.   Down with them when I bid thee, quickly! I'll make thy bones rattle in thy skin else.
MOTHER.   You won't, churl, cutthroat, miser. There they be. Would they stuck 'cross thy throat, thy bowels, thy maw,[2] thy midriff!

1   Puts a curse on.
2   Stomach.

BANKS.   Say'st thou me so? Hag, out of my ground!
MOTHER.   Dost strike me, slave, curmudgeon? Now thy bones aches,
    thy joints cramps, and convulsions stretch and crack thy sinews!
BANKS.   Cursing, thou hag? Take that, and that! (*Exit.*)
MOTHER.

    Strike, do, and wither'd may that hand and arm,
    Whose blows have lam'd me, drop from the rotten trunk!
    Abuse me? Beat me? Call me hag and witch?
    What is the name, where, and by what art learn'd,
    What spells, what charms, or invocations,
    May the thing call'd 'familiar' be purchas'd?
                  [. . .]
                  I have heard old beldams[3]
    Talk of familiars in the shape of mice,
    Rats, ferrets, weasels, and I wot not what,
    That have appear'd and suck'd, some say, their blood.
    But by what means they came acquainted with them
    I'm now ignorant. Would some power, good or bad,
    Instruct me which way I might be reveng'd
    Upon this churl, I'd go out of myself,
    And give this fury leave to dwell within
    This ruin'd cottage ready to fall with age,
    Abjure all goodness, be at hate with prayer,
    And study curses, imprecations,
    Blasphemous speeches, oaths, detested oaths,
    Or anything that's ill, so I might work
    Revenge upon this miser, this black cur
    That barks and bites and sucks the very blood
    Of me and of my credit.[4] 'Tis all one
    To be a witch or to be counted one.
    Vengeance, shame, ruin light upon that canker!

Enter Dog.

DOG.

    Ho! Have I found thee cursing? Now thou art
    Mine own.
MOTHER.   Thine? What art thou?
DOG.   He thou hast so oft
    Importun'd to appear to thee, the devil.
MOTHER.   Bless me! The devil?
DOG.

    Come, do not fear; I love thee much too well
    To hurt or fright thee. If I seem terrible,

3 Hags, witches.
4 Sawyer's way of imagining Banks determines the form her familiar will take; the dog can be seen as a projection of her own hatred.

It is to such as hate me. I have found
Thy love unfeign'd, have seen and pitied
Thy open wrongs, and come, out of my love,
To give thee just revenge against thy foes.

MOTHER.
May I believe thee?

DOG.   To confirm't, command me
Do any mischief unto man or beast,
And I'll effect it, on condition
That, uncompell'd, thou make a deed of gift
Of soul and body to me.

MOTHER.   Out, alas!
My soul and body?

DOG.   And that instantly,
And seal it with thy blood. If thou deniest,
I'll tear thy body in a thousand pieces.

MOTHER.
I know not where to seek relief. But shall I,
After such covenants seal'd, see full revenge
On all that wrong me?

DOG.   Ha, ha, silly woman!
The devil is no liar to such as he loves.
Didst ever know or hear a devil a liar
To such as he affects?

MOTHER.
When I am thine, at least so much of me
As I can call mine own, –

DOG.   Equivocations?[5]
Art mine or no? Speak, or I'll tear –

MOTHER.   All thine!

DOG.
Seal't with thy blood.
                    Sucks her arm. Thunder and lightning.
                         See, now I dare call thee mine.
For proof, command me. Instantly I'll run
To any mischief; goodness can I none.

MOTHER.
And I desire as little. There's an old churl,
One Banks –

DOG.
That wrong'd thee; he lam'd thee, call'd thee witch.

MOTHER.
The same! First upon him I'ld be reveng'd.

---

5   In *Macbeth* it is the powers of darkness that equivocate. This devil demands plain speaking, a clear
commitment from his victim.

DOG.
    Thou shalt. Do but name how.

MOTHER.   Go, touch his life.

DOG.
    I cannot.

MOTHER.   Hast thou not vow'd? Go, kill the slave!

DOG.
    I wonnot.

MOTHER.   I'll cancel then my gift.

DOG.   Ha, ha!

MOTHER.
    Dost laugh! Why wilt not kill him?

        DOG.   Fool, because I cannot.
    Though we have power, know it is circumscrib'd
    And tied in limits. Though he be curs'd to thee,
    Yet of himself he is loving to the world,
    And charitable to the poor. Now men
    That, as he, love goodness, though in smallest measure,
    Live without compass of our reach. His cattle
    And corn I'll kill and mildew, but his life,
    Until I take him, as I late found thee,
    Cursing and swearing, I have no power to touch.

MOTHER.
    Work on his corn and cattle then.

DOG.   I shall.
    The witch of Edmonton shall see his fall,
    If she at least put credit in my power,
    And in mine only, make orisons to me,
    And none but me.

MOTHER.   Say how and in what manner.

DOG.
    I'll tell thee. When thou wishest ill,
    Corn, man or beast would spoil or kill,
    Turn thy back against the sun
    And mumble this short orison:
    'If thou do death or shame pursue 'em,
    Sanctibicetur nomen tuum.'[6]

MOTHER.
    'If thou to death or shame pursue 'em,
    Sanctibecetur nomen tuum.'

DOG.
    Perfect. Farewell. Our first-made promises
    We'll put in execution against Banks. (*Exit.*)

---

6 'Hallowed be thy name', a blasphemous quotation from the Lord's Prayer, the basic prayer in the Christian Tradition.

2

Interpretations

Critical History

The history of *Macbeth* criticism, like that of the criticism of any significant work of art, cannot be reduced to a simple pattern. Different schools of thought operate at the same time, and allowance must always be made for the individuality of particular critics. With that caution kept in mind, this introduction will trace the major movements represented by the extracts that follow, with occasional glances at critics not represented here.

One of the play's special characteristics is its tight focus on the two leading roles, and from the eighteenth century into the early twentieth a dominant strain in the play's criticism was its study of the characters of Macbeth and Lady Macbeth. At the same time the criticism of the eighteenth century in particular had a strong moralizing streak, represented here in its purest form by Arthur Murphy (1753) (see Early Critical Reception, **pp. 45–6**). For Murphy *Macbeth* is an edifying play, and it teaches a lesson: the danger of ambition. As we shall see in the section on performance history, William Davenant at the beginning of this period and David Garrick near its end both rewrote the play to give Macbeth a final speech pointing this moral (see The Work in Performance, **pp. 106–7**). Samuel Johnson's (1745) more subtle analysis of the arguments Lady Macbeth uses on her husband is concerned with the moral issues at stake, and Johnson himself characteristically shows a clear sense of right and wrong (see Early Critical Reception, **pp. 44–5**). Throughout this period the analysis of the central characters dwelt on Macbeth as a good man corrupted by ambition, and on Lady Macbeth as the wicked instrument of that corruption. (Another moral: beware of strong-minded women.) Not everyone followed this line, of course. Elizabeth Montagu (1769) has a more balanced reading of Lady Macbeth, showing her capable of moments of tenderness – of showing, in effect, what was conventionally seen as a feminine virtue (see Early Critical Reception, **pp. 46–9**). And for Francis Gentleman (1770) Macbeth is not a good man fallen but a monster from the beginning (see Early Critical Reception, **pp. 49–53**). This interest in the central characters comes to its climax early in the twentieth century in the influential interpretation of A. C. Bradley (1904) (see Early Critical Reception, **pp. 54–7**). Bradley, no less than previous critics, is concerned with good and evil in the play; but this takes the special form of judging the imaginations of the main characters. Macbeth is a man with a limited but powerful imagination, and that imagination utters warnings on behalf of his better nature. Lady Macbeth, on the other hand, is pragmatic and unimaginative – or if she has an imagination her indomitable will holds it in check.

In the years following the First World War, a reaction against character criticism in general, and Bradley in particular, set in. The close study of language came to the forefront and *Macbeth*, whose language is particularly daring and concentrated, was used as a test case. L. C. Knights's essay 'How Many Children Had Lady Macbeth?' (1933) (see Modern Criticism, **pp. 58–61**) is generally taken as a turning point. Its title is a joke against Bradley's tendency to write about Shakespeare's characters as real people with lives beyond the action of the play. At least it can be said that Bradley's focus on character keeps him in touch with the fact that *Macbeth* is a play: a theatre audience watches characters in action. Knights goes to the other extreme, reading *Macbeth* not as a play but as a poem, focusing on the language and downplaying the importance of character. To risk a broad cultural generalization, this turn away from character is typical of the first half of the twentieth century, which marked the advent of the cultural movement known as modernism. It was in this period that Pablo Picasso broke the human form apart and rearranged the fragments; Bertolt Brecht in his play *Man Equals Man* (1926) demonstrated that one human being can be remade into another; and expressionist film and theatre turned actors into abstract types and choreographed crowds, their individuality erased. Knights explicitly puts *Macbeth* in the same category as T. S. Eliot's *The Waste Land* (1922), a work in which human identities are reduced to fragmented voices. More than story or character, it is language that matters.

Yet for a long time this new concentration on the play's language reflected some much older critical concerns. The examination of moral opposites, which earlier critics conducted through looking at the characters, became in Knights and others a function of the play's poetry. Knights, studying the imaginative impact of that poetry, finds an opposition of the unnatural and chaotic to the natural and the fertile. In the American school of New Criticism represented here by Cleanth Brooks (1947) (see Modern Criticism, **pp. 61–5**) imagery does moral work. Brooks shows the emptiness of Macbeth's power through clothing imagery; and children represent Macbeth's failure to control the future. G. Wilson Knight, an imaginative and highly individual (sometimes eccentric) critic, published two complementary essays on the play's language, 'Macbeth and the Metaphysic of Evil' and 'The Milk of Concord: An Essay on Life-Themes in Macbeth', in which he contrasted the play's atmosphere of evil with its vision of positive good centred on nature.[1] Eighteenth-century critics had misgivings about Shakespeare's language in general: John Dryden in the preface to his own version of *Troilus and Cressida* (1679) complains that it can be coarse, obscure and ungrammatical, and 'his whole stile is so pester'd with Figurative expressions, that it is as affected as it is obscure'.[2] What to later critics would seem the daring and the figurative richness of *Macbeth*'s language were for an earlier time the strongest evidence in

---

1 The first essay appears in *The Wheel of Fire* (repr. London: Methuen, 1949; first published by Oxford University Press in 1930), pp. 140–59; the second in *The Imperial Theme* (London: Oxford University Press, 1931), pp. 125–53.

2 John Dryden, *The Dramatic Works*, ed. Montague Summers, vol. V (repr. New York: Gordian Press, 1968; first published by the Nonesuch Press, 1932), p. 11.

favour of Dryden's complaint. The misgivings of Francis Gentleman (see Early Critical Reception, **pp. 51–2**) are characteristic, and we shall see Davenant's adaptation (1664) trying to correct Shakespeare's faults (see The Work in Performance, **pp. 100–6**). But the figurative expressions with which Dryden thought Shakespeare was pestered were for twentieth-century critics the chief riches of the play. One of the most influential books of Shakespeare criticism in this period was Caroline Spurgeon's *Shakespeare's Imagery and What it Tells Us*.[3] The title sums up a whole school of critical thought.

Even Bradley took time to register the play's distinctive atmosphere of darkness. And the opposing force of fertility led to what might broadly be called anthropological readings like that of John Holloway (1961) (see Modern Criticism, **pp. 65–8**), in which the march of Birnam Wood becomes a fertility ritual, a May Day celebration. We can detect a link here with the archetypal criticism of the Canadian Northrop Frye, whose *Anatomy of Criticism* (1957) classified different types of literature according to the seasons. In such criticism, as in the language-centred criticism of Knights, Brooks and others, there is an underlying assumption of universal forces at work, linked to the pattern of the seasons, the barrenness of winter succeeded by the fertility of spring (universal, one might add, so long as one lives in a temperate zone). And in such criticism the moral certainty of the eighteenth century, or something like it, is still in place.

It is in place no longer. Later twentieth-century criticism is more sceptical and ironic, and suspicious of such notions as universal good – suspicious, indeed, of the whole notion that anything can be seen as universal: to make such a claim is to be guilty of 'essentialism', in some quarters an argument-settling term of rebuke. Duncan, a centre of goodness in earlier criticism, is for Janet Adelman (1992) a figure of dangerous weakness, his gentleness a sign not of grace but of masculine failure (see Modern Criticism, **pp. 78–80**).[4] Naomi Conn Liebler casts equivalent doubts on the ending, seeing in the new order not a restoration of fertility, much less a May game, but in Malcolm and Macduff a 'combination of unusual birth, childlessness, and virginity [that] suggest no potential for procreative renewal'.[5] The restoration of order at the end was a commonplace of earlier criticism. Stephen Booth (1983) challenges the whole notion of such an order by challenging the narrative pattern of beginning, middle and end on which it depends (see Modern Criticism, **pp. 74–5**). David Scott Kastan (1999) in his turn questions the stability of the idea of kingship, on which the play's political order has been thought to rest (see Modern Criticism, **pp. 86–8**). At least the witches are clearly a centre of evil, we might have thought. But for Stephen Greenblatt (1994) nothing is clear about them (see Modern Criticism, **pp. 83–5**); and in one of the quirkiest readings the play has so far received, Terry Eagleton proposes that we see them as the unacknowledged heroines of the play, a sisterhood living apart from a violent society obsessed with power, and as such the centre of positive value.[6]

---

3   Cambridge: Cambridge University Press, 1935.
4   For another critical reading of Duncan, see Harry Berger, Jr., 'The Early Scenes of *Macbeth*: Preface to a New Interpretation', *English Literary History* 47 (1980), pp. 1–31.
5   *Shakespeare's Festive Tragedy: The Ritual Foundations of Genre* (London and New York: Routledge, 1995), p. 222.
6   *William Shakespeare* (Oxford: Basil Blackwell, 1986), pp. 1–8.

The word 'sisterhood' leads us to one of the crucial developments in the later twentieth century, the advent of feminist criticism. This movement of course has had implications far beyond the study of Shakespeare; it is part of a momentous change in social thinking and social behaviour. Earlier criticism, for the most part, saw Lady Macbeth as a dangerous virago, a wicked woman leading her husband into crime. If she occasionally aroused sympathy, it was for touches of 'womanliness'; she could not kill a man who looked like her father, and under the strain of the murder's discovery she was feminine enough to faint. Such criticism tended to focus on the Lady Macbeth of the first half of the play. In the extract given here, Joan Larsen Klein (1980) focuses on the Lady Macbeth of the play's second half, marginalized in her society, ignored by her husband, not so much the action's instigator as its victim, who may seem powerful at the beginning but whose ultimate collapse is what we really have to think about (see Modern Criticism, **pp. 68–71**). This, we might say, is a character study as close as Bradley's but turned to different ends. Janet Adelman (**pp. 78–83**) shares the tendency of earlier critics to see broad underlying forces in the play: but for her these are not disorder versus fertility but male versus female, with the play's men perceiving female power as destructive and attempting to deny it by creating an all-male world in which even childbirth is done through men. Stephen Orgel takes a similar approach, seeing *Macbeth* as a male-oriented, misogynist play which does everything it can to exclude or degrade women.[7] Other feminist studies, including those of Coppélia Kahn and Philippa Berry, show the difficulty Macbeth has in constructing or following male ideals in the play, with a corresponding scepticism about those ideals.[8] Jenijoy La Belle's essay (1980) puts the focus back on Lady Macbeth – not on her character but on her body, dwelling on the all-important fact that it is a woman's body, and exploring the medical implications of her invocation of the spirits (see Modern Criticism, **pp. 71–4**).

In their different ways, Klein and La Belle take us back to the persons of the play: Klein activates our awareness of Lady Macbeth's social role, La Belle concentrates on the importance of her body. (A concern with the body is another prominent element in late twentieth-century criticism).[9] Elsewhere in this collection Barbara Everett's (1989) close study of the Macbeths as a married couple, while demonstrating that the old view of a decent man corrupted by his wicked wife is not the full story, shows that attention to the people of the play did not exhaust its value with Bradley, and was not put out of court by Knights (see Modern Criticism, **pp. 75–7**).

There is another strain in *Macbeth* criticism that may be mentioned more briefly. It does not figure prominently in bibliographies, because it is not the sort of thing academics are comfortable writing about: it is the play's capacity to induce terror. It is something that hits the instincts and the nervous system, and as such not easy to analyse, though De Quincey's famous essay (1823) (see

7   'Macbeth and the Antic Round', *Shakespeare Survey* 52 (1999), pp. 143–53.
8   See Kahn, *Man's Estate: Masculine Identity in Shakespeare* (Berkeley, Los Angeles and London: University of California Press, 1981), pp. 172–92; and Berry, *Shakespeare's Feminine Endings: Disfiguring Death in the Tragedies* (London and New York: Routledge, 1999), pp. 102–34.
9   See, for example, Gail Kern Paster, *The Body Embarrassed: Drama and the Disciplines of Shame in Early Modern England* (Ithaca, NY: Cornell University Press, 1993).

Early Critical Reception, **p. 54**) makes a notable attempt. That essay belongs to the Romantic period, where the ability of *Macbeth* to induce terror may link with the popularity of the Gothic novel and with a new fascination with Scotland as a wild, picturesque country, a place of rugged hills, roaring water and strange legends. It was in this period that the great English actress Sarah Siddons reported reading *Macbeth* at night and finding herself, when she came to the murder, unable to read further, and frightened by the rustling of her own dress as she fled upstairs to bed.[10] But the Romantic period had no monopoly on feelings of terror; the roots of the Gothic lie deep in the sensibility of the eighteenth century, and Samuel Johnson reports, in anticipation of Sarah Siddons, that the reader of *Macbeth* may look up alarmed at finding himself alone (see Early Critical Reception, **p. 45**). In comparing *Macbeth* to a werewolf movie, Harriett Hawkins (1990) tries to revive this sense of terror in twentieth-century terms, tapping into an aspect of the play that cannot be controlled by academic criticism, with its patterns of images and ideas (see Modern Criticism, **pp. 77–8**). It is this aspect of the play that links up with its twentieth-century reputation, discussed in the Introduction (**pp. 1–2**), of being bad luck in the theatre. Yet the play was designed for the theatre, and another important element in recent Shakespeare criticism is a new concentration on Shakespeare in performance. That will be the business of a later chapter, The Work in Performance (**pp. 89–120**).

10 Roger Manvell, *Sarah Siddons: Portrait of an Actress* (London: Heinemann, 1970), pp. 21–2.

Early Critical Reception

From **Samuel Johnson, *Miscellaneous Observations on the Tragedy of 'Macbeth': with Remarks on Sir T.H.'s Edition of Shakespeare***
(1745). Reprinted in Brian Vickers, ed., *Shakespeare: the Critical Heritage*, Vol. III
(London: Routledge and Kegan Paul, 1975), pp. 172–4

Samuel Johnson was the leading critic and literary personality of his age. His notes on *Macbeth* appear to be a preparation for his own edition of Shakespeare, which came twenty years later. The first note given here shows Johnson's characteristic interest in literature as a reflection of the workings of human nature. As he does in his periodical essays, he uses the stance of a generalizing observer. In the second note, comparing two passages on night, one in a play by the influential poet, critic and playwright John Dryden and one in *Macbeth*, Johnson's final interest is in the imaginative power of the play, particularly its ability to generate terror. An interest in terror was characteristic of his age (the Hamlet of David Garrick, the leading actor of Johnson's time, was best remembered for his frightened reaction to the Ghost) and was one of the forces that helped create the Gothic novel.

NOTE XVI.
SCENE X.

The Arguments by which Lady *Macbeth* persuades her Husband to commit the Murder afford a proof of *Shakespeare's* Knowledge of Human Nature. She urges the Excellence and Dignity of Courage, a glittering Idea which has dazzled Mankind from Age to Age, and animated sometimes the Housebreaker and sometimes the Conqueror; but this Sophism *Macbeth* has for ever destroyed by distinguishing true from false Fortitude in a Line and a half, of which it may almost be said that they ought to bestow Immortality on the Author though all his other Productions had been lost.

> I dare do all that may become a Man,
> Who dares do more is none. [1.7.46–7]

This Topic, which has been always employed with too much Success, is used in this Scene with peculiar propriety, to a Soldier by a Woman. Courage is the distinguishing Virtue of a Soldier, and the Reproach of Cowardice cannot be borne by any Man from a Woman without great Impatience.

She then urges the Oaths by which he had bound himself to murder *Duncan*, another Art of Sophistry by which Men have sometimes deluded their Consciences and persuaded themselves that what would be criminal in others is virtuous in them; this Argument *Shakespeare*, whose Plan obliged him to make *Macbeth* yield, has not confuted, though he might easily have shown that a former Obligation could not be vacated by a latter. [. . .]

NOTE XX.
ACT II. SCENE II.

(I) . . . Now o'er one half the World [*sic*]
Nature seems dead. [2.1.49–50]

That is, *over our Hemisphere all Action and Motion seem to have ceased*. This Image, which is perhaps the most striking that Poetry can produce, has been adopted by *Dryden* in his *Conquest of Mexico*:

All things are hush'd as Nature's self lay dead,
The Mountains seem to nod their drowsy Head;
The little Birds in Dreams their Songs repeat,
And sleeping Flow'rs beneath the Night-dews sweat.
Even Lust and Envy sleep!

These Lines, though so well known, I have transcrib'd that the Contrast between them and this Passage of *Shakespeare* may be more accurately observed.

Night is described by two great Poets, but one describes a Night of Quiet, the other of Perturbation. In the Night of *Dryden* all the Disturbers of the World are laid asleep; in that of *Shakespeare* nothing but Sorcery, Lust, and Murder is awake. He that reads *Dryden* finds himself lull'd with Serenity, and disposed to Solitude and Contemplation. He that peruses *Shakespeare* looks round alarmed, and starts to find himself alone. One is the Night of a Lover, the other that of a Murderer.

From **Arthur Murphy, 'Criticism on the Tragedy of *Macbeth*'**
(1753). Reprinted in Brian Vickers, ed., *Shakespeare: the Critical Heritage*, Vol. IV (London: Routledge and Kegan Paul, 1976), p. 86

Arthur Murphy was a lawyer, critic and dramatist whose extensive comments on Shakespeare are often copied from other critics. This passage evidently is his own; it puts in its purest form the moral view of *Macbeth* as a play with a message for its audience, in line with the view of theatre stated at the end of Hugh Kelly's comedy *False Delicacy* (1768): 'The stage should be a school of morality'.

This Tragedy may be considered in a twofold View: with regard to the imaginary Existences introduced, and likewise with respect to the Characters drawn from the Page of human Nature. In this latter Sense it must be allowed to teach a very important Lesson, *viz.* the intoxicating Power and rapid Progress of Vice. In the person of *Macbeth* we see a Mind enriched with many noble Qualities, and, after a severe Conflict, subdued by Invincible Ambition, in spite of the Suggestions of a Conscience naturally tender and sensible. All his sentiments of Loyalty, Gratitude and Hospitality give place by imperceptible Degrees to his unbounded Lust of Power and to the Instigations of a wicked Woman, till at length he is transformed from a Man of many moral Virtues to as great a Monster of Iniquity as ever debased human Nature. Who is there that does not Startle at the Moral here inculcated? Who, though adorned with every amiable Quality, can reflect on *Macbeth*'s unhappy Fate without Shuddering to think on what a precarious Tenure he holds the most valuable of all his Possessions?

From **Elizabeth Montagu, *An Essay on the Writings and Genius of Shakespeare, Compared with the Greek and French Dramatic Poets, with Some Remarks Upon the Misrepresentations of Mons. de Voltaire*** (1769). Reprinted in Brian Vickers, ed., *Shakespeare: the Critical Heritage*, Vol. V (London: Routledge and Kegan Paul, 1979), pp. 336–41

Elizabeth Montagu was a leading member of the so-called 'Blue Stocking' circle, a group of intellectual woman who in the second half of the eighteenth century demonstrated that, contrary to some conventional thinking, women could be among the intelligentsia and could have literary careers. Montagu's essay on Shakespeare, defending him from the pedantic criticisms of the French critic, playwright and social agitator Voltaire, established her as one of the leading commentators on the figure who had become England's national poet. Like Johnson, she generalizes about human nature, and pays tribute to the play's frightening power. Like Murphy, she sees Macbeth as a good man corrupted, but she traces the process more subtly; and she sees Lady Macbeth as capable, if only for a moment, of a humanity that complicates her character too.

This piece is perhaps one of the greatest exertions of the tragic and poetic powers that any age or any country has produced. Here are opened new sources of terror, new creations of fancy. The agency of witches and spirits excites a species of terror that cannot be effected by the operation of human agency or by any form or disposition of human things. For the known limits of their powers and capacities set certain bounds to our apprehensions; mysterious horrors, undefined terrors are raised by the intervention of beings whose nature we do not understand, whose actions we cannot control, and whose influence we know not how to escape. Here we feel through all the faculties of the soul and to the utmost extent of her capacity. The apprehension of the interposition of such agents is the most salutary of all fears. It keeps up in our minds a sense of our connection with awful and invisible spirits to whom our most secret actions are apparent, and from whose chastisement innocence alone can defend us. . . .

The dexterity is admirable with which the predictions of the witches (as Macbeth observes) prove true to the ear but false to the hope, according to the general condition of vain oracles. With great judgment the poet has given to Macbeth the very temper to be wrought upon by such suggestions. The bad man is his own tempter. Richard III. had a heart that prompted him to do all that the worst demon could have suggested, so that the witches had been only an idle wonder in his story. Nor did he want such a counsellor as Lady Macbeth: a ready instrument like Buckingham to adopt his projects and execute his orders was sufficient. But Macbeth, of a generous disposition and good propensities, but with vehement passions and aspiring wishes, was a subject liable to be seduced by splendid prospects and ambitious counsels. This appears from the following character given of him by his wife:

> Yet do I fear thy nature;
> It is too full o'th' milk of human kindness
> To catch the nearest way. Thou wouldst be great;
> Art not without ambition; but without
> The illness should attend it. What thou wouldst highly,
> That wouldst thou holily; wouldst not play false,
> But yet wouldst wrongly win. [1.5.16–22]

So much inherent ambition in a character without other vice, and full of the milk of human kindness, though obnoxious[1] to temptation yet would have great struggles before it yielded, and as violent fits of subsequent remorse.

If the mind is to be medicated by the operations of pity and terror,[2] surely no means are so well adapted to that end as a strong and lively representation of the agonizing struggles that precede and the terrible horrors that follow wicked actions. Other poets thought they had sufficiently attended to the moral purpose of the drama in making the furies pursue the perpetrated crime. Our author waives their bloody daggers in the road to guilt, and demonstrates that as soon as a man begins to hearken to ill suggestions terrors environ and fears distract him. Tenderness and conjugal love combat in the breasts of a Medea and a Herod in their purposed vengeance. Personal affection often weeps on the theatre while jealousy or revenge whet the bloody knife; but Macbeth's emotions are the struggles of conscience, his agonies are the agonies of remorse. They are lessons of justice, and warnings to innocence. I do not know that any dramatic writer except Shakespeare has set forth the pangs of guilt separate from the fear of punishment. Clytemnestra is represented by Euripides as under great terrors on account of the murder of Agamemnon; but they arise from fear, not repentance. It is not the memory of the assassinated husband which haunts and terrifies her but an apprehension of vengeance from his surviving son; when she is told Orestes is dead her mind is again at ease. It must be allowed that on the Grecian stage it is the office of the Chorus to moralize, and to point out on every occasion the advantages of

---

1   Exposed.
2   According to a much-debated passage in Aristotle's *Poetics*, these are the emotions aroused, and purged, by tragedy. Montagu's way of describing the process picks up the medical implications.

virtue over vice. But how much less affecting are their animadversions than the testimony of the person concerned! . . .

Our author has so tempered the constitutional character of Macbeth by infusing into it the milk of human kindness and a strong tincture of honour, as to make the most violent perturbation and pungent remorse naturally attend on those steps to which he is led by the force of temptation. Here we must commend the poet's judgment, and his invariable attention to consistency of character. But more amazing is the art with which he exhibits the movement of the human mind, and renders audible the silent march of thought; traces its modes of operation in the course of deliberating, the pauses of hesitation, and the final act of decision; shews how reason checks and how the passions impel; and displays to us the trepidations that precede and the horrors that pursue acts of blood. No species of dialogue but that which a man holds with himself could effect this. The soliloquy has been permitted to all dramatic writers; but its true use has been understood only by our author, who alone has attained to a just imitation of nature in this kind of self-conference. [. . .]

Macbeth, in debating with himself, chiefly dwells upon the guilt, and touches something on the danger of assassinating the king. When he argues with Lady Macbeth, knowing her too wicked to be affected by the one and too daring to be deterred by the other, he urges with great propriety what he thinks may have more weight with one of her disposition, the favour he is in with the king, and the esteem he has lately acquired of the people. In answer to her charge of cowardice he finely distinguishes between manly courage and brutal ferocity.

> I dare do all that may become a man;
> Who dares do more is none. [1.7.46–7]

At length, overcome rather than persuaded, he determines on the bloody deed.

> I am settled, and bend up
> Each corp'ral agent to this terrible feat. [1.7.80–1]

How terrible to him, how repugnant to his nature we plainly perceive when, even in the moment that he summons up the resolution needful to perform it, horrid phantasms present themselves: murder alarumed by his centinel, the wolf stealing towards his design, witchcraft celebrating pale Hecate's offerings, the midnight ravisher invading sleeping innocence, seem his associates, and bloody daggers lead him to the very chamber of the king. [. . .]

The difference between a mind naturally prone to evil, and a frail one warped by force of temptations, is delicately distinguished in Macbeth and his wife. There are also some touches of the pencil that mark the male and female character. When they deliberate on the murder of the king the duties of host and subject strongly plead with him against the deed. She passes over these considerations; goes to Duncan's chamber resolved to kill him, but could not do it because, she says, he resembled her father while he slept. There is something feminine in this, and perfectly agreeable to the nature of the sex, who even when void of principle are seldom entirely divested of sentiment; and thus the poet who, to use his own phrase, had overstepped the modesty of nature in the exaggerated fierceness of her character, returns back to the line and limits of humanity, and that very judiciously, by a sudden impression which has only an instantaneous effect. Thus she may relapse into her former wickedness, and from the same susceptibility, by the force of other impressions, be afterwards driven to distraction. As her character was not composed of those gentle elements out of which regular repentance could be formed, it was well judged to throw her mind into the chaos of madness; and as she had exhibited wickedness in its highest degree of ferocity and atrociousness she should be an example of the wildest agonies of remorse. As Shakespeare could most exactly delineate the human mind in a regular state of reason so no one ever so happily caught its varying forms in the wanderings of delirium.

From **Francis Gentleman, *The Dramatic Censor; or, Critical Companion*** (1770). Reprinted in Brian Vickers, ed., *Shakespeare: the Critical Heritage*, Vol. V (London: Routledge and Kegan Paul, 1979), pp. 384–97

Francis Gentleman was an actor and playwright as well as a critic. His misgivings about *Macbeth* demonstrate that not everyone has seen Shakespeare as a universal genius who can do no wrong, though his view of the play as unsuitable for the young is a backhanded tribute to its power. His reading of Macbeth as monstrous from the beginning sets him at odds with other critics of his time (Montagu included). He is more characteristic in censuring some of Shakespeare's risky poetic effects as risks not worth taking, and in his view of Lady Macbeth's language as offending propriety. He pays tribute to the dramatic skill of the work, but his dark view of the two principal characters finally leads him to declare the play unfit for presentation.

Preternatural beings afford the widest, most luxuriant field for genius to sport, and ideas to vegetate in. Of this, being truly sensible and willing to give his *muse of fire*[1] unlimited scope, Shakespeare has in several pieces availed himself, but in none more powerfully than the tragedy now before us. However, though critically we must admire that characteristic peculiarity of sentiment and expression which distinguishes the Witches, it is nevertheless necessary to remark that exhibiting such personages and phantoms as never had any existence but in credulous or heated imaginations tends to impress superstitious feelings and fears upon weak minds. For which reason we consider every dramatic piece which treats the audience with a ghost, fairy or witch as improper for young, inexperienced spectators in particular. If, as is well known, old womens stories of such impress a timidity upon every child who hears their terrifying tales, a timidity which lasts to the conclusion of life, may we not infer apprehensions of their having a more forceable effect from being realized on the stage?

It may be said that interdicting such poetical auxiliaries would cramp genius, and deprive us of many unparalelled beauties. To this the answer is plain, that

---

1   *Henry V*, Prologue, 1.

nothing which has not a good effect, or at least an inoffensive tendency, should be deemed beautiful or stand estimation. [. . .]

Macbeth's feelings upon this unexpected acquisition [of the title of Cawdor], verifying in part the prediction which has been so lately pronounced to him, the dawnings of ambition which break out upon his unconnected [meditation], are extremely natural; but his adverting to murther for obtaining the state of royalty in view shew him much too susceptible of villainous impressions.

There are many circumstances and events to bring about the most unthought-of changes in human affairs. Wherefore that man who premeditates the worst means at first must have by nature a deep depravation of heart; and such Macbeth will appear infected with from the whole of that speech which begins 'Two truths are told,' &c [1.3.127] notwithstanding somewhat like palliation is offered in two or three lines. Indeed, his conclusion seems to banish what he beautifully stiles *fantastical murther*, but cannot banish from spectators his barbarous ideas so suddenly conceived. We have dwelt upon this circumstance to strengthen our opinion that the author meant to draw him a detestable monster, which some critics have rather disputed, allowing him a generous disposition which we find no instance of; even the conscientious struggles which we shall presently find him engaged with might arise in the most villainous nature. He who does a bad action precipitately, or without knowing it to be such, may stand in some measure excusable. But when a man has scrupulously weighed every relative circumstance in the nicest scale of reflection, and after all determines upon what nature, gratitude, and justice would avoid, he must be composed of the worst materials.

To corroborate the general idea of Macbeth's character which we have here offered and which will be enlarged upon when we go through the whole piece, let us view him in the very next scene, where, after a most cordial reception from the king, with unbounded promises of future favours, he is so possessed of his base purpose that, void even of common gratitude, he replies upon Duncan's appointing Malcolm prince of Cumberland,

> The prince of Cumberland! that is a step   [*aside*.
> On which I must fall down, or else o'er leap:
> For in my way it lies—Stars hide your fires,
> Let not light see my black and deep desires;
> The eye wink at the end [*sic*]—yet let that be,
> Which the eye fears, when it is done, to see. [1.4.48–53]

From this passage it appears that, not content with the simple idea of regicide he determines to cut off the whole family; in return for being loaded with honours by royal favour, and at the very instant when this unsuspecting monarch and friend places himself upon his hospitable reception. If this does not prove Macbeth an exception to the satirist's remark, *Nemo repente fuit turpissimus*,[2] we know not what can.

Lady Macbeth, and her husband's letter, are judiciously introduced. But sure

---

2 [Vickers's note.] Juvenal, *Satires*, 2.83: 'no one reaches the depths of turpitude all at once'.

such sympathetic barbarity was never in nature as suddenly, on the instant, breaks out in these words,

> Glamis thou art and Cawdor—and shalt be
> What thou art promised. [1.5.15–16]

What follows accuses Macbeth of a milky softness in his nature, of which he does not seem at all possessed, for unsuccessful struggles of conscience cannot justly be called so. However, that he may not have the whole load of aggravated guilt to bear alone, our author has made this matchless lady—we lament so detestable, though a possible picture of the fair sex—exert uncommon talents of temptation. On hearing of the king's visit, with most unrelenting precipitation of thought she dooms the royal visitant. Her invocation to spirits of evil influence is worthy of a powerful imagination, and Macbeth's interruptive entrance extremely well timed; but we must offer some doubt whether the word *blanket* of the dark does not convey a low and improper idea.[3]

Macbeth's mention of Duncan's approach without making any previous reply to his wife's cordial reception is a natural effect of what sits nearest his heart; and her coming to the main point at once is well devised for working him up to her great purpose. Her confining the sentiment of murther in less than a line, and warning him to disguise those looks which appear too intelligible, impress us with a strong idea of her policy, as does her second hint of Duncan's death, and promising to take a great part of the dreadful business on herself. [. . .]

In such a state of guilty perturbation as Macbeth now appears, no mode of expression could be so suitable as that of soliloquy. It were to be wished, however, that our great author, pursuing energy, had not in some sentences bordered upon obscurity, especially if we consider those passages as only repeated on the stage, where the ear must inevitably be too quick for reception. In an alteration of this play which has been often performed,[4] there are some attempts to render the lines we speak of more intelligible; but, like most other paraphrases, they destroy the essential spirit.

The reflection that if he could but gain ease even in this life he would jump the life to come is rather wildly impious; but the inevitable temporal punishment of a conscience loaded with guilt is very well and commendably inculcated. The arguments for declining the murther are so forcible that nothing but the most hardened heart, under such conviction, would proceed. Where he personifies pity, and mounts her astride on the *blast*, fancy takes a very vigorous flight, nor does expression fall beneath. Yet we are afraid they leave propriety behind; the following lines are in our opinion very exceptionable:[5]

> —I have no spur
> To prick the sides of my intent, but only
> Vaulting ambition, which o'er-leaps itself
> *And falls on the other*— [1.7.25–8]

---

3 Davenant's adaptation anticipates this complaint, changing 'blanket' to 'curtains' (see The Work in Performance, **p. 103**).
4 Presumably Davenant's version (see The Work in Performance, **pp. 100–6**).
5 Open to criticism.

To embody *intention*, that *ambition* may be a *spur* to prick its sides, leans towards the burlesque; and then turning the *spur* into another body, that it may vault over, instead of gaining the *saddle* of *intent*, corroborates this idea; indeed the speech should always end at 'The deep damnation of his taking off' [1.7.20]. For 'pity'—'heaven's cherubim' and 'ambition', all upon the full gallop, are strained figures at least; not at all adapted to a man deliberating upon one of the foulest, most important murthers he could commit.

Lady Macbeth comes to speak in rather plainer terms. Yet, unless we allow great latitude of expression, what follows evidently admits of objection:

>   —Was the hope drunk
> Wherein you drest yourself? Hath it slept since,
> And wakes it now to look so pale and sickly [*sic*]. [1.7.35–7]

Suppose we pass over the literal acceptation[6] of *hope* being drunk, surely we must blame a lady of high rank for descending to such a vulgar and nauseous allusion as the paleness or sickness of an inebriated state; nor is her comparison of the cat in the adage much more the effect of good breeding.

Macbeth's reply to the very gross rebuff he has just received is as concise, significant, and noble a one as ever was uttered; but his bloody-minded virago's next speech, towards the conclusion, wounds humanity with such a sentiment as no woman should utter, nor any rational being hear. Yet that strange, horrid picture of dashing a smiling infant's brains out, and laying a plan for complicated destruction, occasions Macbeth to say 'Bring forth men children only' [1.7.73–5]. Should he not rather have said,

> Bring forth fierce tygers only,
> For thy relentless nature should compose
> Nothing but beasts.

If it should be urged that such characters have been, and may be, we still contend that they are among the frightful deformities and essential concealments of nature, which should be excluded from the stage. [. . .]

> At this point there is an interesting turn in Gentleman's argument. He summar-
> izes Macbeth as a monster who seems to be outside nature. Yet this monster is
> a great acting part, and – paradoxically – Gentleman, having declared the play
> unfit for presentation, pays tribute to its central character as acted by David
> Garrick, the greatest English actor of his time. Faced with the power of the
> actor's performance, the critic's objections fall away.

To delineate Macbeth is not easy. The author seems, like Prometheus, to have made a man of his own, but to have stolen his animation rather from Hell than

---

6   i.e., suppose we do not take the speech literally.

Heaven.[7] By the account we hear of him previous to his entrance, magnanimity and courage appear conspicuous in his conduct. Yet no sooner does he present himself, but with all the weakness of unpractised youth he receives a strong impression from old women's prognostications; and with all the aptness of a studied villain suggests the most pernicious practices, which from that moment, with a very few slight intervals, take entire possession of his heart. From his future proceedings we perceive him more actuated by jealous apprehensions than sound policy, more influenced by rage and desperation than any degree of natural resolution; credulous, impatient, vindictive; ambitious without a spark of honour; cruel without a gleam of pity. In short, as compleat a tool for ministers of temptation to work upon as ever fancy formed, and too disgraceful for nature to admit amongst her works.

However, considered in the view of theatrical action, there is not one personage to be found in our English drama which more strongly impresses an audience, which requires more judgment and greater powers to do him justice. Many passages are intricate, some heavy, but for the greater part powerfully impassioned. The mental agitation he is thrown into requires expression peculiarly forcible of action, look, and utterance, even so far as to make the hearts of spectators shrink and to thrill their blood. Indeed, every assistance from externals is given the actor, such as daggers, bloody hands, ghosts, &c. but these must be treated judiciously or the effect, as we have sometimes seen it, may take a ludicrous turn.

Through all the soliloquies of anxious reflections in the first act; amidst the pangs of guilty apprehensions and pungent remorse in the second; through all the distracted terror of the third; all the impetuous curiosity of the fourth, and all the desperation of the fifth, Mr. GARRICK shows uniform, unabating excellence; scarce a look, motion, or tone but takes possession of our faculties and leads them to a just sensibility.

As SHAKESPEARE rises above himself in many places so does this his greatest and best commentator, who not only presents his beauties to the imagination but brings them home feelingly to the heart. Among a thousand other instances of almost necromantic merit let us turn our recollection only to a few in the character of Macbeth. Who ever saw the *immortal actor* start at, trace the imaginary dagger previous to Duncan's murder, without embodying, by sympathy, unsubstantial air into the alarming shape of such a weapon? Who ever heard the low but piercing notes of his voice when the *deed is done*, repeating those inimitable passages which mention the sleeping grooms and murder of sleep, without feeling a vibration of the nerves? Who ever saw the guilty distraction of features he assumes on Banquo's appearance at the feast without sacrificing reason to real apprehension from a mimic ghost? Who has heard his speech after receiving his death wound, uttered with the utmost agony of body and mind, but trembles at the idea of future punishment and almost pities the expiring wretch, though stained with crimes of deepest dye?[8]

---

7 According to mythology, Prometheus created men out of mud and water, then stole fire from Heaven to improve their lives, a crime for which Zeus punished him. Seeing Shakespeare as creating a man of his own, outside the order of nature, Gentleman seems to anticipate Mary Shelley's *Frankenstein, or the Modern Prometheus* (1818).

8 Garrick wrote this speech himself (see The Work in Performance, **pp. 106–7**).

54   INTERPRETATIONS

From **Thomas De Quincey, 'On the Knocking on the Gate in "Macbeth" '** (1823). Reprinted in D. Nichol Smith, ed., *Shakespeare Criticism: a Selection 1623–1840* (London: Oxford University Press, 1916, repr. 1958), pp. 335–6

Thomas De Quincey, one of the leading essayists of his day, made his living by writing for periodicals; this essay was first published in *The London Magazine*. In it he attempts to account for the curious power the knocking that follows Duncan's murder had on him when he first read the play as a boy (see Key Passages, **p. 154**). He argues that in his presentation of the murder, Shakespeare reverses the usual sympathies, making us concerned not for the victim but for the murderers. In order for them to do the deed, normal human nature has to be suspended. While Gentleman's view of Macbeth focuses on the character, De Quincey's account describes a general state of consciousness that begins with the characters but, as he writes, seems to float free of them.

Here, as I have said, the retiring of the human heart, and the entrance of the fiendish heart was to be expressed and made sensible. Another world has stept in; and the murderers are taken out of the region of human things, human purposes, human desires. They are transfigured: Lady Macbeth is 'unsexed;' Macbeth has forgot that he was born of woman; both are conformed to the image of devils; and the world of devils is suddenly revealed. But how shall this be conveyed and made palpable? In order that a new world may step in, this world must for a time disappear. The murderers, and the murder must be insulated—cut off by an immeasurable gulf from the ordinary tide and succession of human affairs—locked up and sequestered in some deep recess; we must be made sensible that the world of ordinary life is suddenly arrested—laid asleep—tranced—racked into a dread armistice; time must be annihilated; relation to things without abolished; and all must pass self-withdrawn into a deep syncope and suspension of earthly passion. Hence it is, that when the deed is done, when the work of darkness is perfect, then the world of darkness passes away like a pageantry in the clouds: the knocking at the gate is heard; and it makes known audibly that the reaction has commenced; the human has made its reflux upon the fiendish; the pulses of life are beginning to beat again; and the re-establishment of the goings-on of the world in which we live, first makes us profoundly sensible of the awful parenthesis that had suspended them.

From **A. C. Bradley, *Shakespearean Tragedy: Lectures on Hamlet, Othello, King Lear and Macbeth*** (1904; repr. London: Macmillan, 1956), pp. 352–6

At the beginning of the twentieth century, A. C. Bradley ranked as the most important contemporary Shakespeare critic, and *Shakespearean Tragedy* was considered his crowning achievement. (There was an often-repeated comic verse in which Shakespeare's ghost failed an exam on his own plays because he had not read Bradley.) His impact can be measured by the fact that so many critics in the years that followed spent so much time arguing against him; and his work still repays reading. Bradley saw the plays as embodying a cosmic struggle between good and evil, in a world where conventional religious belief had no answers. He saw the tragic hero's fate as stemming from his character, and this led him to a close analysis of character, conceived in realistic terms, that became the most controversial aspect of his work. In the extract that follows, he considers Macbeth's imaginative language as a function of Macbeth himself, not so much of the author or the play. In a sense it is Macbeth, not Shakespeare, who is the poet.

In the character as so far sketched there is nothing very peculiar, though the strength of the forces contending in it is unusual. But there is in Macbeth one marked peculiarity, the true apprehension of which is the key to Shakespeare's conception. This bold ambitious man of action has, within certain limits, the imagination of a poet,—an imagination on the one hand extremely sensitive to impressions of a certain kind, and, on the other, productive of violent disturbance both of mind and body. Through it he is kept in contact with supernatural impressions and is liable to supernatural fears. And through it, especially, come to him the intimations of conscience and honour. Macbeth's better nature—to put the matter for clearness' sake too broadly—instead of speaking to him in the overt language of moral ideas, commands, and prohibitions, incorporates itself in images which alarm and horrify. His imagination is thus the best of him, something usually deeper and higher than his conscious thoughts; and if he had obeyed it he would have been safe. But his wife quite misunderstands it, and he himself understands it only in part. The terrifying images which deter him from crime and follow its commission, and which are really the protest of his deepest self, seem to his wife the creations of mere nervous fear, and are sometimes referred by himself to the dread of vengeance or the restlessness of insecurity. His conscious or reflective mind, that is, moves chiefly among considerations of outward success and failure, while his inner being is convulsed by conscience. And his inability to understand himself is repeated and exaggerated in the interpretations of actors and critics, who represent him as a coward, coldblooded, calculating, and pitiless, who shrinks from crime simply because it is dangerous, and suffers afterwards simply because he is not safe. In reality his courage is frightful. He strides from crime to crime, though his soul never ceases to bar his advance with shapes of terror, or to clamour in his ears that he is murdering his peace and casting away his 'eternal jewel.'

It is of the first importance to realise the strength, and also (what has not been so clearly recognised) the limits, of Macbeth's imagination. It is not the universal meditative imagination of Hamlet. He came to see in man, as Hamlet sometimes did, the 'quintessence of dust'; but he must always have been incapable of Hamlet's reflections on man's noble reason and infinite faculty, or of seeing with Hamlet's eyes 'this brave o'erhanging firmament, this majestical roof fretted with golden fire.' Nor could he feel, like Othello, the romance of war or the infinity of love. He shows no sign of any unusual sensitiveness to the glory or beauty in the world or the soul; and it is partly for this reason that we have no inclination to love him, and that we regard him with more of awe than of pity. His imagination is excitable and intense, but narrow. That which stimulates it is, almost solely, that which thrills with sudden, startling, and often supernatural fear. There is a famous passage late in the play [. . .] which is here very significant, because it refers to a time before his conscience was burdened, and so shows his native disposition:

> The time has been, my senses would have cool'd
> To hear a night-shriek; and my fell of hair
> Would at a dismal treatise rise and stir
> As life were in't. [5.5.10–13]

This 'time' must have been in his youth, or at least before we see him. And, in the drama, everything which terrifies him is of this character, only it has now a deeper and a moral significance. Palpable dangers leave him unmoved or fill him with fire. He does himself mere justice when he asserts he 'dare do all that may become a man,' or when he exclaims to Banquo's ghost,

> What man dare, I dare:
> Approach thou like the rugged Russian bear,
> The arm'd rhinoceros, or the Hyrcan tiger;
> Take any shape but that, and my firm nerves
> Shall never tremble. [3.4.98–102]

What appals him is always the image of his own guilty heart or bloody deed, or some image which derives from them its terror or gloom. These, when they arise, hold him spell-bound and possess him wholly, like a hypnotic trance which is at the same time the ecstasy of a poet. As the first 'horrid image' of Duncan's murder—of himself murdering Duncan—rises from unconsciousness and confronts him, his hair stands on end and the outward scene vanishes from his eyes. Why? For fear of 'consequences'? The idea is ridiculous. Or because the deed is bloody? The man who with his 'smoking' steel 'carved out his passage' to the rebel leader, and 'unseam'd him from the nave to the chaps,' would hardly be frightened by blood. How could fear of consequences make the dagger he is to use hang suddenly glittering before him in the air, and then as suddenly dash it with gouts of blood? Even when he *talks* of consequences, and declares that if he were safe against them he would 'jump the life to come,' his imagination bears witness against him, and shows us that what really holds him back is the hideous vileness of the deed:

> He's here in double trust;
> First, as I am his kinsman and his subject,
> Strong both against the deed; then, as his host,
> Who should against his murderer shut the door,
> Not bear the knife myself. Besides, this Duncan
> Hath borne his faculties so meek, hath been

So clear in his great office, that his virtues
Will plead like angels, trumpet-tongued, against
The deep damnation of his taking-off;
And pity, like a naked new-born babe,
Striding the blast, or heaven's cherubim, horsed
Upon the sightless couriers of the air,
Shall blow the horrid deed in every eye,
That tears shall drown the wind. [1.7.12–25]

It may be said that he is here thinking of the horror that others will feel at the deed—thinking therefore of consequences. Yes, but could he realise thus how horrible the deed would look to others if it were not equally horrible to himself?

It is the same when the murder is done. He is well-nigh mad with horror, but it is not the horror of detection. It is not he who thinks of washing his hands or getting his nightgown on. He has brought away the daggers he should have left on the pillows of the grooms, but what does he care for that? What *he* thinks of is that, when he heard one of the men awaked from sleep say 'God bless us,' he could not say 'Amen'; for his imagination presents to him the parching of his throat as an immediate judgment from heaven. His wife heard the owl scream and the crickets cry; but what *he* heard was the voice that first cried 'Macbeth doth murder sleep,' and then, a minute later, with a change of tense, denounced on him, as if his three names gave him three personalities to suffer in, the doom of sleeplessness:

Glamis hath murdered sleep, and therefore Cawdor
Shall sleep no more, Macbeth shall sleep no more. [2.4.41–2]

There comes a sound of knocking. It should be perfectly familiar to him; but he knows not whence, or from what world, it comes. He looks down at his hands, and starts violently: 'What hands are here?' For they seem alive, they move, they mean to pluck out his eyes. He looks at one of them again; it does not move; but the blood upon it is enough to dye the whole ocean red. What has all this to do with fear of 'consequences'? It is his soul speaking in the only shape in which it can speak freely, that of imagination.

Modern Criticism

From **L. C. Knights, 'How Many Children Had Lady Macbeth? An Essay in the Theory and Practice of Shakespeare Criticism'**
(1933). Reprinted in *Explorations: Essays in Criticism Mainly on the Literature of the Seventeenth Century* (London: Chatto and Windus, 1946; repr. Harmondsworth: Penguin Books, 1964), pp. 30–3

L. C. Knights was a leading English Shakespeare critic, and an associate of the influential F. R. Leavis, whose insistence on a rigorous and principled analysis of literature transformed English studies in Britain. Knights himself was noted for provocative re-evaluations of literature – including, for example, a scathing attack on Restoration comedy. In his essay, 'How Many Children Had Lady Macbeth? An Essay in the Theory and Practice of Shakespeare Criticism' (which first appeared in 1933, and was based on a paper read to the Shakespeare Association) Knights takes on Bradley. Bradley's tendency to write about Shakespeare's characters as though they were real people led him to speculate about their lives outside the plays. In the second appendix to *Shakespearean Tragedy* (1904), for example, he asked where Hamlet was when his father was murdered. (I remember Knights, at a public lecture, giving the answer: 'in the tiring house'.) Hence the ironic title of Knights's essay.

It is the subtitle that proclaims the essay's real business, which is to analyse Shakespeare's plays as one would analyse a poem. In fact, at one point in this extract Knights proposes that we think of *Macbeth* as a poem; and just before the extract begins he declares that *Macbeth* has more in common with T. S. Eliot's *The Waste Land* than with Henrik Ibsen's *Doll's House*. Accordingly, he pays close attention to the language and its effect on the reader. Through the analysis runs an awareness of the play's concern with what is natural, and what is unnatural.

Each theme is stated in the first act. The first scene, every word of which will bear the closest scrutiny, strikes one dominant chord:

> Faire is foule, and foule is faire,
> Hover through the fogge and filthie ayre. [1.1.11–12]

It is worth remarking that 'Hurley-burley' implies more than 'the tumult of sedi-
tion or insurrection'. Both it and 'when the Battaile's lost, and wonne' suggest the
kind of metaphysical pitch-and-toss that is about to be played with good and evil.
At the same time we hear the undertone of uncertainty: the scene opens with a
question, and the second line suggests a region where the elements are disintegrated as they never are in nature; thunder and lightning are disjoined, and
offered as alternatives. We should notice also that the scene expresses the same
movement as the play as a whole: the general crystallizes into the immediate
particular ('Where the place?' – 'Upon the Heath' – 'There to meet with Macbeth')
and then dissolves again into the general presentment of hideous gloom. All is
done with the greatest speed, economy, and precision. [See Key Passages,
pp. 126–8.]

The second scene is full of images of confusion. It is a general principle in the
work of Shakespeare and many of his contemporaries that when A is made to
describe X, a minor character or event, the description is not merely immediately
applicable to X, it helps to determine the way in which our whole response shall
develop. This is rather crudely recognized when we say that certain lines 'create
the atmosphere' of the play. Shakespeare's power is seen in the way in which
details of this kind develop, check, or provide a commentary upon the main
interests that he has aroused. In the present scene the description

> – Doubtfull it stood,
> As two spent Swimmers, that doe cling together,
> And choake their Art – [1.2.7–9]

applies not only to the battle but to the ambiguity of Macbeth's future fortunes.
The impression conveyed is not only one of violence but of unnatural violence ('to
bathe in reeking wounds') and of a kind of nightmare gigantism:

> Where the Norweyan Banners flowt the Skie[,]
> And fanne our people cold. [1.2.50–1]

(These lines alone should be sufficient answer to those who doubt the authenticity
of the scene.)[1] When Duncan says, 'What he hath lost, Noble *Macbeth* hath
wonne,' we hear the echo,

> So from that Spring, whence comfort seem'd to come,
> Discomfort swells, [1.2.27–8]

– and this is not the only time the Captain's words can be applied in the course of
the play. Nor is it fantastic to suppose that in the account of Macdonwald Shakespeare consciously provided a parallel with the Macbeth of the later acts when
'The multiplying Villanies of Nature swarme upon him.' After all, everybody has
noticed the later parallel between Macbeth and Cawdor ('He was a Gentleman,
on whom I built an absolute Trust'). [See Key Passages, p. 130.]

---

1   For most readers this is now a non-issue; but some earlier critics, concerned to relieve Shakespeare
     of anything they thought unworthy of him, had doubted his authorship of this scene.

A poem works by calling into play, directing, and integrating certain interests. If we really accept the suggestion, which then becomes revolutionary, that *Macbeth* is a poem, it is clear that the impulses aroused in Act I, scenes i and ii, are part of the whole response, even if they are not all immediately relevant to the fortunes of the protagonist. If these scenes are 'the botching work of an interpolator', he botched to pretty good effect.

In Act I, scene iii, confusion is succeeded by uncertainty. The Witches

> looke not like th' Inhabitants o' th' Earth,
> And yet are on't. [1.3.41–2]

Banquo asks Macbeth,

> Why doe you start, and seeme to feare
> Things that doe sound so faire? [1.3.51–2]

He addresses the Witches,

> You should be women,
> And yet your Beards forbid me to interprete
> That you are so. . . .
> . . . i' th' name of truth
> Are [ye] fantasticall, or that indeed
> Which outwardly ye shew? [1.3.45–7, 52–4]

When they vanish, 'what seem'd corporall' melts 'as breath into the Winde'. The whole force of the uncertainty of the scene is gathered into Macbeth's soliloquy,

> This supernaturall solliciting
> Cannot be ill; cannot be good . . . [1.3.130–1]

which with its sickening see-saw rhythm completes the impression of 'a phantasma, or a hideous dream'.[2] [See Key Passages, **p. 138.**] Macbeth's echoing of the Witches' 'Faire is foule' has often been commented upon.

In contrast to the preceding scenes, Act I, scene iv, suggests that natural order which is shortly to be violated. It stresses: natural relationships – 'children', 'servants', 'sons', and 'kinsmen'; honourable bonds and the political order – 'liege', 'thanes', 'service', 'duty', 'loyalty', 'throne', 'state', and 'honour'; and the human 'love' is linked to the natural order of organic growth by images of husbandry. Duncan says to Macbeth,

> I have begun to plant thee, and will labour
> To make thee full of growing.

When he holds Banquo to his heart Banquo replies,

2   The phrase comes from a passage in Shakespeare's *Julius Caesar* (2.1.65) in which Brutus contemplates the murder of Caesar, rather as Macbeth contemplates the murder of Duncan.

> There if I grow,
> The Harvest is your owne.

Duncan's last speech is worth particular notice,

> . . . in his commendations, I am fed:
> It is a Banquet to me. [1.4.12–29, 32–3, 55–6]

At this point something should be said of what is meant by 'the natural order'. In *Macbeth* this comprehends both 'wild nature' – birds, beasts and reptiles – and humankind since 'humane statute purg'd the gentle Weale'. The specifically human aspect is related to the concept of propriety and degree:

> Degrees in Schooles and Brother-hoods in Cities,
> Peacefull Commerce from dividable shores,
> The primogenitive, and due of byrth,
> Prerogative of Age, Crownes, Scepters, Lawrels.[3]

In short, it represents society in harmony with nature, bound by love and friendship, and ordered by law and duty. It is one of the main axes of reference by which we take our emotional bearings in the play.

In the light of this the scene of Duncan's entry into the castle gains in significance. The critics have often remarked on the irony. What is not so frequently observed is that the key words of the scene are 'loved', 'wooingly', 'bed', 'procreant Cradle', 'breed, and haunt', all images of love and procreation, supernaturally sanctioned, for the associations of 'temple-haunting' colour the whole of the speeches of Banquo and Duncan. We do violence to the play when we ignore Shakespeare's insistence on what may be called the 'holy supernatural' as opposed to the 'supernaturall solliciting' of the Witches. I shall return to this point. Meanwhile it is pertinent to remember that Duncan himself is 'The Lords anoynted Temple' [2.3.69].

From **Cleanth Brooks, *The Well Wrought Urn: Studies in the Structure of Poetry*** (1947; repr. New York: Harcourt Brace and World, n.d.), pp. 34–48.

As the 'Leavisite' school to which L. C. Knights belonged was an important critical movement in Britain in the middle years of the twentieth century, 'New Criticism' dominated literary study in North America around the same time. Its leading exponent, along with W. K. Wimsatt, was Cleanth Brooks. New Criticism concentrated on a close reading of the language of a text, looking for patterns of words and images, tracing tensions and ironies. In its purest form it claimed to regard historical context and information about the author as

3   William Shakespeare, *Troilus and Cressida*, 1.3.104–7.

irrelevant. (This was a factor in the strong reaction against it, when criticism turned to seeing literary texts as closely bound up with the cultures that created them.) *The Well Wrought Urn* is a key text in this critical movement, and its title shows a characteristic interest in craft and structure. In his chapter 'The Naked Babe and the Cloak of Manliness' Brooks traces two patterns of imagery – clothing and children – as a way of establishing the underlying thought structures of *Macbeth*. He is interested not just in obvious meanings but in cases where the language is difficult and paradoxical. The first extract begins with an analysis of Angus's claim that Macbeth's title hangs loosely on him, 'like a giant's robe / Upon a dwarfish thief' (5.2.21–2).

The crucial point of the comparison, it seems to me, lies not in the smallness of the man and the largeness of the robes, but rather in the fact that—whether the man be large or small—these are not *his* garments; in Macbeth's case they are actually stolen garments. Macbeth is uncomfortable in them because he is continually conscious of the fact that they do not belong to him. There is a further point, and it is one of the utmost importance; the oldest symbol for the hypocrite is that of the man who cloaks his true nature under a disguise. Macbeth loathes playing the part of the hypocrite—and actually does not play it too well. If we keep this in mind as we look back at the instances of the garment images which Miss Spurgeon has collected for us,[1] we shall see that the pattern of imagery becomes very rich indeed. Macbeth says in Act I:

> *The Thane of Cawdor lives: why do you dress me*
> *In borrow'd robes?* [1.3.108–9]

Macbeth at this point wants no honors that are not honestly his. Banquo says in Act I:

> *New honours come upon him,*
> *Like our strange garments, cleave not to their mould,*
> *But with the aid of use.* [1.3.145–7]

But Banquo's remark, one must observe, is not censorious. It is indeed a compliment to say of one that he wears new honors with some awkwardness. The observation becomes ironical only in terms of what is to occur later.

Macbeth says in Act I:

> *He hath honour'd me of late; and I have bought*
> *Golden opinions from all sorts of people,*
> *Which would be worn now in their newest gloss,*
> *Not cast aside so soon.* [1.7.32–5]

---

1   Caroline Spurgeon, *Shakespeare's Imagery and What It Tells Us* (Cambridge: Cambridge University Press, 1935), catalogues different categories of imagery in Shakespeare, using them to draw conclusions about his imagination.

Macbeth here is proud of his new clothes: he is happy to wear what he has truly earned. It is the part of simple good husbandry not to throw aside these new garments and replace them with robes stolen from Duncan.

But Macbeth has already been wearing Duncan's garments in anticipation, as his wife implies in the metaphor with which she answers him:

> Was the hope drunk,
> Wherein you dress'd yourself? [1.7.35–6]

(The metaphor may seem hopelessly mixed, and a full and accurate analysis of such mixed metaphors in terms of the premises of Shakespeare's style waits upon some critic who will have to consider not only this passage but many more like it in Shakespeare.) For our purposes here, however, one may observe that the psychological line, the line of the basic symbolism, runs on unbroken. A man dressed in a drunken hope is garbed in strange attire indeed—a ridiculous dress which accords thoroughly with the contemptuous picture that Lady Macbeth wishes to evoke. Macbeth's earlier dream of glory has been a drunken fantasy merely, if he flinches from action now. [. . .]

The clothes imagery, used sometimes with emphasis on one aspect of it, sometimes, on another, does pervade the play. And it should be evident that the daggers "breech'd with gore"—though Miss Spurgeon does not include the passage in her examples of clothes imagery—represent one more variant of this general symbol. Consider the passage once more:

> Here lay Duncan,
> His silver skin lac'd with his golden blood;
> And his gash'd stabs look'd like a breach in nature
> For ruin's wasteful entrance: there, the murderers,
> Steep'd in the colours of their trade, their daggers
> Unmannerly breech'd with gore. . . . [2.3.111–16]

The clothes imagery runs throughout the passage; the body of the king is dressed in the most precious of garments, the blood royal itself; and the daggers too are dressed—in the same garment. The daggers, "naked" except for their lower parts which are reddened with blood, are like men in "unmannerly" dress—men, naked except for their red breeches, lying beside the red-handed grooms. The figure, though vivid, is fantastic; granted. But the basis for the comparison is *not* slight and adventitious. The metaphor fits the real situation on the deepest levels. As Macbeth and Lennox burst into the room, they find the daggers wearing, as Macbeth knows all too well, a horrible masquerade. They have been carefully "clothed" to play a part. They are not honest daggers, honorably naked in readiness to guard the king, or, "mannerly" clothed in their own sheaths. Yet the disguise which they wear will enable Macbeth to assume the robes of Duncan—robes to which he is no more entitled than are the daggers to the royal garments which they now wear, grotesquely. [. . .]

It is because of his hopes for his own children and his fears of Banquo's that he has returned to the witches for counsel. It is altogether appropriate, therefore, that two of the apparitions by which their counsel is revealed should be babes, the crowned babe and the bloody babe.

For the babe signifies the future which Macbeth would control and cannot control. It is the unpredictable thing itself—as Yeats has put it magnificently, "The uncontrollable mystery on the bestial floor."[2] It is the one thing that can justify, even in Macbeth's mind, the murders which he has committed. Earlier in the play, Macbeth had declared that if the deed could "trammel up the consequence," he would be willing to "jump the life to come." But he cannot jump the life to come. In his own terms he is betrayed. For it is idle to speak of jumping the life to come if one yearns to found a line of kings. It is the babe that betrays Macbeth—his own babes, most of all.

The logic of Macbeth's distraught mind, thus, forces him to make war on children, a war which in itself reflects his desperation and is a confession of weakness. Macbeth's ruffians, for example, break into Macduff's castle and kill his wife and children. The scene in which the innocent child prattles with his mother about his absent father, and then is murdered, is typical Shakespearean "fourth act" pathos. But the pathos is not adventitious; the scene ties into the inner symbolism of the play. For the child, in its helplessness, defies the murderers. Its defiance testifies to the force which threatens Macbeth and which Macbeth cannot destroy. [See Key Passages, **pp. 171–5.**]

But we are not, of course, to placard the child as The Future in a rather stiff and mechanical allegory. *Macbeth* is no such allegory. Shakespeare's symbols are richer and more flexible than that. The babe signifies not only the future; it symbolizes all those enlarging purposes which make life meaningful, and it symbolizes, furthermore, all those emotional and—to Lady Macbeth—irrational ties which make man more than a machine—which render him human. It signifies preeminently the pity which Macbeth, under Lady Macbeth's tutelage, would wean himself of as something "unmanly." Lady Macbeth's great speeches early in the play become brilliantly ironical when we realize that Shakespeare is using the same symbol for the unpredictable future that he uses for human compassion. Lady Macbeth is willing to go to any length to grasp the future: she would willingly dash out the brains of her own child if it stood in her way to that future. But this is to repudiate the future, for the child is its symbol.

Shakespeare does not, of course, limit himself to the symbolism of the child: he makes use of other symbols of growth and development, notably that of the plant. And this plant symbolism patterns itself to reflect the development of the play. For example, Banquo says to the Weird Sisters, early in the play:

> If you can look into the seeds of time,
> And say which grain will grow and which will not,
> Speak then to me. . . . [1.3.58–60]

A little later, on welcoming Macbeth, Duncan says to him:

> I have begun to plant thee, and will labour
> To make thee full of growing. [1.4.28–9]

After the murder of Duncan, Macbeth falls into the same metaphor when he comes to resolve on Banquo's death. The Weird sisters, he reflects, had hailed Banquo as

> ... *father to a line of kings.*
> *Upon my head they placed a fruitless crown,*
> *And put a barren sceptre in my gripe* .... [3.1.59–61]

Later in the play, Macbeth sees himself as the winter-stricken tree:

> *I have liv'd long enough: my way of life*
> *Is fall'n into the sear, the yellow leaf* .... [5.3.22–3]

The plant symbolism, then, supplements the child symbolism. At points it merges with it, as when Macbeth ponders bitterly that he has damned himself.

> *To make them kings, the seed of Banquo kings!* [3.1.69]

And, in at least one brilliant example, the plant symbolism unites with the clothes symbolism. It is a crowning irony that one of the Weird Sisters' prophecies on which Macbeth has staked his hopes is fulfilled when Birnam Forest comes to Dunsinane. For, in a sense, Macbeth is here hoist on his own petard. Macbeth, who has invoked night to "Scarf up the tender eye of pitiful day," and who has, again and again, used the "false face" to "hide what the false heart doth know," here has the trick turned against him. But the garment which cloaks the avengers is the living green of nature itself, and nature seems, to the startled eyes of his sentinels, to be rising up against him.

But it is the babe, the child, that dominates the symbolism. Most fittingly, the last of the prophecies in which Macbeth has placed his confidence, concerns the child: and Macbeth comes to know the final worst when Macduff declares to him that he was not only "born of woman" but was from his "mother's womb/ Untimely ripp'd." The babe here has defied even the thing which one feels may be reasonably predicted of him—his time of birth. With Macduff's pronouncement, the unpredictable has broken through the last shred of the net of calculation. The future cannot be trammelled up. The naked babe confronts Macbeth to pronounce his doom.

From **John Holloway, *The Story of the Night: Studies in Shakespeare's Major Tragedies*** (London: Routledge and Kegan Paul, 1961), pp. 63–6.

British critic and poet John Holloway is concerned, like Cleanth Brooks, with patterns of imagery in *Macbeth*. The difference is that he makes links with material outside the play – with the Book of Revelation, the final book of the Bible; and with folk festival. On the latter point in particular, Holloway's interest in seasonal folk customs is characteristic of his time, and in the criticism of Shakespeare this vein is still being tapped.

There is another 'apparition' (as it might be called) besides that of the bloody man, which haunts this play, and expresses and symbolizes this aspect of Macbeth's rôle, his journey in the direction of universal chaos. It is that of riders and horses, and it seems to have gone unnoticed by critics up to now. To register the full contribution which this image makes to the play, one should call to mind something of what the armed rider, and indeed the horse itself (that almost extinct animal, at least in the *milieu* of critics) stood for in Shakespeare's society, as for millennia before. The armed rider was the surest and swiftest of all human messengers, and the signal embodiment of violence, warfare, brigandage, revolt. The horse was the most powerful and valuable of the species which served man, and at the same time, if it rebelled, the most spirited, mischievous and formidable. Both were deeply ambiguous figures, inviting admiration and fear at once.

How these images contribute to *Macbeth* becomes clearer, in fact, once their contribution to *Lear* is seen as well; but even without anticipating this feature of that play, the facts are plain enough. The oft-quoted horses of Duncan that 'turned wild in nature' and ate each other like monsters [2.4.16] should be seen in this light: their monstrous act is the more terrifying because it brings to life what within the world of the play is a permanently latent fear. A passage from the *Homily against Wilful Rebellion*[1] illuminates this episode. When married men revolt, it runs, they leave their wives at home, which is bad enough. It is much worse when the unmarried revolt: 'being now by rebellion set at liberty from correction of laws, they pursue other men's wives and daughters . . . *worse than any stallions or horses*'. Unexpectedly perhaps for our own time, it is the horse which proves to be the obvious illustration of unbridled violence. The disturbing image runs throughout the play. The crucial scenes of the murder in Macbeth's castle at Inverness are set in the context of the arrival first of the Macbeth's messenger:

> One of my fellows had the speed of him,
> Who, almost dead for breath, had scarcely more
> Than would make up his message. [1.5.35–7]

and then of the furiously galloping Macbeth himself:

> *Duncan:* Where's the Thane of Cawdor?
>   We coursed him at the heels and had a purpose
>   To be his purveyor; but he rides well,
>   And his great love, sharp as his spur, hath holp him
>   To his home before us. [1.6.20–4]

The murderers waiting for Banquo and Fleance hear their horses' hooves as they stand waiting in the dark. 'Hark, I hear horses', says the Third Murderer [3.3.8]: and Macbeth's earlier 'I wish your horses sure and swift of foot' [3.1.37] has

---

1   The two Books of Homilies (1547 and 1563) were issued by the Church of England and meant to be read aloud in churches to edify the congregation. They represented official doctrine.

made it clear that the horses (in imagination, or by theatrical device) are at a gallop. We are to envisage the same before Macbeth's last battle:

> Send out more horses, skirr the country round,
> Hang those that talk of fear [5.3.35–6]

and it is this sound again which Macbeth hears after his last meeting with the witches:

> Infected be the air whereon they ride;
> And damn'd all those that trust them! I did hear
> The galloping of horse. Who was't came by? [4.1.138–40]

What he hears, moreover (or so the spectator's impression should run), is not the presumably soundless riding away of the witches, nor merely that of the men who bring him news of Macduff's flight to England. In the last analysis, he hears also those who properly preside unseen at such a meeting; and these are the

> heaven's cherubim hors'd
> Upon the sightless couriers of the air

of his first soliloquy [1.7.22–3]. Nor is the word 'hors'd' here wholly figurative: a more literal interpretation of it will bring to mind heavenly cherubim that belong to this context, and that come down from a then universally known passage of scripture:

> And I sawe, and beholde, a white horse, and hee that sate on hym had a bowe, and a crowne was geuen vnto hym, and he went foorth conquering, and for to overcome. . . . And there went out another horse that was redde: and power was geuen to him that sate thereon to take peace from the earth, and that they should kyl one another. . . . And I behelde, and loe, a blacke horse: and he that sate on hym hadde a pair of ballances in his hande. . . . And I looked, and beholde a pale horse, & his name that sate on hym was death, and hel folowed with him: and power was geuen vnto them, ouer the fourth part of the earth, to kyl with sworde, & with hunger, and with dearth, and with the beastes of the earth.
> (Rev. 6, 2–8)

The horses that Macbeth hears galloping are the Four Horsemen of the Apocalypse: bringing, as they ride over the earth, the disasters which are the proper result of, proper retribution for, human evil.

  That the play depicts disorder spreading throughout a whole society ('bleed, bleed poor country': [4.3.31]) is a commonplace. So is it, indeed, that this is seen as an infringement of the whole beneficent order of Nature; and that nothing less than that whole beneficent order gears itself, at last, to ending the state of evil ('. . . the pow'rs above / Put on their instruments' [4.3.238–9]). That the coming of Birnam Wood to Dunsinane is a vivid emblem of this, a dumbshow of nature overturning anti-nature at the climax of the play, has gone unnoticed. Professor Knights once suggested that in this scene, 'nature becomes unnatural in order to rid itself of Macbeth', or rather, that it was 'emphasizing the disorder' by showing the forces of good in association with deceit and with the *un*natural.[2] To a contemporary audience, however, the scene must have presented a much more familiar and less unnatural appearance than it does to ourselves. The single figure, dressed in his distinctive costume (one should have Macbeth in his war equipment in mind) pursued by a whole company of others carrying green branches, was a familiar sight as a Maying procession, celebrating the triumph of new life over the sere and yellow leaf of winter. Herrick's *Corinna's Going a-Maying* brings out not only the gaiety of the occasion, and its intimate connections with procreation and new life even in the human sphere, but also how familiar such scenes must have been in Shakespeare's time and indeed long after:

> There's not a budding youth, or girl, this day
> But is got up, and gone to bring in May.
> A deal of youth, ere this, is come
> Back, and with white-thorn laden home.
> And some have wept, and wooed, and plighted troth,
> Many a green-gown has been given
> Many a kiss both odd and even . . .
> Many a jest told of the keys betraying
> This night, and locks picked, yet we're not a-Maying.

One should remember that the May procession, with its green branches, survived even in the London Strand until as late as the 1890s.[3]

From **Joan Larsen Klein, 'Lady Macbeth: "Infirm of Purpose" '**, in Carolyn Ruth Swift Lenz, Gayle Greene and Carol Thomas Neely, eds, *The Woman's Part: Feminist Criticism of Shakespeare* (Urbana: University of Illinois Press, 1980), pp. 246–50

The Woman's Part was a breakthrough collection of American feminist essays on Shakespeare. While early discussions of Lady Macbeth tended to make her a powerful, alarming, somewhat inhuman figure, Joan Larsen Klein's essay puts the focus on her vulnerability, in the context of the conventional gender roles within which she has to operate. She emerges as a very human figure, isolated and even victimized in a male-dominated world. Klein's view of Lady Macbeth's marriage as broken and empty contrasts sharply with that of Barbara Everett (see Modern Criticism, **pp. 75–7**).

As soon as Duncan's murder is a public fact, Lady Macbeth begins to lose her place in society and her position at home. She does so because there is no room for her in the exclusively male world of treason and revenge. Therefore, her true

---

2   [Holloway's note, expanded.] L. C. Knights, *Explorations* (London: Chatto and Windus, 1946), p. 34.
3   Janet Adelman presents a very different reading of Birnam Wood (see Modern Criticism, **p. 82**).

weakness and lack of consequence are first revealed in the discovery scene. Lady Macbeth's feeble and domestic response, for instance, to the news she expected to hear—"What, in our house?" [2.3.88]—is very different from the cries and clamors she said she would raise. When she asks Macduff the domestic question, "What's the business" that wakes the "sleepers of the house?" [2.3.82–4], he refuses to answer a "gentle lady": "'Tis not for you to hear what I can speak" [2.3.84–5]. It is apparent, therefore, that Lady Macbeth has as little place in the male world of revenge as she had in the male world of war. Thus it may be that her faint is genuine, a confirmation of her debility. On the other hand, if her faint is only pretended in order to shield Macbeth, it is still a particularly feminine ploy. True or false, it dramatically symbolizes weakness. It has the further effect of removing her from the center of events to the periphery, from whence she never returns. It is characteristic that Macbeth, busy defending himself, ignores his lady's fall. Only Banquo and Macduff in the midst of genuine grief take time to "Look to the lady" [2.3.119, 125].

After Macbeth becomes king, he, the man, so fully commands Lady Macbeth that he allows her no share in his new business. No longer his accomplice, she loses her role as housekeeper. Macbeth plans the next feast, not Lady Macbeth. It is Macbeth who invites Banquo to it, not Lady Macbeth, who had welcomed Duncan to Inverness by herself. When Macbeth commands his nobles to leave him alone, Lady Macbeth withdraws silently and unnoticed along with them [3.1.39–43]. Macbeth does not tell Lady Macbeth that he plans to murder Banquo before his feast or even that he wanted Macduff to attend it. Although Macbeth needed Lady Macbeth to keep house during Duncan's murder, he disposes of Banquo well outside the castle walls. Thus Lady Macbeth is neither companion nor helpmate. Finally, in the great banquet scene, she loses even her faltering role as hostess. Because Macbeth is there beyond her reach and her comprehension, she is powerless. Ross, not Lady Macbeth, gives the first command to rise. When Lady Macbeth twice tries to tell the nobles that Macbeth has been thus since his youth, no one pretends to believe her. When she attempts to preserve the "good meeting" [3.4.108], even Macbeth ignores her. As soon as she is forced by Macbeth's actions to give over her last role, she dissolves in confusion the very society upon whose continuance that role depends. With her husband out of reach and society in shambles, Lady Macbeth no longer has any reason for being.

As soon as Macbeth abandons her company for that of the witches, Lady Macbeth is totally alone. In fact, Macbeth's union with the witches symbolizes the culmination of Lady Macbeth's loss of womanly social roles as well as her loss of home and family. But her growing isolation had been apparent from the moment her husband became king. Unlike Portia or Desdemona or even Macbeth himself, Lady Macbeth was never seen with friends or woman-servants in whose presence she could take comfort. Even when she appeared in company, she was the only woman there. Consequently, once she begins to lose her husband, she has neither person nor occupation to stave off the visitings of nature. All she has is time, time to succumb to that human kindness which, said Bright, no one could forget and remain human.[1] Thus, in Lady Macbeth's short soliloquy before

---

1   [Klein's note, expanded.] T. Bright, *A Treatise of Melancholy* (1586), p. 193.

Macbeth's feast, even though she still talks in terms of "we," she seems to be speaking only of herself. Alone and unoccupied, she is visited by the remorse and sorrow she had hoped to banish:

> Naught's had, all's spent,
> Where our desire is got without content.
> 'Tis safer to be that which we destroy
> Than by destruction dwell in doubtful joy. [3.2.4–7]

Lady Macbeth's existence now is circumscribed by the present memory of past loss. Absent from her mind is the sense of future promise she had anticipated before Duncan's murder when she thought herself transported beyond the "ignorant present" and felt "The future in the instant" [1.5.56–7]. In her words we also hear, I think, what Bright calls the afflictions of a guilt-ridden conscience, that "internal anguish [which] bereve[s] us of all delight" in "outward benefits."[2] Even after Macbeth joins Lady Macbeth, her words seem to continue her own thoughts, not to describe his: "Why do you keep alone, / Of sorriest fancies your companions making" [3.2.8–9]. For we know, as Lady Macbeth does not, that Macbeth is thinking of the coming murder of Banquo, not the past murder of Duncan. We know his recent companions have been murderers, not "fancies." Only Lady Macbeth suffers now the "repetition" of the "horror" of Duncan's death which Macduff had feared "in a woman's ear / Would murder as it fell" [2.3.81, 85–6]. When Lady Macbeth thinks to quiet her husband, she does so with advice she has already revealed she cannot herself take: "Things without all remedy / Should be without regard" [3.2.11–12]. But Macbeth no longer needs her advice: "Duncan is in his grave," he says, "nothing / Can touch him further" [3.2.22–6]. Thus Shakespeare shows that the differences between husband and wife are extreme. Macbeth wades deeper and deeper in blood in order to stifle the tortures of a mind which fears only the future: Banquo's increasing kingliness, Fleance and his unborn children, all living things and their seed. Lady Macbeth, her husband's "Sweet remembrancer" [3.4.36], does little else but think of horrors past: of the "air drawn" dagger which led Macbeth to Duncan [3.4.61], of the king slaughtered and her hands bloodied, of Banquo dead and Lady Macduff in realms unknown.

In the banquet scene, Lady Macbeth's words reveal an increase in weakness, emphasize the loss of her womanly roles, and lay bare her present isolation. Her scolding, for instance, is no more than a weak, futile imitation of the cruelty of her earlier goading. Her images, correspondingly, are more obviously feminine: "these flaws and starts," she tells Macbeth, "would well become / A woman's story at a winter's fire, / Authorized by her grandam" [3.4.62–5]. But her images also evoke a kind of homeliness and comfort she can never know: the security that other women feel when they sit at their warm hearths and tell tales to their children. In fact, Lady Macbeth's words describe the comforts of a home she so little knows that she uses the picture her words evoke to castigate a man who will soon destroy the only real home we see in the play. Thus it is not surprising that

---

2   [Klein's note.] Bright, *Treatise*, p. 185.

Lady Macbeth at the end of the banquet scene does not seem to realize that Macbeth is leaving her as well as the community of men to join the unsexed witches in an unholy union—one wherein they joy to "grieve his heart" [4.1.110]. As soon as Macbeth joins the witches, Lady Macbeth no longer has any place anywhere. Offstage, she is neither wife, queen, housekeeper, nor hostess. When we see her next, she will have lost the memories of motherhood and childhood she remembered so imperfectly and used so cruelly at the beginning of the play. She will also have lost that fragmented glimpse of womanly life she repudiates during her last banquet. [. . .]

Our final glimpse into the afflicted and brainsick mind of Lady Macbeth reveals that her doctor is either mistaken or lying when he says she is troubled with "thick-coming fancies" [5.3.38]. Her madness is not that melancholy which springs from delusion, but rather that which stems from true and substantial causes. Her mind, like her being as mother, child, wife, and hostess, has also been twisted by her destructive longing for Macbeth to murder cruelly and deliberately. When we see Lady Macbeth at the end, therefore, she is "womanly" only in that she is sick and weak. All the valor of her tongue is gone, as is her illusion of its power. The hands which she cannot sweeten with the perfumes of Arabia are the little hands of a woman. As long as she lives, Lady Macbeth is never unsexed in the only way she wanted to be unsexed—able to act with the cruelty she ignorantly and perversely identified with male strength. But she has lost that true strength which Shakespeare says elsewhere is based on pity and fostered by love.

From **Jenijoy La Belle, ' "A Strange Infirmity": Lady Macbeth's Amenorrhea'**, *Shakespeare Quarterly* 31 (1980), pp. 381–5

The new interest in historical context in later twentieth-century criticism included fresh research into the medical beliefs that informed the literature of the time. While Joan Larsen Klein is concerned with Lady Macbeth's role as a woman in social terms, Jenijoy La Belle is concerned with her as the possessor of a woman's body. Her analysis of Lady Macbeth's invocation of the spirits (1.5.40–54; see Key Passages, **p. 142**) is not poetic or spiritual but physiological; and it shows the links between the physiological and the psychological. La Belle also gives a medical grounding to the imagery of fertility noticed by earlier critics like L. C. Knights (see Modern Criticism, **pp. 60–1**).

To understand how Lady Macbeth hopes to achieve a change in her personality, it is important to read the speech in light of its simultaneous references to the physiological and the psychological. When Lady Macbeth commands the spirits of darkness to "unsex" her, it is not just a wish for a psychological movement away from the feminine. To free herself of the basic *psychological* characteristics of femininity, she is asking the spirits to eliminate the basic *biological* characteristics of femininity. Since there is a bond between mind and body, one way for Lady Macbeth to achieve an unfeminine consciousness capable of murdering Duncan is for her to attain an unfeminine physiology. My purpose here is not to reduce *Macbeth*, with its magnificent ethical and spiritual treatment of guilt, to a medical tract, but rather to elucidate this physiological dimension of the play in such a way as to give a more complete sense of *Macbeth*'s full literal and metaphoric meanings.

Lady Macbeth asks that "no compunctious visitings of Nature" shake her "fell purpose." Sylvan Barnet's edition of *Macbeth* interprets these "visitings of Nature" as "natural feelings of compassion." The Neilson and Hill edition interprets them as "conscientious scruples."[1] But "compunctious visitings" also has a biological meaning. Thomas Brugis, in *Vade Mecum: Or, A Companion For A Chyrurgion* (London, 1652), discusses "the overmuch flowing of womens naturall visits," defining "visits" as occurrences of menstruation. For a woman, menstruation is the most apparent natural visitation associated with her sexuality. More than any other natural and usually unavoidable event in a woman's life, it is menstruation that repeatedly reminds her of her sex.

Because of this biological reference, earlier images in Lady Macbeth's speech take on added significance. When she pleads "make thick my blood, / Stop up th' access and passage to remorse" [1.5.43–4], she is asking for the periodic flow to cease, the genital tract to be blocked. Renaissance medical texts generally refer to the tract through which the blood from the uterus is discharged as a "passage." The author of *The Byrth of Mankynde, otherwyse named the Womans Booke* (London, 1545) writes, "The necke of this wombe, otherwise callyd the womans privite, we wyll call the womb passage, or the privy passage." John Sadler explains in *The Sicke Womans Private Looking-Glasse wherein Methodically are handled all uterine affects, or diseases arising from the wombe* (London, 1636), that during "the suppression of the Termes [menses]," the blood thickens and coagulates: it becomes "viscuous and grosse, condensing and binding up the passages, that it cannot flow forth" (p. 15). Sadler also points out that "the wombe communicates to the heart by the mediation of those Arteries which come from Aorta" (p. 20). If the thickened blood blocks the passage of the womb, then, it also stops up the access to the heart from which remorse could flow.

In a very literal and physical way, Lady Macbeth is asking the spirits to "unsex" her. And this request has both a metaphoric and a causal relationship to the psychological transformation that must occur before she can participate in the murder of Duncan. That is, the suggestions of biological unsexing foreshadow Lady Macbeth's mental defeminization, her blocking of pity and remorse. Given the causal links between body and mind of Elizabethan physiological psychology, the biological unsexing will help to bring about the spiritual unsexing. For Lady Macbeth, then, this murder of her femininity is an essential preparation for the murder of the King.

After her entreaty for the suppression of menstruation, Lady Macbeth urges the "murth'ring ministers" to come to her "woman's breasts" and exchange her "milk for gall." There is a movement from the image of the womb (which would become infected from what one seventeenth-century medical directory for midwives calls "the burden of putrified blood") to the image of the corrupted breasts. Since both images deal with the pollution of the primary and secondary feminine

---

1 [La Belle's note.] *Macbeth*, ed. Sylvan Barnet (New York: New American Library, 1963), p. 51; *The Complete Plays and Poems of William Shakespeare*, eds William Alan Neilson and Charles Jarvis Hill (Boston, Mass.: Houghton Mifflin, 1942), p. 1189.

organs, the progression seems generally appropriate, but once again the context of Elizabethan medical beliefs shows that there is a direct causal connection between the two. In *The Sicke Womans Private Looking-Glasse*, Sadler defines the menstruals as "a monethly flux of excrementitious blood," the "finall cause" of which is "the propagation and conservation of mankinde":

> And all will grant it for a truth, that the childe, while it is in the matrice [womb] is nourished with this blood; and it is as true, that being out of the womb, it is still nourished with the same; for the milke is nothing but the menstruous bloud made white in the breasts; and I am sure womans milke is not thought to bee venomous, but of a nutritive quality, answerable to the tender mature of an infant.
>
> (pp. 9–10)

The Complete Midwife's Practice also characterizes "the menstruous Blood" as "the matter of the womans seed" (p. 87):

> Whilst the Birth remains in the Womb, it is cherished up with blood attracted through the Navel, which is the reason that the flowers [menses] do cease alwayes in Women, as soon as they have conceived.
>
> Now this blood, presently after conception, is distinguished into . . . parts; the purest part of it drawn by the Child for the nourishment of its self; the second, which is less pure and thin, the Womb forces upwards to the breast, where it is turned into milk.
>
> (pp. 92–93)

Menstrual blood is meant to nourish the infant—during pregnancy as blood and after pregnancy in its transformed state as milk. A stoppage of the menstrual blood therefore prevents the formation of mother's milk. In its place, Lady Macbeth wishes for a venomous liquid ("gall" or bile rather than "nutritive" fluid) to rise to her breasts. [. . .]

The most devastating outcome of Lady Macbeth's call to be unsexed is that she thereby renders herself barren. She calls for the same destruction of generative faculties that [M]acbeth wishes for in his curse against "Nature's germens"[2] [4.1.59]. And at the end of the play, her way of life, like Macbeth's, "is fall'n into the sere." "If you would have children," Nicholas Culpeper admonishes, "see that the Menstruis come down in good order" (*A Directory for Midwives*, p. 96). According to *The Complete Midwife's Practice*, if "the Menstruous blood . . . come not down according to their accustomed times, and seasons, or do not come down at all, the woman neither can conceive nor engender" (p. 87). As Lady Macbeth wills away her feminine sympathies, she wills away her ability to conceive. She is "blasted" like the heath—both barren and accursed—and "withered" like the "secret, black, and midnight hags." The play is full of images of fertility and growth, embodied primarily in Duncan. And just as Macbeth kills this royal symbol of fruitfulness, Lady Macbeth destroys her own fruitfulness. The spirits she calls on are indeed "murth'ring ministers" because they murder

---

2   Seeds, sperm.

the very possibility of children for her. Macbeth comes to learn that his crown is "fruitless," his scepter "barren," the succession "unlineal." What he may not realize is that his sterility is in part a consequence of Lady Macbeth's fruitless and barren womb. The destruction of the menstrual flow ultimately destroys the lineal flow. Like the Scotland described by Ross, Lady Macbeth is not the mother of her children, but their grave [4.3.166]. Because it is Lady Macbeth's own will to murder that causes her sterility, she is like the sow that "hath eaten / Her nine farrow" [4.1.64–5] and whose blood is used by the witches in their hellbroth.

From **Stephen Booth, *King Lear, Macbeth, Indefinition, and Tragedy*** (New Haven, Conn.: Yale University Press, 1983), pp. 93–4

American critic Stephen Booth is one of the masters of close reading, noted particularly for his work on Shakespeare's *Sonnets*. His close attention to language often leads to provocative, unorthodox conclusions. Here he challenges the apparently commonsense view, derived from Aristotle's *Poetics*, that a tragedy has a beginning, a middle and an end. This has implications for the traditional view of the play's conclusion as a decisive restoration of moral order; but, as Booth argues, a difficulty about endings – not to mention beginnings and middles – is pervasive in the play.

Finality is regularly unattainable throughout *Macbeth*: Macbeth and Lady Macbeth cannot get the murder of Duncan finished: Lady Macbeth has to go back with the knives. They cannot get done with Duncan himself: his blood will not wash off. Banquo refuses death in two ways: he comes back as a ghost, and (supposedly) he lives on in the line of Stuart kings into the actual present of the audience. The desirability and impossibility of conclusion is a regular concern of the characters, both in large matters ("The time has been / That, when the brains were out, the man would die, / And there an end"—[3.4.77–9]) and in such smaller ones as Macbeth's inability to achieve the temporary finality of sleep and Lady Macbeth's inability to cease her activity even in sleep itself. The concern for finality is incidentally present even in details like Macbeth's incapacity to pronounce "Amen."

What is true of endings is also true of beginnings. Lady Macbeth's mysteriously missing children present an ominous, unknown, but undeniable time before the beginning. Doubtful beginnings are also incidentally inherent in such details of the play as Macduff's nonbirth. Indeed, the beginnings, sources, causes, of almost everything in the play are at best nebulous.

Cause and effect do not work in *Macbeth*. The play keeps giving the impression that Lady Macbeth is the source of ideas and the instigator of actions that are already underway. For example, in III.ii the audience may have an impression that Lady Macbeth has some responsibility for the coming attack on Banquo and Fleance, but Macbeth has already commissioned the murderers. People have also tried to show that Lady Macbeth is as much the source of the idea of murdering Duncan as she seems to be. In fact, it is almost impossible to find the source of any idea in *Macbeth*; every new idea seems already there when it is presented to us.

The idea of regicide really originates in the mind of the audience, which comes into a world that presents only the positive action of treason or the negative action of opposing it.

The play, as play, has definition—a beginning, a middle, and an end—but its materials, even those that are used to designate its limits, provide insistent testimony to the artificiality, frailty, and ultimate impossibility of limits. A sense of limitlessness infuses every element of the play.

From **Barbara Everett, *Young Hamlet: Essays on Shakespeare's Tragedies*** (Oxford: Clarendon Press, 1989), pp. 102–4

The work of British critic Barbara Everett is not bound by a particular school or theoretical approach. Through close, imaginative reading of the text itself she draws out the human dimension of the action. In her chapter '*Macbeth*: Succeeding' she analyses the closeness of the Macbeths' marriage. Her view of it may be contrasted with that of Joan Larsen Klein (see Modern Criticism, **pp. 68–71**).

Macbeth is a tragedy extremely bare in human relationship: which is what gives that between Macbeth and Lady Macbeth such intensity, such strength and life. The two Macbeths between them sacrifice every other possibility of relationship that might have opened round them. But every now and again there is a kind of curtain lifted in the tragedy and we see one of these lost possibilities. While Macbeth is murdering Duncan Lady Macbeth tells us, 'Had he not resembled | My Father as he slept, I had don't' [2.2.12–13]. Lady Macbeth with a father is a troublingly different thing. The Witches have a somewhat similar effect on Macbeth. Because of his murders, he needs them—he is drawn into their company, he hunts them out, it is almost an infatuation. He is even, we might say, like a weak and childish man who is always abandoning his family and allows himself to be drawn back into the spoiling care and comfort of a collection of elderly female relatives. The Witches are dingy, bad pre-Volumnias,[1] who locate in the play the faintest hint of that destructive power-relationship of mother and son more sharply present in *Coriolanus*: 'Give me, quoth I'. The resemblance is just enough to make us see how Macbeth lacks that human rootedness as well. Certainly these unreal 'mothers' give him nothing except a form of knowledge he would in any case have been infinitely better without.

The simplest form of the evil that the Witches do to Macbeth—though the truth is that he does it to himself—is to draw him away from Lady Macbeth. Because of the play's marked thinness in terms of character, we feel the coexistence of these two acutely. Though the soul, as it were, of Macbeth's tragedy is the slow destruction of his inner self—the luminous moral imagination that understands everything that is happening to him—the heart of his tragedy is the destruction of his marriage. Lady Macbeth is all relationship to Macbeth—she is his rooting in human life.

---

1   Volumnia is the domineering mother of the title character in Shakespeare's *Coriolanus*.

In a recent interview about his production of *Macbeth*, Sir Peter Hall remarked—and he said it several times, with insistence—that Lady Macbeth is 'very, very sexy'. I find this modish jazzing up of the part saddening; it almost ideally misses by overshooting the real point of the darkly ironical fact that the Macbeths are probably Shakespeare's most thoroughly married couple. Not just lecherous but married: and these aren't the same things. The Macbeths have an extraordinary community and complicity. Some of the play's most troubling moments are those which reach ahead through (say) Chekhov and Ibsen and Strindberg, and many current writers, into 'the woe that is in marriage':[2] the Macbeths become that terrible couple who appear so early in the play, 'two spent Swimmers, that doe cling together[,] | And choake their Art' [1.2.8–9]—their love is so corrupted by the struggle to survive as to pull each other down. Macbeth, to put it simply, loves Lady Macbeth; they love each other; at the painful III. ii, where they first show a marked drift away from each other, each minds. Macbeth addresses his wife with troubled extra care, as 'Love', 'deare Wife', and 'dearest Chuck'. The tragic mutual destructiveness of the marriage is summed up by a simple fact. Married couples invariably, if it is a true marriage, grow like each other. The Macbeths slowly exchange qualities in the course of the play. From the beginning Lady Macbeth has brought to their life a directness, a practicality, an inability to see difficulties in a good cause. Only, she can't see difficulties in a bad cause, either. 'But screw your courage to the sticking place[,] | And wee'le not fayle' [1.7.61–2]. The crux over what precisely her first 'We faile?' [1.7.60] means is interesting: she genuinely can't imagine—she can't cope with ifs; she simply throws Macbeth's phrases back at him. And this practicality moves into Macbeth in the form of brutality—which is why he starts not to need her any more. Lady Macbeth for her part inherits his imagination, but only in the form of nightmare. And she can't live with it: it stops her sleeping ever again.

I want to stress the fact of Shakespeare's depth and seriousness and even tenderness in depicting their marriage. One of the play's most touching and subtle moments is that which brings Lady Macbeth before us for the first time, and she is reading Macbeth's letter: he exists for her when he isn't there. He exists too much for her when he isn't there, she plans and thinks ahead too much for him, she too much connives, putting her image of Macbeth's future where her conscience should be: as the Doctor says, staring at her wide-open but out-of-touch gaze, 'You have knowne what you should not.' And the Gentlewoman adds, 'Heaven knowes what she has known' [5.1.45–7]. Lady Macbeth is Macbeth's 'Dearest Partner of Greatnesse', the tender yet arrogant phrase Macbeth uses to her in his letter, as if the one thing in the world a good marriage were for, were getting a throne. And there begins from that point the insidious corruption of the good which I mentioned earlier:

> yet I doe feare thy Nature,
> It is too full o'th' Milke of humane kindnesse,
> To catch the neerest way . . . [1.5.16–18]

For Lady Macbeth's immediate action, when she knows that the King is coming,

2   Geoffrey Chaucer, *The Wife of Bath's Prologue*, l.3.

is to call to spirits to 'Unsex me here'—to make herself no more a woman. She is sacrificing to Macbeth's success his succession—their hope of children: When the two of them meet at I. vii, it is the hope of children, and the destruction of children, that is a theme of what they say to each other.

From **Harriett Hawkins,** *Classics and Trash: Traditions and Taboos in High Literature and Popular Modern Genres* (Toronto: University of Toronto Press, 1990), pp. 124–5

Harriett Hawkins, an American scholar who taught in Britain, enjoyed challenging the solemnities of academic writing. As its title implies, *Classics and Trash* breaks the barrier between high culture and popular culture. This extract comes from a chapter titled 'From "King Lear" to "King Kong" and back'. By relating *Macbeth* to the conventions of the werewolf movie, Hawkins restores in new terms the terror that eighteenth-century and Romantic critics felt in the play.

An unforgettable experience of pity and terror[1] shared by everyone who saw it at an early and impressionable age was evoked by the original werewolf movie *The Wolf Man* (1941), starring Lon Chaney, Jr, as a man who had been attacked by what appeared to be a wolf. Soon after, we in the audience, along with the horrified hero, were informed by an old woman that, ever after, when the moon was full, he would turn into a werewolf:

> Even a man who is pure at heart
> And says his prayers by night
> Can become a wolf when the wolfbane[2] blooms
> And the moon is shining bright.

As the moon rose we – and he – watched with horror as the mutation began and the wolf fur started to grow on his hands and face. The force compelling the mutation was indeed inexorable and subsequently drove him to commit murder after murder. The only way the werewolf himself could be killed was with a silver-tipped cane displaying the head of a wolf and the design of a pentagon. This is essentially the same movement that occurs in *Macbeth*. But before going on to discuss the structural and thematic similarities, it should be observed that [. . .] the line of succession between *Macbeth* and werewolf films moves on and on through time, even as the lycanthropic[3] hero of *An American Werewolf in London* (1981) himself most vividly remembered having seen the original werewolf movie under discussion here.

---

1   According to Aristotle's *Poetics* – a High Culture text if ever there was one – these are the emotions roused by tragedy.
2   Aconite.
3   Lycanthropy is an illness in which a person imagines he is a wolf; here the word is used for the actual transformation.

At the beginning of Shakespeare's tragedy Macbeth is, as a result of the witches' prophecies, bitten and infected by the external–internal werewolf of ambition and inexorably mutates into a monster. Subsequently driven to commit murder after murder Macbeth, like the hero-victim-villain of *The Wolf Man*, looks on *himself* as if he were an alien creature:

What hands are here? Ha! they pluck out mine eyes.

To know my deed, 'twere best not know myself.

Had I but died an hour before this chance,
I had lived a blessed time.

                    Better be with the dead,
Whom we, to gain our peace, have sent to peace.
Than on the torture of the mind to lie,
In restless ecstasy. [2.2.58, 72; 2.3.91–2; 3.2.19–22]

Macbeth thus describes the fate worse than death familiar to all of us from countless horror movies depicting the state of the 'undead' who cannot find peace in life and envy the dead. For Macbeth himself cannot be killed save by the Shakespearian equivalents of a silver-tipped cane displaying the head of a wolf and the design of a pentagon. He cannot die until Birnam Wood comes to Dunsinane; only a man who was 'not of woman born' can kill Macbeth.

From **Janet Adelman, *Suffocating Mothers: Fantasies of Maternal Origin in Shakespeare's Plays, Hamlet to The Tempest*** (New York: Routledge, 1992), pp. 132–4, 142–4

American scholar Janet Adelman combines feminist and psychoanalytic approaches in her analysis of *Macbeth*. Here, maleness and femaleness are not social roles, as for Joan Larsen Klein (see Modern Criticism, **pp. 68–71**), but archetypal forces. They have a social dimension, but they affect both society and individuals at a deep, even subconscious level. The extract begins with an analysis of Duncan as an ineffective father figure – like Holinshed's Duncan (see Source, **pp. 18–20**), too soft for kingship.

Heavily idealized, this ideally protective father is nonetheless largely ineffectual: even while he is alive, he is unable to hold his kingdom together, reliant on a series of bloody men to suppress an increasingly successful series of rebellions. The witches are already abroad in his realm; they in fact constitute our introduction to that realm. Duncan, not Macbeth, is the first person to echo them ("When the battle's lost and won" [1.1.4]; "What he hath lost, noble Macbeth hath won" [1.2.69]). The witches' sexual ambiguity terrifies: Banquo says of them, "You should be women, / And yet your beards forbid me to interpret / That you are so" [1.3.45–7]. Is their androgyny the shadow-side of the King's, enabled perhaps by his failure to maintain a protective masculine authority? Is their strength a consequence of his weakness? (This is the configuration of *Cymbeline*, where the power of the witch-queen-stepmother is so dependent on the failure of Cymbeline's masculine authority that she obligingly dies when that authority returns to him.) Banquo's question to the witches may ask us to hear a counter-question about Duncan, who should be man. For Duncan's androgyny is the object of enormous ambivalence: idealized for his nurturing paternity, he is nonetheless killed for his womanish softness, his childish trust, his inability to read men's minds in their faces, his reliance on the fighting of sons who can rebel against him. Macbeth's description of the dead Duncan—"his silver skin lac'd with his golden blood" [2.3.112]—makes him into a virtual icon of kingly worth; but other images surrounding his death make him into an emblem not of masculine authority but of feminine vulnerability. As he moves toward the murder, Macbeth first imagines himself the allegorical figure of Murder, as though to absolve himself of the responsibility of choice. But the figure of murder then fuses with that of Tarquin:

> wither'd Murther,
> . . . thus with his stealthy pace,
> With Tarquin's ravishing strides, towards his design
> Moves like a ghost. [2.1.52–6]

These lines figure the murder as a display of male sexual aggression against a passive female victim: murder here becomes rape; Macbeth's victim becomes not the powerful male figure of the king but the helpless Lucrece. Hardened by Lady Macbeth to regard maleness and violence as equivalent, that is, Macbeth responds to Duncan's idealized milky gentleness as though it were evidence of his femaleness. The horror of this gender transformation, as well as the horror of the murder, is implicit in Macduff's identification of the king's body as a new Gorgon ("Approach the chamber, and destroy your sight / With a new Gorgon" [2.3.72–3]). The power of this image lies partly in its suggestion that Duncan's bloodied body, with its multiple wounds, has been revealed as female and hence blinding to his sons: as if the threat all along was that Duncan would be revealed as female and that this revelation would rob his sons of his masculine protection and hence of their own masculinity.

In *King Lear*, the abdication of protective paternal power seems to release the destructive power of a female chaos imaged not only in Goneril and Regan but also in the storm on the heath. Macbeth virtually alludes to Lear's storm as he approaches the witches in Act IV, conjuring them to answer though they "untie the winds, and let them fight / Against the Churches," though the "waves / Confound and swallow navigation up," though "the treasure / Of Nature's germens tumble all together, / Even till destruction sicken" [4.1.52–60; see *King Lear*, 3.2.1–9]. The witches merely implicit on Lear's heath have become in *Macbeth* embodied agents of storm and disorder, and they are there from the start. Their presence suggests that the paternal absence that unleashes female chaos (as in *Lear*) has already happened at the beginning of *Macbeth*. That absence is merely made literal in Macbeth's murder of Duncan at the instigation of female forces: from the start, this father-king cannot protect his sons from powerful mothers, and it is the son's—and the play's—revenge to kill him, or, more precisely, to kill him first and love him after, paying him back for his excessively "womanish" trust and then memorializing him as the ideal androgynous parent. The reconstitution of manhood becomes a central problem in the play in part, I think, because the vision of manhood embodied in Duncan has already failed at the play's beginning.

The witches constitute our introduction to the realm of maternal malevolence unleashed by the loss of paternal protection; as soon as Macbeth meets them, he becomes (in Hecate's probably non-Shakespearean words) their "wayward son" [3.5.11]. This maternal malevolence is given its most horrifying expression in Shakespeare in the image through which Lady Macbeth secures her control over Macbeth:

> I have given suck, and know
> How tender 'tis to love the babe that milks me:
> I would, while it was smiling in my face,
> Have pluck'd my nipple from his boneless gums,
> And dash'd the brains out, had I so sworn
> As you have done to this. [1.7.54–9]

This image of murderously disrupted nurturance is the psychic equivalent of the witches' poisonous cauldron; both function to subject Macbeth's will to female forces. For the play strikingly constructs the fantasy of subjection to maternal malevolence in two parts, in the witches and in Lady Macbeth, and then persistently identifies the two parts as one. Through this identification, Shakespeare in effect locates the source of his culture's fear of witchcraft in individual human history, in the infant's long dependence on female figures felt as all-powerful: what the witches suggest about the vulnerability of men to female power on the cosmic plane, Lady Macbeth doubles on the psychological plane. [. . .]

The answer to the malevolent power of the female begins with a violent subduing of the female, conveyed in the language that describes the war sequence at the play's beginning (see Key Passages, **pp. 128–32**).

In effect, then, the battle that supports the father's kingdom plays out the creation of an all-conquering male erotics that marks its conquest by its triumph over a feminized body, simultaneously that of Fortune and Macdonwald. Hence, in the double action of the passage, the victorious unseaming happens twice: first on the body of Fortune and then on the body of Macdonwald. The lines descriptive of Macbeth's approach to Macdonwald—"brave Macbeth . . . Disdaining Fortune, with his brandish'd steel, / . . . carv'd out his passage" [1.2.16–19]—make that approach contingent on Macbeth's first carving his passage through a female body, like Richard III hewing his way out (3 Henry VI, 3.2.181). The language here perfectly anticipates Macduff's birth by caesarian section, revealed at the end of the play: if Macduff is ripped untimely from his mother's womb, Macbeth here manages in fantasy his own caesarian section, carving his passage out from the unreliable female to achieve heroic male action, in effect carving up the female to arrive at the male. Only after this rite of passage can Macbeth meet Macdonwald: this act of aggression toward the female body, with its accompanying fantasy of self-birth, marks Macbeth's passage to the contest that will define his maleness partly by attributing femaleness to Macdonwald. For the all-male community surrounding Duncan, then, Macbeth's victory is allied with his triumph over femaleness; self-born, he becomes invulnerable, "lapp'd in proof" [1.2.55] like one of Lady Macbeth's armored men-children. Even before his initial entry into the play, that is, Macbeth becomes the bearer of the shared fantasy that secure male community depends on the prowess of the man not born of woman, the man who can carve his own passage out, the man whose very maleness is the mark of his exemption from maternal origin and the vulnerabilities that are its consequence.

Ostensibly, the play rejects the version of manhood implicit in the shared fantasy of the beginning. Macbeth himself is well aware that his capitulation to Lady Macbeth's definition of manhood entails his abandonment of his own more inclusive definition of what becomes a man [1.7.46]; and Macduff's response to the news of his family's destruction insists that humane feeling is central to the definition of manhood [4.3.221]. Moreover, the revelation that even Macduff had a mother sets a limiting condition to the fantasy of a bloody masculine escape from the maternal matrix and hence on the kind of manhood defined by that escape. Nonetheless, even at the end, the play enables one version of the fantasy that heroic manhood is exemption from the female even while it punishes that fantasy in Macbeth. The key figure in whom this double movement is invested at the end of the play is Macduff; the unresolved contradictions that surround him are, I think, marks of ambivalence toward the fantasy itself. In insisting that mourning for his family is his right as a man, he presents family feeling as central to the definition of manhood; and yet he conspicuously leaves his family vulnerable to destruction when he goes off to offer his services to Malcolm. The play moreover insists on reminding us that he has inexplicably abandoned his family: both Lady Macduff and Malcolm question the necessity of this abandonment [4.2.6–14, 4.3.26–8], and the play never allows Macduff to explain himself. This unexplained abandonment severely qualifies Macduff's force as the play's central exemplar of a healthy manhood that can include the possibility of relationship to women: the play seems to vest diseased familial relations in Macbeth and the possibility of healthy ones in Macduff; and yet we discover dramatically that Macduff has a family only when we hear that he has abandoned it. Dramatically and psychologically, he takes on full masculine power only as he loses his family and becomes energized by the loss, converting his grief into the more "manly" tune of vengeance [4.3.235]; the loss of his family here enables his accession to full masculine action even while his response to that loss insists on a more humane definition of manhood. The play here pulls in two directions; and it then reiterates this doubleness by vesting in Macduff his final fantasy of exemption from woman. The ambivalence that shapes the portrayal of Macduff is evident even as he reveals to Macbeth that he "was from his mother's womb | Untimely ripp'd" [5.8.15–16]: the emphasis on untimeliness and the violence of the image suggest that he has been prematurely deprived of a nurturing maternal presence; but the prophecy construes just this deprivation as the source of Macduff's strength. The prophecy itself both denies and affirms the fantasy of exemption from women: in affirming that Macduff has indeed had a mother, it denies the fantasy of male self-generation; but in attributing his power to his having been untimely ripped from that mother, it sustains the sense that violent separation from the mother is the mark of the successful male. The final battle between Macbeth and Macduff thus replays the initial battle between Macbeth and Macdonwald. But Macduff has now taken the place of Macbeth: he carries with him the male power given him by the caesarian solution, and Macbeth is retrospectively revealed as Macdonwald, the woman's man.

The doubleness of the prophecy is less the equivocation of the fiends than Shakespeare's own equivocation about the figure of Macduff and about the fantasy vested in him in the end. For Macduff carries with him simultaneously all the values of family and the claim that masculine power derives from the unnatural abrogation of family, including escape from the conditions of one's birth. Moreover, the ambivalence that shapes the figure of Macduff similarly shapes the dramatic structure of the play itself. Ostensibly concerned to restore natural order at the end, the play bases that order upon the radical exclusion of the female. Initially construed as all-powerful, the women virtually disappear at the end. Increasingly cribbed and confined by the play, Lady Macbeth's psychic power and subjectivity are increasingly written out of it. At first a source of terror, she increasingly becomes the merely helpless wife, alienated from her husband's serious business, pleading with him to come to bed, cooperatively dying offstage in her separate sphere, amidst a cry of women. Even when she is at the center of the stage, her own subjectivity is denied her: the broken object of others' observation in the sleep-walking scene, she has become entirely absent to herself. By the end, she is so diminished a character that we scarcely trouble to ask ourselves whether the report of her suicide is accurate or not. At the same time, the witches who are her avatars disappear from the stage and become so diminished in importance that Macbeth never alludes to them, blaming his defeat only on the equivocation of their male masters, the fiends. Even Lady Macduff exists only to disappear.

With the excision of all the female characters, nature itself can in effect be reborn male. The bogus fulfillment of the Birnam Wood prophecy emphasizes the extent to which the natural order of the end depends on this excision of the female. Critics sometimes see in the march of Malcolm's soldiers bearing their green branches an allusion to the Maying festivals in which participants returned from the woods bearing branches, or to the ritual scourging of a hibernal figure by the forces of the oncoming spring.[1] The allusion seems to me clearly present; but it serves I think to mark precisely what the moving of Birnam Wood is not. Malcolm's use of Birnam Wood is a military maneuver. His drily worded command [5.4.4–7] leaves little room for suggestions of natural fertility or for the deep sense of the generative world rising up to expel its winter king; nor does the play later enable these associations except in a scattered and partly ironic way. These trees have little resemblance to those in the Forest of Arden; their branches, like those carried by the apparition of the "child crowned, with a tree in his hand"

---

1   For example, John Holloway (see Modern Criticism, pp. 65–8).

[4.1.86], are little more than the emblems of a strictly patriarchal family tree. This family tree, like the march of Birnam Wood itself, is relentlessly male: Duncan and sons, Banquo and son, Siward and son. There are no daughters and scarcely any mention of mothers in these family trees. We are brought as close as possible here to the fantasy of family without women. In that sense, Birnam Wood is the perfect emblem of the nature that triumphs at the end of the play: nature without generative possibility, nature without women. Malcolm tells his men to carry the branches to obscure themselves, and that is exactly their function: insofar as they seem to allude to the rising of the natural order against Macbeth, they obscure the operations of male power, disguising them as a natural force; and they simultaneously obscure the extent to which natural order itself is here reconceived purely as male.

From **Stephen Greenblatt, 'Shakespeare Bewitched'**, in Tetsuo Kishi, Roger Pringle and Stanley Wells, eds, *Shakespeare and Cultural Traditions* (Newark, NJ: University of Delaware Press, 1994), pp. 31–3

Stephen Greenblatt has been a leading figure in the critical school called New Historicism, which in the later twentieth century enjoyed the kind of dominance New Criticism once had. In this approach, literary texts are seen in relation to other documents and events of their time (and sometimes other times), not with the literary work as foreground and the rest as background, but in a mutually constructive interplay. 'Shakespeare Bewitched' raises the question of belief in witchcraft, setting the dogmatic certainties of the 1484 *Malleus Mallefi-carum* (written by the Dominican inquisitors Heinrich Kramer and James Sprenger) against the scepticism of the English author Reginald Scot's *The Discoverie of Witchcraft* (1584). This was no mere academic debate; lives were at stake. In the extract given here, Greenblatt argues that *Macbeth* participates in the debate by questioning the very certainty about the supernatural that it exploits on its theatrical surface. Like Stephen Booth and David Scott Kastan (see Modern Criticism, **pp. 74–5, 86–8**), Greenblatt stresses not the moral certainties other critics have found in the play but its radical uncertainties. In this extract his discussion concentrates on 1.3 (see Key Passages, **pp. 132–9**).

The demonic in Shakespeare's early history play makes history happen: it accounts for the uncanny success of the French peasant girl, for her power to fascinate and to inspire, and it accounts too for her failure.[1] The witches in *Macbeth* by contrast account for nothing. They are given many of the conventional attributes of both Continental and English witch lore, the signs and wonders that [Reginald] Scot traces back to the poets: they are associated with tempests, and particularly with thunder and lightning; they are shown calling to their familiars and conjuring spirits; they recount killing livestock, raising winds, sailing in a sieve; their hideous broth links them to birth-strangled babes and

---

1   The reference is to Joan in *Henry VI Part One* (see Contemporary Documents, **pp. 28–30**).

blaspheming Jews; above all, they traffic in prognostication and prophecy. And yet though the witches are given a vital theatrical *enargeia*,[2] though their malevolent energy is apparently put in act—"I'll do, I'll do, and I'll do"—it is in fact extremely difficult to specify what, if anything they do or even what, if anything, they are.

"What are these," Banquo asks when he and Macbeth first encounter them,

> So withered, and so wild in their attire,
> That look not like th'inhabitants o'th' earth
> And yet are on't? [1.3.39–41]

Macbeth echoes the question, "Speak, if you can. What are you?" to which he receives in reply his own name: "All hail, Macbeth!" Macbeth is evidently too startled to respond, and Banquo resumes the interrogation:

> I'th' name of truth,
> Are ye fantastical or that indeed
> Which outwardly ye show? [1.3.52–4]

The question is slightly odd, since Banquo has already marveled at an outward show that would itself seem entirely fantastical: "You should be women, / And yet your beards forbid me to interpret / That you are so" [1.3.45–7]. But "fantastical" here refers not to the witches' equivocal appearance but to a deeper doubt, a doubt not about their gender but about their existence. They had at first seemed to be the ultimate figures of the alien—Banquo initially remarked that they did not look like earthlings—but now their very "outwardness," their existence outside the mind and its fantasies, is called into question.

What is happening here is that Shakespeare is staging the epistemological and ontological dilemmas that in the deeply contradictory ideological situation of his time haunted virtually all attempts to determine the status of witchcraft beliefs and practices. And he is at the same time and by the same means staging the insistent, unresolved questions that haunt the practice of the theater. For *Macbeth* manifests a deep, intuitive recognition that the theater and witchcraft are both constructed on the boundary between fantasy and reality, the border or membrane where the imagination and the corporeal world, figure and actuality, psychic disturbance and objective truth meet. The means normally used to secure that border are speech and sight, but it is exactly these that are uncertain; the witches, as Macbeth exclaims, are "imperfect speakers," and at the moment he insists that they account for themselves, they vanish.

The startled Banquo proposes a theory that would keep the apparition within the compass of nature: "The earth hath bubbles, as the water has, / And these are of them" [1.3.79–80]. The theory, whose seriousness is difficult to gauge, has the virtue of at once acknowledging the witches's material existence—they are "of the earth"—and accounting for the possibility of their natural disappearance. If witches are earth bubbles, they would consist of air around which the earth takes form; hence they could, as Macbeth observes, vanish "into the air." But Banquo's

---

theory cannot dispel the sense of a loss of moorings, for the hags' disappearance intensifies the sense of the blurring of boundaries that the entire scene has generated: "what seemed corporal," Macbeth observes, "Melted as breath into the wind" [1.3.81–2].

Virtually everything that follows in the play transpires on the border between fantasy and reality, a sickening betwixt-and-between where a mental "image" has the uncanny power to produce bodily effects "against the use of nature," where Macbeth's "thought, whose murder yet is but fantastical" can so shake his being that "function / Is smothered in surmise, and nothing is / But what is not" [1.3.139–42], where one mind is present to the innermost fantasies of another, where manhood threatens to vanish and murdered men walk, and blood cannot be washed off. If these effects could be securely attributed to the agency of the witches, we would at least have the security of a defined and focused fear. Alternatively, if the witches could be definitively dismissed as fantasy or fraud, we would at least have the clear-eyed certainty of grappling with human causes in an altogether secular world. But instead Shakespeare achieves the remarkable effect of a nebulous infection, a bleeding of the demonic into the secular and the secular into the demonic.

The most famous instance of this effect is Lady Macbeth's great invocation of the "spirits / That tend on mortal thoughts" to unsex her, fill her with cruelty, make thick her blood, and exchange her milk with gall.[3] The speech appears to be a conjuration of demonic powers, an act of witchcraft in which the "murdering ministers" are directed to bring about a set of changes in her body. She calls these ministers "sightless substances": though invisible, they are—as she conceives them—not figures of speech or projections of her mind, but objective, substantial beings. But the fact that the spirits she invokes are "sightless" already moves this passage away from the earth-bubble corporeality of the weird sisters and toward the metaphorical use of "spirits" in Lady's Macbeth's words, a few moments earlier, "Hie thee hither, / That I may pour my spirits in thine ear" [1.5.24–5]. The "spirits" she speaks of here are manifestly figurative—they refer to the bold words, the undaunted mettle, and the sexual taunts with which she intends to incite Macbeth to murder Duncan, but, like all of her expressions of will and passion, they strain toward bodily realization, even as they convey a psychic and hence invisible inwardness. That is, there is something uncannily literal about Lady Macbeth's influence on her husband, as if she had contrived to inhabit his mind—as if, in other words, she had literally poured her spirits in his ear. Conversely, there is something uncannily figurative about the "sightless substances" she invokes, as if the spirit world, the realm of "Fate and metaphysical aid," were only a metaphor for her blind and murderous desires, as if the weird sisters were condensations of her own breath.

3   See Key Passages, p. 142.

From **David Scott Kastan, *Shakespeare after Theory*** (New York and London: Routledge, 1999), pp. 168–9, 178–81

> As Stephen Greenblatt destabilizes the play's presentation of the supernatural, American scholar David Scott Kastan, in a chapter titled '*Macbeth* and the "Name of King" ', destabilizes its presentation of kingship and royal lineage. The show of eight kings in the cauldron scene (see Key Passages, **p. 169**) may be thought of as representing the continuity of kingship embodied in the Stuart line, with an obvious compliment to King James, particularly if he is in the audience. (See The Work in Performance, **p. 99**.) Kastan, however, sees a conflict between this vision of royal succession and the installation of Malcolm as king, succeeding his father Duncan, at the end of the play. In effect, there are two royal lines, and this disrupts the whole notion of kingship as resting on an orderly succession from father to son.

If the Stewart line is seen to derive from Banquo, then Malcolm's claim to the throne and James's own seem to conflict. The play offers two seemingly incompatible sources of legitimacy: it is Banquo who will plant the "seeds of kings" [3.1.69] that will flower into the Stewart dynasty, but the play asserts as well that Malcolm's restoration of the line of Duncan reestablishes legitimate rule in Scotland.

Macbeth thus makes evident that Stewart legitimacy rests on something less certain than patrilineal descent, though the play is oddly silent about the contradiction that it makes visible. Historically (and that may be the wrong word since "Fleance" seems to be an invention of Hector Boece in 1527),[1] the dynastic lines eventually merge some six generations after the events of the play, when Walter, putatively the descendant of Fleance, marries Marjory, the daughter of Robert I. Their son, Robert II, is the first of the Stewart kings, claiming, however, his throne from his mother [. . .]. The play's emphasis upon Banquo as "father to a line of kings" [3.1.59] rather than Duncan has, then, the effect of avoiding the vexed problem of inheritance through the female, comfortably locating authority in the male body. But if this is appropriate for a play, if not a culture, that consistently demonizes female power, a play in which to be not "of woman born" [4.1.80] is to be invulnerable and to be "unknown to woman" [4.3.126] is to be virtuous, it leaves unmistakable the fault line in the play's, if not the culture's, understanding of legitimacy—and not least because James inherits his crown through the female, a fact at issue in the Witches' "show of eight kings," as the eighth monarch of the Stewart line was in fact James's mother, Mary, whose presence in, no less than her absence from the pageant must necessarily trouble its putative assertion of patrilineal succession.[2]

---

1 [From Kastan's note.] See *The Chronicles of Scotland, Compiled by Hector Boece*, trans. into Scots by John Belledon (1531) and ed. Edith C. Baltho and H. Winifred Husbands (Edinburgh: William Blackwood and Sons, 1941), Vol. II, pp. 154–5.
2 James's mother, Mary Queen of Scots, spent the last eighteen years of her life as a political prisoner in England, and was executed by Queen Elizabeth in 1587. Tributes to James on his accession to the throne of England were notably silent about her.

Kastan goes on to another problem: that the final image of Macbeth's severed head on a pole is an image not just of the defeat of a tyrant, but of the killing of a king.

"Behold, where stands / Th'usurper's cursed head" [5.8.20–1], proudly proclaims Macduff, but the visual image that in its spectacular assertion of legitimate power would resolve the political instability produced by the play's violence in fact reanimates the problematic. If it marks the end of Macbeth's savage tyranny, it marks as well the vulnerability of sacred kingship.

The image of the severed head certainly recalls the heads of traitors fixed on Tower Bridge, but, alternatively, it resonates as well with the crucial term of James's absolutism, characteristically articulated in the anthropomorphizing metaphor of the body politic. James, of course, conceived of the king as "the head of a body composed of diuers members,"[3] and the similitude produces a clear, if predictable, political logic. [. . .] The head cut off, the body must wither. "It may very well fall out that the head will be forced to garre cut off[4] some rotten members . . . to keep the rest of the body in integritie," James wrote, "but what state the body can be in, if the head, for any infirmitie that can fall to it, be cut off, I leaue to the readers iudgement."[5] [. . .] The severed head of Macbeth would, at least for James, mark not the restoration of legitimate authority but its violation: the unwarranted and blasphemous "butchery" of a "tyrannical King." It could not be a sign of renewed sovereignty but must appear as a "breach in nature" [2.3.113] no less awful than the "gashed stabs" in Duncan's sacred body, a breach that within a generation would find its form in the severed head of James's son shockingly displayed upon another "bloody stage" [2.4.6].[6]

My point, however, is obviously not that the play demands to be read in the context of James's own political thought or ambitions, though this has been a familiar critical assertion; it is more to show the impossibility of any such reading, to see the way the play inscribes not merely the contradictions present in the source material but in the absolutist logic itself. [. . .]

Kastan concludes that what looks like the restoration of true kingship at the end of the play is made problematic by the fact that the very word 'King' has been demystified.

Certainly, in *Macbeth* "the name of King" has a "Plenitude of power in it," though not a power inhering in the word itself but in the social relations its speaking defines. Acknowledged "king," the monarch can effectively mobilize the

3   [Kastan's note, expanded.] *The Trew Law of Free Monarchies*, in *The Political Works of James I*, ed. Charles Howard McIlwain (Cambridge, Mass.: Harvard University Press, 1918), p. 64.
4   Cause to be cut off.
5   James I, *The Trew Law* (see Note 3 above), p. 65. It was an important part of James's political thinking that subjects had no right to rebel against a tyrannical king.
6   Charles I, publicly beheaded in 1649.

institutions and agencies of power that define and defend his sovereignty. For Malcolm, Edward the Confessor, the English king, is the type of sacred and efficacious majesty: "sundry blessings hang about his throne, / That speak him full of grace" [4.3.158–9].[7] But what "speaks" his plenitude are less the "blessings" that "hang about his throne" than the loyalty of the "ten thousand warlike men" [4.3.134] who will fight to uphold it. And if the name of king activates the power of the state that constitutes and maintains the crown, it also works to naturalize that power, sanctioning violence, converting it into valor. Thus Malcolm and the avenging nobles insistently deny the name to Macbeth. He is always "the tyrant," whose violent acts make him unworthy of loyalty; Duncan and Malcolm alone are called "King of Scotland" [1.2.28; 5.9.25], a name that turns the acts of violence done on their behalf into loyal and heroic action.

Indeed, though Macbeth enters "*as King*" at the beginning of act three, and is lawfully "named" before he goes "to Scone / To be invested" [2.4.31–2], the word "King" seems to stick even in his own mouth. He speaks it only five times, on three occasions referring to the witches' prophecy [1.3.73; 1.3.144; 3.1.57], once to the apparition of a "child crowned" [4.1.87], and once to Duncan: "Let us toward the King" [1.3.153]. Many critics have remarked on the euphemisms Macbeth uses to describe the murders he plans and commits, but "the name of king" is subject to exactly the same verbal displacements. "When 'tis, It shall make honor for you," he says to Banquo [2.1.25–6], exactly like the pronominal evasions of "If it were done, when 'tis done, then 'twere well / It were done quickly" [1.7.1–2]. Even Lady Macbeth cannot fully articulate his prophesied progress to the throne: "Glamis thou art, and Cawdor; and shalt be / What thou art promis'd" [1.5.15–16], not "King," as the witches' three-fold prophecy demands, but merely the paraphrastic "What thou art promised." The name of king, with its plenitude of power, is not so easily spoken, not quite so "sweet," when one admits the fearsome agency necessary to achieve and defend it.

The Work in Performance

Introduction

Written in or around 1606, *Macbeth* would have been first performed by Shakespeare's company, the King's Men, at the Globe playhouse, with Richard Burbage in the leading role. Immediately we confront a paradox: a play that constantly invokes darkness, a play many of whose crucial scenes take place at night, would have been performed in an open-roofed theatre in daylight. It is the imagination of the audience, triggered by the language, that creates the darkness. It may be that when the King's Men moved into the smaller, indoor Blackfriars (which they leased in 1608) *Macbeth* acquired a literal darkness to match the darkness of the language; but that is more than we know. The Blackfriars would have been lit by candlelight, and candles could be snuffed or removed; but to create full darkness would have required darkening the auditorium, and that would have been a cumbersome business. The elaborate lighting effects we are now used to, and the custom of darkening the auditorium, are products of the nineteenth century. Theatre habits die hard, and it may be that even when it moved indoors *Macbeth* still relied on language to create its peculiar atmosphere.

The theory that the play was written as a compliment to King James I includes speculation about a court performance. We know that in late 1606 Shakespeare's company was paid for putting on three plays before the King and his visiting father-in-law the King of Denmark, two at Greenwich, and one at Hampton Court. But we do not know which plays they were, and while it is perfectly possible that at some point *Macbeth* was played before the King,[1] we have no evidence for such a performance. What we do know is that some time before its publication in the 1623 Folio, the collected edition of Shakespeare's works, *Macbeth* was revised along lines that offered a foretaste of its immediate theatrical future. New scenes were added centring on a new character, Hecate, who commands the three witches and changes their dramatic role from mysterious figures who act on their own to servants of a superior power. The additions feature songs and dances, with extra witches and spirits to swell the chorus, and

---

1 Peter Thompson describes the possible effect of the show of kings in the cauldron scene with King James in the audience (see The Work in Performance, p. 99).

may have included flying effects to show off the descent machinery of the Blackfriars. The new material may have been written by Thomas Middleton, a leading playwright of the Jacobean period; the new *Macbeth* songs also appear in his play *The Witch*. To ask why *Macbeth* was revised is to enter again into speculation. It may have been an attempt to spruce up a relatively unpopular play. There are not many contemporary allusions to *Macbeth*, suggesting it did not have the impact of, for example, *Romeo and Juliet* or *Hamlet*. Or it may have been that the play was popular enough, but Shakespeare's company wanted to keep it in the repertoire by giving the audience new reasons to see it. Two of the long-running hits of the Elizabethan period, Thomas Kyd's *The Spanish Tragedy* and Christopher Marlowe's *Doctor Faustus*, were kept in the repertoire with additional scenes that exploited their most popular elements, mad scenes in Kyd's play and clown-and-devil scenes in Marlowe's. Making *Macbeth* more spectacular also brings it closer to the court masque, raising the possibility that if it was not a play for the court from the beginning, it became one later.

Music, dancing and spectacle were the keynotes of William Davenant's adaptation (see The Work in Performance, **pp. 100–6**), which held the stage after the Restoration and continued to influence later generations. Samuel Pepys, the Secretary to the Navy, whose diary is one of the most fascinating life-records in English, spent a lot of time at the playhouse when he should have been at the office, and he was impressed with this version of *Macbeth*, which he saw several times. He called it 'a most excellent play in all respects, but especially in divertisement, though it be a deep tragedy; which is a strange perfection in a tragedy, it being most proper here and suitable' (7 January 1667), and later 'one of the best plays for a stage, and variety of dancing and music, that ever I saw' (19 April 1667).[2] Davenant's chorus of singing, dancing witches now strikes us as incongruous. Pepys notes the incongruity, but it does not trouble him; the play works as a theatrical entertainment, and that is what matters. Joseph Addison, writing in *The Spectator*, number 45 (21 April 1711), reports that some years earlier he attended *Macbeth* and 'unfortunately' sat near 'a Woman of Quality' who asked, even before the curtain went up, '*When will the dear Witches enter?*' and immediately upon their first Appearance, asked a Lady that sate three Boxes from her, . . . if those Witches were not charming Creatures'.[3] Davenant, building on the Folio Hecate scenes, established a tradition that lasted: John Philip Kemble's 1788 production had a chorus of fifty or sixty witches to support Hecate, and when he toured the production in 1803 an audience in Bristol demanded 'the usual dance'.[4] In 1888 Henry Irving ended the cauldron scene with sixty witches apparently flying across a mountain landscape with the sea in the background, singing as they flew (words by Middleton, music by Sir Arthur Sullivan of Gilbert and Sullivan). The last appearance of such a chorus in Shakespeare's play seems to have been in Sir Herbert Beerbohm Tree's 1911

2   *The Diary of Samuel Pepys*, ed. Robert Latham and William Matthews, Vol. VIII (London: G. Bell and Sons, 1974), pp. 7, 171.

3   Joseph Addison, Richard Steele and others, *The Spectator*, Vol. I (London: J. M. Dent and Sons, repr. 1945), pp. 137–8.

4   John Wilders, ed., *Shakespeare in Production: Macbeth* (Cambridge: Cambridge University Press, 2004), pp. 171, 23–4.

production,[5] though a chorus of witches can still be seen in Giuseppe Verdi's operatic version.

Davenant also made significant changes to the text, smoothing and clarifying the language, and filling out the action with new material. As the extract given here shows (**pp. 100–6**), he builds up Lady Macduff considerably, giving her new scenes with her husband and with Lady Macbeth. He has Lady Macbeth haunted by the ghost of Duncan, which Macbeth cannot see. He builds up Malcolm, evidently as a compliment to the Restoration of Charles II.[6] A freedom in handling Shakespeare's text was characteristic of Davenant's time (Davenant himself, in his 1662 *The Law Against Lovers*, cheered up *Measure for Measure* by adding Beatrice and Benedick from *Much Ado About Nothing*) and it was a habit that died hard. When David Garrick acted Macbeth in 1744 he added the death-speech that Shakespeare had neglected to provide (see The Work in Performance, **pp. 106–7**). Whatever we may think of this, as an actor Garrick served the play well: he had great emotional power, and could sway the feelings not just of his audience but of his fellow performers. His Lear had not only the audience but Goneril and Regan in tears. And at one performance, when he told Banquo's murderer 'There's blood upon thy face', he did it with such intensity that the actor forgot he was in a play and replied, 'Is there, by God?'[7] His death speech now seems quaint and dated. But a contemporary observer records the impact of Garrick's performance:

> At last he fell, at that moment his crimes peopled his thoughts, with the most horrible forms; terrified at the hideous pictures which his past acts revealed to him, he struggled against death; nature seemed to make one supreme effort. His plight made the audience shudder, he clawed the ground and seemed to be digging his own grave, but the dread moment was nigh, one saw death in reality, everything expressed that instant which makes all equal.[8]

Garrick, as was customary, performed the play in the dress of his time; paintings of his Macbeth show an eighteenth-century gentleman in a powdered wig, with daggers in his hands. However, a new interest in what might be called the Scottish Picturesque was reflected in the rugged, barbaric scenery of Charles Macklin's 1773 production.[9] That production died an early death; but in 1842 Charles Kean, who was obsessed with historical accuracy, brought a fully realized, elaborately picturesque vision of ancient Scotland to the stage, and later productions, well into the twentieth century, followed his lead.

Throughout the eighteenth and nineteenth centuries the playing of the central characters shifted according to the talents and interest of the actors. At the end of

5   ibid., p. 177.
6   ibid., p. 8.
7   ibid., p. 151.
8   George Winchester Stone, Jr. and George M. Kahrl, *David Garrick: a Critical Biography* (Carbondale and Edwardsville: Southern Illinois University Press, 1979), p. 559. For Francis Gentleman's response to Garrick's performance, see Early Critical Reception, **pp. 52–3**.
9   James Macpherson's Ossian poems, allegedly the work of a Scottish equivalent of Homer, appeared in the 1760s and helped to create this vogue.

the eighteenth century John Philip Kemble, whose keynote as an actor was statuesque nobility, played Macbeth as a fine man led astray by a domineering wife.[10] Towards the end of the nineteenth century Henry Irving, whose first major success as an actor had been as a guilt-haunted murderer in Leopold Lewis's melodrama *The Bells*, played Macbeth as a craven villain. When he first acted the part in 1875, he scribbled in the margins of his copy, 'LIAR, TRAITOR, COWARD' – all with reference to Macbeth's first two scenes.[11] There was a long-established theatrical tradition whereby Lady Macbeth was played as a virago. This corresponds to the majority view of her in the criticism of the time. Sarah Siddons, John Philip Kemble's sister and Lady Macbeth to his Macbeth, played her that way, though her private view of the character was very different. On the line 'Shalt be / What thou art promised' 'The amazing burst of energy upon the words *shalt be* perfectly electrified the house'.[12] Her performance became one of the legends of the English theatre, overpowering Kemble's Macbeth as by some accounts Mrs Pritchard overwhelmed Garrick, compelling though he was. Towards the end of the century Ellen Terry, the Lady Macbeth of Irving's 1888 production, played her as loving and (in the Victorian sense) womanly. In her notes on the character she asked, 'Surely did she not call on the spirits to be made bad, because she knew she was *not* so *very* bad?'[13] In her gentler approach to Lady Macbeth she had been anticipated in 1843 by Helen Faucit, described by Henry Morley as 'too exclusively gifted with the art of expressing all that is most graceful and beautiful in womanhood, to succeed in inspiring anything like awe and terror'.[14] On the other hand, roughly contemporary with Terry's gentle Lady Macbeth, the great French actress Sarah Bernhardt was playing the character as a seductive siren, working on her husband with sensuous embraces more than with words.[15]

Moving into the twentieth century, we enter the period in which *Macbeth* was regarded as a jinxed play (see Introduction, **pp. 1–2**). It remains one of Shakespeare's most frequently performed plays, yet its stage history in the last century is littered with failures, some of them humiliating. Even major talents have come to grief in the so-called Scottish play.[16] The difficulties include finding a convincing way to stage the witches for a modern audience without falling into merely comic witchiness on the one hand or pretentious abstraction on the other;[17] and the problem of Macbeth's shrinking from a complex, guilt-ridden character to a mere

---

10 Wilders, *Shakespeare in Production*, p. 7.
11 Laurence Irving, *Henry Irving: the Actor and his World* (repr. London: Columbus Books, 1989; first published London: Faber and Faber, 1951), p. 260.
12 Wilders, *Shakespeare in Production*, p. 99.
13 Nina Auerbach, *Ellen Terry: Player in her Time* (New York and London: W. W. Norton and Company, 1987), p. 258.
14 A. R. Braunmuller, Introduction to the New Cambridge Shakespeare edition of *Macbeth* (Cambridge: Cambridge University Press, 1997), p. 70.
15 Wilders, *Shakespeare in Production*, p. 49.
16 These include Ralph Richardson at Stratford-upon-Avon in 1952, in a production directed by John Gielgud; Alec Guinness at the Royal Court in 1966; and Peter O'Toole in a Prospect Theatre Company production in 1980. For anyone who enjoys dwelling on misfortune, sample reviews may be found in Diana Rigg, ed., *No Turn Unstoned: the Worst Ever Theatrical Reviews* (London: Arrow Books, 1983), pp. 222–32.
17 I recall one production in which the witches, played as young women, did what looked like acting-school exercises with large white bedsheets. These conveyed no message whatever to the audience.

brutal tyrant, with a corresponding loss of dramatic interest in the second half. Another problem, perhaps, is that the key emotion in *Macbeth* is fear, and this is an emotion difficult to keep fresh through weeks of rehearsal and performance. *The Tempest*, whose key emotion is wonder, presents a similar problem, and has a similar record of theatrical failure.

Success in *Macbeth* has lately been the exception rather than the rule; but there have been successes, two of which are represented in reviews in this section. When Laurence Olivier performed Macbeth at Stratford-upon-Avon in 1955, some reviewers had reservations about the production and about Vivien Leigh's small-scale Lady Macbeth; but Olivier's Macbeth electrified the audience, particularly in the way he reversed the traditional view of the character's decline, beginning low-key and tentative and gaining power as he went along (see The Work in Performance, **pp. 107–9**). The real breakthrough came in 1976, with Trevor Nunn's production at the Other Place, the Royal Shakespeare Company's smallest theatre. In that intimate space, with a small company of actors working close to the audience on a simple set whose most striking feature was a chalk circle, and costumes that ranged from the mediaeval to the modern to the timeless, the production was both a closely observed personal drama and a ritual. Ian McKellen's tortured Macbeth and Judi Dench's commanding, intelligent Lady Macbeth were powerful as individual performances, and the relationship between them was urgent and intense, two characters operating together under incredible pressure. The production was adapted for Thames television in 1979, and released on videotape (see The Work in Performance, **pp. 113–16**).

There have been other screen versions. Orson Welles in 1948 did a quickly shot version on cheap-looking sets that nonetheless uses imaginative camerawork to convey the claustrophobic power of evil. Reflecting the criticism of the time that saw in the play's language images of grace that counteracted that evil, it is full of Christian imagery associated with Macbeth's adversaries. Akira Kurosawa's 1957 *Throne of Blood* (see The Work in Performance, **pp. 109–11**) finds an equivalent for the play's violent society in the world of the samurai, and for its sense of violated domestic space in the contrast between the decorous rituals of social life and the bloodstained room in which the character equivalent to Duncan is murdered. Borrowing a convention from Japanese theatre, the film begins and ends with the sound of a chorus chanting about the ruin brought about by ambition. Davenant, Garrick and their contemporaries would have recognized the same moral.

Roman Polanski's 1971 film has produced a divided response. Some critics cannot get over the fact that it was financed by Playboy Productions and includes naked witches and a nude sleepwalking scene for Lady Macbeth. Others find its graphic violence excessively literal (for Kenneth Rothwell's description, see The Work in Performance, **pp. 111–13**). But it has its supporters,[18] and it puts an interesting spin on the central characters (Jon Finch and Francesca Annis) by casting them as very young, making their ambition that of an upwardly mobile couple in the audience's world, creating a link between that world and the violent mediaeval past the film portrays. Polanski also anticipates recent criticism's lack

---

18 There is a recent, thoughtful defence by Braunmuller, Introduction, pp. 86–7.

of confidence in a final moral order. Ross is a shifty double agent who always plays for the winning side. His final support for Malcolm and Macduff undermines any sense that good has triumphed; and the film ends with Donalbain riding off to consult the witches. Trevor Nunn's stage and screen production has a similarly ironic ending: Macduff enters from killing Macbeth with two blood-stained daggers held in trembling hands, exactly recalling Macbeth's entrance after the murder of Duncan. Some recent stage productions have been equally sceptical: in Dominic Cooke's 2004 Royal Shakespeare Company production, Malcolm in the England scene was not a noble prince waiting for his country's call but a dishevelled figure who seemed to have spent his exile drinking in a garret. *Macbeth* continues to show new faces to its stage interpreters, as it has to literary critics; and for all the difficulties it presents it continues to haunt the theatre.

Performance

From **Simon Forman, *The Book of Plays and Notes thereof per Forman for Common Policy*** (1611). Reprinted in William Shakespeare, *The Tragedy of Macbeth*, ed. Nicholas Brooke (Oxford: Oxford University Press, 1990), pp. 235–6

What wouldn't we give for an eye-witness account of *Macbeth* performed by Shakespeare's company at the Globe, in Shakespeare's own lifetime? In fact we have one, and a somewhat strange account it is. Simon Forman, a physician and astrologer with an interest in magic, recorded his impressions of the play, noting what he found striking, and muddling some of the details. His account of Macbeth and Banquo riding through a wood does not sound like an account of an Elizabethan performance; it has been suggested that it comes from Forman's memory of a woodcut illustration to Holinshed's *Chronicles* (see Figure 1, p. 21), which corresponds to the scene he describes. His reference to the witches as fairies or nymphs seems at odds with their appearance as described in the dialogue; it too comes from Holinshed. Forman recalls the gist of their prophecies, but understandably gets the wording wrong. He speaks of Lady Macbeth in the sleepwalking scene as having 'confessed all', making her sound like the villain at the end of a conventional play. On the other hand that scene obviously stuck in his mind as noteworthy – so much so that he reads back from it into the middle of the play and has both Macbeth and Lady Macbeth failing to wash the blood from their hands. His account of Banquo's ghost appearing behind Macbeth and sitting in his chair, with Macbeth seeing him as he turns around, may well be an authentic report of stage business. On the whole Forman seems to have found the banquet scene and the sleepwalking scene to be the play's highlights. One clue that the contemporary reception of Shakespeare was different from ours is that Forman takes no notice of the fact that he is seeing a play by the great William Shakespeare, one of the world's leading authors. He is simply seeing a play at the Globe. Shakespeare's overwhelming reputation was a later construction.

In *Macbeth* at the Globe 1610, the 20 of April, Saturday,[1] [. . .] there was to be observed first how Macbeth and Banquo, two noblemen of Scotland, riding through a wood, there stood before them three women, fairies or nymphs, and saluted Macbeth, saying three times unto him: 'Hail Macbeth, king of Codon [. . .], for thou shalt be a king, but shall beget no kings, etc.' Then said Banquo: 'What, all to Macbeth, and nothing to me?' 'Yes' said the nymphs, 'hail to thee, Banquo, thou shalt beget kings, yet be no king.'

And so they departed and came to the court of Scotland, to Duncan, King of Scots, and it was in the days of Edward the Confessor. And Duncan bad them both kindly welcome; and made Macbeth forthwith Prince of Northumberland [. . .],[2] and sent him home to his own castle; and appointed Macbeth to provide for him, for he would sup with him the next day at night, and did so. And Macbeth contrived to kill Duncan, and through the persuasion of his wife did that night murder the king in his own castle, being his guest. And there were many prodigies seen that night, and the day before. And when Macbeth had murdered the king, the blood on his hands could not be washed off by any means, nor from his wife's hands, which handled the bloody daggers in hiding them; by which means they became both much amazed and affronted.[3]

The murder being known, Duncan's two sons fled, the one to England, the [other to] Wales,[4] to save themselves. They being fled, they were supposed guilty of the murder of their father, which was nothing so. Then was Macbeth crowned king; and then he, for fear of Banquo his old companion, that he should beget kings but be no king himself, he contrived the death of Banquo, and caused him to be murdered on the way as he rode. The next night, being at supper with his noblemen whom he had bid to a feast, to the which also Banquo should have come, he began to speak of noble Banquo, and to wish that he were there. And as he thus did, standing up to drink a carouse to him, the ghost of Banquo came and sat down in his chair behind him; and he, turning about to sit down again, saw the ghost of Banquo, which fronted[5] him so, that he fell into a great passion of fear and fury, uttering many words about his murder by which, when they heard that Banquo was murdered, they suspected Macbeth.

Then Macduff fled to England to the king's son. And so they raised an army and came to Scotland, and at [Dunsinane] overthrew Macbeth. In the meantime, while Macduff was in England, Macbeth slew Macduff's wife and children; and after, in the battle, Macduff slew Macbeth.

Observe how Macbeth's queen did rise in the night in her sleep, and walk, and talked and confessed all, and the doctor noted her words.

---

1 In his introduction to the extract (p. 234), Brooke explains: '20 April was not a Saturday in 1610, but it was in 1611, and no doubt 1610 was a slip. The year was still commonly dated in the old style from Lady's Day, 25 March, and slips must have been common in April (as nowadays they are in January).'
2 Forman seems to be confusing two of Duncan's actions: making Macbeth Thane of Cawdor (which happens earlier in any case) and making Malcolm Prince of Cumberland.
3 Dismayed.
4 In the play, and in Holinshed, Donalbain flees to Ireland.
5 May have a double sense, confronted and offended.

From **Peter Thomson, Shakespeare's Theatre** (London: Routledge and Kegan Paul, 1983), pp. 150–5

British scholar Peter Thomson has written extensively on Shakespeare in performance. In *Shakespeare's Theatre* he stresses that for Shakespeare and his fellows putting on a play was a practical business. These extracts are from a chapter called '*Macbeth* from the tiring house'. (The tiring house was the backstage area where actors and stage crew prepared.) Thomson begins his account of each scene with a list of sound effects, special effects, and stage properties, reminding us that, however we may read these details for their symbolism, for Shakespeare's company they were practical matters. Daggers, tapers and severed heads are laid out backstage on a prop table. Thomson also notes the decisions actors have to make in the playing of a scene, and the effect of those decisions. Simon Forman (**pp. 94–5**) gives us the Globe *Macbeth* (not quite accurately) from the audience's point of view. Thomson gives us the Globe *Macbeth* (with, inevitably, a certain amount of speculation) from the company's point of view.

Act Three Scene Four[1]

Sound effect	–	hautboys (?)
Special effect	–	Banquo's ghost
Properties	–	throne (possibly two thrones)
		table fully spread with food and wine

The scene of Banquo's murder gives just about enough time for some intensive preparation in the tiring house. The table has to be prepared and brought out, and the actors have to be called to stand by for their massed entry. The absence of any reference to music in the Folio stage direction is surprising. A royal feast without instrumental accompaniment would not be normal, and Macbeth is concerned that everything should look as normal as possible. Perhaps Shakespeare intended that the feast should be obviously false from the start – or perhaps the Folio fails to record what happened on stage.

Each of the three preceding scenes in Act Three has pointed forward to the feast, and the repetition here of Macbeth's contradictory hopes that Banquo should attend the event *and* that he should be prevented provide the context for the appearance of the ghost, equivocally answering both of Macbeth's demands. There is no doubt that the ghost was a palpable physical presence on the Globe stage, played by the actor of Banquo. He needed no further disguise than blood – a love of significant pattern would have recommended that he be made to look like the bloody soldier who appeared before the last king shortly before his death. We can only guess at the effect the ghost was intended to have on the audience. The probability is that no special tricks were used, no concealed entry or sudden emanation through a trapdoor, since an upstage entry through the stage door

---

1   See Key Passages, **pp. 155–62.**

would be more impressive.[2] That would have involved the 'corpse' of Banquo in a seen-but-not-seen resurrection at the end of III.iii. – back into the tiring house for a hurried application of blood by the tireman.

Emrys Jones, having drawn attention to the play-within-a-play qualities of the feast, describes the effect on Macbeth of the apparition:

> What happens in terms of the play-within-a-play is that Macbeth is put out of his part. The dramatic effect – the effect on the audience of *Macbeth* – is extraordinarily intense. For just as at a real-life performance of a play the experience of seeing an actor forget his part can be quite unforeseeably jarring, so the spectacle of Macbeth lapsing into helpless confusion arouses a feeling of acute tragic embarrassment.[3]

This is an acute observation. The whole scene is set up by Macbeth as a performance, with the moves written in. It is clear, for instance, that as the feast starts Macbeth mingles with his guests, whilst Lady Macbeth advertises her apartness by remaining seated in her throne of state. His own place is 'i' the midst' [3.4.10], and it is to that central position that the ghost will make its way. The ragged inset, when Macbeth talks with the Murderer, must be set apart from the formal grouping of the feast. It is an uncomfortable hiatus for the feasters, who can eat and drink nothing until Macbeth has given the cheer [3.4.32]. How did the actors at the table pass the twenty lines of Macbeth's dialogue with Banquo's killer? The 'unheard conversation' convention is a possibility, but the sense is rather of embarrassed silence that will be felt with even greater intensity when Macbeth addresses the invisible ghost. It is the critical moment in Macbeth's fortune. He may pull himself together, but he can never again hope to pull his court together. A piece of stage business that became traditional in later productions of *Macbeth* may well have originated with Burbage. We have to picture the moment when the host raises his glass:

> Now good digestion wait on appetite,
> And health on both! [3.4.37–8]

Steeling himself against the disappointment of Fleance's escape, Macbeth has turned back to the feast to play the part of genial host – and suddenly Banquo is there. Fingers numbed, Burbage lets the glass slip from his hand. Is it to this that Jasper, his face mealed in grotesque imitation of a ghost, refers in Beaumont's *The Knight of the Burning Pestle* (1607)?

> When thou art at thy table with thy friends,
> Merry in heart, and fill'd with swelling wine,
> I'll come in midst of all thy pride and mirth,
> Invisible to all men but thyself,
> And whisper such a sad tale in thine ear

---

2   This is consistent with Forman's account of Banquo appearing *behind* Macbeth.
3   [Thomson's note.] Here, and elsewhere in this chapter, I am indebted to the work of Emrys Jones in chapter seven of *Scenic Form in Shakespeare*, Oxford, 1971.

Shall make thee let the cup fall from thy hand,
And stand as mute and pale as Death itself. (V.i.22–8)

The resemblance is unmistakable. Beaumont is surely referring to a famous moment in Burbage's performance of Macbeth – one of those hair-raising 'natural' touches that put the audience in touch with the real world without breaking their concentration on the world of the play. [. . .]

Act Four Scene One[4]

Sound effects	–	thunder
		music and a song
		music for a dance
		hautboys
		galloping of horses
Special effects	–	Three apparitions
		entrance and exit (flying) of Hecate
		dumb show of eight kings and Banquo
		mirror effect
		vanishing of witches
Properties	–	cauldron
		ingredients of cauldron (twenty-four are mentioned)
		severed head (Macbeth's)
		branch of a tree
		eight crowns
		ten orbs
		twelve sceptres

The list of theatrical prerequisites for this scene makes its own point. It is a nightmare for the stage-hands and a pantomime for the audience. If we assume, as I think we must, that the Hecate episode is an indoor theatre interpolation, we can ignore the clumsy flying mechanism of the Globe. The Folio text's insistence that the three apparitions 'descend' may also refer to the more elaborate trap-doors of the Blackfriars or the second Globe. If the first Globe had traps amenable enough to spectacular descents and ascents for the effective presentation of the three apparitions and the vanishing Witches, it is surprising that the extant Globe plays make so little use of them. We simply cannot be sure that the performance of *Macbeth* seen by Forman[5] employed any of the vanishing and appearing tricks called for in the Folio stage directions. Much more challenging is the reconstruction of the business implied by the dumb-show mirror, 'the last king with a glass in his hand' [4.1.111]. Macbeth describes the effect from his point of vantage:

And yet the eighth appears, who bears a glass
Which shows me many more. [4.1.119–20]

But an effect that is visible only to the actor is not an effect at all. There is a fascinating possibility that, in the Hampton Court performance of 1606, the silent presenter of the eighth king held the mirror in front of James I himself, the latest guarantee of the continuing Stuart line;[6] but it would take some clever handling of the mirror on the Globe stage to contrive for the audience a sight of the reflected seven kings preceding the mirror-carrier. Such a refinement looks forward to Pepper's awe-inspiring nineteenth-century stage ghost.[7]

The three apparitions probably made lesser demands. The first presents the severed head of Macbeth, carried by a boy actor. It is a property that will be needed again. The second seems to represent Macduff, and the third Malcolm, but it is only by suggestive costuming of the boys who walk on in their place that the point could have been clearly made: another job for the tireman. The dumb show of kings, introduced by the ominous playing of hautboys, was probably a parade round the stage, brought to a halt in a static line prior to a final exit through the other stage door.

The opening of the scene is another 'quotation' from the spell-casting section of a sabbat. It is unlikely that each of the mentioned ingredients was faithfully imitated by the property makers. The theatrical stress is less on the objects than on the words, and on the ritualistic, rhythmic dance for which the words provide the music. The later, probably interpolated, dance would have required much more elaborate choreography. It is a theatrical show rather than a dramatic necessity.

The final sound effect is of the galloping of horses. Since Macbeth tells us that *he* hears them, *we* do not need to. But there is evidence that this was an off-stage noise often enough heard in the Elizabethan and Jacobean theatres, and it has a nice ambiguity here. It *could* be the sound of the vanishing Witches – 'Infected be the air whereon they ride' [4.1.138] – but it *is* the sound of messengers bringing news that Macduff has fled to England.

Act Four Scene Two[8]

The spectacular scene is followed by an indoor – almost a parlour – scene. The various visitors to Lady Macduff are ushered, or break, into intimacy. The actor of Lady Macduff has a strange job to do. This is her only scene, and she stands in necessary contrast to Lady Macbeth. She is emphatically a mother – which Lady Macbeth is not – and she is also the wife of a good man; but, far from being heroic, her opening words to Ross are petulant and ill-considered. She accuses Macduff of lacking 'the natural touch', of deserting her and his children. Like Banquo, but unlike Macbeth, Macduff is fertile; but he stands accused of being a bad father. One modern director, George Roman, has told me that he found it helpful to the actress of Lady Macduff to play the part as if in the late stages of pregnancy, giving her ill temper a source in her physical discomfort. It is a

---

6   David Scott Kastan offers a more sceptical view of the theme of royal lineage (see The Work in Performance, **pp. 86–8**).

7   'Pepper's Ghost' (named for its exponent John Henry Pepper, director of the Polytechnic Institute, London) was a stage trick by which the reflection of an actor standing in the orchestra pit was projected on to a sheet of glass on stage, creating the effect of a ghost.

8   See Key Passages, **pp. 171–6**.

sophisticated touch, that serves to highlight a dramatic contrast between the fertile and the barren. What is of more importance in the construction of the play is this scene's reference forward to the next, when Macduff's 'nature' will be tried and proved. This, in theatrical terms, is a stage door scene. Ross carries the tensions of Macbeth's court into Lady Macduff's house – 'I dare not speak much further' [4.2.17] – and the unnamed messenger who next appears at a stage door might, for all the audience knows, be a murderer. The arrivals in this scene are soundless and sudden. It ends with the shrieking exit of Lady Macduff at one stage door, and the entrance of her husband at the other.

From **Sir William D'Avenant, *Macbeth a Tragedy. With all the Alterations, Amendments, Additions and New Songs*** (1664). Reprinted in Brian Vickers, ed., *Shakespeare: the Critical Heritage*, Vol. I (London: Routledge and Kegan Paul, 1974), pp. 51–61

William Davenant, who liked to claim that he was Shakespeare's illegitimate son, was a leading playwright and theatre manager in the years following the Restoration of Charles II (1660). His adaptation of *Macbeth* (first performed 1664) is best remembered for turning the play into a spectacle with singing and dancing witches; but it did more than that. Davenant built up the roles of Macduff and Lady Macduff (who never appear on stage together in Shakespeare) into a domestic drama in its own right, whose pathos introduces softer emotions into the play. In the process he created a relationship between Lady Macbeth and Lady Macduff, of which the play gives only one hint, Lady Macbeth's 'The Thane of Fife had a wife; where is she now?' (5.1.41–2) in the sleepwalking scene. (Orson Welles's 1948 film also builds up the role of Lady Macduff, and her relationship with Lady Macbeth, by reassigning lines of dialogue.) Davenant's changes are purposeful, and like many adaptations of Shakespeare his work highlights what is different, difficult and unconventional in the original. Davenant creates a sedately ordered drama, in place of Shakespeare's sometimes jagged construction. He smooths over moments that Shakespeare left abrupt. He makes the witches more entertaining than alarming by turning them into a musical act; whatever else Shakespeare's witches may be they are not (or should not be) simply entertaining. In rewriting speeches, Davenant turned Shakespeare's difficult, daring writing, which to many in Davenant's time would have seemed barbarous, into clearer, more logical speech, full of edifying sentiments. Davenant's version held the stage until the middle of the eighteenth century, and some of its effects lingered after that.

Shakespeare's 1.5 (see Key Passages, **pp. 139–43**) begins with Lady Macbeth coming on stage alone, reading her husband's letter. The first words she speaks are not hers, but his. Some performers have found this introduction of the character difficult, and wished they could have had more preparation. Davenant provides it. His 1.5 opens with Lady Macbeth consoling Lady Macduff for her husband's absence in war. This gives Lady Macbeth something Shakespeare denies her, a scene with another woman; it also allows the actor a much longer warm-up before the intense excitement of the soliloquy and the meeting with Macbeth that follows it. In Shakespeare, Lady Macbeth enters alone; solitude is habitual for her, and her only relationship, with her husband, is correspondingly intense. Davenant's Lady Macbeth has to create a moment of privacy in order to read her husband's letter. Davenant also solves what to a tidy mind might seem a problem in Shakespeare, the fact that Macduff appears for the first time only after the murder of Duncan; before that there is no hint of his existence. It seems an odd way to treat a major character. Shakespeare gives us only the painful separation of the Macduffs, and Lady Macduff's resentment; Davenant makes them much more a couple, developing an affectionate relationship we have to take largely on trust in Shakespeare.

[Act I, Scene v.] Inverness. Macbeth's Castle.

Enter Lady Macbeth and Lady Macduff, Lady Macbeth having a Letter in her Hand.

LADY MACBETH.
    Madam, I have observ'd since you came hither,
    You have been still disconsolate. Pray tell me,
    Are you in perfect health?
LADY MACDUFF.   Alas! how can I?
    My Lord, when Honour call'd him to the War,
    Took with him half of my divided soul,
    Which lodging in his bosom, lik'd so well
    The place, that 'tis not yet return'd.
LADY MACBETH.   Methinks
    That should not disorder you: for, no doubt
    The brave *Macduff* left half his soul behind him,
    To make up the defect of yours.
LADY MACDUFF.   Alas!
    The part transplanted from his breast to mine,
    (As 'twere by sympathy) still bore a share
    In all the hazards which the other half
    Incurr'd, and fill'd my bosom up with fears.
LADY MACBETH.
    Those fears, methinks, should cease now he is safe.
LADY MACDUFF.
    Ah, Madam, dangers which have long prevail'd
    Upon the fancy; even when they are dead
    Live in the memory a-while.
LADY MACBETH.
    Although his safety has not power enough to put
    Your doubts to flight, yet the bright glories which
    He gain'd in Battel might dispel those Clouds.
LADY MACDUFF.
    The world mistakes the glories gain'd in war,
    Thinking their Lustre true: alas, they are

> But Comets, Vapours! by some men exhal'd
> From others bloud, and kindl'd in the Region
> Of popular applause, in which they live
> A-while; then vanish: and the very breath
> Which first inflam'd them, blows them out agen.
>
> LADY MACDUFF. (*Aside.*)
>   I willingly would read this Letter; but
>   Her presence hinders me; I must divert her.
>   [*Aloud*] If you are ill, repose may do you good;
>   Y'had best retire; and try if you can sleep.
>
> LADY MACDUFF.
>   My doubtful thoughts too long have kept me waking,
>   Madam! I'll take your Counsel.   [*Exit Lady Macduff.*]
>
> LADY MACBETH.
>   Now I have leisure, peruse this Letter.
>   His last brought some imperfect news of things
>   Which in the shape of women greeted him
>   In a strange manner. This perhaps may give
>   More full intelligence.   (*She reads.*

The last speech is an example of Davenant's concern to make things clearer and easier. In Shakespeare, the opening of the letter, 'They met me in the day of success' (1.5.1) is abrupt and leaves us wondering for a moment who 'they' are. We also wonder if the letter actually begins so abruptly, or if we are picking it up part way through. Davenant, by explaining that this is the second of two letters, and by filling in the background information, clarifies the exposition. In doing so he of course sacrifices some of the unease created by the original.

Davenant's version of Lady Macbeth's soliloquy at 1.5.38–54 ('The raven himself is hoarse . . .') shows him improving Shakespeare's language according to contemporary notions of decorum. (For the original, see Key Passages, **p. 142.**) What is physical becomes abstract, in the change from 'fill me, from the crown to the toe, top-full / Of direst cruelty' to 'Empty my nature of humanity / And fill it up with cruelty'. There is a reduced concentration on Lady Macbeth's body, in favour of a more general idea of nature. The redundancy of 'access and passage' is trimmed. The difficulty of 'compunctious visitings of nature' is clarified: 'relapses into mercy'. The ambiguity of 'take my milk for gall' (drink my milk as though it were gall, or turn my milk to gall?) is resolved, and we do not have to imagine the spirits suckling at Lady Macbeth's breasts. Finally, 'the blanket of the dark', which Francis Gentleman and others were to find inappropriately common (see Early Critical Reception, **p. 151**), has its dignity raised.

> There wou'd be musick in a Raven's voice,
> Which should but croke the entrance of the King
> Under my Battlements. Come all you spirits

That wait on mortal thoughts: unsex me here:
Empty my Nature of humanity,
And fill it up with cruelty: make thick
My bloud, and stop all passage to remorse;
That no relapses into mercy may
Shake my design, nor make it fall before
'Tis ripened to effect: you murthering spirits,
(Where ere in sightless substances you wait
On Natures mischief) com[e], and fill my breasts
With Gall instead of Milk: make haste dark night,
And hide me in a smoak as black as hell;
That my keen steel see not the wound it makes:
Nor Heav'n peep through the Curtains of the dark,
To cry, hold! hold!

After the murder of Duncan, Davenant adds a scene for the Macduffs that builds
up their relationship and allows the singing and dancing witches an opportunity
to show their art. It also creates a strong parallel between Macbeth and Macduff:
the latter too receives riddling prophecies from the witches. (Davenant may be
remembering that in the final act of Shakespeare's *Richard III* the villain Richard
and the hero Richmond are addressed in turn by a procession of ghosts, creating
a theatrical symmetry that draws the characters together.) Though the witches
are gloating over the murder of Duncan, their second song in particular has a
jovial, prancing quality that stamps it as an entertainment, not a vision of evil.

[Act II, Scene v.]
SCENE; *An Heath*

Enter Lady Macduff, Maid, and Servant.

LADY MACDUFF.
    Art sure this is the place my Lord appointed
    Us to meet him?
SERVANT.
    This is the entrance o'th'Heath; and here
    He order'd me to attend him with the Chariot.
LADY MACDUFF.
    How fondly did my Lord conceive that we
    Should shun the place of danger by our flight
    From *Everness*? The darkness of the day
    Makes the Heath seem the gloomy walks of death.
    We are in danger still: they who dare here
    Trust Providence, may trust it any where.
MAID.
    But this place, Madam, is more free from terror:
    Last night methoughts I heard a dismal noise
    Of shrieks and groanings in the air.

LADY MACDUFF.

    'Tis true, this is a place of greater silence;

    Not so much troubled with the groans of those

    That die; nor with the out-cries of the living.

MAID.

    [Yet], I have heard stories, how some men

    Have in such lonely places been affrighted

    With dreadful shapes and noises.   (*Macduff hollows.*[1]

LADY MACDUFF.

    But hark, my Lord sure hollows;

    'Tis he; answer him quickly.

SERVANT.   Illo, ho, ho, ho.

Enter Macduff.

LADY MACDUFF.

    Now I begin to see him: are you afoot,

    My Lord?

MACDUFF.

    Knowing the way to be both short and easie,

    And that the Chariot did attend me here,

    I have adventur'd. Where are our Children?

LADY MACDUFF.

    They are securely sleeping in the Chariot.

First Song by Witches.

FIRST WITCH.

    Speak, Sister, speak; is the deed done?[2]

SECOND WITCH.

    Long ago, long ago:

    Above twelve glasses since have run.

THIRD WITCH.

    Ill deeds are seldom slow;

    Nor single: following crimes on former wait.

    The worst of creatures fastest propagate.

    Many more murders must this one ensue,

    As if in death were propagation too.

SECOND WITCH.   He will.

FIRST WITCH.   He shall.

THIRD WITCH.

    He must spill much more bloud;

    And become worse, to make his Title good.

FIRST WITCH.   Now let's dance.

SECOND WITCH.   Agreed.

THIRD WITCH.   Agreed.

---

1   Calls out.

2   The murder of Duncan.

FOURTH WITCH.   Agreed.

CHORUS.

We shou'd rejoice when good Kings bleed.
When Cattel die, about we go,
What then, when Monarchs perish, should we do?

MACDUFF.   What can this be?

LADY MACDUFF.

This is most strange: but why seem you affraid?
Can you be capable of fears, who have
So often caus'd it in your Enemies?

MACDUFF.

It was an hellish Song; I cannot dread
Ought that is mortal, but this is something more.

Second Song.

Let's have a dance upon the Heath;
We gain more life by *Duncan*'s death.
Sometimes like brinded[3] Cats we shew,
Having no musick but our mew.
Sometimes we dance in some old Mill,
Upon the Hopper, Stones, and Wheel.
To some old Saw, or Bardish Rhime,
Where still the Mill-clack[4] does keep time.
Sometimes about an hollow tree,
A round, a round, a round dance we.
Thither the chirping Cricket comes,
And Beetle, singing drowsie hums.
Sometimes we dance o're Fens and Furs,[5]
To howls of Wolves, and barks of Curs.
And when with none of those we meet,
We dance to th'Ecchoes of our feet.
At the night-Raven's dismal voice,
Whilst others tremble, we rejoice;
And nimbly, nimbly dance we still
To th'Ecchoes from an hollow Hill.

MACDUFF.

I am glad you are not affraid.

LADY MACDUFF.

I would not willingly to fear submit:
None can fear ill, but those that merit it.

MACDUFF. (*Aside.*)

Am I made bold by her? How strong a guard

---

3 Tabby.
4 The clapper that shakes the grain on to the millstones.
5 Marsh and shrubs.

Is innocence! [*Aloud*] If any one would be
Reputed valiant, let him learn of you;
Vertue both courage is, and safety too.   (*A dance of Witches.*

Enter three Witches.

MACDUFF.
These seem foul spirits; I'll speak to 'em.
If you can any thing by more than nature know;
You may in these prodigious times fore-tell
Some ill we may avoid.

FIRST WITCH.
Saving thy bloud will cause it to be shed;

SECOND WITCH.
He'll bleed by thee, by whom thou first hast bled.

THIRD WITCH.
Thy Wife shall shunning danger, dangers find,
And fatal be, to whom she most is kind.   (*Ex[eunt] Witches*

LADY MACDUFF.
Why are you alter'd, sir? Be not so thoughtful:
The Messengers of Darkness never spake
To men, but to deceive them.

MACDUFF.
Their words seem to fore-tell some dire Predictions.

LADY MACDUFF.
He that believes ill news from such as these,
Deserves to find it true. Their words are like
Their shape; nothing but Fiction.
Let's hasten to our journey.

MACDUFF.
I'll take your counsel; for to permit
Such thoughts upon our memories to dwell,
Will make our minds the Registers of Hell.   (*Exeunt omnes.*

From **David Garrick's adaptation of Macbeth** (1744) in *Bell's Edition of Shakespeare's Plays I* (1773). Reprinted in Brian Vickers, ed., *Shakespeare: the Critical Heritage*, Vol. III (London: Routledge and Kegan Paul, 1975), pp. 133–4

David Garrick was the leading English actor and theatre manager of the late eighteenth century. He was also a playwright, and for all his reverence for Shakespeare he was never averse to improving the script by cutting and rewriting. His version of *Macbeth* is much closer to the original than is Davenant's, but he evidently thought Macbeth, the part he himself would play, needed the proper death scene Shakespeare had failed to provide. It is an edifying conclusion, underlined by Macduff's naming the principal crimes for which Macbeth is being punished. Macbeth's last speech draws a moral by identifying ambition as the principal cause of his tragedy. (The last speech of Davenant's Macbeth is one

line: 'Farewell vain world, and what's most vain in it, ambition'.) Macduff's decision to take Macbeth's sword as a trophy spares the audience the indecorous
sight of a severed head. It is typical of the eclecticism of theatrical scripts at this
period that in this short passage there are three writers at work: Macbeth's first
speech is by Shakespeare; Macduff's speech is by Davenant (with revisions);
Macbeth's last speech is by Garrick. On the power of Garrick's acting, in the
play as a whole and in this scene in particular, see Early Critical Reception,
pp. 52–3 and The Work in Performance, **p. 91**.

MACBETH.   Lay on *Macduff*,
    And damn'd be he that first cries, hold, enough.
MACDUFF.
    This for my royal master *Duncan*.
    This for my bosom friend, my wife; and this for
    The pledges of her love and mine, my children.

    Sure there are remains to conquer—I'll   [*Macbeth falls*]
    As trophy bear away his sword, to
    Witness my revenge.   [*Exit Macduff*]
MACBETH.
    'Tis done! the scene of life will quickly close.
    Ambition's vain, delusive dreams are fled,
    And now I wake to darkness, guilt and horror;
    I cannot bear it! Let me shake it off—
    'Tw'o not be; my soul is clogg'd with blood—
    I cannot rise! I dare not ask for mercy—
    It is too late, hell drags me down; I sink,
    I sink—Oh!—my soul is lost for ever!
    Oh!   [*Dies*]

From **Kenneth Tynan, *Curtains*** (London: Longmans, 1961), pp. 98–9

Kenneth Tynan was arguably the leading English drama critic in the middle years
of the twentieth century, and Laurence Olivier was (with John Gielgud) one of
England's two leading Shakespearean actors in the same period. Tynan's review
of the 1955 production of *Macbeth* at the Shakespeare Memorial Theatre in
Stratford-upon-Avon brings the talents of the actor and the critic together.
(They would join again in the 1960s, not always comfortably, when Olivier
became director of Britain's National Theatre with Tynan as its literary manager.) Tynan begins by touching on the paradox of *Macbeth* in the theatre:
though one of Shakespeare's most popular and frequently produced plays, it is
formidably difficult to perform, and its stage history, particularly from the early
twentieth century onward, is littered with failures. Besides reporting and analys-
ing Olivier's success in the leading role, Tynan touches on traditonal areas of
difficulty, particularly the playing of the witches. He also thinks, as Garrick did,
that Macbeth should really have a death scene.

Figure 2 **Laurence Olivier as Macbeth and Vivien Leigh as Lady Macbeth in the 1955 production at Stratford-upon-Avon.**

Nobody has ever succeeded as Macbeth, and the reason is not far to seek. Instead of growing as the play proceeds, the hero shrinks; complex and many-levelled to begin with, he ends up a cornered thug, lacking even a death scene with which to regain lost stature. Most Macbeths, mindful of this, let off their big guns as soon as possible, and have usually shot their bolt by the time the dagger speech is out. The marvel of Sir Laurence Olivier's reading is that it reverses this procedure, turns the play inside out, and makes it (for the first time I can remember) a thing of mounting, not waning, excitement. Last Tuesday Sir Laurence shook hands with greatness, and within a week or so the performance will have ripened into a masterpiece: not of the superficial, booming, have-a-bash kind, but the real thing, a structure of perfect forethought and proportion, lit by flashes of intuitive lightning.

He begins in a perilously low key, the reason for which is soon revealed. This Macbeth is paralysed with guilt before the curtain rises, having already killed Duncan time and again in his mind. Far from recoiling and popping his eyes, he greets the air-drawn dagger with sad familiarity; it is a fixture in the crooked furniture of his brain. Uxoriousness leads him to the act, which unexpectedly purges him of remorse. Now the portrait swells; seeking security, he is seized with fits of desperate bewilderment as the prize is snatched out of reach. There was true agony in "I had else been perfect"; Banquo's ghost was received with horrific torment, as if Macbeth should shriek "I've been robbed!," and the phrase about the dead rising to "push us from our stools" was accompanied by a convulsive shoving gesture which few other actors would have risked.

The needle of Sir Laurence's compass leads him so directly to the heart of the role that we forget the jagged rocks of laughter over which he is travelling. At the heart we find, beautifully projected, the anguish of the *de facto* ruler who dares not admit that he lacks the essential qualities of kingship. Sir Laurence's Macbeth is like Skule in Ibsen's chronicle play *The Pretenders*, the valiant usurper who can never comprehend what Ibsen calls "the great kingly thought." He will always be a monarch *manqué*.

The witches' cookery lesson is directed with amusing literalness; the Turk's nose, the Jew's liver, and the baby's finger are all held up for separate scrutiny; but the apparitions are very unpersuasive, and one felt gooseflesh hardly at all. On the battlements Sir Laurence's throttled fury switches into top gear, and we see a lion, baffled but still colossal. "I 'gin to be a-weary of the sun" held the very ecstasy of despair, the actor swaying with grief, his voice rising like hair on the crest of a trapped animal. "Exeunt, fighting" was a poor end for such a giant warrior. We wanted to see how he would die; and it was not he but Shakespeare who let us down.

Vivien Leigh's Lady Macbeth is more niminy-piminy than thundery-blundery; more viper than anaconda, but still quite competent in its small way. Macduff and his wife, actor-proof parts,[1] are played with exceptional power by Keith Michell and Maxine Audley. The midnight hags, with traditional bon-homie, scream with laughter at their own jokes: I long, one day, to see whis-pering witches, less intent on yelling their sins across the country-side. The production has all the speed and clarity we associate with Glen Byam Shaw, and Roger Furse's settings are bleak and serviceable, except for the England scene, which needs only a cat and a milestone to go straight into *Dick Whittington*.[2]

From **James Goodwin, *Akira Kurosawa and Intertextual Cinema***
(Baltimore, Md., and London: The Johns Hopkins University Press, 1994), pp. 178–83

In his 1957 film *Throne of Blood* the Japanese director Akira Kurosawa adapted *Macbeth* to mediaeval Japan, the world of the samurai. These extracts from James Goodwin's analysis show how Kurosawa found cinematic equivalents for Shakespeare's language. Early in the film, the confusing journey through Cobweb Forest (the film's original Japanese title is *Castle of the Spider Woman*) reflects the murky language of Shakespeare's 1.2, with its equally confusing reports of the war (see Key Passages, **pp. 128–32**). The sense of entrapment recalls the

---

1   i.e., parts in which an actor cannot fail.
2   Tynan's reference is to that popular form of English theatre, the Christmas pantomime; the suggestion is that the set was inappropriately pretty, and a bit tacky.

prophecies that make Macbeth's fate seem predetermined. Shakespeare's images become pictures on the screen, noises on the soundtrack. Lady Macbeth talks of a raven; in the film we hear and see the crows, and Kurosawa draws on their symbolic power in Japanese culture. (The character equivalents are as follows: Washizu = Macbeth; Miki = Banquo; Tsuzuki = Duncan; Asaji = Lady Macbeth.)

Washizu is forewarned about the futility of ambition.[1] The initial movement of Washizu and Miki in their ride through Cobweb Forest is swift and determined, as accented through camera tracks and pans in a consistent direction from screen left to right. In a subsequent shot, however, they enter from screen right. Realizing that after two hours in the forest their ride has taken them full circle, Washizu and Miki fear they are held captive by a spirit. In trying to break the spell, Washizu rides on with bow drawn, an action suggestive of a Buddhist ceremony in which priest-archers shoot arrows to ward off evil spirits. The two samurai are led to a ghostly hut containing a mysterious old woman at a spinning wheel.

As the spinner works at her device, an image that suggests the thread of fate and a tragic wheel of fortune, her soft chant warns

Nothing in this world will save
Or measure up man's actions here
Nor in the next, for there is none.
This life must end in fear.

In her prediction of the rise in his political fortunes, the spinner dismisses Washizu's show of loyalty to Tsuzuki as a self-deception. The spinner scolds Washizu for denying his deeper ambitions for power. (In the subsequent reunion with her husband, Asaji expresses the same criticism of him.) When she gives voice to his inner desires, the spinner accelerates her movements and speech. Several visual analogies between this spirit and Asaji are developed, but one fundamental distinction between them is the spinner's cautions on the vanity of ambition. In leaving the forest, Washizu and Miki pass mounds of unburied human skeletons still dressed in battle gear. On his second visit to the forest spirits, Washizu will vow to leave a mountain of slain enemies, yet the only death that follows is his own.

Cobweb Forest is a paradoxical environment that contains utter contrasts in physical conditions. In the midst of sunlight there is a rainstorm, and though it is daytime there is immense darkness. The ride of Washizu and Miki is rapid and unimpeded, but in the foreground of each successive shot appears a tangle of tree trunks, branches, and undergrowth. They drive their horses furiously through a tempest but they find absolute calm around the mysterious hut. The forest offers the greatest strategic defense for Tsuzuki's forces, yet his two leading commanders

1   The film opens and closes with speeches by an unseen chorus proclaiming, like Garrick's death-speech (see The Work in Performance, pp. 106–7), the ruin produced by ambition.

become lost in it. Even when they have left the forest, Washizu and Miki remain lost. Though in completely open terrain, a dense fog protracts the labyrinthian confusion of their ride towards Forest Castle. Sparse, repetitive chords of music measure the futility of their ride in the fog. Once visibility is restored, they find themselves in front of the castle at a distance of only several hundred yards. [. . .]

The film brilliantly reconceives the play's elaborate bird imagery, which is inaugurated by Lady Macbeth's murderous allusion, "The raven himself is hoarse / That croaks the fatal entrance of Duncan / Under my battlements" [1.5.37–9]. Dialogue references, sound effects, and filmic images are combined to form similar metaphors that encompass the film drama. When Washizu's men prepare the forbidden chamber for their master and lady, a passing crow's cry is heard over visuals dominated by the room's walls, discolored by blood. The crow is a symbol of death within traditional Japanese culture, and Washizu's men react to the cry as an omen of evil. In urging her husband toward the first murder, Asaji hears a similar cry and assures her husband that the crow has signaled, "The throne is yours." Just before Washizu goes to commit the assassination, the visuals cut away to a night sky. Prominent in the sky is a crescent moon, which is the symbol of Tsuzuki's reign. Across this night sky a crow flies and sharply caws.

Against all logic, Washizu insists at his last war council that the sudden, unexplained flight of forest birds into the castle's chambers is a good omen. After making this assertion he sits down in a show of defiance, but a bird then calmly perches on his shoulder. The frightened screams of women draw Washizu from the council chamber. In the corridor he encounters attendants in terrified flight from Lady Asaji.

When the forest finally approaches the castle, Washizu's soldiers turn against their master. With a sustained barrage of arrows, they entrap him within Forest Castle. The protracted death scene is an ironic manifestation of Washizu's tenacity and firm will to power, attained, finally, at the point of his own destruction. The baroque prolongation and overstatement of this event[2] is a culmination of the visual figures for forces—the spinner-prophet's exposure of his inner ambitions, Asaji's manipulations, a heritage of political intrigue—that ultimately ensnare him.

From **Kenneth S. Rothwell, *A History of Shakespeare on Screen: a Century of Film and Television*** (Cambridge: Cambridge University Press, 1999), pp. 155–6

Roman Polanski's 1971 film version of *Macbeth* brings the violence on to the screen, and as we watch it we realize by comparison how little violence Shakepeare shows on stage. In the film Duncan is murdered, and Macbeth is beheaded, before our eyes. In the previous extract we saw how Akira Kurosawa found cinematic equivalents for Shakespeare's language. In this account by Kenneth S. Rothwell, a leading American scholar in the field of Shakespeare on film, we see how Polanski translated Shakespeare's pervasive sense of evil into graphic images. Characteristically, his symbol of entrapment is a very literal one,

---

2   At the climax of this sequence Washizu has so many arrows in his body he looks like a porcupine.

a chain. In *Macbeth* we are constantly aware of the pressure of the language, with its images of blood and darkness; Polanski's visual images, and his sound-track, exert a similar, even more relentless, pressure.

The pre-credit, spectacular long take subliminally gives portents of the events to follow, and predicts what it means for Macbeth to "have supp'd full with horrors" [5.5.13] before he suffers death by beheading at the hands of MacDuff. First, there is a hazy sunrise and seascape of a lonely beach, and then a crooked stick enters the frame from the right followed by two withered crones and a young woman, whose fairness contrasts with the foulness of the older women: "Fair is foul, and foul is fair" [1.1.11]. From a squeaky, dilapidated cart, these less than supernatural hags remove an assortment of macabre objects, among them a hangman's noose and a severed arm, into the hand of which they insert a dagger (is that a sufficient portent?). In closeup, the cackling trio bury the arm in the sand and pour a vial of blood over it. A gull squawks, a talisman of a galaxy of birds' cries to follow, all of which echo Shakespeare's own ornithological obsession in *Macbeth*: "Light thickens, and the crow / Makes wing to th' rooky wood" [3.2.50–1]. Fog and mist roll in with superimposed titles fading in and out, while the Third Ear Band provides discordant violin and bagpipe music for the depart-ure of the witches' rickety cart. The soundtrack reverberates with horses' hooves, shouting and screaming, clashing of swords, the whinnying of horses, human wailing, coughing, and moaning, while the superimposed credits continue to roll on the now completely fog-bound screen. After the fog dissipates, dead and wounded litter the battlefield at Forres. In mid-shot a soldier stops by an injured man lying face down on the ground, pulls at his boot, and the man stirs. The injured man feebly lifts his head and the soldier shatters his spine with two or three sickening whacks with an iron ball on a chain. The camera moves on to the bleeding sergeant's battle report and then to a bloodied Thane of Cawdor (Vic Abbott) bound and stretched out on a horse-drawn litter.

Polanski husbands his aural and visual images the way a good writer squeezes words. The mist and fog again suggest the play's leitmotif – the equivocal nature of reality – "Is this a dagger which I see before me [?]" [2.1.33]. The beauty of nature contrasts with the ugliness of battle. The medallion and ceremonial chain that Duncan (Nicholas Selby) lifts from the defeated Thane of Cawdor fore-shadows more chain images, to include the iron collar and chain around the neck of Cawdor at his grisly execution, an episode only reported in the play. A defiant endomorph, Cawdor oozes contempt for his captors, especially the double-dealing Rosse, and leaps off a castle parapet to die brutally at the end of a chain fastened to an iron collar around his size twenty-two neck, "Nothing in his life / Became him like the leaving it" [1.4.7–8], reports Malcolm (Stephan Chase) to Duncan. Chains hold the bear to the stone column in the baiting scene[1] before the disastrous banquet. Later, Macbeth awards Lennox's medallion and chain to Seyton (Noel Davis) as a payoff for his corrupt services. The chain motif also

1   In the final battle Macbeth compares himself to a bear tied to a stake for a bear-baiting (5.7.1–2).

stands for Macbeth's self-enchainment, who, as has rightly been said, murdered himself when he murdered Duncan.

Hanged men dangle, slowly twisting in the wind, from a crudely constructed gallows, while below several more of the condemned are queued up awaiting their turns. Those uncooperative with their hangmen are pummeled into submission. A twitching and jerking wretch is hoisted up high by a rope around his neck. Muffled cries, grunts, groans. Off in the distance, a mounted Macbeth (Jon Finch) and Banquo (Martin Shaw) impassively watch the chamber of horrors, a Brueghel-like nightmare. In the words of the bleeding sergeant, "another Golgotha" [1.2.41], the place of the skull.

Marion D. Perret, 'Double, Double: Trevor Nunn's *Macbeth* for Television', *Shakespeare Bulletin* 52 (Summer 1992), pp. 38–9

Trevor Nunn's 1976 production of *Macbeth*, which began in the Royal Shakespeare Company's smallest theatre, The Other Place, was not only one of the most successful twentieth-century productions of the play, but one of the most effective transfers of a stage production of Shakespeare to television. The intimacy of the original performance conditions suited the intimacy of the medium. Marion D. Perret's account of the 1978 Thames Television version (released on videotape by HBO) stresses its close observation of the actors, its ritualistic and metatheatrical qualities, and its use of repeated gestures which encourage a close observation of social behaviour. She also shows how the production, in line with some late twentieth-century criticism, makes it difficult to draw a pat moral contrast between Macbeth as evil and his adversaries as good. Macbeth's capacity for love, and the misgivings created about the final victory of Malcolm and Macduff, work against conventional distinctions.

This video recording of Trevor Nunn's 1976 production of *Macbeth*, with Ian McKellen and Judi Dench, grips us and will not let go. Powerful acting by the Royal Shakespeare Company turns even minor moments into revelations. For example, in the sleepwalking scene, when Dench's astonishing Lady Macbeth draws us into the anguish of the self-damned, shifting our gaze brings small relief: we see the Doctor visibly shaken by horror, pity, and helplessness. Nunn's production both intensifies our emotional involvement and challenges our understanding by persistent ambiguity.

This *Macbeth* makes us consider carefully what we see: the first shot forces us to interpret a pattern. We look down on a ring of dark blocks within a spotlit circle, puzzling until the ceremonial entrance of the actors, who sit on the blocks, reveals the inner circle to be the stage. (Our point of view will usually be that of the circle of actors, looking inward upon the action, though occasionally we will look outward to see characters emerge from darkness or the mist of the light spill.) A slow pan of the actors' faces gives more information than meaning. We cannot tell, unless we know who plays what part, which of the expressionless men is a hero, which a villain. Nor can we tell when or where the action occurs.

Figure 3 Ian McKellen (as Macbeth) and the witches in the 1976–8
Royal Shakespeare Company production.

Without visual cues as to time or place, we have to follow with a concentration seldom demanded of television audiences. To verify our understanding, we can do nothing more than look where pinspotting or closeups direct us and weigh what we hear against what we see, which sometimes underscores the words, sometimes undercuts them. Striking visual images, such as the opening overhead shot of the stage, also tend to take on a life of their own: associations of circularity—community, ritual, repetition, entrapment—become visual texts within the play. This stark, intense, metatheatrical *Macbeth* turns us into active participants in creating meaning: we are caught with the characters in a dangerous world and forced to deal with its disturbing possibilities.

To perceive a pattern is not necessarily to resolve its ambiguities. Repetition of the simple act of kneeling to kiss the ruler's hand can expand the gesture's range of significances. As Macbeth, cheered by the thanes, enters to Duncan, the bloody sergeant impulsively falls to his knees and presses his lips to the hero's hand; as quickly, he pulls himself stiffly erect, clicks his heels together in salute, and disappears. He may merely pay tribute to his brave captain, but Macbeth may find his obeisance another confirmation of the witches' prophecy, and Duncan may find it a reason for proclaiming Malcolm forthwith. Macbeth's kneeling to kiss Duncan's hand shows warmth, love, and loyalty; to kiss Malcolm's, cold observance of protocol.

The most ambiguous repetition of this gesture comes in 3.1. Banquo formally declares his loyalty to the royal party but bows only slightly before turning to leave. "Goes Fleance with you?" stops him short. Banquo hesitates, then kneels to kiss his friend's hand with enough fervor to make Lady Macbeth eye him narrowly. What does this ostentation reflect? Awareness that he has violated decorum? Fear that Macbeth might harm his son? Reversal or concealment of a decision to speed fulfillment of the witches' prophecy? We do not know how to read Banquo here, and Macbeth's subsequent musing on his friend's "royalty of nature" serves as epitaph rather than clarification.

Nor do we know how to read Macduff. In 1.1, as images of Christian worship are intercut with the witches' unholy rites, he watches while Duncan and his followers kneel in prayer—Macduff is at once part of this community and detached from it. Our final view of him is likewise equivocal. Just as Macbeth entered from killing Duncan, with the bloody daggers clutched in his hands, Macduff enters from killing Macbeth. Macduff's halting "Hail, King of Scotland!" reveals a sudden recognition that he has killed an anointed king and that the new king is weak. The much-needed champion is already following Macbeth's footsteps. This production closes with what seems an emblem: bloody hands holding daggers opposite clean hands holding the crown. The striking image overpowers our memory of Macduff's "The time is free," disquieting us with an ambiguity not in the text.

Like Macbeth, we may itch to resolve what "cannot be ill, cannot be good" into one or the other; like him, we may be misled or mislead ourselves. The intercutting in 1.1 invites us to expect a contest between forces of supernatural good and evil, like that in [Orson] Welles' film. Although there are many visual references to religion, we see, in fact, little of such a struggle in Scotland or in Macbeth. His faltering in determination comes not from depth of moral scruples but fear that his "vaulting ambition" will o'erleap itself and fall.

This Macbeth is very much a warrior. Hair slicked back, leather-coated, at the witches' hail he whirls, whipping his dagger out as a street punk pulls a switchblade. Before killing Duncan, he rolls up his sleeve, workmanlike. In the banquet scene, he is both "a soldier and afeard": despite the fit of terror that has him literally foaming at the mouth, he plunges his dagger again and again into that "horrid imagining." Though temporarily so "unmanned in folly" that he clings to his wife in public, when she collapses after their guests leave, he lifts her up and drags her off to face knowledge of other dark deeds.

Disturbingly, we are not allowed to forget the loving man when Macbeth becomes a monster. McKellen makes us feel in his Macbeth a genuine warmth gradually giving way to pretended cordiality. The gore we expect to see on Macbeth's hands may strike us less than the love those hands show after the murder: sustaining Macduff as he struggles to voice the unspeakable, comforting Donalbain in his grief, protectively embracing Lady Macbeth. Her growing recognition that the man she so loves has murdered his ability to care for her— or anyone but himself—is what kills the spirit of this Lady. Intuiting that he plans the murder of his battle partner, she pulls back in horror from the man Macbeth has become, but she can never "be innocent of the knowledge" or free of the deed.

Foul and fair are inextricable in what is at once a horror story and a love story. Lips explore lips, pausing only to plan murder. Both Macbeth and his wife express and seek union of mind through touch; when their thoughts match, their bodies mesh. The dying of their passion is as wrenching to watch as the dying of their souls. Preoccupied with killing, he turns to irony and action. Shut out, unable to bear the change in him or between them, she has nowhere to turn for relief. Nor do we, if we seek to respond unequivocally.

Difficult to endure, Nunn's powerful Macbeth is impossible to forget.

From **Sinead Cusack with Carol Rutter, 'Lady Macbeth's Barren Sceptre'**, in Carol Rutter *et al.*, *Clamorous Voices: Shakespeare's Women Today* (New York: Routledge, 1989), pp. 70–2

Clamorous Voices is a series of conversations conducted by British scholar Carol Rutter, whose work on Shakespeare in performance is strongly feminist, with a number of actresses who have played leading women's parts in Shakespeare. This extract comes from the chapter 'Lady Macbeth's Barren Sceptre', a conversation with Sinead Cusack, who played Lady Macbeth in a 1986 Royal Shakespeare Company production directed by Adrian Noble. Cusack describes how she thought her way through the sleepwalking scene (see Key Passages, **pp. 177–80**), showing the variety of sources a performer draws on: personal experience, details of costume, a sense of the language. She begins with very practical offstage preparation – and relaxation – during the long wait the character has before this scene.

I would go to my dressing room and have a great time – a strong cup of tea, a fag – and then I messed myself up. People hated the way I looked in the sleepwalking scene and I don't give a tuppenny! I loved it.

I had on this gown of white cotton, almost like a hospital gown, and then I had Macbeth's jumper on – the one he'd worn under his armour: she'd been sleeping in it. I wanted to give the impression that she'd been in that nightgown for a long time, that she wasn't dressing during the day, and the nightgown was soiled. And then one day in rehearsal – it's ridiculous how these things happen, they have no logic to them – Adrian said to me, 'Tuck the nightie up into your knickers; I think you're going to paddle in the sea.' Of course – washing her hands!

I'm a sleepwalker myself. Once when I was a child my parents were having a party; at about eleven o'clock I emerged from my bedroom and I walked through the hallway into the garden and took off my nightie. I dug a hole in the garden and I buried my nightdress. And then I went back to bed. My parents told me that my sleepwalking was characterised by speed. I was very *busy* in my sleep, and I found that a great help, coming down fast, in the sleepwalking scene. I felt that her particular brand of unrest would be those frantic little devil-thoughts that you

Figure 4 **Sinead Cusack as Lady Macbeth in the 1986 Royal Shakespeare Company production.**

can't knock out of your mind, devil-thoughts that keep coming back – about blood, about *blood*. You know when you're panicking, frantically panicking, and these little shooting thoughts are hitting you and getting embroiled and all mixed up in your head and you can't stop the voices, you can't stop the sounds: that's the sort of unrest I pictured her as having, and that's certainly the way the sleepwalk-ing speech is written – erratic, disjointed.

What I found I had to do in rehearsal was to clarify absolutely in my head what each of those thoughts reminded me of, what situations they were pictures of. It's terribly easy to generalise madness or unrest or panic into one long blur, but you have to isolate each single thought so that it's absolutely clear to you where the picture – where those words – comes from. It took me ages and ages to do that.

I ran down the stairs and then I turned and I held out my hands – it was that same spasmodic child gesture from after the murder when I showed Macbeth Duncan's blood on my hands – only it wasn't Macbeth standing there, it was my gentlewoman and the physician. I saw Macbeth. As I thrust out my hands to display the blood to him, the candle slipped out of my hand and my woman caught it, but I was already walking forward. I knelt and starting putting stuff all over my face. I was looking in a mirror and making myself up to be Queen. To be the very, very beautiful Queen.

Then I was rubbing, rubbing. 'Yet here's a spot.' 'Out, damned spot!' Each of those angle turns in the speech was a new picture. 'One: two', – the clock strikes, she's hearing the bell she signalled Macbeth with when everything was 'provided' – 'why then, 'tis time to do't.' And *we've got to do it*. The next thought that came – 'Hell is murky!' – was utterly bereft. She was using loss, the loss of him, the loss of the child. Without him she didn't know where to go. Hell is murky and she's lost her way; she doesn't know the way through.

Then all the old gestures began to echo what had gone before. 'Fie, my lord, fie! A soldier and afeard?' was very prim; 'What need we fear? . . . none can call our power to accompt' was irritable and steely together – one can imagine that she said many times, '*We are untouchable!*' But the next picture pushes in – talk about untouchable! 'Yet who would have thought the old man to have had so much blood in him?' I was looking at Duncan's body again. Those Scottish castles have lots of very small stone rooms. It was easy to imagine one of those little bedchambers covered in blood from wall to wall.

I played a madness in this scene that I don't think has been there in other productions. It was a mind that had disintegrated into shards – that's how I imagined her – rather than a retrospective, reflective consideration of my life. I couldn't play that option. I tried a few times in rehearsals, but it didn't work. I felt this desolate child saying, 'We can do it – we can – no we can't – I've lost him. I've lost him!' A mind in shards.

On the 'Oh! Oh! Oh!' I collapsed on the floor. But then I pulled myself together, in queenly fashion, took my little pot of carmine, made up my lips with that queen-red lipstick, put my carmine away, looked down at my hand – and saw blood on my fingers! It was the carmine, but I *saw* Duncan's blood! I went berserk then and began scrabbling in the earth. I tried to rub the blood off the floor, but then the floor suddenly shot out – a plank in the boards shot forward – and this place was turning into a gallery built over hell!

Technically, one of the things I found useful was the idea that when the plank shot out, I had my battlement: I walked forward, out on the battlement, and I was going to throw myself over! That was the moment when I was going to kill myself – only I couldn't, and I retreated, pulling myself together, saying, 'Wash your hands; put on your nightgown.'

And then that last line, 'I tell you yet again, Banquo's buried, he cannot come out on's grave.' Adrian Noble gave me a note on that line: she's saying, 'No – please – this *can't* be happening,' she's trying to persuade herself, to hold their madness at bay. It's an absolute panic attack. She's shaking. '*Don't* say he's come out of his grave, because if we admit to that one, we're lost.'

From **Derek Jacobi, 'Macbeth'**, in Robert Smallwood, ed., *Players of Shakespeare 4* (Cambridge: Cambridge University Press, 1998), pp. 196–7

Derek Jacobi played Macbeth in 1993, in a Royal Shakespeare Company production directed by Adrian Noble. Here he describes his playing of Macbeth's reaction to his encounter with the witches (see Key Passages, **pp. 132–9**). Macbeth has come on stage in a mood of high exuberance after his victory; he himself is beating on the drum whose sound cues his entrance. Then the witches startle him by speaking his own thoughts of ambition. The extract begins with Macbeth noticing that Banquo is watching his reaction. We are used to concentrating on Macbeth and Lady Macbeth; Jacobi reminds us that Macbeth's relationship with Banquo is also important, and warrants close attention. Later in his account he reveals how helpful a stage prop – like those listed by Peter Thomson (see The Work in Performance, **pp. 96–9**) – can be to an actor constructing a performance.

The sudden awareness that Banquo is deeply intrigued and looking at him very searchingly is something I tried to use to whip Macbeth out of his reverie and bring him back into focus. He listens to what the witches prophesy for Banquo and tries to detain them, to hear more, as they begin to leave. I tried to suggest at this point that he attempts to wipe these things from his mind, to make a joke of them with Banquo, their little exchange finishing with them both laughing.[1] But there is an odd edge to it, because they are not exactly sure what they are laughing at; the end of the conversation is strained and awkward. This is a significant moment, for it marks the beginning of their divergence, of their ceasing to trust each other. It must be plotted, because their relationship is so important, but it must not be overdone. They have been shown as pals (there's just a few seconds to do that), but if you show the distrust here too big and too soon you've got nowhere to go. It is merely a thought at this point. At the end of the scene, after the news of Macbeth's elevation has come from Ross and Angus, Macbeth says to Banquo 'Think upon what hath chanced' [1.3.154] and it seems as though they are about to talk to each other again in the old way. Then Macbeth says 'Till then, enough', and I tried to suggest that he was about to say something serious and confidential, then paused and instead said 'enough', implying uncertainty about sharing his thoughts with him: the process of separation has gone a little further. Even the final 'Come, friends' seemed to have a double edge: 'Come, . . .' – and what am I to call them? Are they friends? Yes, everyone is a friend at the moment. What *am* I worrying about?

Macbeth's response to the witches' greeting is hesitant and interrogative. He considers the idea, the pause I used on the word *king* in 'to be king / Stands not within the prospect of belief' [1.3.73–4] seeming to hold it up for momentary examination. To the news from Ross and Angus, on the other hand, his reaction is much more fearful. The very thought of it makes his heart beat and his hair stand

1   In Holinshed Macbeth and Banquo initially treat the witches' prophecies as a joke (see Source, pp. 21–2).

on end. This was very important to me, one of the through-lines for Macbeth. I went through the play marking the times he speaks of fear, particularly in relation to himself. He does so in every scene: it is paramount for him; the man is constantly fearful. He says so to himself, he says so to his wife: it never changes. When the witches said he was going to be king, I had dropped the dagger which I'd been using to beat the drum and bent to pick it up and put it away. I took it out again in the middle of Macbeth's long aside [1.3.127–42] and was very conscious of it on 'Present fears / Are less than horrible imaginings' [1.3.137–8] because those imaginings are already of killing the king. It was only a momentary thing, but still the dagger came out when he thought of being king. The dagger was a constant emblem for me: the physical dagger, one of his essential accoutrements for battle, was from the beginning connected with the idea of his kingship, leading inevitably to 'Is this a dagger that I see before me?' [2.1.33] and to the drawing of the dagger in earnest to commit the terrible murder. Obviously this is just an actor's finessing: it doesn't have to be there for this aside, but it seemed to me to create a link with the next stage of the play – and it was no doubt useful for the other actors, biding my soliloquizing, to look across at Macbeth and see that he has a dagger in his hand that he is twisting and looking at and yet not really seeing.

Macbeth, then, before the end of his first scene, has faced the thought of killing the king. 'Why do I yield to that suggestion', he asks [1.3.13], and the word is *yield*. The thought could have been repulsed immediately, but it's not repulsed, it's accepted. And the thought terrifies him. He is in an extraordinary mood; the adrenalin is coursing through him and he's not thinking totally straight. Because of the victory he is in a state of high excitement and of emotional exhaustion. He has been killing all day: he is covered with blood. In this state he gets the news: in this state he must react to it. The speed with which things happen in the next phase of the play is to a large extent conditioned by Macbeth's physical and mental state when he receives the witches' greeting.

3

Key Passages

Introduction

Our only source for *Macbeth* is the text in the Folio of 1623, the collection of Shakespeare's works published after his death. It appears to be based on a playhouse manuscript used by Shakespeare's company. Given the general suspicion that the Hecate scenes are later additions, not part of the original play, it represents a version performed some years (we cannot be sure how many) after the first performance. The original *Macbeth*, if there ever was such a thing as a single original version, is lost. In cases in which we have Quarto as well as Folio texts for a Shakespeare play – *Hamlet* and *King Lear* are prime examples – we can tell that cuts have been made in the Folio version. Lacking a Quarto *Macbeth*, we will likely never know if the same is true of this play. Not that cutting Shakespeare is necessarily a bad thing; it has been argued that some of the cuts in *Hamlet* and *Lear* were probably made by Shakespeare himself. In any case this *Macbeth*, for good or ill, is the only *Macbeth* we have.

The text used in this selection of key passages is a modernized version of the Folio, emended where emendation seems necessary. The commentary analyses each passage for its dramatic function, the special problems it may present, and in some cases the theatrical choices it offers. The footnotes offer help with the language, and suggestions on more detailed matters of interpretation. The key passages have been selected, first of all, to show crucial developments in the two central characters, particularly in the lead-in to the murder of Duncan, the immediate aftermath of the murder, and the final deterioration of both characters in the later scenes. The witches, who figure prominently in the Contexts section of this Sourcebook, are fully represented. In any Shakespeare play scenes with secondary characters make important contributions. Of the selections given here, the second scene helps create the play's atmosphere of confusion and moral uncertainty; the scene with Lady Macduff puts a human face on Macbeth's reign of terror, which elsewhere is described in general terms; and the brief description of Edward the Confessor from the England scene offers a vision of good kingship to counter the play's depiction of evil. Reading these Key Passages is of course no substitute for reading the full play. But it is hoped that the guidance provided here will help the reader work through the play as a whole by suggesting the sorts of details to notice and the sorts of questions to ask.

Summary of the Action

Duncan, King of Scotland, is faced with a rebellion by the Thane of Cawdor and an invasion by the King of Norway. His captains Macbeth and Banquo win victories for him on both fronts, and Duncan, ordering the execution of Cawdor, bestows his title on Macbeth (**pp. 128–32**) (page references in bold refer to the Key Passages). Macbeth and Banquo, returning from battle, encounter three witches, who were glimpsed briefly in the play's opening scene (**pp. 126–8**). The witches hail Macbeth as Thane of Glamis, Thane of Cawdor and King hereafter. The witches also predict that Banquo, though he will not be king, will be father to a line of kings (**pp. 132–9**). Macbeth initially seems willing to leave his future kingship to chance; but Duncan's proclamation of his son Malcolm as his heir turns Macbeth's thoughts towards murder. In a letter, he tells Lady Macbeth of his encounter with the witches. This sparks Lady Macbeth's own ambition for her husband, and her determination that they will kill Duncan. When Macbeth returns he seems hesitant about the deed; she prepares to overcome that hesitation (**pp. 139–43**). Duncan arrives as a guest at Macbeth's castle. Macbeth argues himself out of killing the King, but Lady Macbeth conquers his scruples (**pp. 143–8**). On the night of the murder Macbeth sees an imaginary dagger leading him to Duncan's chamber (**pp. 148–9**). After the murder itself he panics, hearing strange voices; Lady Macbeth tries to get him under control (**pp. 150–4**). Macduff discovers Duncan's corpse. Duncan's sons Malcolm and Donalbain flee, and Macbeth is named king.

Not satisfied with the crown, Macbeth broods on the prophecy that Banquo's descendants will be kings, while he himself has no heirs. He hires murderers to kill Banquo and his son Fleance, on the night of a banquet in which Banquo is to be chief guest. The murderers kill Banquo, but Fleance escapes. Banquo's ghost appears at the banquet; only Macbeth sees it, and his wild reaction causes the banquet to break up in disorder (**pp. 155–62**). Macbeth consults the witches, who call up three apparitions: the first tells Macbeth to beware Macduff; the second promises that no one born of woman can harm him; the third, that he will never be defeated until Birnam Wood comes to Dunsinane. The witches also present him with a show of eight kings, the line of Banquo, confirming the prophecy about Banquo's descendants (**pp. 162–70**). Macduff has fled to England; unable to reach him there, Macbeth has Macduff's family murdered (**pp. 171–5**). In England, at the court of Edward the Confessor, whose virtues contrast with Macbeth's tyranny (**pp. 175–7**), Macduff and Malcolm lament the state of Scotland. After Ross brings word of the slaughter of Macduff's family, Malcolm plans to claim the throne of Scotland, backed by Scottish exiles and English soldiers, with Macduff joining in both to save his country and to avenge his family.

In Scotland, Macbeth, who has become a hated tyrant, is plagued by desertions and reports of the impending invasion. Lady Macbeth sleepwalks, trying in vain to wash imaginary blood from her hands (**pp. 177–80**). She dies off stage; at the end of the play Malcolm reports a rumour that she committed suicide. To Macbeth, life now seems meaningless (**pp. 181–6**). He clings to the prophecies as his final hope. But Malcolm orders his soldiers to cut boughs from Birnam Wood, and use them as camouflage for their attack on Macbeth's castle; Birnam Forest comes to Dunsinane. And in the final conflict Macduff reveals that he was not born of woman, but torn from his mother's womb by caesarian section. Macduff kills and beheads Macbeth; Malcolm becomes king of Scotland.

The Characters

Duncan, King of Scotland
Malcolm, his older son
Donalbain, his younger son

Macbeth, captain of Duncan's army
Lady Macbeth, his wife

Banquo, captain of Duncan's army
Fleance, his son

Macduff, a thane of Scotland
Lady Macduff, his wife
Boy, their son

Lennox
Ross
Menteith $\Big\}$ thanes
Angus
Caithness

Siward, Earl of Northumberland
Young Siward, his son

Seyton, Macbeth's attendant
A Captain
English Doctor
Scottish Doctor
Gentlewoman attending Lady Macbeth
Porter
Old Man
Messengers, murderers, soldiers and servants

Hecate, goddess of sorcery
Three witches
Apparitions

Key Passages

Act 1, Scene 1: The witches

This is the shortest opening scene in Shakespeare, and it introduces one of his shortest plays. Its sheer abruptness is startling, and grips the audience's attention. Thunder and lightning, a favourite stage effect with Jacobean popular audiences, take the place of the dialogue, or the trumpet fanfare, that tells the audience, which in Shakespeare's time could be voluble and restless, that the play has begun and they had better settle down and listen.

The scene is not just startling but mysterious, and the mystery centres on the witches – beginning with the question of what to call them. The word 'witch', used in speech headings and stage directions, and in most critical writing about the play, appears only once in the dialogue (1.3.6). In this scene there is no name for these characters; they are simply 'we three', and we make what we can of their words and their appearance. In the rest of the play they are called, by themselves and others, the weird sisters, or weird women. 'Weird' comes from an old English word for 'fate'; this, and the fact that there are three of them, suggests an association with the Parcae, the three Fates who in classical mythology control human destiny. Whether they control Macbeth's destiny or merely start him on a course for which he himself is responsible is one of the many questions the play provokes. (On the play's sense of indeterminacy as explored by Stephen Booth and Stephen Greenblatt, see Modern Criticism, pp. 74–5, 83–5.)

The scene in fact opens with a question, one that leads to further questions: 'When shall we three meet again?' shows that we have come in not at the beginning of a witches' meeting, but at the end. They are planning their next meeting. What have they been up to in this one? Characteristically, we never know. The clearest idea we have of their next meeting is that they are going to meet with Macbeth. Is that all? Just meet with him? Why? Already the hidden-ness of their motives creates a tension that makes us look forward to what is coming.

Their dialogue, with its references to thunder, lightning, rain, fog and filthy air, establishes the murky atmosphere in which the play will unfold, coming to a climax in Lady Macbeth's cry during her sleepwalking scene: 'Hell is murky' (5.1.35). It is as though the play itself, beginning with this opening scene, takes place in a figurative hell, a place of darkness. The witches also introduce a riddling language that will run through the play: 'When the battle's lost, and won' (4); 'Fair is foul, and foul is fair' (11). The riddles can be decoded: the battle will be lost by one side and won by another; foul will look fair when Lady Macbeth graciously welcomes Duncan to her house; fair will look foul when Malcolm slanders himself as a monster of wickedness in order to test Macduff. But a feeling remains that language is unstable and unreliable; the witches will use its ambiguity in 4.1, in the riddling prophecies that give Macbeth a false sense of security. Moreover, the witches do not say that fair will look like foul – they say that fair *is* foul. Reversing the meanings of words, they reverse the poles of the moral universe. When in Milton's *Paradise Lost* Satan declares, 'Evil, be thou my good', we feel the effort he has to make to change the meanings of words. For the witches it is no effort at all: words slide easily into their opposites. We shall see that Macbeth, like Satan, has to make an effort to steel himself to evil. For the witches it comes naturally. At the end of the scene they speak together, combining their voices with an ominous sense of purpose.

Productions sometimes add their own atmospheric touches to this scene. As the audience entered for Peter Hall's 1967 Royal Shakespeare Company production they saw a white sheet covering the entire stage opening. As the play began there were three thunderclaps accompanied by flashes of lightning: in each flash the witches were glimpsed as giant silhouettes projected on to the sheet. The sheet was then whisked away and they were discovered holding a crucifix upside down and pouring blood on it. At the other extreme was the opening of Robin Phillips's production at Stratford, Ontario, in 1978. Before the house lights went down the witches appeared on the stage, and simply stared at the audience for a few moments. The effect was in its own way as unsettling as Hall's more spectacular opening.

Thunder and lightning.
Enter three Witches.

FIRST WITCH
        When shall we three meet again?
        In thunder, lightning, or in rain?
SECOND WITCH
        When the hurly-burly's[1] done,
        When the battle's lost, and won.
THIRD WITCH
        That will be ere the set of sun.
FIRST WITCH
        Where the place?

---

1   Noisy confusion, tumult (referring to the battle).

SECOND WITCH   Upon the heath.[2]
THIRD WITCH
        There to meet with Macbeth.
FIRST WITCH   I come, Graymalkin!
SECOND WITCH   Paddock calls.[3]
THIRD WITCH   Anon!   10
ALL
        Fair is foul, and foul is fair,
        Hover through the fog and filthy air.   *Exeunt*

Act 1, Scene 2: Rebellion and enemy invasion; Macbeth as war hero

We are thrown abruptly into what looks at first like a very different kind of scene. Instead of three nameless and mysterious figures speaking in short rhymed lines, we have a stage full of more or less identifiable characters, a king, his sons, his lords and soldiers, speaking blank verse in iambic pentameter, the normal staple of dramatic writing in Shakespeare's time. We have not just cryptic, riddling hints but a narrative: King Duncan's enemies, the traitors Macdonwald and Cawdor and the foreign invader the King of Norway, are defeated by his loyal generals Macbeth and Banquo. Up to a point, the moral clarity the witches tried to blur with their reversal of fair and foul is restored. The King's followers are valiant and victorious, his enemies, 'merciless' (9) and 'terrible' (52). For the witches, the battle is simply 'lost, and won' (1.1.4); who loses and who wins does not seem to matter to them. In 1.2 Duncan's forces win, and treason and foreign invasion lose.

Yet the scenes are not so unlike as they may at first appear. Act 1, Scene 2, like 1.1, opens with a question, 'What bloody man is that?' Though Duncan later sees the Captain as a morally coherent figure, whose words and wounds both 'smack of honour' (45), the appearance of a man covered in blood is bound to evoke horror. More specifically, he anticipates the bloodstained ghost of Banquo who disrupts the royal banquet in 3.4; the second apparition, a bloody child, in the cauldron scene (4.1); and – most ironically – the bloodstained body (off stage but described vividly) of Duncan himself, who in this scene tells the Captain that his wounds become him, and whose own wounds will be a terrible symbol of order violated. When the Captain describes the heroic feats of Macbeth and Banquo, he wonders if they meant 'to memorize another Golgo-

---

2 Open land, with stunted vegetation.
3 Graymalkin (a cat) and Paddock (a toad) are the witches' familiars, attendant spirits taking animal form. (For an onstage familiar in *The Witch of Edmonton*, see Contemporary Documents, pp. 34–6.) They have evidently called to the witches, but (though a production could decide otherwise by adding offstage noises) the audience does not hear them. This anticipates the disembodied voices heard by Macbeth in the murder sequence.

tha' (41). This links the King's loyal soldiers with the Roman soldiers who crucified Jesus Christ. Finally, Macbeth's reward for loyalty is to be given the title of a traitor, the Thane of Cawdor. Fair is foul, and foul is fair – the witches' words are echoing just below the surface of a scene that seems to have left them behind, a scene full of characters who have no inkling of their existence.

Nor is it altogether clear who is losing and who is winning. A certain murkiness in the writing of the scene is likely to leave a first-time reader or audience member feeling disoriented. (In Dominic Cooke's 2004 Royal Shakespeare Company production lines were cut or rewritten to remove the confusion; however important that confusion may be thematically, theatre artists tend to prefer clarity.) In the Captain's account of Macbeth's confrontation with Macdonwald the antecedents of the pronouns are unclear, so that on first reading it may seem that Macdonwald is killing Macbeth, not the other way around (16–23). It is implied, but never directly stated, that 'Bellona's bridegroom' (55) is Macbeth, and when he confronts the enemy with 'self-comparisons . . . rebellious arm 'gainst arm' the loyal general and the enemy, both faceless, seem alike – not to mention the fact we are not sure whom Macbeth is fighting. The structure of the speech suggests the King of Norway, but 'rebellious' is an odd word to apply to that character; it fits Macdonwald, and it fits Cawdor, and in turn it will fit Macbeth; but Norway is a foreign invader, not a rebel. Who is fair and who is foul, and who is fighting whom? The moral uncertainty is developed in a later scene, when Malcolm reports that the traitor Cawdor died a noble death, begging the King's forgiveness and accepting his own end with courage (1.4.1–11). Meanwhile the loyal Macbeth, the new Thane of Cawdor, is already embarked on a career of treachery in which one of his key emotions is fear. (For L. C. Knights's analysis of the language of 1.2, see Modern Criticism, **pp. 58–61**; for a cinematic equivalent of its linguistic confusion in Kurosawa's *Throne of Blood*, see The Work in Performance, **pp. 109–11**.)

The scene, then, celebrates the victory of Duncan's generals, but in language that works against the assertion of order by allowing unsettling ambiguities. And the clearest thing we learn about Duncan in this scene is that others do his fighting for him. Is there a power vacuum here, a personal weakness that has tempted rebels and foreign invaders to try their chances? And is this part of what tempts Macbeth?

Alarum within.[1]
Enter King Duncan, Malcolm, Donalbain, Lennox, with Attendants, meeting a Bleeding Captain.

DUNCAN
　　What bloody man is that? He can report,
　　As seemeth by his plight, of the revolt
　　The newest state.

1　Trumpet-call off stage, theatrical shorthand for a nearby battle.

MALCOLM   This is the sergeant[2]
              Who like a good and hardy soldier fought
              'Gainst my captivity; Hail, brave friend:
              Say to the King the knowledge of the broil,
              As thou didst leave it.
     CAPTAIN   Doubtful it stood,
              As two spent swimmers that do cling together
              And choke their art: the merciless Macdonwald
              (Worthy to be a rebel, for to that[3]   10
              The multiplying villainies of nature
              Do swarm upon him) from the Western Isles
              Of Kerns and Gallowglasses[4] is supplied,
              And Fortune on his damnèd quarry[5] smiling
              Showed like a rebel's whore; but all's too weak:
              For brave Macbeth (well he deserves that name)
              Disdaining Fortune, with his brandisht steel,
              Which smoked with bloody execution,
              Like Valour's minion[6] carved out his passage
              Till he faced the slave: 20
              Which[7] ne'er shook hands, nor bade farewell to him,
              Till he unseamed him from the nave to th' chops,[8]
              And fixed his head upon our battlements.
     DUNCAN
              O valiant cousin, worthy gentleman!
     CAPTAIN
              As whence the sun 'gins his reflection[9]
              Shipwracking storms and direful thunders break,
              So from that spring, whence comfort seemed to come,
              Discomfort swells: mark, King of Scotland, mark,
              No sooner Justice had, with Valour armed,
              Compelled these skipping Kerns to trust their heels,[10]   30
              But the Norweyan lord, surveying vantage,[11]
              With furbished[12] arms, and new supplies of men,
              Began a fresh assault.
     DUNCAN
              Dismayed not this our captains, Macbeth and Banquo?

---

  2 Speech headings and stage directions call this character a Captain. Sergeant and Captain are
    distinct offices in modern English, but were not in Shakespeare's time; he can be imagined as a staff
    officer.
  3 i.e., to that end.
  4 Kerns are foot-soldiers, armed with swords or bows; gallowglasses are horsemen usually armed
    with axes.
  5 Quarrel, cause.
  6 Favourite, lover (continuing the sexual associations of Fortune as a rebel's whore).
  7 Could be either Macbeth or Macdonwald; 'he' in the next line is evidently Macbeth.
  8 Split him open from the navel to the jaw.
  9 At the spring equinox.
 10 i.e., beat a quick retreat.
 11 Seeing an opportunity.
 12 Newly cleaned, implying a fresh effort.

CAPTAIN
    Yes, as sparrows eagles, or the hare the lion:
    If I say sooth, I must report they were
    As cannons over-charged with double cracks,
    So they doubly redoubled strokes upon the foe;
    Except they meant to bathe in reeking wounds,   40
    Or memorize another Golgotha,[13]
    I cannot tell: but I am faint,
    My gashes cry for help.
DUNCAN
    So well thy words become thee as thy wounds,
    They smack of honour both. Go get him surgeons.

                    Enter Ross and Angus.

    Who comes here?
MALCOLM   The worthy Thane of Ross.
LENNOX
    What a haste looks through his eyes! So should he look
    That seems to speak things strange.
ROSS   God save the King.
DUNCAN
    Whence cam'st thou, worthy Thane?
ROSS   From Fife, great King,
    Where the Norweyan banners flout[14] the sky   50
    And fan our people cold.
    Norway himself, with terrible numbers,
    Assisted by that most disloyal traitor,
    The Thane of Cawdor, began a dismal conflict,
    Till that Bellona's bridegroom,[15] lapped in proof,[16]
    Confronted him with self-comparisons,
    Point against point, rebellious arm 'gainst arm,
    Curbing his lavish[17] spirit; and to conclude,
    The victory fell on us.
DUNCAN
    Great happiness!
ROSS   That now   60
    Sweno, the Norways' King, craves composition;[18]
    Nor would we deign him burial of his men
    Till he disbursed, at Saint Colme's Inch,[19]
    Ten thousand dollars,[20] to our general use.

13 i.e., recall the place where Jesus Christ was crucified.
14 Mock.
15 Macbeth (continuing the train of imagery that begins with Fortune as a rebel's whore). Bellona was the Roman goddess of war, and a virgin. Macbeth's marriage is childless.
16 In armour of proven quality.
17 Wild.
18 A negotiated peace.
19 An island in the Firth of Forth, associated with Saint Columba.
20 Different explanations have been offered for this term, which may refer to the German *thaler* or the Danish *rigsdaler*.

DUNCAN
    No more that Thane of Cawdor shall deceive
    Our bosom interest: go pronounce his present death,
    And with his former title greet Macbeth.
ROSS   I'll see it done.
DUNCAN
    What he hath lost, noble Macbeth hath won.   *Exeunt*

Act 1, Scene 3: Macbeth and Banquo encounter the witches

In the first part of this scene the witches begin their next meeting, anticipated in the play's opening line. This scene too opens with a question: 'Where hast thou been, sister?' As the witches report their activities, we get a clearer sense of them than in 1.1. They are malicious and destructive: one has been 'killing swine' (2), a reflection of conventional belief about witches in rural communities. Another has had a quarrel with a sailor's wife: the witch begged food from her, which the sailor's wife refused; the witch's response is to threaten the woman's husband, then at sea, with tempests and with lack of sleep (insomnia will be one of Macbeth's torments). She also threatens to 'drain him dry as hay' (18), a curse that links with the sterility of Macbeth's marriage.

The witches are interrupted by the sound of a drum, a military effect that signals the entrance of the victorious generals Macbeth and Banquo for the encounter anticipated in 1.1. Macbeth's entrance line, 'So foul and fair a day I have not seen' (38), is an eerie echo of the witches' riddling statements in 1.1: not just 'Fair is foul, and foul is fair' but 'When the battle's lost, and won'. The day is foul because of the weather; fair because Macbeth has been victorious in battle. This link between Macbeth and the witches can be read more than one way: perhaps the characters are simply participating in the general riddling idiom of the play, and the echo is no more significant than that. But it can be argued that at some subliminal level the mind of Macbeth and the minds of the witches are in contact, even before they meet. This latter reading plays off against the strangeness Banquo sees in the witches; to him they are other, incomprehensible, not of this world. As he speaks to them, they remain silent. When Macbeth speaks to them, they respond at once. This may recall the effect of the opening scenes of *Hamlet*, where the Ghost meets Horatio's questions with silence, and speaks only to Hamlet.

The witches' greetings to Macbeth combine past, present and future; he has been for some time Thane of Glamis; he is now, though he does not yet know it, Thane of Cawdor; he will be king hereafter. The last greeting is the only one that counts as a prophecy; it looks fair but turns out to be foul, both for Scotland and for Macbeth. It is worth noting that the witches say only that Macbeth will be king. They say nothing of how this will happen, and in his long aside later in this scene Macbeth is torn between the fear that he is being tempted to murder Duncan and the hope that since he will be king in any case, all he has to do is wait for it to happen. He is startled by the witches' greeting, even deprived of speech; if we wonder what is going on in his mind, that later aside may provide a clue.

Banquo too is torn: he claims to be indifferent to the witches (60–1), yet he still itches to know his own future. That he will be both lesser and greater than Macbeth is yet another riddle; it has an obvious answer and a more deeply buried ambiguity. He will be lesser, in that he will never be king; greater, in that unlike Macbeth he will father a line of kings. The deeper ambiguity of this prophecy is that its fair promise will cause Banquo's death: Macbeth will kill him out of fear and jealousy, trying to stop the prophecy from coming true.

Both Macbeth and Banquo find the encounter so strange that when the witches suddenly vanish they wonder if they were ever real at all. (This is one of Shakespeare's favourite effects: throughout his work characters have experiences so extraordinary they wonder if these experiences are real; the waking of the lovers after their night in the forest in *A Midsummer Night's Dream* is a classic example.) The entrance of Ross and Angus restores familiar characters and ordinary reality, not unlike the shift in the audience's own experience between 1.1 and 1.2. And in that ordinary reality the second greeting, the one that made Macbeth incredulous, has come true: he is Thane of Cawdor. Macbeth now has to take the third greeting (king hereafter) with a new seriousness, and the fact that he goes into a long aside, heard by the audience but not by his fellows, anticipates in theatrical terms the way Macbeth will be cut off from human fellowship, moving into a nightmare of his own. The audience will follow him into that nightmare. (For Derek Jacobi's playing of Macbeth in this scene, see The Work in Performance, **pp. 119–20**.)

Thunder. Enter the three witches.

FIRST WITCH   Where hast thou been, sister?
SECOND WITCH   Killing swine.
THIRD WITCH   Sister, where thou?
FIRST WITCH
    A sailor's wife had chestnuts in her lap,
    And munch'd, and munch'd and munch'd. Give me, quoth I.
    Aroint thee,[1] witch, the rump-fed ronyon cries.[2]
    Her husband's to Aleppo[3] gone, master o'th'Tiger;[4]
    But in a sieve I'll thither sail,
    And like a rat without a tail,[5]
    I'll do, I'll do, and I'll do.[6]   10

---

1   Get away from me.
2   Scholarly explanations of this insult have varied in detail, but the general sense is 'fat bitch'. This line also contains the only use of the word 'witch' in the play's dialogue. Like Mother Sawyer in *The Witch of Edmonton* (see Contemporary Documents, **pp. 32–6**) the weird sister is labelled a witch by someone she has offended.
3   A trading city in Syria.
4   A common name for a ship in Shakespeare's time. An actual ship of that name had a particularly troubled voyage in 1604–6.
5   It was believed that witches could take animal form, but would lack tails if they did so.
6   'Do' can be slang for sexual intercourse; this would explain 'drain him dry as hay' at l.18.

SECOND WITCH   I'll give thee a wind.
FIRST WITCH   Th'art kind.
THIRD WITCH   And I another.
FIRST WITCH
    I myself have all the other,
    And the very ports they blow,
    All the quarters that they know
    I'th' ship-man's card.[7]
    I'll drain him dry as hay;
    Sleep shall neither night nor day
    Hang upon his pent-house lid;[8]   20
    He shall live a man forbid;[9]
    Weary sev'nnights, nine times nine,
    Shall he dwindle, peak, and pine;
    Though his bark cannot be lost,
    Yet it shall be tempest-tost.
    Look what I have.
SECOND WITCH   Show me, show me.
FIRST WITCH
    Here I have a pilot's thumb,
    Wrack't, as homeward he did come.

Drum within.

THIRD WITCH
    A drum, a drum;   30
    Macbeth doth come.
ALL
    The Weird Sisters, hand in hand,
    Posters[10] of the sea and land,
    Thus do go about, about,
    Thrice to thine, and thrice to mine,
    And thrice again, to make up nine.
    Peace, the charm's wound up.

Enter Macbeth and Banquo.

MACBETH
    So foul and fair a day I have not seen.
BANQUO
    How far is't called[11] to Forres? What are these,[12]
    So withered, and so wild in their attire,   40

---

7 Chart; also, a card showing points of the compass.
8 Eyelid.
9 Cursed.
10 Swift travellers.
11 Supposed to be.
12 For a line and a half Macbeth and Banquo fail to notice the witches, creating a quick moment of suspense.

That look not like th'inhabitants o'th' earth,
And yet are on't? Live you, or are you aught
That man may question? You seem to understand me,
By each at once her choppy[13] finger laying
Upon her skinny lips. You should be women,
And yet your beards forbid me to interpret
That you are so.

MACBETH
                    Speak if you can; what are you?

FIRST WITCH
    All hail Macbeth, hail to thee Thane of Glamis.

SECOND WITCH
    All hail Macbeth, hail to thee Thane of Cawdor.

THIRD WITCH
    All hail Macbeth, that shalt be King hereafter.   50

BANQUO
    Good sir, why do you start,[14] and seem to fear
    Things that do sound so fair? [*To the Witches*] I'th' name of truth,
    Are ye fantastical,[15] or that indeed
    Which outwardly ye show? My noble partner
    You greet with present grace,[16] and great prediction
    Of noble having,[17] and of royal hope,
    That he seems rapt withal; to me you speak not.
    If you can look into the seeds of time,
    And say which grain will grow, and which will not,
    Speak then to me, who neither beg, nor fear   60
    Your favours, nor your hate.

FIRST WITCH
    Hail.

SECOND WITCH
    Hail.

THIRD WITCH
    Hail.

FIRST WITCH
    Lesser than Macbeth, and greater.

SECOND WITCH
    Not so happy,[18] yet much happier.

THIRD WITCH
    Thou shalt get[19] kings, though thou be none:
    So all hail Macbeth, and Banquo.

13 Chapped.
14 Look startled.
15 Imaginary.
16 Immediate honour.
17 Possession.
18 Fortunate.
19 Beget.

FIRST WITCH
    Banquo, and Macbeth, all hail.
MACBETH
    Stay, you imperfect speakers, tell me more: 70
    By Sinell's death I know I am Thane of Glamis,[20]
    But how, of Cawdor? The Thane of Cawdor lives
    A prosperous gentleman;[21] and to be King
    Stands not within the prospect[22] of belief,
    No more than to be Cawdor. Say from whence
    You owe this strange intelligence, or why
    Upon this blasted[23] heath you stop our way
    With such prophetic greeting? Speak, I charge you.

                                                    Witches vanish[24]

BANQUO
    The earth hath bubbles, as the water has,
    And these are of them; whither are they vanished?   80
MACBETH
    Into the air; and what seemed corporal[25]
    Melted, as breath into the wind. Would they had stayed!
BANQUO
    Were such things here, as we do speak about?
    Or have we eaten on the insane[26] root
    That takes the reason prisoner?
MACBETH
    Your children shall be kings.
BANQUO   You shall be King.
MACBETH
    And Thane of Cawdor too; went it not so?[27]
BANQUO
    To th' self-same tune, and words. Who's here?

                        Enter Ross and Angus.

ROSS
    The King hath happily received, Macbeth,

---

20 In Holinshed, Sinel (a mistake for Finel) is Macbeth's father.
21 In line with the narrative confusion of 1.2, Macbeth makes no reference to Cawdor's treason or his own combat with him.
22 Possibility.
23 Blighted.
24 A film or television production can use the resources of the medium to make the witches vanish instantly; at the Globe, the effect (possibly using either the trap door or flying machinery) would have depended more on the audience's imagination.
25 Physical.
26 Causing insanity.
27 At this point in Holinshed, Banquo and Macbeth treat the whole matter as a joke (see Source, pp. 21–2). It is possible for the actors to play these lines in the same spirit, setting up the shock of what follows (see The Work in Performance, p. 119).

The news of thy success; and when he reads[28]   90
Thy personal venture in the rebels' fight,
His wonders and his praises do contend,
Which should be thine, or his.[29] Silenced with that,
In viewing o'er the rest o'th' self-same day,
He finds thee in the stout Norweyan ranks,
Nothing afeard of what thyself didst make –
Strange images of death. As thick as hail
Came post[30] with post, and every one did bear
Thy praises in his kingdom's great defence
And poured them down before him.

ANGUS   We are sent   100
To give thee from our royal master thanks,
Only to herald thee into his sight,
Not pay thee.

ROSS
And for an earnest[31] of a greater honour,
He bade me, from him, call thee Thane of Cawdor:
In which addition,[32] hail most worthy Thane,
For it is thine.

BANQUO   What, can the devil speak true?

MACBETH
The Thane of Cawdor lives; why do you dress me
In borrowed robes?[33]

ANGUS   Who was the Thane, lives yet,
But under heavy judgement bears that life   110
Which he deserves to lose.
Whether he was combined with those of Norway,
Or did line the rebel with hidden help
And vantage;[34] or that with both he laboured
In his country's wrack, I know not.
But treasons capital,[35] confessed, and proved,
Have overthrown him.

MACBETH [aside]   Glamis, and Thane of Cawdor:
The greatest is behind.[36] [To the others] Thanks for your pains.
[To Banquo] Do you not hope your children shall be kings,
When those that gave the Thane of Cawdor to me
Promised no less to them?

28 Considers.
29 A difficult passage, the gist of which is that Duncan is torn between silent wonder at Macbeth's
    achievements and the impulse to praise him.
30 Messenger.
31 Promise, foretaste.
32 With which title.
33 This introduces a series of clothing images that runs through the play. The strongest link is with
    Angus's claim that kingship hangs on Macbeth 'like a giant's robe / Upon a dwarfish thief' (5.2.22–
    3). (Cleanth Brooks explores the play's clothing imagery: see Modern Criticism, pp. 61–3.)
34 Extra aid, or opportunity.
35 Deserving death.
36 The biggest step is already taken.

BANQUO   That trusted home[37]   120
    Might yet enkindle[38] you unto the crown,
    Besides the Thane of Cawdor. But 'tis strange;
    And oftentimes, to win us to our harm,
    The instruments of darkness tell us truths,
    Win us with honest trifles, to betray's
    In deepest consequence.[39]
    [To the others] Cousins,[40] a word, I pray you.
MACBETH [aside]   Two truths are told[41]
    As happy prologues to the swelling act
    Of the imperial theme.[42] [To the others] I thank you gentlemen.
    [Aside] This supernatural soliciting[43]   130
    Cannot be ill; cannot be good.
    If ill, why hath it given me earnest[44] of success,
    Commencing in a truth? I am Thane of Cawdor.
    If good, why do I yield to that suggestion
    Whose horrid image doth unfix my hair,
    And make my seated heart knock at my ribs,
    Against the use[45] of nature? Present fears
    Are less than horrible imaginings:[46]
    My thought, whose murther yet is but fantastical,[47]
    Shakes so my single state[48] of man,   140
    That function is smothered in surmise,[49]
    And nothing is, but what is not.[50]
BANQUO   Look how our partner's rapt.
MACBETH [aside]
    If chance will have me King, why chance may crown me,

---

37 Fully.
38 Encourage (the image is of lighting a fire, suggesting ambition is both natural and dangerous).
39 In the most serious matters.
40 This word is vaguer in Shakespeare's English than in ours. It can be used for a variety of relationships, familial and otherwise; here it suggests that Duncan's followers form a kind of extended
   family. (The sleeping Duncan will remind Lady Macbeth of her father (2.2.13–14).) This word of
   relationship is used just as Macbeth separates himself from his fellows and goes into his own
   thoughts.
41 Macbeth uses the passive voice, the voice that conceals agency. (He and Lady Macbeth use this
   device continually when discussing the murder of Duncan.) Banquo has reminded him that the
   news comes from the powers of darkness; Macbeth suppresses that fact.
42 The imagery suggests both a play beginning and a piece of music rising to a crescendo.
43 Encouragement, enticement.
44 At l.104 Ross uses the same word when he says that Duncan's making Macbeth Thane of Cawdor
   is a promise of greater honours to come.
45 Custom.
46 The horror I can imagine is greater than what I fear now.
47 i.e., the murder that so far I have only imagined. After several lines in which Macbeth refuses to
   name the horrible thought that shakes him, he finally speaks the word, 'murder'. Paul Scofield
   (Royal Shakespeare Company, 1967) hesitated before speaking the word, and it came out with the
   extra horror that had accumulated during the pause.
48 Integrity.
49 Thought overwhelms action.
50 Macbeth takes the riddling ambiguity of the witches (fair is foul, and foul is fair) to a new depth of
   absurdity: nothing exists except that which does not exist. One possible meaning is that the
   thought which overwhelms his mind is the one thought that is unthinkable.

Without my stir.

BANQUO   New honours come upon him
Like our strange garments, cleave not to their mould[51]
But with the aid of use.[52]

MACBETH [*Aside*]   Come what come may,
Time, and the hour, runs through the roughest day.[53]

BANQUO
Worthy Macbeth, we stay upon your leisure.

MACBETH
Give me your favour: my dull brain was wrought   150
With things forgotten. Kind gentlemen, your pains
Are registered where every day I turn
The leaf to read them. Let us toward the King.
[*To Banquo*] Think upon what hath chanced, and at more time,
The interim having weighed it,[54] let us speak
Our free hearts each to other.

BANQUO   Very gladly.[55]

MACBETH
Till then enough. [*To the others*] Come, friends.   *Exeunt*

Act 1, Scene 5: Lady Macbeth reads Macbeth's letter, and prepares to urge him to murder

In 1.4 Duncan declares his gratitude to Macbeth and Banquo, and they profess their loyalty to him. Duncan then names Malcolm as his heir, putting one more barrier between Macbeth and the crown, and dashing his hope that he can become king without taking action. It is Lady Macbeth who spurs him to action. Her entrance at the beginning of 1.5 is striking in a number of ways. This is the first scene to begin with a single character alone on stage; this puts a strong focus on her. It is the first scene to begin with a statement, not a question, as though anticipating her own decisiveness. (Act 1, Scene 4 opens with Duncan asking, 'Is execution done on Cawdor?') And Lady Macbeth enters reading a letter from her husband: his words, spoken in her voice. It is the first hint of the bond between them.

There is also a gap. Macbeth is afraid of the deed he might commit to become king; Lady Macbeth is afraid he might not commit it. Both fears strike quickly. Our first impression is that Lady Macbeth has the resolution her husband lacks.

---

51 i.e., the body beneath the garments, that gives them their shape. Banquo continues Macbeth's clothing imagery (108–9).
52 Regular wearing.
53 Whatever happens, time runs its course.
54 Once we have had time to think.
55 The frank conversation Macbeth proposes never happens. At 2.1.21–30 Banquo broaches the subject, and Macbeth puts him off till some time in the future, with the hint that he has new honours in mind for Banquo. Banquo bridles at the suggestion, insisting on his own loyalty to Duncan. From this point the two men view each other with suspicion.

While in 1.3 Macbeth was frozen in horror, 1.5 has a sense of urgency that comes from Lady Macbeth. But she cannot prepare her husband without first preparing herself. She talks of pouring her spirits in her husband's ear (26), but she also calls on unnamed evil spirits to enter her own body. The supernatural, embodied on stage in the mysterious witches, is now an unseen power evoked by Lady Macbeth's language. The witches' bodies were unnatural: Lady Macbeth wants her own body unsexed, its capacity for nurture turned to poison. The witches simply are what they are, whatever that is; we feel the effort Lady Macbeth makes to turn herself into something unnatural.

Here and in 1.7 the language stresses the femininity of Lady Macbeth's body: her breasts, her milk, her ability to conceive. When in the modern theatre the part is played by a woman, the performer's own body is aligned with the language. But in Shakespeare's theatre Lady Macbeth would be played by a boy. What effect would this have? Sometimes in his comedies, especially when the heroine goes into male disguise, Shakespeare jokingly calls attention to the male body beneath the female character. In *Twelfth Night* the disguised Viola, caught up in a duel, declares, 'A little thing would make me tell them how much I lack of a man' (3.4.302–3). Lines like this suggest that when Shakespeare wants us to be aware of the boy actor, he takes steps to activate that awareness. Normally in the tragedies we accept the illusion seriously, and I think that is the case here. (For the medical implications of Lady Macbeth's invocation, see Modern Criticism, **pp. 71–4**; for Davenant's rewritten version, see The Work in Performance, **pp. 102–3**.)

It is important that Lady Macbeth registers as a woman just as seriously as Macbeth registers as a man, since much of this scene depends on evoking, and challenging, conventional gender roles: the hardness and aggressiveness of men, the soft and nurturing qualities of women. Declaring her husband is 'too full o'th' milk of human kindness' (17), Lady Macbeth makes him sound like a woman. Talking of pouring her spirits in his ear, she sounds as though she plans to impregnate him (26, and note). She talks of the castle as hers ('my battlements' (40)). When they meet, she takes the conversational lead and does most of the talking: his part in this scene is confined to a mere fifteen words. Conservative moralists in Shakespeare's time saw modesty of speech as one of the principal female virtues. Like the effort Lady Macbeth makes to have her body unsexed, these reversals play off against the sense of the 'normal', as most of Shakespeare's audience would have seen it, embodied (literally) in the fact that Macbeth is a man and Lady Macbeth is a woman.

Macbeth's guardedness, his putting off the decision they have to make, show that Lady Macbeth still has work to do. As he hesitates to kill, he hesitates even to confront his wife. The issue between them has not yet been faced, as it will be in 1.7.

Enter Macbeth's wife alone, with a letter.

LADY MACBETH 'They met me in the day of success; and I have learned by the perfectest report, they have more in them than mortal knowledge. When I burnt in desire to question them further, they made themselves air, into which they vanished. Whiles I stood rapt in the wonder of it, came missives[1] from the King, who all-hailed me Thane of Cawdor, by which title, before, these Weird Sisters saluted me, and referred me to the coming-on of time with "Hail King that shalt be". This have I thought good to deliver thee, my dearest partner of greatness, that thou mightst not lose the dues of rejoicing by being ignorant of what greatness is promised thee. Lay it to thy heart, and farewell.'   14

    Glamis thou art, and Cawdor, and shalt be
What thou art promised; yet do I fear thy nature,
It is too full o'th' milk of human kindness[2]
To catch the nearest way.[3] Thou wouldst be great,
Art not without ambition, but without
The illness[4] should attend it. What thou wouldst highly,   20
That wouldst thou holily: wouldst not play false,
And yet wouldst wrongly win. Thou'dst have, great Glamis,
That which cries, 'Thus thou must do', if thou have it;
And that which rather thou dost fear to do,
Than wishest should be undone.[5] Hie thee hither,
That I may pour my spirits in thine ear,[6]
And chastise with the valour of my tongue
All that impedes thee from the golden round[7]
Which Fate and metaphysical[8] aid doth seem
To have thee crowned withal.

Enter Messenger.

                 What is your tidings?   30

MESSENGER
    The King comes here tonight.
LADY MACBETH   Thou'rt mad to say it.[9]
    Is not thy master with him? who, were't so,
Would have informed for preparation.
MESSENGER
    So please you, it is true; our Thane is coming;
One of my fellows had the speed of him,[10]

1 Messengers.
2 Naturalness (as well as the modern meaning, benevolence).
3 Take the most direct path.
4 Capacity for evil.
5 You know what you have to do to get what you want, and once it's done you won't regret it; but you're afraid to do it. (Like Macbeth, Lady Macbeth avoids naming the deed, and her language becomes convoluted as she circles around it.)
6 'Spirit' can mean 'semen'. Planning to use words to give Macbeth her own courage, she thinks of impregnating him. There was a tradition that the Virgin Mary, who gave birth to Jesus without losing her virginity, was impregnated through the ear by the Holy Spirit. Lady Macbeth's blasphemous adaptation of a Christian image fits with her later evocation of the powers of darkness.
7 Crown.
8 Supernatural.
9 Either Lady Macbeth thinks the news is too good to be true, or (her mind racing ahead) she thinks the servant is referring to Macbeth as king, and she rebukes him for giving away the secret. If that is the case, she makes a quick recovery in the next line.
10 Outran him.

Who almost dead for breath, had scarcely more
Than would make up his message.
LADY MACBETH   Give him tending,
He brings great news.   *Exit Messenger*
                              The raven himself is hoarse[11]
That croaks the fatal entrance of Duncan
Under my battlements. Come, you spirits,   40
That tend on[12] mortal thoughts,[13] unsex me here,
And fill me from the crown to the toe, top-full[14]
Of direst cruelty; make thick my blood,
Stop up th'access and passage to remorse,
That no compunctious visitings of nature[15]
Shake my fell[16] purpose, nor keep peace between
Th'effect and it.[17] Come to my woman's breasts,
And take my milk for gall,[18] you murth'ring ministers,[19]
Wherever, in your sightless[20] substances,
You wait on nature's mischief.[21] Come, thick night,   50
And pall[22] thee in the dunnest[23] smoke of Hell,
That my keen[24] knife see not the wound it makes,
Nor Heaven peep through the blanket of the dark,
To cry, 'Hold, hold!'

                              Enter Macbeth.

                    Great Glamis, worthy Cawdor,
Greater than both, by the all-hail hereafter!
Thy letters have transported me beyond
This ignorant present, and I feel now
The future in the instant.
MACBETH   My dearest love,
Duncan comes here tonight.
LADY MACBETH   And when goes hence?

---

11 The image combines the bird of ill omen with the breathless messenger.
12 Wait on (picking up on Lady Macbeth's command that the messenger should be looked after (36)
    and giving it a sinister twist).
13 Human thoughts; thoughts of death.
14 From head to foot, full to the brim.
15 Natural feelings of remorse.
16 Cruel.
17 Come between my purpose and the end at which it aims.
18 Turn my milk into gall; or, drink my milk as though it were gall.
19 Attendants (picking up the idea of attendance from l. 40, and anticipating the claim that Duncan
    was murdered by his servants).
20 Invisible.
21 Attend on natural disasters, or on harm done to nature ('mischief' is a stronger word in Shake-
    speare's English than in ours).
22 Cover.
23 Darkest.
24 Sharp. (Is Lady Macbeth thinking of Macbeth as her knife, or does she for a moment imagine doing
    the deed herself?)

MACBETH
  Tomorrow, as he purposes.
LADY MACBETH   O never   60
  Shall sun that morrow see.[25]
  Your face, my Thane, is as a book, where men
  May read strange matters; to beguile[26] the time,
  Look like the time, bear welcome in your eye,
  Your hand, your tongue; look like th'innocent flower,
  But be the serpent under't. He that's coming
  Must be provided for;[27] and you shall put
  This night's great business into my dispatch,[28]
  Which shall to all our nights, and days to come
  Give solely sovereign sway, and masterdom.[29]   70
MACBETH
  We will speak further.
LADY MACBETH   Only look up clear;[30]
  To alter favour, ever is to fear.[31]
  Leave all the rest to me.   *Exeunt*

Act 1, Scene 7: Macbeth hesitates; Lady Macbeth breaks his reluctance

In 1.6 Lady Macbeth, playing the gracious hostess, welcomes Duncan to her castle. Macbeth (unable to face the man he has to kill?) is conspicuously absent. Act 1, Scene 7 opens with music and a procession of servants on their way to lay the table for a formal meal. All of this invokes the idea of hospitality, and the host–guest relationship that early societies held sacred. Against this, Macbeth's entrance – the first time we have seen him alone on stage – shows he has abruptly left the table in the middle of the meal, echoing the moment in 1.3 when he turns aside from his companions and goes into his own thoughts. The opening of his soliloquy suggests that he hesitates to murder Duncan because he is afraid of the consequences. But as he goes on he thinks of his responsibilities as kinsman, subject and host, and of Duncan's virtues – as though the occasion he has just left has brought home to him forcefully the values that the murder would violate.

25 Duncan will never leave, because he will die tonight. Lady Macbeth's words also anticipate 2.4.7–10, where Duncan's death is followed by a sunless day. 'Tomorrow', repeated three times, begins the speech in which Macbeth reacts to his wife's death (5.5.19).
26 Deceive.
27 Lady Macbeth ironically conflates hospitality and murder.
28 Into my hands ('dispatch' implies a speedy end).
29 Absolute power.
30 Look as though nothing is troubling you.
31 If you look fearful, you will be fearful. (Lady Macbeth reverses normal cause and effect, suggesting that by controlling his appearance Macbeth can control his feelings.)

Lady Macbeth's entrance forces him at last to make a decision: he will not kill Duncan. What follows is the confrontation Lady Macbeth anticipated in 1.5. Picking up one of the key issues of that scene, she challenges his manhood, and they debate what it means to be a man. Is killing manly? Or does true manhood lie in following the values that have turned Macbeth against the murder? Lady Macbeth's clinching argument is that Macbeth has sworn to do the deed, and should keep his oath. Men should keep their promises. But that argument would not have the power it does without the startling image with which she reinforces it. If she had sworn to kill a child she was breastfeeding she would do it, and she gives a graphic image of the action she imagines. As in the invocation of the spirits, it matters that her body is a woman's body: she would deny the values implicit in that body – quite literally, the milk of human kindness – if she had sworn to do so. Nor is she speculating about the tender feelings that accompany breastfeeding; she knows them from experience. If she can thus surrender her sense of what it is to be a woman, Macbeth can surrender his sense of what it is to be a man. Most performers playing Lady Macbeth display indomitable will power in this scene. Judi Dench, in the Trevor Nunn production, adds quick-working argumentative intelligence. Francesca Annis, in the Roman Polanski film, takes an unusual line: she becomes tearful with disappointment, using emotional blackmail.

Shakespeare does not bother to reconcile Lady Macbeth's experience of breastfeeding with the childlessness of her present marriage, by explaining either that (like her historical counterpart) she had children by another marriage, or that she has had children by Macbeth who died. A modern realistic drama might need explanations of this kind; amid the speed and urgency of Shakespeare's play they would simply be clutter. More recently, the theatre of Beckett and Pinter has taught us not to expect explanations. What matters is the image in front of us, not its logical underpinnings in a past action. Yet the childlessness of this marriage is relevant at another level. We see this in the way Macbeth signals his decision to kill Duncan: 'Bring forth men-children only' (73). This is not only a tribute to Lady Macbeth's manly valour (picking up the gender theme) but a suggestion that the frustration of parenthood and the frustration of ambition will end together, in an action the couple will share.

Macbeth began the scene afraid of consequences, and it helps that Lady Macbeth has a practical plan for avoiding them: get Duncan's chamber attendants drunk, and blame the murder on them. Macbeth adds to this the plan of using the attendants' own daggers, and smearing them with blood. The moral and spiritual horror of the murder, expressed in the mind-blowing imagery of Macbeth's soliloquy, has vanished, to be replaced by practical problems with practical solutions. Lady Macbeth is instrumental in turning the scene in this direction. (The effect is repeated in 2.2, where Macbeth's moral horror comes back, and his wife continues to think in practical terms.) The scene ends with a new bonding between the couple, as Macbeth picks up from the end of 1.5 Lady Macbeth's idea of hiding their true intentions under a false appearance.

Hautboys.[1] *Torches.*[2] *Enter a sewer*[3] *and divers*[4] *servants with dishes and service*[5] *crossing over the stage. Then enter Macbeth.*

MACBETH

If it were done, when 'tis done, then 'twere well
It were done quickly; if th'assassination
Could trammel up[6] the consequence, and catch
With his surcease, success;[7] that but this blow
Might be the be-all and the end-all – here,
But here, upon this bank and shoal of time –
We'd jump[8] the life to come. But in these cases
We still have judgement here, that we but teach
Bloody instructions, which being taught, return
To plague th'inventor. This even-handed justice   10
Commends th'ingredience[9] of our poisoned chalice
To our own lips.[10] He's here in double trust:
First, as I am his kinsman, and his subject,
Strong both against the deed; then, as his host,
Who should against his murtherer shut the door,
Not bear the knife myself. Besides, this Duncan
Hath borne his faculties[11] so meek; hath been
So clear[12] in his great office, that his virtues
Will plead like angels, trumpet-tongued against
The deep damnation of his taking-off;   20
And pity, like a naked new-born babe,
Striding the blast,[13] or Heaven's cherubim,[14] horsed
Upon the sightless[15] couriers of the air,
Shall blow the horrid deed in every eye,
That tears shall drown the wind. I have no spur.
To prick the sides of my intent, but only
Vaulting ambition, which o'erleaps itself
And falls on th' other –[16]

1 Wind instrument, often used on courtly occasions.
2 Torchbearers.
3 Superior domestic officer, in charge of organizing meals.
4 Several.
5 Either eating utensils, or the food itself.
6 Capture and control, as with nets.
7 Make Duncan's death a successful end to the business.
8 Risk.
9 Ingredients.
10 In the last scene of *Hamlet*, Claudius is made to drink from the chalice he himself has poisoned. In both cases there is a parody of the Christian service of Holy Communion.
11 Kingly powers.
12 Pure.
13 Wind; also, the trumpet-blast of the angels.
14 The second of the nine orders of angels.
15 Invisible (also, perhaps, blind, anticipating the next few lines).
16 Presumably Macbeth's next word would have been 'side', but Lady Macbeth's entrance interrupts him. He sees her at once, as opposed to the brief delay before he notices the witches (1.3.38–9). The whole passage (18–28), with its rapidly overlapping images, shows Shakespeare's writing at its most daring, as Macbeth's imagination operates at white heat.

Enter Lady Macbeth.

How now? What news?

LADY MACBETH
He has almost supped; why have you left the chamber?

MACBETH
Hath he asked for me?

LADY MACBETH   Know you not he has?   30

MACBETH
We will proceed no further in this business:
He hath honoured me of late, and I have bought
Golden opinions from all sorts of people,
Which would be worn now in their newest gloss,
Not cast aside so soon.[17]

LADY MACBETH   Was the hope drunk
Wherein you dressed yourself? Hath it slept since?[18]
And wakes it now to look so green,[19] and pale,
At what it did so freely? From this time,
Such I account thy love. Art thou afeard
To be the same in thine own act and valour   40
As thou art in desire? Wouldst thou have that
Which thou esteem'st the ornament of life,
And live a coward in thine own esteem,
Letting 'I dare not' wait upon 'I would',
Like the poor cat i'th' adage?[20]

MACBETH   Prithee peace:
I dare do all that may become a man,
Who dares do more is none.

LADY MACBETH   What beast was't then
That made you break[21] this enterprise to me?
When you durst do it, then you were a man;
And to be more than what you were, you would   50
Be so much more the man. Nor time, nor place
Did then adhere,[22] and yet you would make both;
They have made themselves, and that their fitness now
Does unmake you. I have given suck, and know
How tender 'tis to love the babe that milks me;
I would, while it was smiling in my face,

17 Macbeth makes his refusal a practical matter; he does not want to lose the high reputation he has just earned. He cannot share with his wife the imaginative horror he has just experienced.
18 Lady Macbeth's accusation that Macbeth has been in a drunken stupor plants an idea that will return in the drugging of the grooms, and in the drunken comedy of the Porter at the opening of 2.3.
19 Suggesting not only the sick complexion of a hangover, but 'maiden green-sickness', a form of anaemia affecting young women; a taunt at Macbeth's manhood.
20 The cat in the old saying wants to eat fish but is afraid to get her feet wet.
21 Disclose.
22 Come together.

Have plucked my nipple from his boneless gums,
And dashed the brains out, had I so sworn
As you have done to this.

MACBETH   If we should fail?

LADY MACBETH   We fail?[23]   60
But screw your courage to the sticking place,
And we'll not fail. When Duncan is asleep
(Whereto the rather shall his day's hard journey
Soundly invite him) his two chamberlains[24]
Will I with wine, and wassail,[25] so convince[26]
That memory, the warder of[27] the brain,
Shall be a fume, and the receipt[28] of reason
A limbeck[29] only; when in swinish sleep
Their drenchèd natures lies as in a death,
What cannot you and I perform upon   70
Th'unguarded Duncan? What not put upon
His spongy[30] officers, who shall bear the guilt
Of our great quell?[31]

MACBETH   Bring forth men-children only:
For thy undaunted mettle should compose
Nothing but males. Will it not be received[32]
When we have marked with blood those sleepy two
Of his own chamber, and used their very daggers,
That they have done't?

LADY MACBETH   Who dares receive it other,
As we shall make our griefs and clamour roar
Upon his death?

MACBETH   I am settled, and bend up   80
Each corporal[33] agent to this terrible feat.
Away, and mock the time with fairest show,
False face must hide what the false heart doth know.

Exeunt

---

23 There is an editorial choice here which is also a performance choice. The Folio, like most modern
    editions, reads 'fail?' But printers in Shakespeare's time often used question marks where modern
    printers would use exclamation marks, and some editors have printed 'We fail!' Lady Macbeth
    could be expressing resignation, or a startled contempt at the idea of failure. In a modern edition,
    the question mark produces contempt, with an edge of incredulity. (We? Fail? What are you talking
    about?)
24 Servants who attend the King in his bedchamber.
25 Drinking toasts.
26 Overcome.
27 Guard over (continuing the idea of an attendant asleep at his post).
28 Receptacle.
29 Vessel used in alchemy for distilling (an image of transformation, linking with the idea of the
    drunken chamberlains as swine).
30 Having soaked up the wine.
31 Slaughter.
32 Believed.
33 Bodily (the only challenge now is physical).

Act 2, Scene 1, lines 33–64: Macbeth sees 'a dagger of the mind'

The first part of the scene (not given here) begins with Banquo and his son Fleance in conversation; Banquo then has a brief encounter with Macbeth. They discuss the prophecies; each man seems a little suspicious of the other. Between Macbeth's decision to murder Duncan and the deed itself Shakespeare has inserted a brief anticipation of the future beyond the murder, the jealousy of Banquo's line (represented here by Fleance) that will lead Macbeth to more killing. Macbeth has tried to think of the murder of Duncan as an end; it is only a beginning.

Left alone, Macbeth has a vivid hallucination: a dagger, its handle towards his hand and its point towards Duncan's bedchamber. It is so vivid he thinks it is real, and he tries to grasp it. Up to this point we have had witches appearing on stage, seen by the audience but so strange that Macbeth and Banquo wonder if they are visions; unseen, unidentified spirits invoked by Lady Macbeth; and now a vision we cannot see, of which Macbeth gives a description so evocative we almost *can* see it. Shakespeare is ringing the changes in his presentation of the supernatural: things seen, and really present; things only imagined; things seen, but not really there. It is as though the border between the palpable world and the invisible one is breaking down.

The dagger changes as Macbeth watches it: clean at first, it is suddenly covered in blood. Macbeth's imagination is taking him through the deed of murder, making him see what it will look like. Whatever agency (outside Macbeth, or in his own mind) is sending the vision, is it meant to warn him against the deed by showing its horror? (That was A. C. Bradley's view; see Early Critical Reception, **pp. 54–7**.) Or is it meant to fascinate him, fixing his determination to do the deed by giving him a clear image of it? If he can visualize it, he can do it. Iago uses this sort of technique on Othello, ostensibly warning him against jealousy but planting in his mind vivid images of what it is like to be jealous, giving Othello something to fix on in his confusion. In any case the dagger, as a vision of the murder, is incomplete. It is just a dagger; then it is suddenly covered in blood, with no image of the actual deed that stains it. Macbeth visualizes the weapon but not the victim, not the deed. His imagination is taking him part way to the murder; the horror of the experience is yet to come.

MACBETH . . .
    Is this a dagger which I see before me,
    The handle toward my hand? Come, let me clutch thee;
    I have thee not, and yet I see thee still.
    Art thou not, fatal[1] vision, sensible[2]

---

1 Evoking both fate and death.
2 Perceptible.

To feeling, as to sight? Or art thou but
A dagger of the mind, a false creation,
Proceeding from the heat-oppressèd[3] brain?
I see thee yet, in form as palpable   40
As this which now I draw.
Thou marshall'st me[4] the way that I was going,
And such an instrument I was to use.
Mine eyes are made the fools o'th' other senses,[5]
Or else worth all the rest; I see thee still;
And on thy blade, and dudgeon,[6] gouts[7] of blood,
Which was not so before. There's no such thing;
It is the bloody business which informs
Thus to mine eyes.[8] Now o'er the one half world[9]
Nature seems dead, and wicked dreams abuse   50
The curtained[10] sleep; witchcraft celebrates
Pale Hecate's[11] off'rings, and withered Murther,[12]
Alarumed[13] by his sentinel, the wolf,
Whose howl's his watch,[14] thus with his stealthy pace,
With Tarquin's ravishing strides,[15] towards his design
Moves like a ghost. Thou sure and firm-set earth,
Hear not my steps, which way they walk, for fear
Thy very stones prate of my whereabout,[16]
And take the present horror from the time,
Which now suits with it. Whiles I threat, he lives;   60
Words to the heat of deeds too cold breath gives.[17]

A bell rings.

I go, and it is done: the bell invites me.
Hear it not, Duncan, for it is a knell[18]
That summons thee to Heaven, or to Hell.   *Exit*

---

3 Disturbed by passion.
4 You guide me.
5 Fooled by my other senses; or, the greatest fools among my senses.
6 Handle.
7 Splashes.
8 At this point the dagger evidently disappears; but the horror it triggers becomes generalized, and seeps into Macbeth's perception of the world around him.
9 Half the globe.
10 Alluding both to closed bed-curtains and to closed eyelids.
11 Goddess of sorcery. She appears later in the play, in scenes generally considered to be later additions.
12 In a last attempt to avoid facing what he is going to do, Macbeth turns himself into an abstraction.
13 Called to action.
14 Continuing the image of the sentinel (sentry), the wolf is a guard calling out the time.
15 Tarquin's rape of the Roman matron Lucrece was the subject of one of Shakespeare's early narrative poems, *Lucrece*. His internal conflict before he does the deed, and his compulsion to do it, anticipate Macbeth. Tarquin attacks Lucrece in her bedchamber, as Macbeth is about to attack Duncan.
16 Give away my position.
17 Words cool action.
18 Bell tolling for the dead. This omen, unlike the dagger, is part of the real world; the audience hears it.

Act 2, Scene 2: Macbeth and Lady Macbeth react to the murder

We never see the murder of Duncan. Shakespeare is observing here something like the restraint of classical tragedy, in which violent acts take place off stage and are reported, often in graphic detail, by a messenger. This is not Shakespeare's usual practice: in *Julius Caesar*, the assassination of the title character is staged before our eyes, and later in this play Banquo is killed on stage. In this case Shakespeare may want us to focus on the imaginative horror created by the deed – in the mind of Macbeth before the murder, in the minds of all the characters after – rather than on the physical act itself. What matters is not the deed but what people think of the deed. In this scene we see the first reactions of Macbeth and Lady Macbeth. The effect is very unlike that of a messenger's speech in classical tragedy. Such speeches are usually long, unbroken narratives, delivered by a minor character with no involvement in the action other than that of a horrified observer. We get all the details, as they happened. The dialogue of the Macbeths is jagged, broken, full of confusion and panic. It is anything but an orderly narrative. It is full not just of statements but of questions, many of which have no answers.

Macbeth, who has done the deed, cannot describe it. Instead he reacts in panic to the soundscape that has suddenly sprung to life in the aftermath of the murder, and to the sight of the blood on his hands. The play back and forth between the real and the imagined continues, intensified. As Macbeth enters he hears a noise, but cannot say what it was. He reports hearing, in reality, the grooms praying; his own voice failed as he could not complete their prayer with an 'Amen'. Then he heard another voice, which seemed to be as hallucinatory as the dagger, crying, 'Macbeth shall sleep no more' (42). As he recounts the speech of this unseen voice, line after line, it becomes his voice, prophesying his own fate. In a way his account of his experience in the bedchamber is as graphic as a messenger's speech; but when in this account does he kill Duncan? Before or after he hears the grooms? Before, after or during the long speech of the voice that cries 'Sleep no more'? As the voice cries, 'Macbeth does murder sleep' (35), is he doing the deed? It is impossible to tell. The memory of the act is overwhelmed by the noises that accompany it. Then a sound comes from the real world, a knocking on the door. The deed was done in secrecy, and now that secrecy is about to be broken. The Macbeths have been in a nightmare world of their own; now the real world is stirring again. (The effect is described by De Quincey; see Early Critical Reception, **p. 154**.) At the end of the dagger soliloquy, Macbeth called for silence, for the stones not to hear his footsteps (2.1.57–9). Now his world is full of noise, all of it out of his control. And sight is as vital as sound. In the previous scene, Macbeth saw an imaginary dagger covered in blood; it remained imaginary, and his own hands were still clean. Now we see him holding two bloody daggers, his own hands red. Hallucination has become reality.

As she has before, Lady Macbeth seems by comparison practical and resolute. Macbeth asks where the knocking comes from, as though it were one more hallucination (56). Lady Macbeth hears 'a knocking / At the south entry' (64–5). Macbeth, in a panic, has forgotten a vital part of the plan; he has brought the daggers out of the chamber instead of leaving them with the grooms, and implicating them in the murder by using the daggers to smear them with blood. He is afraid to return; Lady Macbeth does it for him. Against Macbeth's horror at the sight of his bloodstained hands, Lady Macbeth insists that all they have to do is wash. In her sleepwalking scene, she will find it is not so easy (see Key Passages, **pp. 177–80**).

But we do not have to wait for that scene; there are hints here of the shattered woman we will see later. Her resolution comes with an effort, and at a price. The first thing we learn in this scene is that she has been drinking. She needed something to stir her courage. She hears a noise, as her husband does, and it takes her a moment to realize it was an owl: she has a moment of panic, then a quick return to reality (2–3). As in 1.3 Macbeth takes a line and a half to see the witches, here it takes Lady Macbeth five lines to realize her husband has come on stage. Is this an effect of the darkness? (In the daylight performances in Shakespeare's roofless theatre, dialogue like this would be needed to create darkness for the audience's imagination.) Or is she undergoing a panic and confusion of her own? Most tellingly, she has a chance to kill Duncan, and fails: 'Had he not resembled / My father as he slept, I had done't' (12–13). There may be more here than the coincidental resemblance of one old man to another. Recognizing Duncan as her father, Lady Macbeth evokes the interlinked political and family structures of her society, the order the murder will violate. In the soliloquy that opens 1.7, Macbeth knows what is at stake in killing a king. It may be that Lady Macbeth knows it just as well. She has been better at suppressing it, but here it comes out, her imagination speaking to her as Macbeth's does to him. In the scene that follows, the horror of Duncan's murder, which begins as a private nightmare for Macbeth – and, more than we may at first realize, for Lady Macbeth – will sweep through the whole community.

Enter Lady Macbeth.

LADY MACBETH
> That which hath made them drunk, hath made me bold;
> What hath quenched them, hath given me fire. – Hark, peace;
> It was the owl[1] that shrieked, the fatal bellman,
> Which gives the stern'st good-night.[2] He is about it,
> The doors are open; and the surfeited grooms[3]

---

1 An omen of death.
2 Watchman calling the hours, here imagined as announcing the coming of death. (The image picks up on the sound effect of the bell at the end of the previous scene.)
3 Chamber attendants (the word applies to any male servant).

Do mock their charge[4] with snores. I have drugged their possets,[5]
That Death and Nature do contend about them,
Whether they live, or die.

Enter Macbeth.

MACBETH   Who's there? What ho?[6]
LADY MACBETH
    Alack, I am afraid they have awaked,
    And 'tis not done; th'attempt, and not the deed,   10
    Confounds[7] us. – Hark! – I laid their daggers ready,
    He could not miss 'em. Had he not resembled
    My father as he slept, I had done't. – My husband?[8]
MACBETH
    I have done the deed. Didst thou not hear a noise?
LADY MACBETH
    I heard the owl scream, and the crickets cry.
    Did not you speak?
MACBETH   When?
LADY MACBETH   Now.
MACBETH   As I descended?[9]
LADY MACBETH   Ay.
MACBETH
    Hark! Who lies i'th' second chamber?
LADY MACBETH   Donalbain.
MACBETH   This is a sorry sight.   20
LADY MACBETH   A foolish thought, to say a sorry sight.
MACBETH
    There's one did laugh in's sleep,
    And one cried 'Murther', that they did wake each other;
    I stood, and heard them; but they did say their prayers,
    And addressed[10] them again to sleep.
LADY MACBETH   There are two lodged together.
MACBETH
    One cried 'God bless us', and 'Amen'[11] the other,

---

4 Responsibility.
5 Comforting drinks made with warm milk and alcohol.
6 Does he see but not recognize Lady Macbeth (as she seems not to recognize him)? Or is he reacting
   to a sound he has heard?
7 Ruins.
8 This could be a question or an exclamation (see **p. 147** n. 23). If the former, she does not recognize
   her husband, either because it is dark or because his appearance is transformed by horror. If the
   latter, she recognizes him as never before: this is the first time she has used the word 'husband' for
   him. He has done what she wanted, and become the man she wanted him to be.
9 He did speak, and he seems to have forgotten.
10 Prepared.
11 The word that ends a prayer, meaning 'so be it'. Macbeth's inability to say the word suggests he is
   cut off from religious comfort; also that, as he cannot complete the prayer, he can never finish
   with the consequences of murdering Duncan. (This point is made by Stephen Booth; see **Modern
   Criticism, pp. 74–5**.)

As they had seen me with these hangman's[12] hands;
List'ning their fear, I could not say 'Amen',
When they did say 'God bless us'.

LADY MACBETH   Consider it not so deeply.

MACBETH

But wherefore could not I pronounce 'Amen'?   30
I had most need of blessing, and 'Amen'
Stuck in my throat.

LADY MACBETH   These deeds must not be thought
After these ways:[13] so, it will make us mad.

MACBETH

Methought I heard a voice cry 'Sleep no more;
Macbeth does murder sleep, the innocent sleep,
Sleep that knits up the ravelled[14] sleeve of care,
The death of each day's life, sore labour's bath,
Balm of hurt minds, great nature's second course,
Chief nourisher in life's feast.'

LADY MACBETH   What do you mean?

MACBETH

Still it cried 'Sleep no more' to all the house: 40
'Glamis hath murdered sleep, and therefore Cawdor
Shall sleep no more;[15] Macbeth shall sleep no more.'

LADY MACBETH

Who was it that thus cried? Why worthy thane,
You do unbend your noble strength, to think
So brain-sickly of things; go get some water,
And wash this filthy witness from your hand.
Why did you bring these daggers from the place?[16]
They must lie there; go carry them, and smear
The sleepy grooms with blood.

MACBETH   I'll go no more:
I am afraid to think what I have done;   50
Look on't again, I dare not.

LADY MACBETH   Infirm of purpose;
Give me the daggers; the sleeping, and the dead,
Are but as pictures; 'tis the eye of childhood
That fears a painted devil.[17] If he do bleed,
I'll gild the faces of the grooms withal,

---

12 Sometimes hangmen would not just hang their victims, but disembowel them and cut them in quarters.
13 Don't think like this.
14 Frayed.
15 The voice echoes the first two greetings of the witches, but not the third.
16 Her delay in seeing the daggers recalls her delay in seeing Macbeth; neither of them is thinking clearly.
17 Is Lady Macbeth speaking to her husband, taunting his cowardice, or to herself, screwing up her own courage?

For it must seem their guilt.[18]   *Exit*

Knock within.

MACBETH   Whence is that knocking?
How is't with me, when every noise appals me?
What hands are here? Ha, they pluck out mine eyes.
Will all great Neptune's[19] ocean wash this blood
Clean from my hand? No; this my hand will rather   60
The multitudinous seas incarnadine,[20]
Making the green one red.

Enter Lady Macbeth.

LADY MACBETH
My hands are of your colour, but I shame
To wear a heart so white.

Knock.

I hear a knocking
At the south entry: retire we to our chamber;
A little water clears us of this deed.
How easy is it then! Your constancy
Hath left you unattended.[21]

Knock.

Hark, more knocking.
Get on your nightgown,[22] lest occasion[23] call us,
And show us to be watchers;[24] be not lost   70
So poorly in your thoughts.
MACBETH
To know my deed, 'twere best not know myself.[25]

Knock.

Wake Duncan with thy knocking! I would thou couldst.   *Exeunt.*

---

18 Not all puns are jokes; this one is deadly serious. 'Gild' means 'decorate with gold' (which could be
    imagined as red: Macbeth later speaks of Duncan's 'silver skin laced with his golden blood'
    (2.3.114)).
19 God of the sea.
20 Turn the many seas of the world red. (Shakespeare seems to have invented both 'multitudinous' and
    'incarnadine'; new words are needed to convey the extraordinary horror of Macbeth's imaginings.)
21 Your firmness of purpose has deserted you.
22 Dressing-gown.
23 Circumstances.
24 i.e., awake while others are sleeping.
25 A cryptic line, though its general meaning seems to be that when Macbeth thinks of what he has
    done, he wishes he could avoid thinking of himself as the perpetrator.

Act 3, Scene 4: The banquet; Banquo's ghost

In the intervening scenes the murder of Duncan is discovered; Duncan's sons Malcolm and Donalbain, trusting no one, flee the country. In 2.4 Ross and an Old Man report strange omens – unnatural darkness, an owl killing a hawk, Duncan's horses eating each other – as though Macbeth's capacity for hallucination is spreading to ordinary people, or as though horrors of the sort he has only imagined are now happening in the real world. Amid general unease, Macbeth is named king. He has the prize at which he aimed through the first two acts of the play, yet the play is less than half over. Confirming Macbeth's fear that the deed, once done, will not really be done, the rest of the play is concerned with the consequences.

Macbeth shows no satisfaction at being king; instead he broods on the prophecy that Banquo will be father to a line of kings, while he will have no successor. In an attempt to block the prophecy, he decides to have Banquo and Fleance murdered. With ironic politeness, he insists on Banquo's attendance at a banquet to be held that night; Banquo promises to come, then rides off with Fleance. In the darkness the murderers hired by Macbeth attack them. They kill Banquo, but Fleance escapes. Macbeth's attempt to control the future has failed.

The occasion of 3.4 is a state banquet, a celebration of the new regime. Even in our time, institutions from clubs and colleges to army regiments hold formal dinners to celebrate themselves; in Shakespeare's time, the scene would have a special resonance if the play was performed at court, since the court of King James was known for its lavish entertainments. But this is a court occasion that goes wrong, not because the chief guest, Banquo, is missing but because he turns up. Even before this disruption, Macbeth as host strikes false notes. While Lady Macbeth keeps her state as queen, he mingles with the thanes, not so much a king standing on his dignity as a politician working the room. It is as though he feels already the insecurity of his position, and is trying to cover for it with a slightly false bonhomie. Moreover, he allows himself to be distracted by an intruder who has no business being there, the murderer who reports the half-success of the attack on Banquo. He spends a long time talking with the murderer, while the party has to go on without him. Finally Lady Macbeth rebukes her husband for neglecting his guests, as in 1.7 she rebuked him for leaving the chamber while Duncan was still at supper. The recurring motif of the disrupted meal reflects at a domestic level the general sense of disorder; Macbeth, a great success as a soldier, is never much of a host.

The distraction produced by the murderer is mild compared to the panic caused by the victim. Banquo, dead and bloodstained, recalls the bleeding Captain of 1.2, but this time the effect is straightforward horror. In the lead-in to Duncan's murder Macbeth and his wife agreed on the importance of concealing their true desires beneath a false front. Now Macbeth is completely unable to control himself. What makes the scene especially disconcerting for the audience is that we see what Macbeth sees. We did not see the dagger; we did not hear the voice that cried 'Sleep no more'. Now, just as he is becoming more steeped in fear and evil, more cut off from normal humanity, we start to enter his mind, to share his visions. Some modern productions omit the ghost of Banquo, leaving Macbeth shouting at empty space. It's all in his mind. (As early as 1794 John Philip Kemble experimented with omitting the ghost, but his audience demanded its restoration, and he complied.) Such a staging has a certain value, in letting us share the perspective of the assembled thanes as their king goes berserk; we see how strange it must be from their point of view. But the text is explicit about bringing Banquo on stage; at a time when we might be feeling increasingly detached from Macbeth, it is important to be able to see with his eyes. And while the idea that Macbeth is simply hallucinating may suit contemporary scepticism about ghosts, this is a play that deals unabashedly in the supernatural.

Lady Macbeth cannot see Banquo. This is part of a growing rift in the marriage. At ll. 61–2 we learn that at some point Macbeth told his wife about the imaginary dagger. But earlier in Act 3 he has plotted the murder of Banquo without involving her; he allows her only a general hint of what he is up to. He stirred the murderers up to the job by challenging their manhood, using on them a technique Lady Macbeth used on him (3.1.90–107). He is taking over her role, making her redundant. In 3.4 she tries to restrain him, and to cover for him. She does her best, showing her old acumen and ingenuity in argument; but this time she fails. By the end of the scene she seems quiet and drained, as though the effort has cost her more than she had to spare. We never see them together again, and when we next see Lady Macbeth she is sleepwalking. (Joan Larsen Klein describes the weakening of Lady Macbeth; see Modern Criticism, **pp. 68–71**. For Peter Thomson's reconstruction of the staging of this scene in Shakespeare's theatre, see The Work in Performance, **pp. 96–8**.)

Banquet prepared.[1]
Enter Macbeth, Lady Macbeth, Ross, Lennox, Lords, and Attendants.

MACBETH
    You know your own degrees,[2] sit down; at first
    And last, the hearty welcome.
LORDS   Thanks to your majesty.
MACBETH
    Ourself[3] will mingle with society,
    And play the humble host;
    Our hostess keeps her state,[4] but in best time[5]

---

1   At the opening of 1.7 a procession of servants indicated the preparation of a meal for Duncan. Here we see the meal itself. Theatrically, Shakespeare is raising the stakes. 'Banquet' could mean a modest collection of sweets and snacks, but it also had its modern meaning, an elaborate formal occasion, and this seems to be the meaning that operates here.

2   On an occasion such as this there would be a set order of precedence reflecting the relative importance of the guests. Quarrels could break out over this; Macbeth seems anxious to get this part of the occasion over quickly.

3   Macbeth uses the royal 'we'.

4   A chair of state, indicating her status as queen, and keeping her at some distance from the rest of the guests. There is presumably a similar chair (even a throne) for Macbeth, but it is not clear that he ever uses it.

5   When the time seems right.

We will require her welcome.

LADY MACBETH

Pronounce it for me sir, to all our friends,
For my heart speaks they are welcome.

Enter First Murderer.[6]

MACBETH

See, they encounter thee with their hearts' thanks.
Both sides are even – here I'll sit i'th' midst;   10
Be large[7] in mirth, anon we'll drink a measure
The table round. [*To First Murderer*]
There's blood upon thy face.

FIRST MURDERER   'Tis Banquo's then.

MACBETH

'Tis better thee without than he within.[8]
Is he dispatched?

FIRST MURDERER   My lord, his throat is cut,
That I did for him.

MACBETH   Thou art the best o'th' cut-throats,
Yet he's good that did the like for Fleance;
If thou didst it, thou art the nonpareil.[9]

FIRST MURDERER

Most royal sir –
Fleance is scaped.

MACBETH   Then comes my fit again;   20
I had else[10] been perfect:
Whole as the marble, founded as the rock,
As broad, and general, as the casing[11] air;
But now I am cabined, cribbed,[12] confined, bound in
To saucy[13] doubts and fears. But Banquo's safe?

FIRST MURDERER

Ay, my good lord: safe in a ditch he bides,[14]
With twenty trenchèd gashes[15] on his head,
The least a death to nature.[16]

6 In the dialogue that follows Macbeth and the murderer have a long conversation that no one else
   notices. This would be aided at the Globe by the stage pillars which create inner and outer acting
   areas; the effect can be seen in the modern reproduction of the Globe in London.
7 Unrestrained.
8 The blood is better on your skin than inside his body (with an inner meaning, anticipating Banquo's entrance: it's better to have you outside the room than him inside it).
9 Unequalled.
10 Otherwise.
11 Surrounding (with suggestion of enclosure, leading into the next line).
12 Closed up, as in a small hut (cabin) or an animal's stall (crib).
13 Insolent (a stronger word in Shakespeare's English than in ours).
14 This may be a factor in Banquo's return; he has not been properly buried.
15 Deep cuts.
16 Any one of which would normally kill him.

MACBETH   Thanks for that;
　　There the grown serpent lies, the worm that's fled
　　Hath nature that in time will venom breed,
　　No teeth for th' present. Get thee gone; tomorrow   30
　　We'll hear ourselves again.   *Exit First Murderer*
LADY MACBETH   My royal lord,
　　You do not give the cheer; the feast is sold
　　That is not often vouched while 'tis a-making:
　　'Tis given, with welcome; to feed were best at home:
　　From thence, the sauce to meat is ceremony,
　　Meeting were bare without it.[17]

Enter the Ghost of Banquo, and sits in Macbeth's place.

MACBETH   Sweet remembrancer![18]
　　Now good digestion wait on appetite,
　　And health on both.
LENNOX   May't please your highness sit?
MACBETH
　　Here had we now our country's honour, roofed,[19]
　　Were the graced person of our Banquo present,   40
　　Who may I rather challenge for unkindness
　　Than pity for mischance.[20]
ROSS   His absence, sir,
　　Lays blame upon his promise. Please't your highness
　　To grace us with your royal company?
MACBETH
　　The table's full.
LENNOX   Here is a place reserved, sir.
MACBETH   Where?[21]
LENNOX
　　Here, my good lord. What is't that moves[22] your highness?
MACBETH
　　Which of you have done this?
LORDS   What, my good lord?

---

17 A difficult passage, which may be paraphrased as follows: if you do not offer your guests a proper
    welcome, you are selling a meal (as though you were an innkeeper), not giving it, and they might as
    well eat at home. Away from home, a meal without proper entertainment (ceremony) is like meat
    without sauce.
18 An official whose role it is to issue reminders.
19 The nobility of our country in one room.
20 i.e., I hope I have to rebuke him for breaking his promise rather than pity him for meeting with
    some accident.
21 Macbeth's delay in seeing Banquo (an effect repeated at the Ghost's second appearance) recalls his
    brief delay in seeing the witches in 1.3, and Lady Macbeth's delay in seeing him as he emerges from
    Duncan's chamber. It also suggests a staging in which Banquo's entrance is unobtrusive. In Robin
    Phillips's production (Stratford, Ontario, 1978) the murder of Banquo was staged in a total black-
    out, during which the banquet was assembled. The lights came on to reveal a stage full of actors,
    with Banquo already in his place.
22 Disturbs.

MACBETH [*to the Ghost*]
>   Thou canst not say I did it; never shake
>   Thy gory locks at me.   50
ROSS   Gentlemen rise, his highness is not well.
LADY MACBETH
>   Sit, worthy friends, my lord is often thus.
>   And hath been from his youth. Pray you keep seat,
>   The fit is momentary, upon a thought[23]
>   He will again be well. If much you note[24] him
>   You shall offend him and extend his passion;
>   Feed, and regard him not. [*Aside to Macbeth*] Are you a man?
MACBETH
>   Ay, and a bold one, that dare look on that
>   Which might appal the Devil.
LADY MACBETH [*aside to Macbeth*] O proper stuff![25]
>   This is the very painting of your fear,[26]   60
>   This is the air-drawn dagger which you said
>   Led you to Duncan. O, these flaws and starts,[27]
>   (Impostors[28] to true fear) would well become
>   A woman's story, at a winter's fire,
>   Authorized by her grandam; shame itself,
>   Why do you make such faces? When all's done
>   You look but on a stool.
MACBETH
>   Prithee see there;
>   Behold, look, lo, how say you?

[*To the Ghost*]

>   Why what care I, if thou canst nod, speak too.
>   If charnel houses[29] and our graves must send   70
>   Those that we bury, back, our monuments
>   Shall be the maws of kites.[30]   *Exit Ghost*
LADY MACBETH   What, quite unmanned in folly?
MACBETH
>   If I stand here, I saw him.
LADY MACBETH   Fie, for shame!
MACBETH
>   Blood hath been shed ere now, i'th' olden time
>   Ere humane statute purged the gentle weal;[31]

---

23 In a moment.
24 Notice.
25 Utter nonsense.
26 A picture created by your fear.
27 Sudden bursts of feeling and movement.
28 (Because there is really nothing to fear.)
29 Rooms or buildings for storing the bones of the dead.
30 We will be buried not in tombs but in the stomachs of birds of prey.
31 i.e., before law (both human and humane) cured society ('the gentle weal') of violence.

Ay, and since too, murthers have been performed
Too terrible for the ear. The times has been,
That when the brains were out, the man would die,
And there an end; but now they rise again
With twenty mortal murthers on their crowns,[32]   80
And push us from our stools. This is more strange
Than such a murther is.

LADY MACBETH   My worthy lord,
Your noble friends do lack you.

MACBETH   I do forget:
Do not muse at me, my most worthy friends,
I have a strange infirmity, which is nothing
To those that know me. Come, love and health to all,
Then I'll sit down. Give me some wine, fill full:

Enter Ghost.

I drink to th' general joy o'th' whole table,
And to our dear friend Banquo, whom we miss;
Would he were here; to all, and him, we thirst,   90
And all to all.[33]

LORDS   Our duties, and the pledge.

MACBETH [*to the Ghost*]
Avaunt, and quit my sight, let the earth hide thee;
Thy bones are marrowless, thy blood is cold;
Thou hast no speculation[34] in those eyes
Which thou dost glare with.

LADY MACBETH   Think of this, good peers,
But as a thing of custom: 'tis no other,
Only it spoils the pleasure of the time.

MACBETH   What man dare, I dare:[35]
Approach thou like the rugged Russian bear,
The armed rhinoceros,[36] or th' Hyrcan[37] tiger,   100
Take any shape but that, and my firm nerves
Shall never tremble. Or be alive again,
And dare me to the desert with thy sword;
If trembling I inhabit[38] then, protest me
The baby[39] of a girl. Hence, horrible shadow,
Unreal mock'ry, hence.   *Exit Ghost*[40]

---

32 Heads (recalling the twenty wounds on Banquo's head (26).
33 I long to drink to all of you, including Banquo; let's have a general toast.
34 Ability to see.
35 Echoing 'I dare do all that may become a man' (1.7.46). Once again Macbeth feels his manhood
    challenged, an idea he develops in the rest of the speech.
36 The thick folds of the rhinoceros's skin look like plate armour.
37 Referring to an area around the Caspian sea.
38 Stay indoors.
39 Doll.
40 Since the play observes so carefully the storytelling rule of three (three witches, murderers, greet-
    ings, apparitions, prophecies) the fact that Banquo does not make a third appearance in this scene
    introduces a note of suspense, a sense of unfinished business. He appears for the third time in 4.1.

Why so, being gone
I am a man again; pray you sit still.

LADY MACBETH

You have displaced the mirth, broke the good meeting,
With most admired[41] disorder.

MACBETH   Can such things be,
And overcome us like a summer's cloud,   110
Without our special wonder? You make me strange
Even to the disposition that I owe,[42]
When now I think you can behold such sights
And keep the natural ruby of your cheeks,
When mine is blanched with fear.

ROSS   What sights, my lord?

LADY MACBETH

I pray you speak not; he grows worse and worse,
Question enrages him; at once, good night.
Stand not upon the order of your going,[43]
But go at once.

LENNOX   Good night, and better health
Attend his majesty.

LADY MACBETH   A kind good night to all.   120

Exeunt Lords [and Attendants]

MACBETH

It will have blood they say: blood will have blood.
Stones have been known to move, and trees to speak;
Augures, and understood relations,[44] have
By maggot-pies,[45] and choughs,[46] and rooks brought forth
The secret'st man of blood.[47] What is the night?[48]

LADY MACBETH

Almost at odds with morning, which is which.

MACBETH

How sayst thou that[49] Macduff denies his person
At our great bidding?[50]

LADY MACBETH   Did you send to him, sir?

---

41 Astonishing.
42 You make me feel alienated from my own nature (i.e. less of a man).
43 Don't bother leaving in the proper order (referring to the order of precedence Macbeth invoked at the beginning of the scene). The ghost has not just shocked Macbeth but disturbed the whole occasion.
44 Augurers (fortune-tellers) and their knowledge of how to link signs in nature with forthcoming events.
45 Magpies (augurers read the entrails of birds).
46 Crows.
47 Revealed the most carefully hidden murder. (The 'man of blood' could be the corpse, or the killer; we have seen both in this scene.)
48 What time of night is it?
49 What do you think about the fact that . . .?
50 Macduff (unlike Banquo) has refused Macbeth's invitation to the banquet. The insult introduces Macbeth's next fear, to be confirmed in 4.1.

MACBETH

    I hear it by the way; but I will send;
    There's not a one of them but in his house   130
    I keep a servant fee'd. I will tomorrow
    (And betimes[51] I will) to the Weird Sisters.
    More shall they speak: for now I am bent[52] to know
    By the worst means, the worst; for mine own good,
    All causes shall give way. I am in blood
    Stepped in so far, that should I wade no more,
    Returning were as tedious as go o'er.[53]
    Strange things I have in head, that will to hand,
    Which must be acted, ere they may be scanned.[54]

LADY MACBETH

    You lack the season[55] of all natures, sleep.   140

MACBETH

    Come, we'll to sleep; my strange and self-abuse[56]
    Is the initiate fear, that wants hard use;[57]
    We are yet but young indeed.[58]   *Exeunt*

Act 4, Scene 1: The witches' cauldron; the riddling prophecies

In the play as printed in the Folio, the banquet scene is followed by a scene (3.5) in which Hecate, the goddess of witchcraft, rebukes the witches for not involving her in their dealings with Macbeth. The lightness and jauntiness of the Hecate sequence make it unlike the rest of the play, and the introduction of a song at the end of the scene moves the play towards Davenant's song-and-dance spectacle. It is generally assumed that 3.5 is a later addition, possibly by Middleton, almost certainly not by Shakespeare. The same assumption is made about Hecate's brief appearance in 4.1 (not given here), which includes another song, extra witches and a dance. We are on our way towards *Macbeth: the Musical.*

If we can reconstruct the original play by removing the Hecate material (and we cannot know for certain whether it is that simple), then what follows the banquet scene is a dialogue between Lennox and a nameless Lord, in which Lennox accuses Macbeth of the murders of Duncan and Banquo. The banquet

---

51 Early.
52 Determined.
53 The alert moral horror of the earlier scenes has been replaced by a weariness in which there is no moral element. Macbeth says, in effect, I might as well go on as go back; both are equally tedious.
54 I have to act before I think about what I'm doing. (Earlier in the play, thought paralysed action.)
55 Preservative.
56 My strange tormenting of myself (Macbeth has already called his thoughts 'strange' (138); he is moving into new territory).
57 Beginner's fear, that needs to be treated roughly.
58 Punning on 'in deed' (and sometimes printed that way in modern editions).

scene dramatizes Macbeth's own private sense of guilt; the scene with Lennox shows that Macbeth's guilt is now common knowledge. The Lord reports that Malcolm is now in the English court, and Macduff is on his way there. England has become the centre of resistance, and as Macbeth tries to consolidate his power the counter-movement to him has already begun. In what we might think of as the daylight world of political and military action, Macbeth is already in trouble. It is a doomed man who in 4.1 goes to the witches to learn his fate. But 4.1 gives a deeper vision of that fate. There is something working against Macbeth at another level than the Scottish exiles and the English army, something that links with the uncanny reappearance of the murdered Banquo.

The witches' prophecies are somehow dependent on the strange brew they concoct at the opening of the scene, out of which the apparitions appear. In some productions, including Trevor Nunn's stage and television version, Macbeth drinks the brew, suggesting that the apparitions are the hallucinations it produces. We may assume that when the scene opens the witches are expecting Macbeth, as they do in 1.3, and the brew is being prepared for him. Yet they never say that, and when he asks them what they are doing, they reply, 'A deed without a name' (49). Behind the obvious grotesquerie and the images of black magic there is still something enigmatic. They are putting Macbeth in touch with his future, but the way they do so combines straightforward warnings that confirm his worst fears and deceptive reassurances that give him false hope. They refuse at first to answer his question about Banquo's issue, and reverse themselves a moment later. At the end, as they did before, they simply vanish. They never appear again. In the interpolated Hecate scene, 3.5, Hecate gives a clear underpinning to 4.1. by telling the witches to give Macbeth false hopes that will lure him to his destruction (28–33). If that is their motive in the original play, it is never spelled out; the sense of mystery remains.

Hecate's singing and dancing witches move *Macbeth*, in its revised version, towards spectacle of a kind that seems unnaturally grafted on to it. But Shakespeare is using spectacle in his own way. For the most part he has conveyed the supernatural through language, especially the fevered language of Macbeth. But Banquo's appearance at the feast, in which an ordered state occasion is broken up by the sight of an atrocity, puts a new weight on the visual. In 4.1 Macbeth does not just hear prophecies: he sees visions, and (as with the ghost of Banquo) we see them too. The armed head, the bloody child and the crowned child with the tree in its hand are if anything more troubling, more resistant to simple interpretation, than the words they utter.

The armed head utters a straightforward warning: 'Beware Macduff' (71) that sits oddly with the deceptive reassurances of the next two prophecies, where the warnings are couched in what look like messages of hope. If the first vision's warning is also paradoxical, it may be because, by warning Macbeth to beware of Macduff, it is provoking Macbeth to strike at his enemy, making the latter more dangerous than ever. The armed head itself is more obviously a puzzle: whose head is it? Does it represent Macduff as warrior? Or, since it is *only* a head, does it predict the end, where Macduff will produce Macbeth's severed head on stage? If it is the latter, then the warning to beware Macduff is accompanied by the sight of what Macduff will do to Macbeth. In that sense the warning is futile:

Macbeth is doomed in any case. (In the 1955 production at Stratford-upon-Avon the head was Macbeth's own.) The bloody child is also enigmatic: is it Macduff's murdered child, the victim of the raid that takes place in the next scene? Is it Macduff himself, who was born by caesarian section, torn from his mother's womb? Are we seeing a dead child or a newborn one? To mystery we can add incongruity: the child's exhortation to be 'bloody, bold and resolute' (79) suggests the violence of the battlefield; the words come not from a soldier but from a child, who looks more like one of war's victims. Also, while this prophecy seems opposed to the first one, it turns out to be another way of saying the same thing.

Things happen in threes, but not neatly: we have one straight warning and two riddles; one warrior and two children; two prophecies about Macduff and one about Malcolm. The third vision, the crowned child with a tree in his hand, tells Macbeth that he can never be defeated until Birnam Wood comes to Dunsinane; but the reassurance is cut across by the visual image. The tree in the child's hand shows how the trick will be done; the crown on his head predicts Malcolm's kingship. He holds the tree as a king would hold a sceptre. One child is covered in blood, the other holds the visual attributes of power. Macbeth is later contemptuous of 'the boy Malcolm' (5.3.3). To become king, Macbeth has had to become what Lady Macbeth calls a man. A 'boy' will succeed him.

The most elaborate spectacle in the scene (and in the play) is the procession of eight kings, which has its own paradoxical quality. It is a vision of order and power, of the continuity Macbeth has violated. It celebrates the lineage of the reigning King, James I of England and VI of Scotland. For viewers of a conservative bent it ought to be reassuring. Yet for Macbeth it is a vision of horror, from which he recoils; and as I have suggested, by sharing his visions we have come, in part at least, to share his perspective on the action. The climax of the procession is not the last and most splendid king, but the third appearance of Banquo. In 1.2 good news about the defeat of treason was delivered by a man covered in blood; now a man covered in blood presides over the vision of order. (David Scott Kastan finds the scene problematic in other ways; see Modern Criticism, p. 86.)

Throughout 4.1 the words and pictures cut across each other: children, images of weakness, become signs of power; words reassure and pictures threaten; warnings sound like reassurances; an orderly procession induces terror; a line of kings is presided over by a murder victim. The final effect of the scene on Macbeth is also paradoxical. He finds that the future, which he is desperate to know, is out of his control. Any action of his will be meaningless; and so he takes action. He has seen the most dramatic evidence that he is helpless to prevent the line of Banquo from succeeding. In a pattern that is grimly recognizable to those who live with violence, he reacts to his sense of helplessness by lashing out – not against Banquo (he tried that) or against Macduff (beyond his reach) but against Macduff's family. He has gone from killing traitors to killing the King; and from that to killing the man who represents Scotland's future. He has gone from hand-to-hand combat on the battlefield to killing a sleeping old man, to hiring assassins. His next victims will be a woman and her children.

Thunder. Enter the three Witches.

FIRST WITCH
  Thrice the brinded[1] cat hath mewed.
SECOND WITCH
  Thrice, and once the hedge-pig[2] whined.
THIRD WITCH
  Harpier[3] cries, 'tis time, 'tis time.
FIRST WITCH
  Round about the cauldron go,
  In the poisoned entrails throw:
  Toad, that under cold stone,
  Days and nights has thirty-one
  Sweltered[4] venom sleeping got,[5]
  Boil thou first i'th' charmèd pot.
ALL
  Double,[6] double, toil and trouble;   10
  Fire burn, and cauldron bubble.
SECOND WITCH
  Fillet[7] of a fenny[8] snake
  In the cauldron boil and bake;
  Eye of newt, and toe of frog,
  Wool of bat, and tongue of dog;
  Adder's fork, and blind-worm's[9] sting,
  Lizard's leg, and howlet's[10] wing;
  For a charm of powerful trouble,
  Like a hell-broth, boil and bubble.
ALL
  Double, double, toil and trouble;
  Fire burn, and cauldron bubble.   20
THIRD WITCH
  Scale of dragon, tooth of wolf,
  Witch's mummy,[11] maw and gulf[12]

1 Tabby.
2 Hedgehog.
3 Presumably the Third Witch's familiar (see **p. 128**, n. 3); We do not know what form it takes, though the name suggests 'harpy', a mythological creature, part bird and part woman, that spread contamination.
4 Produced like sweat.
5 Toads were thought to generate poison; it is appropriate that a toad should be the first ingredient. In the lines describing it the natural order of the sentence is reversed, suggesting that in the charm, as in a witches' dance or black mass, things are done backwards.
6 The word can mean 'deceptive' (as in modern expressions like 'double-dealing'), and this will be the effect of the prophecies on Macbeth.
7 Slice.
8 From a marsh.
9 Either a slow-worm (a reptile with small eyes) or an adder, both considered poisonous.
10 Young or small owl.
11 Mummified flesh.
12 Throat and stomach.

Of the ravined[13] salt-sea shark;
Root of hemlock,[14] digged i'th' dark;
Liver of blaspheming Jew,
Gall of goat, and slips[15] of yew,
Slivered[16] in the moon's eclipse;
Nose of Turk, and Tartar's lips;
Finger of birth-strangled babe,   30
Ditch-delivered by a drab,[17]
Make the gruel thick and slab.[18]
Add thereto a tiger's chawdron,[19]
For th' ingredience of our cauldron.

ALL

Double, double, toil and trouble;
Fire burn, and cauldron bubble.

SECOND WITCH

Cool it with a baboon's blood,
Then the charm is firm and good. . . .[20]

SECOND WITCH

By the pricking of my thumbs,
Something wicked this way comes;[21]
Open locks, whoever knocks.

Enter Macbeth

MACBETH

How now, you secret, black, and midnight hags?
What is't you do?

ALL   A deed without a name.

MACBETH

I conjure you, by that which you profess,[22]   50
(Howe'er you come to know it) answer me:

---

13 Greedy.
14 Another poison.
15 Twigs. (The yew tree was associated with death and mourning, and its berries were thought to be poisonous.)
16 Sliced off.
17 Prostitute. Born in a ditch (as the murdered Banquo is tossed into a ditch), the child is unwanted, and strangled at birth. The image resonates with Macbeth's lack of children, and his own turn to infanticide at the end of the scene. Since the child would be unbaptized, it also links with the infidels (Jew, Turk, Tartar) of the previous lines, playing on the stock prejudices of Shakespeare's society.
18 Semi-solid.
19 Entrails.
20 At this point in the revised play Hecate enters with three other witches, and the assembled coven dances 'Like elves and fairies in a ring' (4.1.42) around the cauldron, singing and adding more ingredients. This passage is omitted here. Assuming that the cut restores the original play, the completion of the charm with the baboon's blood is followed immediately by a knocking to signal Macbeth's entrance. (There is no stage direction for it, but the dialogue would seem to call for it.) The sound effect recalls the knocking that followed Duncan's murder, and contrasts with the drum that heralded Macbeth's entrance when he first met the witches. He has gone from warrior to murderer.
21 The suggestion is that however wicked the witches and their brew seem, Macbeth is more wicked still, so steeped in evil that he is no longer human but 'something' unnameable.
22 i.e., by your claim to know the future.

Though you untie the winds, and let them fight
Against the churches; though the yesty[23] waves
Confound and swallow navigation[24] up;
Though bladed corn be lodged,[25] and trees blown down,
Though castles topple on their warders' heads;
Though palaces and pyramids[26] do slope[27]
Their heads to their foundations; though the treasure
Of nature's germen[28] tumble all together,
Even till destruction sicken – answer me   60
To what I ask you.

FIRST WITCH   Speak.
SECOND WITCH   Demand.
THIRD WITCH   We'll answer.
FIRST WITCH
Say, if th'hadst rather hear it from our mouths,
Or from our masters.[29]
MACBETH   Call'em: let me see 'em.
FIRST WITCH
Pour in sow's blood, that hath eaten
Her nine farrow;[30] grease that's sweaten[31]
From the murderer's gibbet,[32] throw
Into the flame.
ALL   Come high or low;
Thy self and office[33] deftly show.

Thunder.
First Apparition, an armed head.

MACBETH
Tell me, thou unknown power –
FIRST WITCH   He knows thy thought:
Hear his speech, but say thou nought.   70
FIRST APPARITION
Macbeth, Macbeth, Macbeth: beware Macduff,
Beware the Thane of Fife. Dismiss me. Enough.

He descends

23 Frothy.
24 Shipping.
25 Flattened.
26 Shakespeare and his contemporaries used the word for what we would call an obelisk.
27 Bend down.
28 Seeds.
29 The First Witch calls the spirits who form the apparitions 'our masters'; yet they appear at the witches' command. What are they, and what is their relation to the witches? We never know.
30 Piglets (here, the animal equivalent of the birth-strangled babe).
31 Exuded (like the toad's poison at l.8).
32 Gallows.
33 Function.

MACBETH
> Whate'er thou art, for thy good caution, thanks.
> Thou hast harped[34] my fear aright. But one word more –

FIRST WITCH
> He will not be commanded: here's another
> More potent than the first.

Thunder.
Second Apparition, a bloody child.

SECOND APPARITION   Macbeth, Macbeth, Macbeth.
MACBETH   Had I three ears, I'd hear thee.
SECOND APPARITION
> Be bloody, bold, and resolute: laugh to scorn
> The power of man; for none of woman born   80
> Shall harm Macbeth.   *Descends*

MACBETH
> Then live, Macduff; what need I fear of thee?
> But yet I'll make assurance double sure,
> And take a bond[35] of fate: thou shalt not live,
> That I may tell pale-hearted fear it lies,
> And sleep in spite of thunder.

Thunder
Third Apparition, a child crowned, with a tree in his hand.

> What is this
> That rises like the issue of a king,
> And wears upon his baby-brow the round
> And top[36] of sovereignty?

ALL   Listen, but speak not to't.
THIRD APPARITION
> Be lion-mettled,[37] proud, and take no care   90
> Who chafes, who frets, or where conspirers are;
> Macbeth shall never vanquished be, until
> Great Birnam Wood, to high Dunsinane Hill[38]
> Shall come against him.   *Descends*

MACBETH   That will never be;
> Who can impress[39] the forest, bid the tree
> Unfix his earthbound root? Sweet bodements,[40] good;
> Rebellious dead, rise never till the Wood

---

34 Guessed.
35 Binding promise.
36 Highest sign.
37 Show the courage of a lion.
38 Birnam is twelve miles from Dunsinane (the site of Macbeth's castle).
39 The image is drawn from impressment, the forced enlistment of soldiers, and soldiers carrying boughs will fulfil the prophecy.
40 Prophecies.

Of Birnam rise, and our high-placed Macbeth
Shall live the lease of nature,[41] pay his breath
To time, and mortal custom.[42] Yet my heart   100
Throbs to know one thing: tell me, if your art
Can tell so much: shall Banquo's issue ever
Reign in this kingdom?

ALL   Seek to know no more.

MACBETH
I will be satisfied. Deny me this,
And an eternal curse fall on you! Let me know.
Why sinks that cauldron? (*Hautboys*)[43] And what noise[44] is this?

FIRST WITCH   Show.
SECOND WITCH   Show.
THIRD WITCH   Show.
ALL
Show his eyes, and grieve his heart,   110
Come like shadows, so depart.

A show of eight kings [the last with a glass[45] in his hand; Banquo at the end].

MACBETH
Thou art too like the spirit of Banquo: down!
Thy crown does sear mine eye-balls. And thy hair,
Thou other gold-bound brow, is like the first;
A third is like the former. Filthy hags,
Why do you show me this? A fourth? Start, eyes![46]
What, will the line stretch out to th' crack of doom?[47]
Another yet? A seventh? I'll see no more;
And yet the eighth appears, who bears a glass
Which shows me many more; and some I see   120
That two-fold balls, and treble sceptres carry.[48]
Horrible sight! Now I see 'tis true,
For the blood-boltered[49] Banquo smiles upon me,
And points at them for his. What, is this so? ....[50]
Where are they? Gone? Let this pernicious hour

41 Live out his natural life.
42 i.e., his death will be the payment of a debt to time and mortality; it will be normal.
43 See p. 145, n. 1. The same instruments played as Macbeth feasted Duncan. They introduce an image of kingship restored.
44 Music, or a group of musicians (not necessarily with the modern connotations).
45 Crystal used for seeing the future.
46 i.e., leap from your sockets.
47 Day of Judgement (in Christian belief, the end of the world).
48 Probably an allusion to King James, who had brought England and Scotland under a single monarchy. As King of Scotland, he would bear an orb and a sceptre; as King of England, an orb and two sceptres.
49 Covered in clots of blood.
50 In the revised play the First Witch answers Macbeth's question, 'Ay, sir, all this is so', then calls for a dance to cheer Macbeth up. The dance is then performed, with no noticeable effect on Macbeth's spirits. The passage is cut here (possibly restoring the original play) with the effect that Macbeth at this point asks his last question of the Witches, and they vanish without answering.

Stand aye accursèd in the calendar.
Come in, without there.[51]

Enter Lennox.

LENNOX   What's your grace's will?
MACBETH
    Saw you the Weïrd Sisters?
LENNOX   No, my lord.
MACBETH
    Came they not by you?
LENNOX   No indeed, my lord.
MACBETH
    Infected be the air whereon they ride,
    And damned all those that trust them! I did hear
    The galloping of horse. Who was't came by?   140
LENNOX
    'Tis two or three, my lord, that bring you word,
    Macduff is fled to England.
MACBETH   Fled to England?
LENNOX   Ay, my good lord.
MACBETH [*aside*]
    Time, thou anticipat'st[52] my dread exploits;
    The flighty purpose never is o'ertook
    Unless the deed go with it.[53] From this moment,
    The very firstlings[54] of my heart shall be
    The firstlings of my hand. And even now
    To crown my thoughts with acts, be it thought and done:
    The castle of Macduff I will surprise,   150
    Seize upon Fife; give to th' edge o'th' sword
    His wife, his babes, and all unfortunate souls
    That trace him in his line.[55] No boasting like a fool,
    This deed I'll do, before this purpose cool;
    But no more sights. [*To Lennox*] Where are these gentlemen?
    Come, bring me where they are.   *Exeunt*

---

51 Macbeth calls to someone outside, who turns out to be Lennox. (The appearance of this character, who criticized Macbeth sharply in the previous scene, turns us back from Macbeth as a man trafficking in the supernatural to a man in political trouble.)
52 You forestall.
53 The deed must be as swift as the purpose.
54 Firstborn children (ironic in view of Macbeth's childlessness, and his dedication to infanticide).
55 i.e., his entire family.

Act 4, Scene 2: Lady Macduff and her son

We go directly from Macbeth's threat against Macduff's family to a brief glimpse of the family itself – the first and only sight the play gives us of a domestic setting other than Macbeth's castle, and the only time we see what might be called a family. Productions sometimes build up the domestic aspect of the scene, with Lady Macduff doing needlework or rocking a cradle, servants tending other children, and so on. The effect is to underline the shock of the violence that ends the scene. Shakespeare's treatment, however, is more austere and in some ways surprising. In the area of the play we are now entering, Macbeth is a tyrant and the Scottish people are his victims. The invasion that destroys him is a purifying force, a restoration of moral order. Shakespeare uses this scene to complicate the simple responses these developments might invite. Macduff will kill Macbeth to avenge his murdered family; but the first part of 4.2 is taken up with Lady Macduff's complaint that her husband has deserted his family. Macduff bears his own weight of guilt, and in 4.3, when he hears of the murder, that guilt overwhelms him: 'Sinful Macduff! / They were all struck for thee' (224–5). When Malcolm asks him why he deserted his wife and children he gives no answer (4.3.26–31). The best case that can be made for him is that he has made a difficult choice, saving himself for the good of Scotland at the price of deserting his family. Even granted that motive, there is no way he can make that choice without guilt, and in the final battle he declares that if anyone else kills Macbeth, 'My wife and children's ghosts will haunt me still' (5.7.16). One haunted man is killed by another. These misgivings about Macduff begin in this scene, with his wife's sharply phrased complaints. It would have been easy to play this character for pathos, but Shakespeare does not take the easy way. This is an angry woman, and she has cause.

It would have been easier still to play Macduff's son for pathos. He is, after all, a child who is about to be murdered. But his prattle is not altogether innocent. He may not know the meaning of the word 'traitor' but he knows that snares are set for rich birds, not poor ones, that there are more liars and swearers in the world than honest men, that if marriage is a market no loyalty is involved, and that his mother is lying to him. He is like one of Shakespeare's clowns, whose jokes convey a bitter wisdom about the world. In the context of the growing horror of life in Scotland, he is looking at the world with the hard eyes of a child who has grown up in a war zone.

In the end Shakespeare turns the scene around. Confronted with the murderers, Lady Macduff stands up for the husband who deserted her. When one murderer calls Macduff a traitor, the son denies it, and the murderer's response is to kill him. He too defends the father who abandoned him. The violence that ends the scene is in some productions elaborate and drawn out. In the actual writing of the scene the shock comes from the speed and simplicity of the violence. One cut of the knife despatches the boy; his mother runs off screaming, and the scene ends. (In the eighteenth and nineteenth centuries some productions cut the killing of the child as too painful. Sometimes the whole scene was cut.)

In the next scene, set in England, Macduff, Malcolm and, later, Ross lament the miserable state of Scotland. Their complaints are couched in general terms, to give a sense of the sheer scale of suffering: 'each new morn, / New widows howl, new orphans cry' (4.3.4–5). But the audience, which has just seen a particular atrocity, has a sense of the reality behind the abstraction. It is one thing to see a casualty list, another to watch particular people killed. And there is grim irony in the words just quoted, since they are Macduff's: he imagines women and children mourning, in a world in which men die. We know that women and children, his own included, are being killed, and he as the man of the family will be left to mourn. We feel the outrage more strongly in that Shakespeare has refused to sentimentalize any of the characters involved. They are not stock figures of pathos, but believable characters, with the difficult, complex feelings of the fully human.

Enter Macduff's wife, her son, and Ross.

LADY MACDUFF
    What had he done, to make him fly the land?
ROSS
    You must have patience, madam.
LADY MACDUFF   He had none;
    His flight was madness; when our actions do not,
    Our fears do make us traitors.
ROSS   You know not
    Whether it was his wisdom, or his fear.
LADY MACDUFF
    Wisdom? To leave his wife, to leave his babes,
    His mansion, and his titles, in a place
    From whence himself does fly? He loves us not,
    He wants the natural touch.[1] For the poor wren
    (The most diminutive of birds) will fight,   10
    Her young ones in her nest, against the owl;
    All is the fear, and nothing is the love;
    As little is the wisdom, where the flight
    So runs against all reason.
ROSS   My dearest coz,[2]
    I pray you school yourself.[3] But for your husband,
    He is noble, wise, judicious, and best knows
    The fits o'th' season.[4] I dare not speak much further,
    But cruel are the times, when we are traitors
    And do not know ourselves: when we hold rumour

---

1   Lady Macbeth, on the other hand, complained that her husband was 'too full o'th' milk of human kindness'.
2   Cousin (not necessarily implying kinship).
3   Bring yourself under control.
4   The violence of the time (imagined here as the convulsions of an illness).

From what we fear, yet know not what we fear,   20
But float upon a wild and violent sea
Each way, and move.[5] I take my leave of you:
Shall not be long but I'll be here again;
Things at the worst will cease, or else climb upward,
To what they were before. [*To Son*] My pretty cousin,
Blessing upon you.

LADY MACDUFF
Fathered he is, and yet he's fatherless.[6]

ROSS
I am so much a fool, should I stay longer
It would be my disgrace, and your discomfort.[7]
I take my leave at once.   *Exit* 30

LADY MACDUFF   Sirrah, your father's dead, and what will you do
now? How will you live?

SON   As birds do, mother.

LADY MACDUFF   What, with worms, and flies?

SON   With what I get, I mean, and so do they.

LADY MACDUFF   Poor bird, thou'dst never fear the net, nor lime,[8] the
pitfall,[9] nor the gin.[10]

SON   Why should I, mother? Poor birds they are not set for. My father
is not dead for all your saying.

LADY MACDUFF   Yes, he is dead; how wilt thou do for a father?

SON   Nay, how will you do for a husband?

LADY MACDUFF   Why, I can buy me twenty at any market.   40

SON   Then you'll buy 'em to sell again.

LADY MACDUFF   Thou speak'st with all thy wit, and yet i'faith with
wit enough for thee.[11]

SON   Was my father a traitor, mother?

LADY MACDUFF   Ay, that he was.

SON   What is a traitor?

LADY MACDUFF   Why, one that swears, and lies.[12]

SON   And be all traitors, that do so?

---

5 The idea seems incomplete (move how? where?) and at this point Ross breaks off. Throughout the
  scene he has met Lady Macduff's sharp accusation of her husband with vague reassurances (saying
  in effect that her husband knows best and she should not question his motives) and his sense of the
  danger of the time is equally vague. It is as though he cannot speak frankly to her; and before he
  leaves he falls back on a conventional, empty hope that things will get better.
6 Lady Macduff has her own version of the riddling language that has run through the first scene.
  (And she will not let Ross have the last word about her husband.)
7 Suggesting he might burst into tears – unmanly and embarrassing in the play's gender code.
8 Bird-lime, a sticky substance. It was spread on branches, and when birds caught their feet in it they
  could not escape.
9 Trap.
10 Snare.
11 You're speaking with all your intelligence, and it's all the intelligence you need. 'Yet' implies a
   turnaround; the point may be that the first part of the line sounded condescending, an impression
   Lady Macduff then corrects.
12 One who swears oaths he never means to keep (Lady Macduff may be thinking of her husband as
   having broken his marriage vows).

LADY MACDUFF   Everyone that does so is a traitor, and must be
hanged.   50
SON   And must they all be hanged, that swear and lie?
LADY MACDUFF   Every one.
SON   Who must hang them?
LADY MACDUFF   Why, the honest men.
SON   Then the liars and swearers are fools: for there are liars and
swearers enow[13] to beat the honest men, and hang up them.
LADY MACDUFF   Now God help thee, poor monkey! But how wilt
thou do for a father?[14]
SON   If he were dead, you'd weep for him; if you would not, it were a
good sign that I should quickly have a new father.   60
LADY MACDUFF   Poor prattler, how thou talk'st!

Enter a Messenger.

MESSENGER
Bless you fair dame: I am not to you known,
Though in your state of honour I am perfect;[15]
I doubt[16] some danger does approach you nearly.
If you will take a homely[17] man's advice,
Be not found here: hence with your little ones.
To fright you thus methinks I am too savage;
To do worse to you were fell cruelty,   70
Which is too nigh your person.[18] Heaven preserve you,
I dare abide no longer.   *Exit Messenger*
LADY MACDUFF   Whither should I fly?
I have done no harm. But I remember now
I am in this earthly world, where to do harm
Is often laudable, to do good sometime
Accounted dangerous folly. Why then (alas)
Do I put up that womanly[19] defence,
To say I have done no harm?

Enter Murderers.

What are these faces?[20]

---

13 Enough.
14 Lady Macduff returns to the question, implying it is a serious one. She is trying to get her son to
adjust to life without a father.
15 I know everything about your status, your honorable reputation.
16 Fear.
17 Plain. With one word, Shakespeare fills out the character. He is not, like most Shakespearean
messengers, a functionary whose role it is to carry news. He is an ordinary man, probably living
nearby, who has entered a house that is normally too grand for him to warn its mistress of
approaching danger. His equivalents in *King Lear* are the servant who tries to stop the blinding of
Gloucester, and the old tenant farmer who helps the blind lord when he is thrust out of his own
house.
18 It is cruel to frighten you like this, but the cruelty that is approaching you is even worse.
19 Implying an innocence of the world.
20 Who are these people? But 'what' implies they are hardly human, and their reduction to 'faces'
suggests their faces are so horrible she can look at nothing else.

MURDERER   Where is your husband?
LADY MACDUFF
      I hope in no place so unsanctified   80
      Where such as thou mayst find him.
MURDERER   He's a traitor.
SON
      Thou li'st, thou shag-eared²¹ villain.
MURDERER   What, you egg?
      Young fry²² of treachery! [*Kills him.*]
SON   He has killed me, mother,
      Run away I pray you.
      Exit [*Lady Macduff*] *crying 'Murther'.* [*The murderers pursue her.*]

Act 4, Scene 3, lines 139–73: Edward the Confessor and Macbeth: a good king and a tyrant

The attack on Macduff's family is followed immediately by the entrance of Macduff and Malcolm, in England, lamenting the state of their country. Macduff has more to lament than he knows. Later in the scene he will learn the truth from Ross. The scene as a whole is the longest and slowest in the play; for once, the quick pace relaxes. This provides a break for the audience, and for the actor playing Macbeth. Shakespeare frequently gives the title character in his tragedies a substantial period off stage (sometimes jokingly called the 'Burbage tea-break', after the leading actor of Shakespeare's company) before he faces the demands of the final scenes. In this case Shakespeare also takes the occasion to widen the significance of the play's issues, to go from the story of Macbeth to general reflections on the nature of kingship, particularly a king's relation to his people. (These may be compared with King James's similar reflections; see Contemporary Documents, **pp. 30–1**.)

   In the first part of the scene (not given here) Malcolm, not quite trusting Macduff, tests his integrity. Macduff is pressing Malcolm to overthrow Macbeth and rule in his place; Malcolm claims for himself a spectacular list of vices that make him unfit to be king. He wants to see if Macduff has a breaking point, if there is a degree of wickedness he will not accept. There is; Macduff finally rejects the idea of Malcolm as king. Malcolm then reverses himself, and declares himself innocent of all the evils he has just listed. One effect of the scene is to list the vices of a tyrant. Malcolm dwells on avarice and lechery. Neither is particularly characteristic of Macbeth; Malcolm is constructing a general formula for a tyrant. He also lists the kingly virtues he claims to lack: 'justice, verity, temp'rance, stableness, / Bounty, perseverance, mercy, lowliness' (4.3.92–3), and so on. Again, he is constructing a general formula.

---

21 Torn ears would imply a criminal record; convicted criminals sometimes had their ears mutilated. (Editors sometimes change this to 'shag-hair'd', suggesting a rough, uncouth appearance.)
22 Offspring.

The idea of a good king is given specific embodiment in the sequence that follows (given here), the description of the saintly English King, Edward the Confessor. His virtue is summarized by his ability to cure the so-called 'King's evil' (scrofula, a swelling of the lymph glands) with a touch of his hand. English monarchs performed the ceremony of touching for the King's Evil well into the eighteenth century. (King James was sceptical about it, and performed it with reluctance.) This magic, curative power sets Edward against Macbeth, who is destroying his kingdom. Edward has a gift of prophecy; Macbeth is the victim of prophecies. Edward can pass the gift to his successors; Macbeth will have no successors (155–7). More powerfully than Duncan, Edward represents an ideal of kingship. He remains off stage, suggesting that such ideals are at a remove from the reality the characters have to live in. Ross then enters, and before telling Macduff what has happened to his family, he gives a general account of Scotland – a sick, suffering country.

Enter a Doctor.

MALCOLM   Well, more anon.
    Comes the King forth, I pray you?   140
DOCTOR
    Ay, sir; there are a crew of wretched souls
    That stay[1] his cure: their malady convinces[2]
    The great assay of art.[3] But at his touch,
    Such sanctity hath Heaven given his hand,
    They presently[4] amend.   *Exit*
MALCOLM   I thank you. Doctor.
MACDUFF
    What's the disease he means?
MALCOLM   'Tis called the Evil.
    A most miraculous work in this good King,
    Which often since my here remain[5] in England,
    I have seen him do. How he solicits Heaven
    Himself best knows; but strangely visited[6] people,   150
    All swoln and ulcerous, pitiful to the eye,
    The mere despair of surgery,[7] he cures,
    Hanging a golden stamp[8] about their necks,
    Put on with holy prayers, and 'tis spoken,
    To the succeeding royalty he leaves
    The healing benediction. With this strange virtue,[9]

1 Wait for.
2 Defeats.
3 The best efforts of medical skill.
4 Immediately.
5 My stay.
6 Afflicted.
7 Medical treatment (not necessarily surgery in the modern sense).
8 Coin or medal.
9 Mysterious power.

He hath a heavenly gift of prophecy,
And sundry blessings hang about his throne
That speak him full of grace.

Enter Ross.

MACDUFF   See who comes here.
MALCOLM
My countryman;[10] but yet I know him not.   160
MACDUFF
My ever gentle cousin, welcome hither.
MALCOLM
I know him now. Good God, betimes[11] remove
The means that makes us strangers.
ROSS   Sir, amen.
MACDUFF
Stands Scotland where it did?
ROSS   Alas poor country,
Almost afraid to know itself. It cannot
Be called our mother, but our grave; where nothing
But who knows nothing, is once seen to smile;[12]
Where sighs, and groans, and shrieks that rent the air[13]
Are made, not marked;[14] where violent sorrow seems
A modern[15] ecstasy;[16] the deadman's knell   170
Is there scarce asked for who,[17] and good men's lives
Expire before the flowers in their caps,
Dying or ere[18] they sicken.

Act 5, Scene 1: Lady Macbeth sleepwalks

For the second time in as many scenes a doctor appears, as though to emphasize the motif of sickness and cure that is becoming increasingly prominent in the play. But while the doctor who described the miracles wrought by the

---

10 The fact that Malcolm recognizes Ross as a fellow Scot before he recognizes the man himself suggests that Shakespeare's company used distinctive costume elements (we can only guess what they were) to identify the characters as Scottish. Malcolm's moment of non-recognition links with Ross's description of Scotland as 'Almost afraid to know itself' (165).
11 Soon.
12 The only people who smile are those who do not know what is going on.
13 This takes us back to the previous scene, which ended with the screams of Lady Macduff.
14 Noticed. Ross declares that the sounds of human suffering are so common no one pays any attention to them.
15 Commonplace.
16 Madness (that madness should be commonplace is part of the horror).
17 At the end of 2.1, as Macbeth set out to murder Duncan he heard a bell, that he took as Duncan's death-knell. Now death is so common no one asks whose knell is being tolled.
18 Before.

English King was redundant, in that the King was going beyond the powers of conventional medicine, the doctor who watches Lady Macbeth is helpless: 'This disease is beyond my practice' (56). Lady Macbeth, once so resolute, is now shattered; she is beyond cure. All that is left of her is a series of echoes of previous dialogues, as though she is trapped in a scrambled version of the past. In this she contrasts with Macbeth, who is trapped by the prophecies in a deceptive vision of the future. She is also in a world of her own; the dialogue of the doctor and the waiting gentlewoman cannot penetrate her consciousness.

She speaks mostly – perhaps entirely – to her husband. Her life was centred on her plans for him, and now that he has drawn away from her she can only repeat, in fragmentary form, scenes they used to have together. The compulsive letter-writing the gentlewoman describes at the beginning of the scene suggests a link with her first entrance reading Macbeth's letter. She has been doing this, we learn, since Macbeth went to war. Is she writing to him? Is she rewriting his first letter, over and over? In any case it is a compulsive action, suggesting entrapment. The other compulsive action is washing her hands, recalling her reassurance after the murder, 'A little water clears us of this deed. / How easy is it then!' (2.2.66–7). Her earlier reassurances, some of which she repeats in this scene, play off against the new knowledge that her hands will never be clean.

For the most part she circles back to situations in which we saw her earlier in the play – the murder of Duncan, the appearance of Banquo's ghost. The key exception is 'The Thane of Fife, had a wife; where is she now?' (41–2). What sounds almost like a nursery rhyme repeated in her sleep is turned to horror by the question that follows it. It is the only connection the play makes between the two women – indeed, the only connection of any kind between Lady Macbeth and another woman. It leaves us wondering: was she in some way complicit in the murder? Did she simply hear about it? And behind her question is there a fear that her husband might kill her next? Is she protesting that he has gone too far? The moment comes and goes, leaving the questions hanging.

Once she leaves, the doctor equates her sickness with the general sickness of the land, picking up a key motif from 4.3. But at the end of his speech he comes back to Lady Macbeth, and his command, 'Remove from her the means of all annoyance' (73), suggests a fear that she might try to kill herself. At the end of the play Malcolm repeats a rumour that Lady Macbeth committed suicide (5.9.36–7). It is only a rumour; we learn later that she has died, but nothing about the manner of her death. In a way it hardly matters: what we see in 5.1 is a woman who is already not just dead but in hell, doomed to a futile repetition of the actions that brought her there. In productions that add an explanation for her death – in the Orson Welles film she leaps from the battlements, in John Wood's production at Stratford, Ontario (2004), she stole Macbeth's sword – the effect is generally anticlimactic. (For Sinead Cusack's approach to acting this scene, see The Work in Performance, **pp. 116–18**.)

Enter a Doctor of Physic, and a Waiting Gentlewoman.

DOCTOR   I have two nights watched[1] with you, but can perceive no truth in your report. When was it she last walked?

GENTLEWOMAN   Since his majesty went into the field, I have seen her rise from her bed, throw her nightgown[2] upon her, unlock her closet,[3] take forth paper, fold it, write upon't, read it, afterwards seal it, and again return to bed; yet all this while in a most fast sleep.

DOCTOR   A great perturbation in Nature, to receive at once the benefit of sleep, and do the effects of watching.[4] In this slumbery agitation, besides her walking, and other actual[5] performances, what (at any time) have you heard her say?   13

GENTLEWOMAN   That, sir, which I will not report after her.

DOCTOR   You may to me, and 'tis most meet[6] you should.

GENTLEWOMAN   Neither to you, nor anyone, having no witness to confirm my speech.

Enter Lady [Macbeth], with a taper.

Lo you, here she comes; this is her very guise,[7] and upon my life fast asleep; observe her, stand close.

DOCTOR   How came she by that light?   20

GENTLEWOMAN   Why, it stood by her; she has light by her continually, 'tis her command.

DOCTOR   You see her eyes are open.

GENTLEWOMAN   Ay but their sense[8] are shut.

DOCTOR   What is it she does now? Look how she rubs her hands.

GENTLEWOMAN   It is an accustomed action with her, to seem thus washing her hands: I have known her continue in this a quarter of an hour.

LADY MACBETH   Yet here's a spot.   30

DOCTOR   Hark, she speaks, I will set down what comes from her, to satisfy[9] my remembrance the more strongly.

LADY MACBETH   Out damned spot; out I say. One; two; why then 'tis time to do't;[10] Hell is murky.[11] Fie, my lord, fie, a soldier, and afeard? What need we fear who knows it, when none can call our

---

1 Stayed awake. (Lady Macbeth appears on the third night, another example of the play's obsession with the number three.)
2 Dressing-gown.
3 Cabinet.
4 Behave as though she were awake.
5 Active.
6 Appropriate.
7 This is just how she behaves.
8 Senses.
9 Confirm.
10 She may be recalling the bell that signalled the time for Duncan's murder; or the striking of a clock that was her cue to ring the bell.
11 This may explain her command to have light by her continually.

power to accompt? Yet who would have thought the old man to
have had so much blood in him?[12]

DOCTOR   Do you mark[13] that?   40

LADY MACBETH   The Thane of Fife, had a wife; where is she now?
What, will these hands ne'er be clean? No more o'that my lord, no
more o' that – you mar all with this starting.[14]

DOCTOR   Go to, go to;[15] you have known what you should not.

GENTLEWOMAN   She has spoke what she should not, I am sure of that;
Heaven knows what she has known.

LADY MACBETH   Here's the smell of the blood still; all the perfumes
of Arabia will not sweeten this little hand. Oh, oh, oh.   50

DOCTOR   What a sigh is there! The heart is sorely charged.[16]

GENTLEWOMAN   I would not have such a heart in my bosom, for the
dignity of the whole body.

DOCTOR   Well, well, well.

GENTLEWOMAN   Pray God it be, sir.

DOCTOR   This disease is beyond my practice; yet I have known those
which have walked in their sleep, who have died holily in their beds.

LADY MACBETH   Wash your hands, put on your nightgown, look not
so pale; I tell you yet again Banquo's buried; he cannot come out
on's[17] grave.   61

DOCTOR   Even so?

LADY MACBETH   To bed, to bed; there's knocking at the gate; come,
come, come, come, give me your hand; what's done, cannot be
undone. To bed, to bed, to bed.   *Exit*

DOCTOR   Will she go now to bed?

GENTLEWOMAN   Directly.[18]

DOCTOR

Foul whisp'rings are abroad; unnatural deeds
Do breed unnatural troubles; infected minds
To their deaf pillows will discharge their secrets;   70
More needs she the divine than the physician;
God, God forgive us all. Look after her,
Remove from her the means of all annoyance,[19]
And still keep eyes upon her; so good night;
My mind she has mated,[20] and amazed my sight.
I think, but dare not speak.

GENTLEWOMAN   Good night, good doctor.   *Exeunt*

---

12   It was a medical belief of the time that old people had less blood in their veins than younger ones.
     This image of copious bleeding also links with Macbeth's vision of turning the seas red with his
     bloodstained hand (2.2.59–62) and Lady Macbeth's inability to wash her hands. In each case,
     blood, escaped from the body, is out of control.
13   Note. (Lady Macbeth's words are evidence of her involvement in the murder of Duncan.)
14   Startled movement.
15   An expression of reproach.
16   Severely burdened.
17   Of his.
18   Immediately.
19   Harm.
20   Stunned.

Act 5, Scene 5: Macbeth hears of the death of Lady Macbeth

Throughout Act 5, the play alternates between scenes in which Malcolm, Macduff and their allies prepare their invasion of Scotland and scenes in which Macbeth, clutching the prophecies that he thinks secure his future, remains defiant. In his defiance he has to confront the invasion, massive desertions from his own side, and an increasing awareness of the bleakness of his own life, which has 'fall'n into the sere, the yellow leaf' and in which kingship has brought him not 'honour, love, obedience, troops of friends' but 'Curses, not loud, but deep, mouth-honour, breath, / Which the poor heart would fain deny, and dare not' (5.3.23–8). In 5.4 we see how one of the prophecies will unravel: Malcolm orders his soldiers to cut boughs from the trees of Birnam Wood, using them as camouflage to conceal their advance. Birnam Wood will come to Dunsinane after all.

At the opening of 5.5, Macbeth seems to have abandoned the idea of meeting his enemies in the field. He is staying in his castle, counting on its strength to withstand a siege as he counts on the prophecies to protect him. The active warrior who, in the reports from the battlefields in 1.2, seemed to be everywhere at once, is now fixed in one spot, awaiting his fate, like Hitler in his bunker in the final days of the Third Reich. He is counting not on winning a battle but on outwaiting his enemies, letting them die of starvation and disease. At the opening of 5.7, he will compare himself to a bear in a bear-baiting, tied to a stake while the dogs attack him. (There was a bear-baiting arena just down the road from the Globe.) Through all of this, he is counting on his own capacity to endure.

That endurance is tested in the rest of the scene, in which Macbeth receives two shocks. The first is the death of Lady Macbeth. The offstage cry of women gives us a hint of something we never see: a community of women around Lady Macbeth, who mourn her. Throughout the play her only relationship has been with her husband; when that relationship collapses, she is alone. The fact that Macbeth does not recognize the cry of women, and claims to be unmoved by it, suggests how confined he is to the male world of military action. Does it also suggest how detached he has become from his wife? He has at least enough curiosity about the cry to ask Seyton for an explanation. But his response to the news of his wife's death leaves us wondering how, and whether, it affects him.

His first reaction, 'She should have died hereafter; / There would have been a time for such a word' (17–18), sounds emotionally dead. Macbeth is a busy man, and doesn't have time for this sort of thing. The speech that follows is one of the bleakest statements of the emptiness of life in Shakespeare (or anywhere else). It can be read as general philosophizing, another failure on Macbeth's part to confront the death of his wife. There is no particular memory of her in it, no sense of the loss of a person who mattered to him. Or is there? When he describes life as a 'brief candle' (23) we may recall the taper Lady Macbeth carried in the sleepwalking scene, her last appearance in the play. Macbeth was not there, of course; but if the audience makes the link it may suggest that this speech is more about Lady Macbeth than it may at first appear. Elsewhere in the final scenes Macbeth complains about the emptiness of his own life (as in 5.3.22–8, quoted above). Here he complains of the emptiness of all life. If we wonder what makes the difference, the answer may be that he has just heard of the death of Lady Macbeth.

Starting with its first line, 'Tomorrow, and tomorrow and tomorrow' (19), the speech picks up themes from earlier in the play, beginning with the theme of time. Macbeth was prepared to let time make him king without taking any action of his own: 'Time and the hour runs through the roughest day' (1.3.148). Time was for him the medium through which fulfilment would naturally come. Lady Macbeth was not content with that. When she read Macbeth's letter, her imagination leapt ahead to the future: 'Thy letters have transported me beyond / This ignorant present, and I feel now / The future in the instant' (1.5.56–8). Far from being willing to wait, she wanted the future now. At the same time, paradoxically, she seemed prepared to stop time: when Macbeth said innocently that Duncan would leave their castle 'Tomorrow', she retorted, 'O never shall sun / That morrow see' (1.5.60–1). Literally, she means that Duncan will never leave; but the way she puts it carries the suggestion that time will stop, tomorrow will never come. In Macbeth's 'Tomorrow, and tomorrow, and tomorrow' the future is at once inevitable and meaningless. One day succeeds another, in a procession that crawls pointlessly forward. The long vowels of 'morrow' allow the actor to stretch the word into a lament, or even a monotonous drone. From the witches' opening question, 'When shall we three meet again?', the play has been fixated on the future. Now the future means nothing.

Macbeth began the soliloquy that opens 1.7 by fretting about judgement in this world, while claiming he could ignore the fear of judgement in the next. But the idea of the Last Judgement, in which the dead would rise and Jesus Christ would decide their fate (heaven or hell) for all eternity, was a live one for Shakespeare's audience. In the scene that follows Duncan's murder, a stage full of characters in their nightclothes, roused from sleep by Macduff's cry 'As from your graves rise up' to see 'The great doom's image' (2.3.79–80), might have suggested to the first audience the dead in their shrouds rising from their graves for the Last Judgement. Now, in Macbeth's imagination, there is no such end to hope for or to fear. The end will be as meaningless as life itself. Time will just, one day, stop.

He speaks of 'the last syllable of recorded time' (21). In the account of the Creation in the Book of Genesis, God creates by speaking: 'And God said, Let there be light, and there was light'. The opening of the Gospel of John picks up the theme: 'In the beginning was the Word'. And so Macbeth imagines the death of all things as the death of language, 'the last syllable'. Throughout the play the powers of evil have abused language, turning it to riddles, doubletalk and euphemisms like Lady Macbeth's way of calling for Duncan's murder: 'He that's coming / Must be provided for' (1.5.65–6). Now language simply dies.

Macbeth also speaks of 'the last syllable of *recorded* time'. Having thought of the future, he thinks of the past, as though there is a collective memory, human or extra-human, that accumulates the whole of time in a record, the ultimate work of history. But when his imagination turns to 'all our yesterdays' (22), the whole of human history becomes a story of fools, and all those fools do is die. Macbeth has been a soldier, a man of action, confronting reality. Now life itself is as unreal as a stage play. It is the commonplace stated by Jaques in *As You Like It*: 'All the world's a stage, / And all the men and women merely players' (2.7.139–40). But while this leads Jaques to a detached, cynical amusement about the play of life it leads Macbeth to deeper despair. The performance of life is simply meaningless noise. Finally, the human actor does not even have the freedom a stage actor has to construct his own performance. He is simply a character in a story, 'a tale / Told by an idiot' (26–7). If earlier in the speech the fools were humanity, who is the idiot who is telling the meaningless story that is all human life? The play has given us glimpses of the power of evil. Is this our glimpse of God?

Then language resumes, and so does story-telling. Macbeth orders the messenger, 'thy story quickly' (29). And his story – the march of Birnam Wood – far from 'signifying nothing' reveals the inner meaning of the witches' prophecy. Macbeth receives his second shock, and while it produces nothing that stretches his imagination (and ours) so terribly as the speech triggered by the death of Lady Macbeth, it produces in more limited terms a sense of meaninglessness. Macbeth, who has been preoccupied with survival, no longer cares whether he lives or dies (40–1). 'Arm, arm, and out' (46) suggests he has abandoned his strategy of waiting out the siege; but 'There is no flying hence, nor tarrying here' (5.6.48) declares that any strategy he adopts will be meaningless. He is left, at the end of the scene, with nothing but the sheer raw courage to go on fighting. That courage sustains him to the end; whether we see it as giving his life meaning depends on whether we see it as rescinding the despair of 'Tomorrow, and tomorrow, and tomorrow' or ironically overshadowed by it.

Enter Macbeth, Seyton,[1] and Soldiers, with drum and colours.[2]

MACBETH
    Hang out our banners on the outward walls,
    The cry is still, 'They come'; our castle's strength
    Will laugh a siege to scorn; here let them lie,
    Till famine and the ague[3] eat them up;
    Were they not forced[4] with those that should be ours,
    We might have met them dareful,[5] beard to beard,
    And beat them backward home. What is that noise?

1 The name of Macbeth's attendant in the final scenes may suggest a pun on 'Satan'. There is an equivalent effect in *Antony and Cleopatra* (written not long after *Macbeth*) where Antony, who has given up the world for love, has an attendant called Eros.
2 Military banners.
3 Fever (it was at least as common for soldiers to die from disease as from enemy action).
4 Reinforced.
5 Bravely.

A cry within of women.

SEYTON
It is the cry of women, my good lord.   [*Exit*]⁶

MACBETH
I have almost forgot the taste of fears;
The time has been, my senses would have cooled   10
To hear a night-shriek, and my fell of hair⁷
Would at a dismal treatise⁸ rouse, and stir
As life were in't. I have supped full with horrors,⁹
Direness¹⁰ familiar to my slaughterous thoughts
Cannot once start¹¹ me.

[*Enter Seyton.*]

Wherefore was that cry?
SEYTON   The Queen, my lord, is dead.
MACBETH   She should have died hereafter;
There would have been a time for such a word;¹²
Tomorrow, and tomorrow, and tomorrow,
Creeps in this petty¹³ pace from day to day,   20
To the last syllable of recorded time;
And all our yesterdays have lighted fools
The way to dusty death. Out, out, brief candle,
Life's but a walking shadow,¹⁴ a poor¹⁵ player
That struts and frets¹⁶ his hour upon the stage,
And then is heard no more. It is a tale
Told by an idiot, full of sound and fury
Signifying nothing.

---

6 Seyton's exit here and his re-entry a few lines later with the news of the Queen's death are editorial
   decisions, which may or may not be followed in production. He has no exit or re-entry in the Folio
   text. If he remains on stage throughout, the effect can be deliberately and disturbingly unrealistic
   (uncannily, he just *knows*); or realistic (he knows from the beginning, and has been holding back).
7 i.e., all the hair on my head.
8 Tale, report.
9 Recalling his encounter with Banquo's ghost, where he showed the fear he now claims he can no
   longer feel.
10 Horror.
11 Startle.
12 i.e., such a word as 'dead', the key word in Seyton's report. This introduces the idea of language
   that runs through the rest of Macbeth's speech. 'Hereafter' in the previous line returns as 'Tomorrow'. At first Macbeth claims that a later time would have been better for Lady Macbeth to die; he
   would have had time to mourn her properly. Just for a moment he sees the future as better than the
   present. Then the future becomes meaningless.
13 Insignificant.
14 Shakespeare uses the same word for actor in *A Midsummer Night's Dream*, in Theseus's line about
   the amateur actors whose incompetent performance has amused him – 'The best in this kind are but
   shadows' (5.1.211) – and in the apology to the audience that begins Puck's epilogue: 'If we
   shadows have offended' (5.1.423). An actor is a shadow in that he presents an unreal image of a
   human figure. This idea creates urbane amusement in the comedy, despair in the tragedy.
15 Badly paid; incompetent.
16 The verbs suggest, respectively, exaggerated movement and exaggerated emotion. The line evokes
   the old-fashioned over-acting against which Hamlet warns the players (3.2.1–35).

Enter a Messenger.

Thou com'st to use thy tongue; thy story quickly.

MESSENGER   Gracious my lord,   30
I should report that which I say I saw,
But know not how to do it.[17]

MACBETH   Well, say, sir.

MESSENGER
As I did stand my watch upon the hill
I looked toward Birnam, and anon methought
The wood began to move.

MACBETH   Liar, and slave.

MESSENGER
Let me endure your wrath, if't be not so;
Within this three mile may you see it coming.
I say, a moving grove.

MACBETH   If thou speak'st false,
Upon the next tree shall thou hang alive
Till famine cling[18] thee; if thy speech be sooth,[19]   40
I care not if thou dost for me as much.
I pull in[20] resolution, and begin
To doubt th'equivocation of the fiend,
That lies like truth. 'Fear not, till Birnam Wood
Do come to Dunsinane', and now a wood
Comes toward Dunsinane. Arm, arm, and out!
If this which he avouches[21] does appear,
There is nor flying hence, nor tarrying here.
I 'gin to be aweary of the sun[22]
And wish th'estate o'th' world[23] were now undone.   50
Ring the alarum bell, blow wind, come wrack,[24]
At least we'll die with harness[25] on our back.   *Exeunt*

---

17 The messenger echoes Macbeth's idea of the failure of language: he does not know how to describe
    what he has seen. 'Say' creates a contradiction in his own speech: I don't know how to say what I'm
    saying.
18 Shrink.
19 Truth.
20 Rein in (as in restraining a horse).
21 Claims as truth.
22 Macbeth committed his earlier crimes under the cover of darkness. Now he is exposed to the light
    of day, and shrinks from it. It is part of the emotional deadness he claims earlier in the scene that he
    is not frightened by sunlight, just tired of it.
23 The whole order of creation.
24 Ruin.
25 Armour.

The desperate courage Macbeth shows at the end of this scene sustains him to the end of the play. Birnam Wood comes to Dunsinane, and Macduff turns out to be of no woman born. In the end Macbeth determines to fight it out with the man he now knows will kill him. Macduff duly kills him, and in the last scene comes on with his severed head, an echo of the first apparition in the cauldron scene. The dominant voices that end the play are those of his triumphant enemies, putting Scotland to rights. Macbeth has no last speech of the sort that Garrick wrote for himself (see The Work in Performance, **pp. 106–7**), no final statement, not even a dying groan. For the central figure in a tragedy of this period, this is a very unusual way to end. Has Shakespeare ended Macbeth's part this way because he has become so empty there is nothing he could say?

It is worth noting that the last we see of Macbeth he is fighting. In a way, this takes us back to the way his story began; when we first heard of him he was fighting. The difference is that in the early scenes we never saw him fighting; his actions were conveyed to us in words, sometimes murky and confusing words. When he finally came on to the stage the battle was over, and his first encounter was not with the sword of an adversary but with the riddling, dangerous words of the witches, a power more deadly than any sword. Now, at the end of the play, Macbeth stops talking and takes up the sword again. We see in the final scenes what was only described at the beginning. Words, in the form of the prophecies, have betrayed him; in 'Tomorrow, and tomorrow, and tomorrow' he imagines the death of language. It is a typical Shakespearean paradox that he does so in some of the most eloquent language in the play. Words having failed him, or just failed, Macbeth ends as a creature of pure action.

In the play's final scene Malcolm, now hailed as king of Scotland, dismisses Macbeth as 'this dead butcher' and Lady Macbeth as 'his fiend-like Queen' (5.9.35). The gift for shedding blood, for which Macbeth was praised in 1.2, is now the final reason to condemn him. In his next words Malcolm reports the rumour that Lady Macbeth committed suicide (5.9.36–7). He spends no more words on either of them; his focus is on the future, which Macbeth saw as meaningless, and which Malcolm sees as a time of restoration and healing for Scotland. The new King is surrounded by cheering supporters. But the general cry of 'Hail, King of Scotland!' (5.9.25) disconcertingly recalls the witches' greeting to Macbeth in 1.3, and Malcolm's view of Macbeth and Lady Macbeth is equally disconcerting in its oversimplification of two complex characters. Characteristically, Shakespeare ends the tragedy not with a simple restoration of order, but with lingering tensions: with misgivings that cut across the hope for the future, and with a sense that the survivors do not really understand the tragedy we have just experienced.

4

Further Reading

Further Reading

The literature on *Macbeth*, as on any of Shakespeare's major plays, is vast, and any list of readings must be highly selective. The following list is organized into five categories: recommended editions, works that concern the play's context, studies of the play in performance, film versions and critical studies.

Recommended Editions of *Macbeth*

Macbeth, ed. A. R. Braunmuller (Cambridge: Cambridge University Press, 1997). Probably the most thorough and helpful edition currently available. The introduction contains useful material on context and performance, and the commentary on the play is unusually full.

Macbeth, ed. Nicholas Brooke (Oxford: Oxford University Press, 1990). A recent edition with full introduction and commentary. Its treatment of the Hecate scenes is particularly interesting: Brooke treats them seriously, and departs from editorial tradition by printing the witches' songs in full.

Macbeth, ed. Robert S. Miola (New York and London: W. W. Norton and Company, 2004). An annotated text with a relatively brief introduction. Its special feature is its collection of extracts from the play's sources, from different theatrical versions (including some Victorian burlesques) and from criticism.

Macbeth, ed. Kenneth Muir (London: Methuen, 1951, frequently reprinted). The Arden (second series) edition. Some of its critical interests and procedures may now look old-fashioned, but it is a solid work by one of the leading Shakespeare scholars of the twentieth century, and it puts the reader in touch with some long-standing editorial issues.

Contexts

K. M. Briggs, *Pale Hecate's Team* (London: Routledge and Kegan Paul, 1962). Surveys beliefs about witchcraft in the dramatic and non-dramatic literature of Shakespeare's time.

Anthony Harris, *Night's Black Agents: Witchcraft and Magic in Seventeenth-Century English Drama* (Manchester: Manchester University Press, 1980). A study of the stage presentation of magic and witchcraft in Shakespeare's time. Includes two chapters on *Macbeth*: one on the weird sisters and one on demonology.

King James VI and I, *Political Writings*, ed. Johann P. Sommerville (Cambridge: Cambridge University Press, 1994). King James's view of kingship in his own words. Includes *Basilicon Doron*, *The Trew Law of Free Monarchies*, and several speeches to Parliament.

Arthur F. Kinney, *Lies Like Truth: Shakespeare, Macbeth, and the Cultural Moment* (Detroit, Mich.: Wayne State University Press, 2001). Studies the play in its political, religious and cultural contexts.

Alan Macfarlane, *Witchcraft in Tudor and Stuart England: a Regional and Comparative Study*, second edition (London: Routledge, 1999). A study of witchcraft by a social historian, relating it to local cultures, including statistics drawn from local records.

Henry N. Paul, *The Royal Play of Macbeth* (New York: Macmillan, 1950). An elaborate and influential (if not always convincing) argument that the play was written for King James and designed to appeal to his interests.

Keith Thomas, *Religion and the Decline of Magic* (New York: Charles Scribner's Sons, 1971). A classic study of supernatural belief in early modern England.

The Play in Performance

Dennis Bartholomeusz, *Macbeth and the Players* (Cambridge: Cambridge University Press, 1969). Surveys the stage history of the play from its first appearance at the Globe to the middle of the twentieth century.

Bernice W. Kliman, *Shakespeare in Performance: Macbeth*, second edition (Manchester: Manchester University Press, 2004). A study of selected stage and screen versions.

Marvin Rosenberg, *The Masks of Macbeth* (Berkeley, Los Angeles and London: University of California Press, 1978). A detailed, scene-by-scene account of performance decisions taken throughout the play's production history.

John Wilders, ed., *Shakespeare in Production: Macbeth* (Cambridge: Cambridge University Press, 2004). Reprints the text of the Cambridge edition, with extensive notes describing what actors and directors have done at particular moments. Special emphasis on the nineteenth century. Includes an introductory essay on the play's stage history.

Gordon Williams, *Macbeth: Text and Performance* (London: Macmillan, 1985). Traces the key themes of the play, and goes on to describe the development of those themes in selected modern performances.

Film Versions

Macbeth, directed by Trevor Nunn. Thames Television, 1978. VHS video: HBO Home Video 91612. DVD: A&E, AAE 71424. A screen version of the 1976 Royal Shakespeare Company production, with powerful performances by Ian McKellen and Judi Dench.

Macbeth, directed by Roman Polanski. Columbia Pictures and Playboy Productions, 1971. VHS video: Columbia Tristar Home Video 60622. DVD: Columbia Pictures 07780. Polanski's version depicts the Macbeths as an upwardly mobile young couple in a violent, politically cynical world.

Macbeth, directed by Orson Welles. Republic Pictures, 1948. VHS video: Morningstar Entertainment 32392. Though it bears the signs of a quick shooting schedule and a small budget, Welles's version show his characteristic flair for cinematic invention.

Throne of Blood, directed by Akira Kurosawa. Toho Company Ltd, 1959. VHS video: Home Vision THR090. DVD Criterion, The Criterion Collection 190. An effective re-telling of Shakespeare's story transposed to mediaeval Japan.

Criticism

Philippa Berry, *Shakespeare's Feminine Endings: Disfiguring Death in the Tragedies* (London and New York: Routledge, 1999). As part of a feminist reading of Shakespearean tragedy, traces the issues of time, lineage and kingship in *Macbeth*.

Ralph Berry, *Tragic Instance* (Newark: University of Delaware Press; London: Associated University Presses, 1999). The chapter on *Macbeth* examines the links between murder and sexuality.

John Russell Brown, ed., *Focus on Macbeth* (London, Boston, Mass., and Henley: Routledge and Kegan Paul, 1982). A collection of essays ranging over critical, contextual and theatrical approaches.

James L. Calderwood, *If It Were Done: Macbeth and Tragic Action* (Amherst: University of Massachusetts Press, 1986). Studies the play first in relation to *Hamlet*, then in terms of its action and its presentation of violence.

Terry Eagleton, *William Shakespeare* (Oxford: Basil Blackwell, 1986). Eagleton's argument that the witches are the centre of the play's positive values is a classic example of reading against the apparent effect of the text.

G. R. Elliott, *Dramatic Providence in Macbeth* (Princeton, NJ: Princeton University Press, 1960). A Christian reading of the play, stressing its presentation of divine grace.

R. A. Foakes, *Shakespeare and Violence* (Cambridge: Cambridge University Press, 2003). Examines the dehumanizing effect of violence on Macbeth and his society.

Michael Goldman, *Acting and Action in Shakespearean Tragedy* (Princeton, NJ: Princeton University Press, 1985). The chapter on *Macbeth* studies the demands the play's language makes on the actor, and the way that language produces an encounter with evil.

Paul A. Jorgensen, *Our Naked Frailties: Sensational Art and Meaning in Macbeth* (Berkeley, Los Angeles and London: University of California Press, 1971). An examination of the supernatural and psychological horror of the play, arguing that while achieving a strong sense of spiritual evil it remains rooted in the world.

Coppélia Kahn, *Man's Estate: Masculine Identity in Shakespeare* (Berkeley, Los Angeles and London: University of California Press, 1981). Traces Macbeth's frustrated attempt to achieve manhood.

G. Wilson Knight, *The Imperial Theme* (London: Oxford University Press, 1931). The chapter on *Macbeth* surveys the play's images of good, drawn mostly from nature.

G. Wilson Knight, *The Wheel of Fire* (Oxford: Oxford University Press, 1930; reprinted London: Methuen, 1949). Studies the play's imaginative atmosphere, focusing on images of evil.

Naomi Conn Liebler, *Shakespeare's Festive Tragedy* (London and New York: Routledge, 1995). Examines the ritual elements in the tragedy, with an emphasis on liminality, and a sceptical reading of the ending.

Michael Long, *Harvester New Critical Introductions to Shakespeare: Macbeth* (New York and London: Harvester Wheatsheaf, 1989). A general account that traces the play's developing action, including references to its symbolism and its Christian context.

David Margolies, *Monsters of the Deep: Social Dissolution in Shakespeare's Tragedies* (Manchester and New York: Manchester University Press, 1992). Studies the collapse of social values in *Macbeth*, taking a sceptical view of the final restoration of order.

S. Schoenbaum, ed., *Macbeth: Critical Essays* (New York and London: Garland Publishing, 1991). A collection of essays ranging from the eighteenth century to the twentieth.

John Wain, ed., *Shakespeare: Macbeth: a Casebook* (London: Macmillan, 1968). A collection of critical essays, mostly from the twentieth century, with special emphasis on the play's language.

Index

Related titles from Routledge

William Shakespeare's Hamlet
Edited by Sean McEvoy

Routledge Guides to Literature

William Shakespeare's *Hamlet* (c.1600) is possibly his most famous play, in which the motives of revenge and love are entangled with the moral dilemmas of integrity and corruption.

Taking the form of a sourcebook, this guide to Shakespeare's remarkable play offers:

- extensive introductory comment on the contexts, critical history and many interpretations of the text, from first performance to the present
- annotated extracts from key contextual documents, reviews, critical works and the text itself
- cross-references between documents and sections of the guide, in order to suggest links between texts, contexts and criticism
- suggestions for further reading.

Part of the Routledge Guides to Literature series, this volume is essential reading for all those beginning detailed study of *Hamlet* and seeking not only a guide to the play, but a way through the wealth of contextual and critical material that surrounds Shakespeare's text.

Hb: 0–415–31432–1
Pb: 0–415–31433–X

Available at all good bookshops
For further information on our literature series, please visit
www.routledge.com/literature/series.asp
For ordering and further information please visit:
www.routledge.com

Related titles from Routledge

William Shakespeare's King Lear
Edited by Grace Ioppolo

This sourcebook clearly introduces the many critical issues surrounding this complex and haunting play. Ioppolo examines sources, from Holinshed to Spencer, and looks at critical readings and notable performances of the play. Examining *King Lear* within its literary and cultural contexts, this book brings together:

- contemporary documents surrounding *King Lear*
- performance history
- early critical reception from major critics
- twentieth-century criticism
- key passages from the play itself.

The volume concludes with a list of recommended editions and further reading, allowing students to pursue their study in the areas that interest them the most. This is the ideal introduction for undergraduates, providing a clear guide to the play, its reception and the critical material which surrounds it.

Hb: 0–415–23471–9
Pb: 0–415–23472–7

Available at all good bookshops
For further information on our literature series, please visit
www.routledge.com/literature/series.asp
For ordering and further information please visit:

www.routledge.com

Related titles from Routledge

William Shakespeare's The Merchant of Venice
Edited by Susan P. Cerasano

With Shylock's pound of flesh and Portia's golden ring, *The Merchant of Venice* is one of Shakespeare's most controversial, disturbing and unforgettable plays.

Combining accessible commentary with a range of reprinted materials, Susan. P. Cerasano:

- explores the contexts of the play, including early modern images of Venice, the commercialism of the play, Shakespeare's theatre and London, and images of Jewishness

- samples modern criticism of Shakespeare's *Merchant*, grouped into sections on The Economic Framework, Choosing and Risking, and Shylock and Other Strangers

- offers an invaluable discussion of the play in performance, considering crucial staging issues and changing interpretations of the roles of Portia and Shylock

- closely examines key passages of the work, providing both commentary and extensively annotated sections of play text

- prepares readers for additional study of the play with a useful guide to further reading.

Assuming no prior knowledge of the play, this sourcebook is the essential guide to one of the most haunting works of English drama.

Hb: 0–415–240514
Pb: 0–415–240522

Available at all good bookshops
For further information on our literature series, please visit
www.routledge.com/literature/series.asp
For ordering and further information please visit:
www.routledge.com